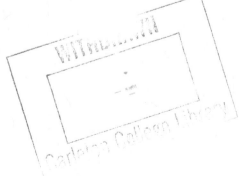

Charity and State
in Late Renaissance Italy

CHARITY AND STATE IN LATE RENAISSANCE ITALY

THE MONTE DI PIETÀ OF FLORENCE

Carol Bresnahan Menning

CORNELL UNIVERSITY PRESS
Ithaca and London

First published 1993 by Cornell University Press.

International Standard Book Number 0-8014-2773-8
Library of Congress Catalog Card Number 92-56788
Printed in the United States of America
Librarians: Library of Congress cataloging information
appears on the last page of the book.

⊗ The paper in this book meets the minimum requirements of the American National Standard for Information Sciences—Permanence of Paper for Printed Library Materials, ANSI Z39.48-1984.

Für die Bären

CONTENTS

FONDI CONSULTED
(AND ABBREVIATIONS)

All these files are located at the Archivio di Stato in Florence.

Acquisti e Doni
Archivio della Repubblica (Arch. della Rep.)—Signori e Collegi
Arti—Arte del Cambio
Auditore delle Riformagioni (Aud. delle Rif.)
Capitani di Parte Guelfa
Carte Alessandre
Carte Strozziane (CS)
Depositeria Generale (DG)
Libri Fabarum
Magistrato Supremo (MS)
Manoscritti (Mano.)
Manoscritti e Codici Litterari (Mano. e Cod. Litt.)—Bardi
Mediceo (Principato) (Med.)
Mercanzia
Miscellanea Medicea
Miscellanea Repubblicana (Misc. Rep.)
Monte di Pietà (MP)
Monte di Pietà del Bigallo
Otto di Guardia e Balìa
Otto di Pratica (Principato)
Pratica Segreta (PS)
Provvisioni (Prov.)
Pupilli
Senato de' Quarantotto
Sindaci (Sin.)

PREFACE

IN THE MINDS of its founders, there was no doubt about the purpose of the Florentine monte di pietà: it had been created, in the words of the statutes, "to be able to lend against pawns to poor persons with as little interest as possible." Until its demise in the nineteenth century with Italian unification, the monte di pietà continued to accept pawns and to offer low-cost small loans. Yet less than half a century after its founding in 1496, the monte also began to undertake other functions far different from those envisioned by its founders and to serve social groups other than the poor. By the late 1530s it agreed to pay 5 percent interest on deposits and by the next decade it was flooded with income, the bulk of which came from middle-class persons seeking a safe if conservative investment. The establishment's liquidity quickly attracted the attention of Duke Cosimo I de' Medici who, seeing the monte, as his son and heir Francesco bluntly put it, "abounding in money," used its resources to finance loans to himself, his family, and friends. The duke's personal, dynastic, and public financial schemes were, in essence, subsidized by the monte di pietà, which was in turn supported by its poor clientele and its middle-class depositors.

With its incomparably rich documentation, the Florentine monte gives us a viewpoint from which to observe issues of importance not just for Florentine history, but for the development of the state in early modern Europe. It offers an excellent example of how a republican charitable establishment was transformed into an instrument of banking, state finance, and patronage under pressure first from a republican regime and then from a ducal one. Much of the pressure, however, came from Cosimo de' Medici, whose great talent lay in his ability to imagine innovative uses for old institutions while still permitting them to carry out their traditional functions.

Along with Cosimo and the various Florentine regimes, the other influences in the monte di pietà's story include the wealthy and middle classes and their investment patterns, the Jews, cycles of wealth and poverty, women and wards, the demands of foreign and domestic affairs, the Medici dukes and their search for political control, and state finance. Together these present a narrative that, while documenting the history of an institution, tells the larger story of the changes that the institution underwent as the demands placed on it by the city and its rulers changed.

This book is not a quantitative examination of the Florentine monte di pietà, although the institution's ledgers contain information that could be quantified by a team of scholars interested in such an approach. Naturally, at times I have balanced accounts, analyzed samples from the ledgers, and compiled statistics where I considered them necessary or useful. After reading all the extant ledgers for the period 1496–1574—from the institution's founding through the death of Cosimo I—I feel certain that I have accurately discerned the trends in the monte di pietà's activities without having had to quantify the figures to the last exhaustive decimal point.

In order to discover the links between the institution and the society in which it operated, I have relied on two sources of documentation. The first is ledgers, income and outgo books, *deliberazioni* (discussions and decisions), correspondence, and miscellanea from the monte di pietà files (*fondi*) in the Archivio di Stato of Florence. The second, and equally important, consists of other republican and ducal records such as those of the Depositeria Generale, Pratica Segreta, Mediceo, and Magistrato Supremo *fondi*. These sources have all helped to set the historical stage, as it were, on which the monte di pietà played its political, economic, and charitable roles and outside of which the story of the institution would be merely an antiquarian curiosity.

I thank the institutions and programs that provided material support for my research: the Renaissance Society of America, the International Telegraph and Telephone Corporation's International Fellowship Program and the Institute of International Education, the

Beneficial Foundation and Brown University, and the University of Toledo's generous Faculty Research Fellowships. I am grateful for their help, which allowed me to spend time in the Florentine archives.

Many colleagues and friends read all or part of the manuscript at various points and offered moral support, advice, and thoughtful criticism. I owe a tremendous debt to Richard Goldthwaite of the Johns Hopkins University, who offered invaluable help with the technical secrets of ledgers and money and forced me to reconsider some of my assumptions about the sixteenth-century economy. Gino Corti of Villa i Tatti in Florence, my paleography teacher, has been a paragon of generosity. Judith Brown of Stanford University shared her ideas on sixteenth-century political economy with me and read the manuscript with a critical eye. William Connell of Rutgers University selflessly shared his own research. Conversations with Stanley Chojnacki of Michigan State University have given me more than, I am sure, I have given in return. I also thank R. Burr Litchfield of Brown University, David Underdown of Yale University, Elena Fasano Guarini of the University of Pisa, and Furio Diaz of the Scuola Normale Superiore of Pisa. Their helpful suggestions saved me from making many errors. Above all, Anthony Molho of Brown has inspired me with his rigor, expertise, and patience.

The staffs of the Archivio di Stato of Florence and the Special Collections Library of the Hatcher Graduate Library of the University of Michigan were immensely helpful to my research. My gratitude also goes to Douglas Johnson of the University of Toledo, who prepared the index.

Parts of Chapter 3 appeared as part of my article, "The Monte's 'Monte': The Early Supporters of Florence's Monte di Pietà," *Sixteenth Century Journal* 23 (Winter 1992): 303–18, © 1992, The Sixteenth Century Journal Publishers. Parts of Chapter 6 were published in my article, "Loans and Favors, Kin and Clients: Cosimo de' Medici and the Monte di Pietà," *Journal of Modern History* 61 (September 1989): 487–511, © 1989, The University of Chicago. These passages are used here with the permission of the publishers.

Finally, I thank my husband, Ralph, the best historian I know, without whose love and support I'd never write anything at all.

CAROL BRESNAHAN MENNING

Toledo, Ohio

INTRODUCTION

IN THE LENTEN SEASON of 1488 the fa-
mous Franciscan preacher Bernardino da Feltre came to Florence to
offer a sermon in the Duomo. Within two days of his arrival Brother
Bernardino had so incited his listeners that they threatened to riot.
The Otto di Guardia e Balìa, faced with this threat to public order,
seized him and escorted him out of the city with the warning not to
return. What were the themes of the oration that had gotten Bernardino into so much trouble? First, he accused Jewish moneylenders in
Florence of usury. Second, he called upon the citizens to follow the
example of their fellows in Perugia, Siena, and elsewhere to establish
a charitable civic pawnshop—a monte di pietà. By providing inexpensive loans to persons with no other source of credit, the monte di
pietà would perform a valuable economic service as well as a charitable one.

Bernardino da Feltre failed in his attempt to prompt the Florentines to found a monte di pietà in their city. But his twin themes—
the evil of Jewish usury and the benefits of a monte di pietà—were
not forgotten, and found a place in the preaching of Savonarola,
who saw usury as one of the deadly sins that Florentines should
drive out. Parting company with his fellow Dominicans, Savonarola
urged his flock to set up a monte di pietà, a call answered late in
1495 when civic legislation appointed a commission to create a charitable pawnshop in Florence.

Run in accordance with the principles of Christian charity, the
monte di pietà saw as its clientele the poor, who could pawn an item

of some small value: a cap, a table knife, a cup, even a book. The owner of the pawn then received a loan based on the value given the pawn by an assessor working for the monte di pietà. The owner might redeem the pawn at any time within a year by paying back the loan plus a low interest charge, usually 5 percent. After one year the monte could sell at auction any unredeemed items. As brokers of small loans against pawns, Italian monti di pietà were expected not only to replace Jewish moneylenders but also to set up the conditions in which all Jews could be expelled.

The contribution the monte di pietà made to Florentine society, the uses to which different groups in that society put it, the internal workings of the monte, the kinds of persons who supported it with their generosity—all are important aspects of a history of the institution in late Renaissance Florence. There was little about its first three decades to distinguish the Florentine establishment from other Italian monti di pietà; it was, in fact, carefully modeled after earlier monti. But later developments did serve to set the monte di pietà of Florence on a unique path. The key to these developments was the relationship between it and the rulers of the state, a relationship that eventually forced upon the charitable establishment an important role in ducal finance and patronage under Duke Cosimo I de' Medici (1519–1574).

The monte di pietà's vitality in the ducal period stemmed not only from the services it offered Florentines, but also from the Medici's interest in it, which in turn stemmed from its potential. Cosimo made astute use of many existing Florentine institutions. When he needed money, he turned to forced loans, taxes, the countryside—all time-honored sources of income. Likewise, once the monte had acquired great liquidity in the mid-sixteenth century, he discovered the practical ways in which the institution might serve dynasty and state. His talent lay in the systematic, rational, and controlled exploitation of the monte's resources. Toward the end of his reign, the charitable pawnshop, while continuing to offer its traditional services to the poor, had become an integral part of the finances of the Medicean state and the maintenance of the Medicean dynasty. In addition, a revived monte di pietà in Siena, consciously modeled after the Florentine institution, served the same functions in that conquered city. Finally, the monte became a means through which Cosimo could exercise that old practice of the Florentine elite, patronage: he could appoint his friends to the board of directors or authorize large loans at low interest to those whom he wished to cultivate. The monte di pietà thus formed part of what John Hale called the "pattern of control" that the Medici tried to impose on the city for a period of three centuries.[1] The institution therefore offers us a viewpoint, a way of examining the Florentine state at close range.

Writings about the monte's early history emphasize the role of the Franciscans, beginning with that of one instrumental in its founding, Marco di Matteo Strozzi. When in 1670 Senator Carlo Strozzi brought together the papers that today comprise the rich family collection in Florence's Archivio di Stato, he hoped to be able "to write the lives of the illustrious men of the Strozzi family."[2] Perhaps bedazzled by the political accomplishments of the better known among them, the senator gave little attention to his forebear Marco di Matteo Strozzi. Carlo Strozzi did not bother to record Marco's date of birth or death and simply listed four milestones in his life: 1481, rector of San Miniato fra le Torri; 1487, vicar-general of Volterra and doctor of decretals; 1506, canon of the Florentine cathedral; 1516, chapter vicar of Florence.[3] He thus omitted any mention of the accomplishment that Marco saw as the center of his life's work: his role in the establishment in Florence of a monte di pietà and in the related attempt to expel the Jews.

Along with the Dominican Savonarola, the Franciscan rector of San Miniato fra le Torri fervently preached the creation of a monte di pietà and, once having seen his sermons bear fruit, personally supported the monte by lending it small sums of his own money and by calling upon his friends and parishioners to remember it in their charity. Marco's memoirs portray a man who worked passionately for the monte's establishment and keenly followed its progress. They also provide a first brief history of the monte's creation and early years.

1. John Hale, *Florence and the Medici: The Pattern of Control* (London, 1979). See Anthony Molho, "Cosimo de' Medici: *Pater Patriae* or *Padrino?*" *Stanford Italian Review* 1 (1979): 5–33, for the methods of Cosimo the Elder.

2. Carte Strozziane, ser. III, 195, "Raccolta di memorie, fatta del Senatore Carlo Strozzi, per scrivere le vite degl'uomini illustri della famiglia Strozzi." Vol. 2: M–Z, title page.

3. On Marco Strozzi, see Carte Strozziane (CS), ser. III, 195, 262r. The church of San Miniato fra le Torri, which no longer exists, was located in or near the Mercato Vecchio (old market) and not far from the Palazzo Strozzi, already under construction in 1489. I am grateful to George Dameron of Saint Michael's College for his assistance in pinpointing the site of this church.

Marco Strozzi was obsessed by the presence of Jews in his native city. His papers enumerate the alleged evil deeds of the Jews throughout history down into his own time, especially their "having placed Christ into the hands of Pilate," among "many other examples." He abhorred what he saw as the crushing usury that the Jews, thinking only of their own profit, callously placed upon the frail shoulders of the Christian poor. He alluded to the distasteful rites of the Jews without, however, treating his readers to the repulsive details often found in such polemics.[4]

Marco Strozzi saw that the creation of a monte di pietà in Florence would allow the expulsion of the hated Jews. He surely knew that in many other Italian towns, his fellow Franciscans preached, in the same breath, the creation of monti and the expulsion not only of Jewish moneylenders but of the entire Jewish community. In nearby Pistoia, for instance, hatred of Jewish moneylending intensified in the second half of the fifteenth century, precisely when that town erected its monte at the urging of the Brothers Minor. Apparently the solitary existence of the town's only Jewish banker was threatening! In Lucca too, the sole Jewish moneylender was forced to leave when that city's monte di pietà was established. Many cities in central and northern Italy—Perugia, site of the first monte, virtually all the towns in the Marches where monti were set up, and many Veneto towns—drove out the Jews once monti di pietà were founded. A rare exception was Siena, where the commune established the monte after the Franciscans preached it but without any other help from that order, and where Jews were permitted to remain even after the monte began operation.[5] When the Florentine authorities finally approved the establishment of a monte di pietà, Strozzi noted with sat-

---

4. The list is endless; for two examples of the Western medieval tradition of depicting the Jews as filthy, criminal, and perverted, consider Chaucer's "Prioress's Tale" from *The Canterbury Tales*, and Guibert of Nogent's memoirs, *Self and Society in Medieval France*, ed. John Benton (New York, 1970), esp. chap. 26.

5. On the expulsions of Jews, see Ilvo Capecchi and Lucia Gai, *Il monte della pietà a Pistoia e le sue origini* (Florence, 1976), 25–26; Domenico Corsi, "Il secondo monte di pietà di Lucca (1493–1502)," *Archivio storico italiano* (*ASI*) 126 (1968): 389–90; and Brian Pullan, *Rich and Poor in Renaissance Venice* (Oxford, 1971). On Siena, see N. Piccolomini, ed., *Il monte dei paschi di Siena e le aziende in esso riunite* (Siena, 1891), 1:171, 215–34; Federico Melis, "Motivi di storia bancaria senese: Dai banchieri privati alla banca pubblica," *Monte dei paschi di Siena: Note economiche* 5 (1972): 58; and *Monte dei paschi di Siena* (Siena, 1955), 23–25.

isfaction that the legislation called for the simultaneous expulsion of the Jews.

In many cases, then, the connection between monti di pietà and the expulsion of Jews was real. Unfortunately, much of the subsequent scholarly investigation into Italian monti di pietà did not proceed beyond these issues. Knowingly or not, an anonymous seventeenth-century writer compiling a record of Florence's monte di pietà repeatedly echoed the rector of San Miniato fra le Torri, emphasizing the monte's origins, reciting the text of the *provvisione* (law) calling for the erection of the monte and the expulsion of the Jews, and dutifully quoting the same figures on Jewish usury that Strozzi had cited. This tendency to emphasize the connection survived to the present century in the wide literature, much of it by Franciscans, tracing the origins of various monti di pietà. Research on their subsequent development has been much more limited.

One of the first scholarly works on the origins of monti di pietà was published in 1903 by the Franciscan Heribert Holzapfel.[6] Holzapfel stressed the ties among monti founded by Franciscan preaching, notably their anti-Semitic nature and their common structures. Other works described the origins of particular monti. Piero Compostella published a valuable study of the monte of Milan and a companion series of documents on that monte, painstakingly examining the origins of the institution in the late 1480s and attempting to place it in its larger historical context. The origins of the monti of Lucca and Pistoia have been treated as well. F. R. Salter's article "The Jews in Fifteenth Century Florence and Savonarola's Establishment of a *Mons Pietatis*" likewise fits into the traditional historiography. Vittorino Meneghin published the valuable *Monti di pietà in Italia dal 1462 al 1562*, the latest in his important series of works on the role of the Franciscan Bernardino Tomitano da Feltre in founding the institutions. Meneghin, himself a Franciscan, focused on these years because he saw them as the period of greatest Franciscan influence; thus he too remained in the traditional historiographical camp.[7]

6. Heribert Holzapfel, "Le origini dei Monti di Pietà," *La Verna* 1 (1905): 407–12, 603–11, 667–73; 2 (1906): 86–95, 164–68, 343–52, 470–76, 547–52; and 3 (1907): 25–33, 293–97, 681–92, 743–56; orig. pub. Munich, 1903.

7. For Milan, see Piero Compostella, *Il monte di pietà di Milano: Le origini (1486–1518)* (Milan, 1966). Also, a second volume, notable for its coverage of a wider sweep

This historiography is supplemented by a body of writing on closely related topics, notably Jews and Jewish banks in Renaissance Italy, usury, and the role of Franciscan preaching in setting up monti. Jewish banking in Florence was treated by Umberto Cassuto and M. Ciardini.[8] Other towns have received similar treatment.[9] A general study of the Jews in Italy by Attilio Milano closely scrutinizes the services provided by Jewish bankers, the growth of anti-Jewish sentiment, and, again, the connection between Jews and monti di pietà.[10] Other writers have closely examined the energetic role played by the friars in establishing the monti. Meneghin's biography of Bernardino da Feltre and Anscar Parson's article on the friar are among the better selections from this group, and they reiterate the theme that Marco Strozzi first sounded concerning the dual purpose of monti: the expulsion of the Jews and the inexpensive extension of Christian charity to the poor.[11]

---

of time, *Il monte di pietà di Milano: L'istituto nella storia milanese attraverso i secoli xv e xvi* (Milan, 1973), and the documents, *Il monte di pietà di Milano: Libro giornale (1506–1535) e ordinazioni capitolari (1497–1580)* (Milan, 1973). For Lucca, see Corsi, "Secondo monte di pietà"; for Pistoia, see Capecchi and Gai, *Monte della pietà a Pistoia.* F. R. Salter, "The Jews in Fifteenth Century Florence and Savonarola's Establishment of a *Mons Pietatis,*" *Cambridge Historical Journal* 5 (1935–37): 193–211. Vittorino Meneghin, *I Monti di pietà in Italia dal 1462 al 1562* (Vicenza, 1985).

8. Umberto Cassuto, *Gli ebrei in Firenze nell'età del Rinascimento* (Florence, 1965; orig. pub. 1918); and M. Ciardini, *Banchieri ebrei in Firenze nel secolo XV e il monte di pietà* (Florence, 1975; orig. pub. Borgo San Lorenzo, 1907).

9. For example, G. Annibaldi, "Banchi degli ebrei ed il monte di pietà di Gesi," *Picenum seraphicum* 9 (1972): 89–129; and M. Cassandro, *Ebrei e il prestito ebraico a Siena nel Cinquecento* (Milan, 1979). Annibaldi does not fully place the role of Franciscans, who "always took a greater part in the life and problems of the city," into context.

10. Attilio Milano, *Storia degli ebrei in Italia* (Turin, 1963). A recent scholarly work on the Jews in one Italian town is Ariel Toaff, *Jews in Medieval Assisi, 1305–1487* (Florence, 1979). See also Massimo D. Papi, "Studi e problemi sull'antigiudaismo medievale," *ASI* 135 (1977): 141–63. Anthony Molho lamented over twenty years ago the lack of diligent, modern scholarship on the Florentine Jewish community, particularly on the problems of the Jews' apparent prosperity and on the organization of the Jewish community itself. See Molho, "A Note on Jewish Moneylenders in Tuscany in the Late Trecento and Early Quattrocentro," in Anthony Molho and John Tedeschi, eds., *Renaissance: Studies in Honor of Hans Baron* (DeKalb, Ill., 1971), 110. Maria Giuseppina Muzzarelli echoed part of Molho's complaint in her article "Luoghi e tendenze dell'attuale storiografica italiana sulla presenza ebraica fra XIV e XVI secolo," *Società e storia* 24 (1984): 369–94.

11. Vittorino Meneghin, *Bernardino da Feltre e i monti di pietà* (Vicenza, 1974); and Anscar Parsons, "Bernardine of Feltre and the *Montes Pietatis,*" *Franciscan Studies* 22,

Historians of banking were among the first to ask questions of a different sort. For these writers, monti di pietà may have begun as charitable, anti-Jewish and anti-usury institutions, but their development quickly took them along quite a different path. Inherent in the structures of these institutions was the germ of modern banking, they argued. A natural evolution changed monti from mere charitable institutions to banks that met the needs of both a clientele in search of credit for which it had no other source and the middle classes who sought an institution where they could safely deposit money at a profit.[12] Such an argument rests upon two premises: first, that the early monti di pietà were endowed from the beginning with structures that encouraged the development of banking activities; and second, that the middle classes chose to deposit money in them in substantial numbers. According to those historians, monti bridged the gap between the *banco* (bench or table) of the medieval moneychanger and the *sportello* (cashier's window) of modern banks. There can be no doubt that those monti di pietà that accepted deposits at interest in the sixteenth century came to furnish some banking services that many people in a broad range of social classes could not find elsewhere. At the same time, however, a close examination of the Florentine model casts doubt upon some of the premises and

n.s. 1 (Mar. 1941): 11–32. Among the literature on usury, Benjamin N. Nelson, *Idea of Usury: From Tribal Brotherhood to Universal Otherhood* (Chicago, 1969; orig. pub. Princeton, 1949) remains seminal, along with idem, "Usurer and the Merchant-Prince: Italian Businessmen and the Ecclesiastical Law of Restitution, 1100–1550," *Journal of Economic History* 7, supp. 7 (1947): 104–22. See also Florence Edler de Roover, "Restitution in Renaissance Florence," in *Studi in onore di Armando Sapori* (Milan, 1957); and John T. Noonan, *The Scholastic Analysis of Usury* (Cambridge, England, 1957). Michele Monaco, in "La questione dei monti di pietà al Quinto Concilio lateranense," *Rivista di studi salernitani* 4 (1971): 86–136, shows that the question of monti di pietà and usury was not settled in the fifteenth century. Also important is Pullan, *Rich and Poor in Renaissance Venice*.

12. The chief proponent of this argument is Giuseppe Garrani, *Il carattere bancario e l'evoluzione strutturale dei primogenii monti di pietà: Reflessi della tecnica bancaria antica su quella moderna* (Milan, 1957). See also Anscar Parsons, "The Economic Significance of Montes Pietatis," *Franciscan Studies* 22, n.s. 1 (Sept. 1941): 3–28. Mario Chiaudano, in "Un contributo alla storia dei monti di pietà e della banca in Italia: L'istituto S. Paolo di Torino," *ASI* 124 (1966): 251, refines the argument: "The monti di pietà, at least until the beginning of the sixteenth century, cannot be considered banks, even though they anticipated, in a certain way, the successive structures [of banks]." The monti's most important contribution was the development and extension of cheap credit (251–52).

conclusions of this thesis and suggests that the banking structures of the late Renaissance Florentine monte di pietà have been exaggerated, for monti came to play roles never envisioned by their founders and for which their original structures ill equipped them.

The emphasis on the evolving banklike nature of the monti di pietà also results from the fact that monti continue to function as banks in several cities, including Lucca and Siena. Some of these banks have published series and journals that naturally tend to stress the origins and evolution of such banks. In one series published in 1956 by the Associazione Bancaria Italiana an important article by Guido Pampaloni appeared, deeply rooted in archival sources, that broke new ground in several ways.[13] First, Pampaloni's work followed the Florentine monte over the course of its history from the first unsuccessful attempts to establish the institution through its demise during the period of Italian unification. Second, by revealing the richness of the sources, Pampaloni suggested ways for scholars to continue investigations into the Florentine monte. Third, he firmly placed the Florentine monte in the context of the flowering of monti di pietà in fifteenth-century Italy, and proceeded to note several important changes and reforms over time. Yet the article remained within a traditional framework. It was largely a narrative, continued the emphasis on origins, stressed administrative change and reforms, and concurred in the standard conclusions about the role of the monte as a middle-class bank.

Historians have now begun to show a growing interest in sixteenth-century Florence and its institutions, although the postrepublican period of Florentine history has no parallel to the rich monographic and synthetic literature on the republican period.[14] Furio Diaz has taken the lead with his comprehensive *Granducato di Toscana: I Medici*.[15] Primarily concerned with political and administrative history, Diaz laid groundwork for inquiry into Florentine politics and society in the sixteenth century and beyond.

One question that has received considerable attention recently concerns the development of the sixteenth-century Tuscan state, a

13. Guido Pampaloni, "Cenni storici sul monte di pietà di Firenze," *Archivi storici delle aziende di credito* 1 (1956): 525–60.

14. Despite Eric Cochrane's call for scholars to examine "Florence in the forgotten centuries." *Florence in the Forgotten Centuries, 1527–1800: A History of Florence and the Florentines in the Age of the Grand Dukes* (Chicago, 1973).

15. This is vol. 13.1 of the *Storia d'Italia* series (Turin, 1976).

question central to this book. Arnaldo D'Addario's work emphasizes continuity in Medici aims, if not in means, and the development, brought to a high point by Cosimo I, of a quasi-absolute state and of a loyal bureaucracy.[16] His work, along with Elena Fasano Guarini's on Cosimo's state, which highlights the growing Medici control over Tuscany, makes clear a fact that is as obvious as it is commonly ignored: Tuscany, unlike virtually every other Italian state, was a growing power in consolidation under a talented and energetic prince, Cosimo I. The Medici duke's personal control over his state, far wider than that enjoyed by any of his ancestors and wielded through efficient and talented functionaries, mirrored tendencies elsewhere in Europe in the sixteenth century, but itself received comparatively little attention until recently.[17] The assumption that the mark of this state builder appeared on the institutions under his direction underlies this work. The monumental changes that marked the monte di pietà of Florence in the mid-sixteenth century were inseparably tied to Cosimo's statecraft.

Historians who studied the origins of the monti di pietà in the fifteenth century emphasized the background of fiscal decline, political crisis, and anti-Semitism that characterized the period of the monti di pietà's foundation. If the monte di pietà is connected to the larger issues in Tuscan history over the course of the sixteenth century, its evolution can at last be seen not as the inevitable result of its supposed banking "structures" nor as the logical outcome of its anti-Jewish origins, but as a flexible, almost organic process shaped by the demands placed on it. By the sixteenth century, the ruler, more so than the populace or even the elite, gained the strength to be able to impose his own demands. This development set the stage for the Florentine monte di pietà to become part of Cosimo de' Medici's strategy of statecraft.

16. Arnaldo D'Addario, *La formazione dello stato moderno in Toscana da Cosimo il Vecchio a Cosimo I de' Medici* (Lecce, 1976); and idem, "Burocrazia, economia, e finanze dello stato fiorentino alla metà del Cinquecento," *ASI* 121 (1963): 362–456.

17. Elena Fasano Guarini, *Lo stato mediceo di Cosimo I* (Florence, 1973). R. Burr Litchfield emphasizes the tenaciousness of the Florentine patriciate and the development of the Tuscan state, in *Emergence of a Bureaucracy: The Florentine Patricians, 1530–1790* (Princeton, 1986). See also Melissa Bullard, *Filippo Strozzi and the Medici* (Cambridge, England, 1980); John N. Stephens, *The Fall of the Florentine Republic, 1512–1530* (Oxford, 1983); and Humfrey Butters, *Governors and Government in Sixteenth Century Florence, 1502–1519* (Oxford, 1985).

In this volume I place the Florentine monte in its context as one of the major social, political, economic, and charitable institutions of the sixteenth century. I also address some of the questions with which scholars are now concerned in their attempts to understand politics, society, and power in Renaissance Florence. Viewing those problems through a close examination of a single institution yields important information about the origins of monti, about the presence of Jewish moneylenders and of anti-Jewish campaigning, about the institution's administrative history, and about the growth of banking services. More important, it reveals much about the lively problems of political patronage, the growth of the early modern state, and the establishment of control by the Medici in the sixteenth century.

1 THE EARLY MONTI DI PIETÀ AND THE ATTEMPTS TO ESTABLISH A MONTE IN FLORENCE

THE BRIGHT IMAGE of prosperity set forth by Benedetto Dei in 1472 represented a proud patrician view of the city of Florence. Surrounded by rich *contado* (countryside) estates, its citizens remarkable for their entrepreneurship, the jewel of the Arno withstood comparison to any other Italian city.

> We have round about us thirty thousand estates, owned by noblemen and merchants, citizens and craftsmen, yielding us yearly bread and meat, wine and oil, vegetables and cheese, hay and wood, to the value of nine hundred thousand ducats in cash. . . . We have two trades greater than any four . . . in Venice put together: the trades of wool and silk. . . . [There are] the banks of the Medici, the Pazzi, the Capponi, the Buondelmonti, the Corsini, the Falconieri, the Portinari, and the Ghini. . . . Our beautiful Florence has seven things, without all of which no city can be called perfect. The first is complete liberty; the second is a prosperous, well-clothed and large population; . . . the seventh and last is banks.[1]

---

1. Benedetto Dei, *La Cronica dall'anno 1400 all'anno 1500*, ed. R. Barducci (Monte Oriolo, 1984), 77–79. The entire text may be found in the Archivio di Stato, Florence, Manoscritti 119. Some excerpts are found in Mary McLaughlin and James Bruce Ross, eds., *The Portable Renaissance Reader* (New York, 1964), 165–66. Previously unpublished parts of the chronicle were published in 1952 by Giustiniano degli Azzi, "Un frammento inedito della Cronaca di Benedetto Dei," *ASI* 110 (1952): 99–111.

Yet turbulence stirred beneath the tranquil surface of wealth and contentment. Dei—and others like him—could never have guessed that before the end of the decade, an assassination attempt, civil strife, and war with the pope would threaten not only Florence's prosperity, but its independence. Banking crises had shocked the city in the 1430s and 1440s and again in the 1460s. Even as Dei wrote, several Florentine banks foundered, and by the early six-teenth century there were too few men enrolled in the bankers' guild to fill its offices. Such wild fluctuations signaled crisis from which the Medici bank was not immune. Loss of much of its lucra-tive business with the pope weakened the bank, already in decline under the indifferent management of Lorenzo.[2]

Florence's prosperity rested upon groups Dei never thought to mention when describing the glories of his native city. The *popolo minuto* (lower classes), the contado sharecroppers and rentiers, the servants, the poor religious, the Jews—none seemed important enough to warrant Dei's attention. Politically quiet since the suppres-sion of the Ciompi Revolt of 1378 and withdrawn into their own parishes, many poor workers continued to walk a narrow line be-tween subsistence and death.[3] Women, children, and the infirm had always been objects of pity and were considered worthy recipients of Christian charity. Many urban charitable institutions were designed to help those considered the worthy poor. But the able-bodied poor were distrusted, the sick feared and shunned.[4]

2. Raymond de Roover, *The Rise and Decline of the Medici Bank, 1397–1494* (New York, 1966), 365–75. The guild's matriculation records show a lack of new blood in the fifteenth and early sixteenth centuries: from 1 January through 31 March 1501, for example, 147 of the 151 matriculants were sons or close relatives of guild mem-bers. The next year marked a steep decline in matriculations: there were only 3. Arti—Arte del Cambio 12, Book of Matriculations, 133r–v. Richard Goldthwaite, in *The Building of Renaissance Florence: An Economic and Social History* (Baltimore, 1980), argues that the Florentine economy was much stronger in the late fifteenth century than has been believed and that Florentine optimism in it was justified (chap. 1). However, some scholars think this revisionist thesis has not yet been proven.
3. For a study of the evolution of Tuscan landholding and landworking, see Mar-ian Malowist, "Capitalismo commerciale e agricoltura," in *Storia d'Italia: Annali* (Turin, 1978), 1:484–91; and Piero Ugolini, "Il podere nell'economia rurale italiana," in *Storia d'Italia*, esp. 1:782–807. On the endogamy of the working classes, see Samuel K. Cohn, *The Laboring Classes in Renaissance Florence* (New York, 1980).
4. For the connection between innocent victims and charity, see Richard Trexler, "The Foundlings of Florence, 1395–1455," *History of Childhood Quarterly* 1 (1973):259–84.

The Jews were despised for a different reason. As non-Christians, they stood outside the canonical ban on usury. As a result, many Italian communes made pacts with their Jewish inhabitants, for they understood the social and economic value of the lending services the Jews could render. In 1422, for example, the commune of Todi granted its Jewish residents freedom to practice their religion, keep their shops closed on Saturdays, and give loans on collateral at a rate of interest not to exceed 50 percent. They were also guaranteed freedom from outside interference, including the Inquisition.[5]

Jews had a long history of moneylending in Jesi, and attempts to expel them and establish a monte di pietà in 1470 failed because of tacit recognition of their economic importance.[6] The commune nonetheless passed laws intended to protect Christian borrowers from Jewish lenders. City fathers also condemned Jews for charging interest on accrued interest rather than on the principal of loans only, but they must have been aware that Christian lenders followed this profitable practice as well. The curious continuity between services rendered by the despised Jewish moneylenders and those that would be rendered by the new monti di pietà is best illustrated by the pacts that Pistoia made with its Jews in the Quattrocento. Convinced that, left to their own devices, the Jews would charge ruinous interest rates, the commune regulated their activities in a series of laws and contracts. Above all, the Pistoians made it clear that they allowed the Jews to charge interest only because these pawnbrokers performed a useful social service. The commune later used this reasoning to justify controlling the interest rates of its monte di pietà. More important, many of the regulations the city placed on the Jewish moneylenders in 1455 would later appear almost verbatim in the statutes of Pistoia's monte di pietà.[7]

The origins of Jews serving as moneylenders to Christians date back to the urban and commercial revolution of the late eleventh and twelfth centuries. By the twelfth century, rabbinic authorities had declared acceptable the practice of lending money to non-Jews at interest. By the thirteenth, Jews had reached their own conception of the workings of the economy, one distinct from the Christian view

---

5. Holzapfel, "Origini," 1:411.
6. Annibaldi, "I banchi degli ebrei."
7. Capecchi and Gai, *Monte della pietà a Pistoia*, 24–25.

in its understanding of money as a commodity.[8] The tremendous demands of the commercial revolution assured these moneylenders a place within many cities. The development of important Jewish moneylending communities helped to spur a growing Christian view of Jews as a separate group. The first known Jewish ghetto dates from 1084, as do attempts by Christendom to require Jews to dress distinctively.[9]

In Italy by the thirteenth century, most important trading towns had established communities of Jews, who were active participants in financial and commercial life.[10] There is no positive evidence that any Jews lived in Florence during the Dugento, but in 1304 the preacher Giordano da Rivalto delivered a sermon urging Florentines to avoid contact with them, which suggests some must have been living in the city by then. Throughout the fourteenth century Jews were free to enter or leave the commune, and some practiced medicine. By the middle of the century Jews had established themselves as moneylenders in nearby areas. From 1341 to 1345 a small consortium of Jews, including at least one residing in Florence, issued loans to the commune of San Gimignano. However, Christians rather than Jews dominated moneylending through the end of that century.

By the fourteenth century, guild statutes and civic legislation began to reveal the city's determination to enforce the canonical ban on usury. The first step was to limit the number of Christians permitted to lend money at interest against a pawn. In 1351 a provvisione limited this privilege to twenty-one bankers in return for a payment of two thousand florins. No others were permitted to collect interest on loans against pawns under penalty of a fine of one hundred florins. The next step, a ban on usury itself, was taken in

---

8. Giacomo Todeschini, *La ricchezza degli ebrei: Merci e denaro nella riflessione ebraica e nella definizione christiana dell'usura alla fine del Medioevo* (Spoleto, 1989), 121–27. Todeschini argues that a scholarly bias that sees Jews as passive in the debate on usury has mistakenly viewed Christian sources as "the complete realm of information useful in reconstructing the commercial conscience of medieval society" (121). The author makes the provocative suggestion that "polemics on Jewish usury . . . did not signify only persecution but also the blossoming in the Christian conscience of a Jewish economic and juridical identity" (142). Todeschini tends to overstate the theoretical nature of Thomist work on usury, which in fact could be quite down-to-earth.

9. Lester K. Little, *Religious Poverty and the Profit Economy in Medieval Europe* (Ithaca, N.Y., 1978), 42–46.

10. For this and the following discussion, see Cassuto, *Ebrei*, 5–13.

1367 when the bankers' guild forbade the practice by its members.[11] This move, however, meant that usurers would ply their trade outside the guild or that guild members would seek ways to disguise any transactions that might appear usurious. For the tax census of 1427, the Catasto, borrowers were not allowed to declare as deductions their debts to Jewish moneylenders, which might also have discouraged some Florentines from resorting to Jewish pawnbrokers.[12]

The difficulties encountered by the commune and the bankers' guild in trying to enforce the laws regulating moneylending emerged in the Catasto. The tax declaration, or *portata*, submitted for the Banca della Vacca showed that the nearly 3000 lire it lent out against pawns earned it 878 lire in interest, a yield of about 30 percent. Moreover, the canonical prohibition against usury was riddled with exceptions, and the application of an apparently clear principle proved difficult.[13] Yet citizens grew disturbed about the existence of usury in their city, for the practice if committed by a Christian was a grave sin; one writer went so far as to call it unforgivable.[14] That a Christian community would permit its practice was no less repugnant. In 1427 San Bernardino reminded his Sienese listeners of the Church's condemnation of those who allowed the practice of usury. "If," he preached, "you have consented to have a Jew lend at usury here in Siena, if you have given your consent to it . . . , you have incurred . . . excommunication."[15]

Convinced that it was impossible to watch over the activities of the

11. Ibid., 14. The fine for usury was set at one hundred lire. R. de Roover adds that proprietors of pawn shops ("banchi di pegni o a pannello"), whether Christian or Jewish, were barred from guild membership. De Roover, *Medici Bank*, 14.

12. This was true for the Catasto of 1427. David Herlihy and Christiane Klapisch-Zuber, *Tuscans and Their Families* (New Haven, 1985); orig. pub. as *Les toscans et leurs familles* (Paris, 1978), 17.

13. On the Vacca, see Ciardini, *Banchieri*, 17. On the ecclesiastical ban, Monaco, in "Questione dei monti di pietà," 102, writes, "It was necessary to consent to and tolerate repeated exceptions."

14. Monte di Pietà (MP) 1, "Legge prima circa l'ordinare il Monte di Pietà," 2r, repeats the condemnation of a community that supported those practicing this "peccato irremissibile." For the thesis that the community as a whole could reach a state of holiness or plunge into sin, see Marvin Becker, "Aspects of Lay Piety in Early Renaissance Florence," and Donald Weinstein, "Critical Issues in Civic Religion," in Charles Trinkhaus and Heiko Obermann, eds., *The Pursuit of Holiness in Late Medieval and Renaissance Religion* (Leiden, 1974).

15. Quoted in Parsons, "Bernardine of Feltre," 14.

Christian banks and influenced by a serious fiscal crisis, the Signoria of Florence in 1430 reached an agreement with the Jews in an effort to regulate canonically questionable lending practices.[16] The city fathers had a second, more practical motive beyond this idealistic one: an attack of the plague had caused hardship among the poor, and the city councils, the Signori and Collegi, hoped that Jewish moneylenders, accepting pawns from the needy, would provide a source of ready cash for this unfortunate group.[17] The provvisione conceded that "the Jews may lend against pledges in the city of Florence" in return for paying a tax of four denari per lira. The Signori then refused to renew the privileges of the Christian pawnbrokers, effectively transferring this activity from Christians to Jews by default. In October 1437 the councils approved the first moneylending concessions to Jews, and in November the first Jewish banks in Florence began operation.

From that time on, the trade of lending money at interest and against collateral gradually devolved to the Jews, a development that sharpened the traditional repugnance Florentines felt toward them. The belief that Jews "trafficked in other people's misfortunes" took hold despite the fact that, until recently, Christians themselves had practiced this same trade, canonical bans notwithstanding.[18] Two centuries later, an anonymous Florentine, compiling a history of the origins of his city's monte di pietà, would recall "this raging pestilence of usury borne in our city and its dominion . . . [and practiced by] that perfidious sect, those enemies of God, the Hebrews."[19] This attitude built on a long history of Christian objection to Jewish pawnbroking. For example, in the twelfth century, stories circulated that not only did Jews accept as pawns such ecclesiastical objects as

16. See Anthony Molho, *Florentine Public Finances in the Early Renaissance, 1400–1433* (Cambridge, Mass., 1971), esp. chaps. 5–6, for the development of this crisis. Interest rates charged by the Christian banks were as high as 66.66 percent. See Cassuto, *Ebrei*, 12. The provvisioni regulating Jewish activities in fifteenth-century Florence have been conveniently compiled in Miscellanea Repubblicana, busta I, inserto 37: "Provvisioni diverse relative alla concessione fatta agli Ebrei di prestare . . . ed all'istituzione del Monte in Firenze."

17. Cassuto, *Ebrei*, 18. See also Misc. Rep., busta I, inserto 37, which contains the statute of 12 June 1430 proposing a 20 percent limit (four denari per lira) on loans by Jews.

18. Pampaloni, "Cenni storici," 526.

19. MP 1, 2r. This account dates from the mid-seventeenth century.

chalices, but, as Peter the Venerable remarked, they did things to them "horrendous to contemplate, detestable to mention." This attitude also built on the increasingly close association of Jews with avarice, a sin depicted in the story of Judas's betrayal of Jesus for silver. At the same time, Christian polemicists began to link the Jews with the devil, who was no longer portrayed as a fallen angel but as a repulsive creature with horns and tail. This image was solidified in the thirteenth century by Raymond Martini's "Pugio fidei" (the dagger of the faithful). "The Jews," he asserted, "do not accept Christianity because of their ancient pact with the devil, to which even the Talmud attests."[20]

The notion of usury originated in what Benjamin Nelson called the "Deuteronomic double standard," which seemed to forbid usurious lending "to thy brother" but to permit such practices in dealings with "strangers."[21] Theologians had difficulty reconciling a conflict inherent in these two passages: how could they identify "strangers" within the universal Christian brotherhood of Jesus' new covenant? The New Testament made Christ's teaching clear: "Lend freely, hoping for nothing thereby" (Luke 6:35). Saint Jerome contended that the gospel of love and brotherhood must take precedence over Deuteronomy's apparent toleration of usury. Saint Ambrose proposed a different answer, suggesting that those heathen who waged war against Christians were the "strangers" of whom Deuteronomy spoke and that usury was licit when exacted from them. These two different conclusions—one forbidding usury outright, the other acknowledging its acceptability in some circumstances—provided the basis for discussion of the problem in the Middle Ages. The dangers inherent in the Ambrosian point of view surfaced in the twelfth century when, despite repeated papal pleas and threats, European Christians lent badly needed money at usury to the Saracens, claiming that the ancient bishop of Milan had authorized such loans to heathen.

20. Peter the Venerable's words to Louis VII of France are quoted in Little, *Religious Poverty*, 52–53. On the diabolical portrait of Jews, see Robert Bonfil, "The Devil and the Jews in the Christian Consciousness of the Middle Ages," in Shmuel Almog, ed., *Antisemitism through the Ages* (Oxford, 1988): 91–98; the quotation from Martini is found on 97.

21. See Nelson, *Idea of Usury*, xx–xxi, and 3–28, for this discussion. Also see the relevant passage in Deuteronomy 23:19–20. A similar distinction between a lender's relations with brothers and with strangers appears in Deuteronomy 15:1–3.

The canonists made a number of important contributions to the debate. Writing in the mid-twelfth century, Gratian declared that persons who had committed usury were barred from holy orders. Furthermore, he warned that even the expectation of gain over and above the principal of a loan was usury and that anyone, layman or cleric, receiving such gain shared the guilt of a thief. Gratian supported his argument by citing texts from the fourth through sixth centuries, for there had been no decrees of more recent date. After the completion of Gratian's landmark *Decretum* in 1140, however, councils took up the question and handed down decisions as contradictory as they were voluminous. Subsequent canon lawyers commented on this body of laws and customs, adding to the discussion.

The fact that civil law as compiled in Justinian's *Corpus juris civilis* clearly permitted usury complicated the issue.[22] Some canonists later argued that in fact no disagreement existed between civil and canon codes on usury because Justinian had called for adherence to the decrees of general councils, which had condemned the practice. Others, however, argued that civil law permitted usury in order to avoid a worse evil, even though usury itself was spiritually dangerous. The civil law, after all, did not forbid everything that was evil, but only regulated those elements that properly fell under its jurisdiction.

In the course of their examination of this difficult question, the canonists suggested that the distinction between *usura* and *interesse*—the former best defined as illicit profit, the latter as licit profit on loans—lay in the question of risk or loss, which could permit a lender licitly to receive compensation. Delay in receiving repayment of a loan, for instance, entitled the lender to collect interest, but calculated only from the point at which the loan became overdue.[23]

Bartolus, or Baldo degli Ubaldi, was the first canonist to treat the subject comprehensively. He reiterated both the divine prohibition of usury and the notion that any delay in repayment of a contracted loan meant that the collection of profit was not usury at all but licit

22. See Terence P. McLaughlin, "The Teaching of the Canonists on Usury," *Mediaeval Studies* 1 (1939): 81–147 and 2 (1940): 1–22, for this and the following discussions.

23. Canonists saw, for instance, that three kinds of cases permitted lenders to expect a return in excess of the money lent: *damnum emergens* (loss resulting), *lucrum cessans* (profit ending; perhaps implying money lying idle), or *periculum sortis* (risk of the principal). Parsons, "Economic Significance," 17.

interest. At the heart of the debate lay the issue of whether the civil law could, in T. P. McLaughlin's words, "legislate against the divine law and the canons."[24] The attempt to reconcile this problem brought up the question of social utility. Here the canonists disagreed, however. Some felt that the plight of the poor made usury acceptable though not desirable because, despite its dangers, it could relieve their want. Bartolus spoke for those who felt instead that canon law must always prevail over mere utility. Nonetheless, the canonists denied that an emperor who permitted usury was a heretic, for he acted not out of obstinacy to God's law but out of concern for the well-being of his people.

The debate concentrated on defining "stranger" rather than articulating an outright prohibition of usury. Christian thinkers of the late twelfth and thirteenth centuries added that Jews had been permitted to practice usury because God knew they would commit worse sins if not allowed this one. Just because a practice was permitted to exist, however, did not mean it was pleasing to God or free from sin, for good Christians ought to choose not to commit the sin of usury. Thomas Aquinas summarized the scholastics' position:

> The Jews were forbidden to lend upon interest to their brothers, that is to say, to their fellow Jews. What we are meant to understand by this is that lending upon interest to any man is wrong in itself, in so far as we ought to treat every man as our brother and neighbour. . . . And the fact that they took interest from foreigners shows not that they were entitled to do so as of right but only that they were allowed to do so in order to avoid the greater evil of taking interest from their fellow Jews, God's own people, out of sheer greed, to which they were prone.[25]

Jews were nonetheless condemned for the practice, as, for example, in a canon of the Fourth Lateran Council of 1215 decrying their "oppressive and immoderate usury." Provincial councils repeated this judgment.[26]

The commercial revolution of the twelfth century sharpened the

---

24. McLaughlin, "Teaching of the Canonists," 91.
25. Thomas Aquinas, *Summa Theologica* (London, 1975), quaestio 38, 38:237.
26. Quoted in McLaughlin, "Teaching of the Canonists," 99: "graves et immoderatas usuras." On the Dominicans and Franciscans and the questions of usury and social utility, see Little, *Religious Poverty*, 173–83.

economic element of the debate, bringing into focus the issue of the just price and when, if ever, it was canonically permissible to take interest on loans.[27] The scholastics, including Henry of Langerstein, John Duns Scotus, Albertus Magnus, and Thomas Aquinas, grappled with this complicated issue and developed a body of literature that took into consideration such market factors as costs of production (including labor), demand, and risk in the determination of the just price. Many of these theories were put into practice through guild regulations that set prices and wages, and otherwise regulated the marketplace.[28]

It was never the canonists' intention to deny merchants and bankers their profit, but rather to insist that such profit be reasonable and legitimate. According to Nelson, canon lawyers saw "a world of difference between usury, that is profit openly demanded or secretly hoped for in a contract of loan (*mutuum*), and justifiable returns derived from partnerships where there was sharing of the risk and venture of the capital."[29] Merchants and bankers had developed ways of evading the ecclesiastical prohibition against usury; the letter of exchange (*cambium*), by which a borrower received a loan in one currency and repaid in another at a rate of exchange favorable to the lender, was one such instrument. Business loans, which usually involved some risk to the lender, could be made by this form of contract. The lender could legitimately accept compensation in exchange for the risk he ran by affixing what amounted to an interest charge to his loan. But loans to individuals generally fell under the rubric of the mutuum, and canon law viewed interest on such loans as usurious. The distinction between these two kinds of loans was crystal clear among the canonists: "Usury occurs only in the mutuum," and "the cambium is not a mutuum."[30]

27. See, for example, F. de Roover, "Restitution in Renaissance Florence," and Raymond de Roover, "'Cambium ad Venetias': A Contribution to the History of Foreign Exchange," in *Studi in onore di Armando Sapori* (Milan, 1957).

28. Raymond de Roover, "Labour Conditions in Florence around 1400: Theory, Policy and Reality," in Nicolai Rubinstein, ed., *Florentine Studies: Politics and Society in Renaissance Florence* (Evanston, Ill., 1968).

29. Nelson, "Usurer and the Merchant Prince," 104. McLaughlin, "Teaching of the Canonists," 100, adds that the object of the transaction of the *mutuum* was something that could be counted, weighed, or measured.

30. Quoted in R. de Roover, *Medici Bank*, 10–11: According to Bernardino of Siena, "Usura solum in mutuo cadit," and "Cambium non est mutuum." De Roover noted that, for most Italian banks, "earnings, instead of being derived from interest charges,

Despite this intense discussion, the question of usury was not easily settled by the theologians. Antipathy toward making money on loans continued to run deep. The banker Giulio di Giovenco de' Medici, for example, made many loans to business entrepreneurs at a rate of 10 to 12 percent per annum, a practice his guild considered legitimate. But since he had demanded collateral on these loans and was therefore guarded against default by his debtors, Giulio worried about the salvation of his eternal soul. Thus he decided to ask his heirs to make restitution to those who had incurred the loans. But as for those loans for which he had received no collateral, he made no such request, as, for example, with the money he advanced to the Spedale degli Innocenti, among others.[31]

San Bernardino da Siena, one of the most famous and captivating preachers of his day, represented the Observant Franciscan position.[32] His sermons bluntly called usury a mortal sin and argued that, in his own lifetime (1380–1444), the sin was on a rampage. He called upon his listeners to direct their civic leaders to elect an official "to set everything to rights . . . and to get everything back to normal." Worst of all, the friar told his audiences, were pawnbrokers. In typical Franciscan fashion, Bernardino's objection lay not only in the usury these men practiced but also in the principles of utility. Selling an item was preferable to pawning it, he said, for "if you had sold it, you would have done some good, first to yourself, then to the townsman who buys or resells it, and everyone would have earned something from it." In the same sermon, Bernardino reiterated this point: "the usurer plays the good-for-nothing. . . . If a man is a soldier, someone benefits from it; if he's a wool merchant, someone

---

originated in exchange differences." The principal instrument of operation for these banks was the letter of exchange (109, 130).

31. F. de Roover, "Restitution in Renaissance Florence," 779–80. For the medieval roots of the practice of deathbed and testamentary restitution, see Philippe Ariès, "Richesse et pauvreté devant la mort," in Michel Mollat, ed., *Etudes sur l'histoire de la pauvreté* (Paris, 1974), Vol. 2; and Georges Duby, *The Early Growth of the European Economy: Warriors and Peasants from the Seventh to the Twelfth Century*, trans. H. Clarke (Ithaca, N.Y., 1974), 258–59. Testamentary bequests have been treated in detail by Samuel K. Cohn, *Death and Property in Siena, 1205–1800: Strategies for the Afterlife* (Baltimore, 1988).

32. The importance of the contribution of Observant spirituality to the Italian Renaissance has been emphasized by George Holmes, *Florence, Rome and the Origins of the Renaissance* (Oxford, 1986).

benefits from it, and every trade does good to someone. Except the usurer."[33] Bernardino was not opposed to business or to business techniques per se and even had a rough conception of the beneficial influence of the marketplace. His wrath descended instead on illicit profit, which damaged individuals and society.

By trying to adhere to canon law's requirements for legitimate profits and by offering restitution when necessary, Italian merchants of the fifteenth century gradually ceased to be thought of—and to think of themselves—as usurers.[34] The Medici family offers an example of this evolution. The bookseller Vespasiano da Bisticci related the "prickings of conscience" felt by Cosimo the Elder, who feared that "certain portions of his fortune . . . had not been rightfully gained." His friend Pope Eugenius advised Cosimo to build a monastery to calm his worries.[35] Two generations later, much of this fear had disappeared. Marsilio Ficino wrote to Lorenzo de' Medici, "Lorenzo, God himself is for sale. But with what coin can he be bought? . . . At the price of generous charity to the poor."[36] Ficino never implied that Lorenzo need worry about having gained his wealth illicitly through usury. Rather than giving to offer restitution, Lorenzo ought to give freely in order to please God through charity. Thus Nelson tells us that in Florence emerged the clear distinction between "the city father, . . . patron of the arts, devout philanthropist, merchant prince" and "the degraded manifest usurer-pawnbroker, as often as not a Jew."[37]

In Florence, debate over the canonical legality of the *monte comune*, the funded public debt, had already thrust the question of usury to center stage.[38] This development occurred as theologians began to

33. From Bernardino's sermon "On Usury," in *Le prediche volgari*, ed. Ciro Cannorozzi (Florence, 1934), 2:113–28. Parts of this sermon have been published (and excellently translated by Lydia Cochrane) in Eric Cochrane and Julius Kirshner, eds., *Readings in Western Civilization*, vol. 5, *The Renaissance* (Chicago, 1986), 128–38.

34. See Nelson, "Usurer and the Merchant Prince," for this thesis.

35. Vespasiano da Bisticci, *Le vite*, ed. Aulo Greco (Florence, 1970–76), 2:177–78.

36. Marsilio Ficino, *The Letters of Marsilio Ficino* (London, 1975), 1:116–17.

37. Nelson, "Usurer and the Merchant Prince," 120–21.

38. See Julius Kirshner, "From Usury to Public Finance: The Ecclesiastical Controversy over the Public Debts of Florence, Genoa, and Venice (1300–1500)," Ph.D. diss., Columbia University, 1970, chaps. 2–3. On the phrase found in the *Decretum*, see ibid., 57, and R. de Roover, *Medici Bank*, 10: "Quidquid sorti accedit, usura est."

question the mechanisms that Italian communes had devised to deal with the growing expenses of government. Did citizens who invested in Florence's funded public debt risk the grave spiritual peril of usury? The answer depended upon one's definition of that sin. Saint Ambrose, in a phrase that would later be found in the *Decretum*, had been clear: "Whatever is added [to the principal of a loan] is usury." That such "usury" might further the common good was irrelevant. Nevertheless, the undeniable usefulness of a funded public debt paved the way for more sophisticated debate on usury.

If, for instance, a person gave a loan of money as a free gift, he or she might reasonably expect the receiver to repay the loan promptly. Further, if a debtor failed to repay a loan on time, the creditor was entitled to exact a penalty. Lenders forced to make loans could licitly receive a profit, one spiritual Franciscan declared, because the state had imposed the loan. Dominicans countered that, although citizens might be forced to make a loan, they were not forced to make a profit, and such profit remained wrong. Lorenzo Ridolfi's treatise on usury aimed specifically at the problem of the funded public debt helped resolve the controversy. Since, Ridolfi claimed, no one could expect to receive prompt repayment of a loan to the state (which was "a debtor in perpetual decay"), persons collecting interest on forced state loans broke no church law.[39] Both Sant'Antonino and San Bernardino echoed Ridolfi's words; the latter, for example, agreed that citizens forced to lend may accept "damages." This viewpoint marked a clear expression of a principle generally accepted by theologians by the end of the fifteenth century: *lucrum cessans* (profit ending). Proponents of this idea saw money as an instrument that persons could put to work in order to make their living through profitable ventures. Giving money in a forced loan cost such persons the opportunity to invest it in a licit money-making enterprise. In lieu of such profit, they could instead receive interest without committing usury.

By the middle of the fifteenth century, then, Florentines had conveniently arrived at a canonical justification for what they wanted to do anyway: place investments at interest in the monte comune. Such a development depended on a less stringent definition of usury. Although by itself this definition did not obviate accusations of usury in the monte di pietà, the Florentines' willingness to discuss the

---

39. Kirshner, "From Usury to Public Finance," 127.

problems and their history of finding moral and spiritual justifications for economic exigencies predicted success for the monte di pietà too. As Nelson put it, "In fifteenth-century Italy, economic expediencies completely overshadowed moral philosophy as a force in the propagation of Christian universalism." In addition, the subsequent debate over the practices of monti di pietà led to landmark decisions about usury.[40]

Once Christians in Florence were no longer permitted to run pawnshops, the identification of usury with the Jews became clearer, a development that would prove crucial in justifying the activities of the monte di pietà. In Florence, one writer calculated the damage done to the citizens' economic well-being by the usury of the Jews: "having begun at the outset with a sum of one hundred lire, this capital increased with usury over the course of fifty years to a total of 49,792,556 lire, seven grossi, and seven denari."[41] This insidious practice had, moreover, caused economic harm to the city as a whole. The Jews had "drawn from the city and its territories an infinite treasure." Along with usury, this anonymous writer continued, the Jews had perpetrated many other frauds and wrongdoings, all of which rightly aroused the hostility of Christians. This writer ignored, however, cases in which Christian, not Jewish, moneylenders admitted having charged high interest rates. One example was recounted by an anonymous and recently reformed "Christian usurer" writing to San Bernardino da Feltre about "how bad a thing usury is. . . . I have offered in loans," the lender continued, "one hundred ducats for fifty years, lending at twenty-five percent per annum . . . , putting earnings and interest back [into the loans]." His profit came, he claimed, to 6,101,632 ducats.[42] The similarities between this letter describing Christian usury and the example cited above are too remarkable to be coincidental and suggest a rhetorical expression of the dangers of usury.

---

40. The quotation is from Nelson, *Idea of Usury*, 18–19. The monte di pietà's long-term contributions to the debate are noted in Parsons, "Economic Significance."

41. MP 1, 2r. Cassuto has shown that this figure was taken directly from the "Tabula della salute" of Marco da Monte Santa Maria, who calculated the accrual of money on an investment of L. 100 at 30 percent per annum for fifty years (simple interest, but with all profits reinvested). Cassuto, *Ebrei*, 68–71. (Marco's calculations were fairly accurate: the total ought to be just over L. 49,792,922.)

42. Letter of a Christian usurer to Bernardino of Feltre, 22 Sept. 1484, in Vittorino Meneghin, ed., *Documenti vari intorno al Beato Bernardino Tomitano da Feltre* (Rome, 1966), 50.

Florentines believed that Jewish moneylenders had ways of doubling or tripling their profits by offering loans equal to less than half
the value of pawns. According to a seventeenth-century writer describing Jewish lending practices in the late fifteenth century, Jewish
loan contracts required Christian borrowers to pay interest every
month, with the result that the moneylenders collected more than
the value of the loan on interest payments alone. Many borrowers
requested an extension of the loan's terms, yet still defaulted. In
these cases the Jew then sold the pawn at its true value, multiplying
his profit well beyond the interest rate the law allowed him to
charge.[43]

The Florentine Signoria made numerous attempts to legislate the
public and private behavior of the Jews. In 1446 all Jews except
moneylenders were ordered to wear a yellow badge under penalty of
one hundred florins. This law was enforced: in April of the same
year, a Jew was thrown into the Stinche prison and fined for failing
to display the badge. Neither his conversion to Christianity nor the
intervention of the archbishop of Florence freed him from the obligation to pay his fine. Eventually he fled the city, and those who had
posted bond (*mallevadori*) against his good behavior forfeited it.[44]
Still, the Signoria regularly renewed the laws that allowed the Jews
to lend money in Florence.

Soon trouble arrived from outside the city when an Observant
Franciscan from Milan came to Florence to preach against the Jews.
Archbishop Antonino, the Signoria, and the Otto di Guardia e Balìa
forbade him to continue, but persist he did, stirring crowds in Florence to anti-Jewish violence. The authorities responded by sending
guards to escort the preacher from the city and giving him three
days to leave Florentine territory. Florentine public officials felt little
sympathy for Jews, but they wanted to regulate and restrict their
activities and had no intention of forfeiting their power to the mob
or to an itinerant friar. The result was more restrictions on the Jews.
In 1463 a set of provvisioni called for a twenty-five lire fine for any
Jew, including moneylenders, who did not wear the yellow badge.
The number of Jews permitted to reside in the city was limited to
seventy, including moneylenders, their families, and the keeper of a
Jewish inn.[45]

43. MP 4, 34.
44. Cassuto, *Ebrei*, 36–41.
45. Ibid., 47–48.

Popular feelings were inflamed by morality plays like *The Tale of Agnolo the Jew*, which tied together the usury of the Jews, the suffering of the poor, and its alleviation by the monte di pietà. In this work by an anonymous playwright, two Jewish usurers, Samuello and Isac, meet on the street. Samuello says,

> Isac, I am disturbed deep in my heart. . . .
> I have felt a knife stab me;
> I have heard one Brother Picciuolo preach.
> He has said—I tell you the truth—
> That loans will be ended, and a monte di pietà built. . . .
> He says and reaffirms that it would be good
> To send us out right away from this land.[46]

The play's rather conventional plot (converted wife prays for Jewish husband's conversion, with uplifting ending) is enlivened by an interesting twist. Agnolo, the Jew, has forty lire to invest. His wife begs, "Give it to my God, and without any doubt / he will return it to you a hundredfold." So Agnolo offers alms to a poor widow and to a destitute man with ten children. He regrets his act of charity until he visits a Christian church, where he is elated to find a silver denaro. Aha! he thinks; this is surely the beginning of God's hundredfold repayment! After haggling with a fishmonger over the price of his wares, Agnolo buys a whole fish and takes it home for his wife to cook. She discovers inside a jewel that Agnolo—still haggling—sells to a banker for two hundred ducats. Impressed with the Christian God's alacrity in repaying his debts, Agnolo agrees to convert and be baptized. Neither prayers nor entreaties had convinced Agnolo, nor did his conversion stem from the basis of Christian life, faith. Only the multiple repayment of his reluctantly offered charitable gift convinced this usurious Jew of the error of his ways and of the universal truth of God's saving grace.

Legal restrictions and popular plays show that the traditional enmity in which Christians held Jews intensified in the late fifteenth century. Throughout Italy, civic and religious leaders sought a new answer to the problem of how to expel the Jews from Christian soci-

---

46. The passages quoted are from the anonymous "Storia di Agnolo ebreo," in Mario Bonfantini, ed., *Le sacre rappresentazioni italiane: Raccolta di testi dal secolo XIII al secolo XVI* (Milan, 1942), 572–73, 576.

ety while at the same time escaping the economic peril that the cessation of usury would pose. Several Franciscan friars proposed a solution: a new, communal charitable institution, the monte di pietà, that would offer small loans against pawns while eliminating usury, thereby rendering the Jews socially superfluous.

Although this answer appears innovative, it nonetheless comprised some old elements. First, it is not surprising that the mendicant friars embraced, with characteristic energy, the task of solving this problem. With their origins in the commercial revolution of the Middle Ages (the Dominicans received papal approval in 1206, the Franciscans in 1210), the friars had traditionally ministered to the needs of the new working and merchant classes of the cities. The central ideal of Franciscan life had always been, at least in theory, absolute, uncompromising poverty for themselves collectively as well as individually and alleviation of the desperate poverty of the urban poor. In the thirteenth century, wherever the Dominicans preached they left behind a legacy of enthusiasm for the creation of charitable institutions and lay confraternities. Florentines knew that their own ancestors had been moved to found the charitable Bigallo as the result of the fervent preaching of the Dominican Peter Martyr in the 1240s.[47]

Second, the notion of forming an economic institution, or monte,[48] had been successfully implemented in Florence as early as 1345 when the Florentines set up their monte comune. Citizens could purchase shares in this funded public debt on which they received interest payments. The purchase of shares would in theory provide the government with sufficient operating capital as well as the means to pay the interest. With this successful example before them, in 1425 the city councils passed legislation setting up the *monte delle doti,*

47. Ugo Morini, ed., *Documenti inediti o poco noti per la storia della Misericordia di Firenze* (Florence, 1940), 33; the institution was "Facta et cominciata Perlo beato messer santo piero martire de l'ordine de frati predicatori."

48. The word *monte,* meaning an accumulation or an institution for accumulating, has an ancient history. Prudentius used the word in its Latin form, *mons,* to denote a sum of alms; it soon came to refer to the donations for support of a group of poor monks. In the mid-twelfth century the city of Venice had formed a *mons profanus,* envisioned as a center for resources to help offset civic expenses, of which there were many as a result of the wars between Pope Alexander III and Emperor Frederick Barbarossa. In other cities, groups of merchants founded a type of monte roughly equivalent to a modern insurance company, which would protect each member against catastrophic losses. Holzapfel, "Origini," 1:408.

or dowry fund, in which citizens were invited to make deposits in their young daughters' names. Once the offsprings' marriages were consummated, the deposits and interest would be paid as the women's dowries.

The Franciscans took up battle against the Jews, indicting in their sermons individual cities for permitting the practice of usury within their walls. Emphasizing the social, financial, and spiritual utility of the monte di pietà, these tireless preachers left in their wake a series of fledgling monti. They scored their first success in Perugia in 1462, a city with a long-standing Jewish community: in 1385 the city had conceded privileges, including the right to open their shops on Christian feast days, to its Jewish inhabitants.[49]

This first monte di pietà, which served as a model for most of the others that followed, was founded almost single-handedly by two Franciscans, Bernaba de' Terni and Antonio da Lodi. Attached to the jurisdiction of Umbria, the two brothers prayed to God to free Perugia from the sufferings caused by the Jews and other usurers. Legend has it that Christ appeared to them in a dream and promised to help them by sending the preacher Fra Michele da Carcano from the Holy Land to give a Lenten sermon urging the establishment of a monte di pietà.[50]

The establishment of the Perugian monte went hand in hand with the expulsion of the Jews. A contemporary document related how, in April 1462, Fra Michele "so moved the citizenry by his excellent arguments, advice and sermons . . . that they all with a single voice revoked the privileges conceded to the Jews."[51] At the same time the magistrates ordered the Jews to support the institution designed to displace them by lending it two thousand florins. Pope Pius II, familiar with Perugia after a three-week stay there in 1459, approved the plan, though he reduced the sum to be obtained from the Jews to twelve hundred florins.[52] The original Perugian monte, allotted an

49. Diego Quaglioni, "I giuristi medioevali e gli ebrei: Due 'consultationes' di G. F. Pavini (1478)," *Quaderni storici*, n.s., 64 (1987): 12. On Perugia's status as the site of the first monte di pietà, see Meneghin, *Monti di pietà*, 25 and 131. Meneghin proved that an institution called the monte di pietà founded in 1458 in Ascoli Piceno did not in fact function as a charitable pawnshop.

50. Holzapfel, "Origini," 1:603 ff.

51. Quoted ibid., 606.

52. Pius's trip is mentioned in his memoirs; Pius II, *Memoirs of a Renaissance Pope: The Commentaries of Pius II*, ed. Leona C. Gabel (New York, 1959), 100–101.

operating capital of three thousand florins, was soon joined by two branches erected in the same city, each given the sum of one thousand florins. By 1472 the three were united under one roof after the city provided them with a large new building.[53]

Encouraged by the Franciscans and bringing in their wake the expulsion of the Jews, monti began to spring up throughout Italy. They flourished first in Umbria, then spread to the Marches, the Veneto, Lombardy, Emilia, Tuscany—in short, almost everywhere in Italy as far south as Sicily.[54] During Lent of 1463, a friar successfully urged the Orvietesi to end usury, expel the Jews, and create a monte. No later than October of the same year, Gubbio founded a monte that imitated the first establishment in Perugia. Others soon followed in Foligno, Monterubbiano, and elsewhere.[55] Genoa's was instituted in 1483, during the dogeship of Paulo Fregoso, at the urging of the jurist Bartolomeo Bosco and the preacher Angelo da Chiavassa.[56] The creation of the monte at Monterubbiano was noteworthy for the role played by Fra Cristoforo, a Dominican. Monti were also established in Recanati, Macerata, Assisi, Urbino, Ancona, Viterbo, and several of the March cities. Some discovered, however, that their new monti di pietà could not replace the Jews. The Lucchesi found it necessary to establish a second monte di pietà in 1493 because of the departure, for unspecified reasons, of the Jewish moneylender Davit di Dattilo.[57]

By 1472 Tuscany's first monte di pietà had taken root in Siena. Within four years, responding to the preaching of the Franciscan Cherubino da Spoleto, the citizens of Prato, near Florence, established their monte di pietà in 1476.[58] Florentines too had begun to

53. Holzapfel, "Origini," 1:610.

54. Meneghin, *Monti di pietà*, 30–33. In their first hundred years (1462–1562), Italian monti di pietà numbered 214 by Meneghin's count.

55. Holzapfel, "Origini," 3:27. Holzapfel errs in stating that the founder of the monte at Foligno in 1465 was a Jesuit, since that order was not founded until the sixteenth century. Most likely the word *Gesuiti* is a misprint for *Gesuati*, an order founded in 1367 by Giovanni Colombini. See Amleto Spicciani, "The 'Poveri Vergognosi' in Fifteenth-Century Florence," in Thomas Riis, ed., *Poverty in Early Modern Europe* (Aalphen aan den Rijn, 1981), 129 and n. 54, where the Company of the Good Men of San Martino gave aid "to the poor *Gesuati* of the Porta a Pinti" (emphasis added).

56. Vito Vitale, *Breviario della storia di Genova* (Genoa, 1955), 1:164, 194.

57. Corsi, "Secondo monte di pietà di Lucca," 390–92.

58. Enrico Stumpo, "Le istituzioni e la società," in *Un microcosmo in movimento*, vol. 2 of Elena Fasano Guarini, ed., *Prato: Storia di una città* (Prato, 1986), 323.

discuss building a monte and were urged on by the rhetorical powers of the Franciscans Fortunato Coppoli da Perugia and Giacomo da Cagli. Finally a provvisione of 24 March 1473 empowered the officials of the monte comune to make the necessary arrangements to set up a *mons subventionis et caritatis* (a monte of relief and charity).[59] Modeled after the first monti di pietà, the Florentine institution would offer loans to the poor against pawns, charging a small fee rather than interest to meet its operating costs. Fortunato Coppoli, defending this last point, composed a treatise that came to be known as the "Florentine Advice" ("Consiglio Fiorentino") because it urged that a monte di pietà in Florence collect a fee from borrowers.[60] The fervor of the Franciscans pervaded the provvisione, which declared that it was evil not only to commit usury, but to allow others to practice it.[61]

But this proposed Florentine monte never began operation. First, the traditional rivalry between the Franciscans and the Dominicans fired the latter's bitter opposition to monti di pietà on the grounds that the institution required interest from the poor. However low the fee, however admirable the cause, argued the Dominicans, this was interest, and interest was usury. Their objection was overturned by Domenico Bocchi, vicar of the archbishop of Florence, but the Dominicans remained, for the time being, opposed to the creation of the monte di pietà.[62]

Second, not even the forceful preaching of the Franciscans could loosen the pursestrings of the cautious Florentines. Although Lorenzo de' Medici pledged the generous sum of five hundred florins, none of his peers followed his lead. The commission that investigated possible sources of capital for the proposed monte di pietà charged the officials of the monte comune with the task of providing part of the necessary sum. However, the newly reformed monte comune held a substantial sum of money from Jewish moneylenders, who paid a handsome annual fee for the privilege of doing business in Florence. The monte comune's officials were not inclined to relin-

59. Libri fabarum, 24 March 1472 (O.S.), 136r–137r. I am grateful to Anthony Molho of Brown University for this reference.
60. Meneghin, *Bernardino da Feltre*, 206, n. 1.
61. Quoted in Capecchi and Gai, *Monte della pietà a Pistoia*, 27.
62. Cassuto, *Ebrei*, 51.

quish this source of revenue and as a result did not lift a finger to help establish the charitable institution.[63]

Finally, it appears that Lorenzo himself, while maintaining a public show of support, worked secretly to undo the monte di pietà. He opposed the attempts to remove the Jews, part and parcel of the creation of the monte in Florence, for he saw economic advantages in their presence. In addition, his humanist training may have instilled in Lorenzo contempt for discrimination on racial or even religious grounds. Among his circle of literate friends were men who questioned whether virtue existed solely in the Western Christian tradition and who appreciated the value of the writings of the ancient Greeks, Romans, Arabs, and Hebrews.[64] Lorenzo himself had protected and patronized Hebrew scholars. In 1478, when a pontifical delegation went to Lorenzo hoping to work out a plan for levying taxes on Florentine Jews, Lorenzo carefully avoided compliance, partly to shield the Jews, partly to avoid the appearance of bowing to pressure during a time of strain in papal-Florentine relations. During Lorenzo's lifetime, though the city passed laws restricting their freedom, Jews nonetheless felt that they had a protector.[65]

Humanists as a group, however, were not always benevolent toward Jews. Fourteenth-century Italy produced only five polemical treatises against Jews, most written by friars. By the fifteenth century the number of such tracts had at least doubled. More important, Quattrocento anti-Jewish polemicists included the Jewish convert

63. On Lorenzo, see ibid., 51–52. A promise made by another Medici almost resulted in a similar outcome in Pistoia when Bishop Donato de' Medici pledged the huge sum of three thousand florins but successfully evaded attempts to force him to pay up. Capecchi and Gai, *Monte della pietà a Pistoia*, 68 and 31.

64. Giovanni Pico della Mirandola is the best example of a humanist within Lorenzo's circle who was well versed in the languages required to pursue this topic. In Ernst Cassirer's words, "Truth [for Pico] is handed down through the ages; but it is generated by no age, by no single epoch." Cassirer, "Giovanni Pico della Mirandola," in Paul O. Kristeller and Philip P. Weiner, eds., *Renaissance Essays from the* "Journal of the History of Ideas" (New York, 1968), 12; originally published in volume 2 (1942) of that journal.

65. Cassuto argues that in Florence, Jews were generally well off under the Medici and persecuted under the republics. See *Ebrei*, 54–58. On Lorenzo's lack of cooperation with the pope, see *Ebrei*, 56, n. 1. For instances of Medici aid to Jews, see idem, *La famille des Médicis et les juifs* (Paris, 1923). Capecchi and Gai concur that "Jewish lenders were protected or tolerated in Florence *at least while Lorenzo de' Medici was alive*" (original emphasis). *Monte della pietà a Pistoia*, 31.

Gianbattista Graziadei, the Bolognese jurist Borrio della Sala, the Venetian man of politics Paolo Morosini, Bishop Pietro Bruti of Cattaro, and the humanist Giannozzo Manetti. The ranks of anti-Semitic propagandists were no longer comprised solely of a small group of friars, but had expanded to include lay intellectuals. Rather than fostering tolerance, the humanist embrace of Hebrew studies in the late fifteenth century led to more anti-Semitism, with scholars now able to attack Jews by using Hebrew sources.[66]

As a result, learned opposition to the Jewish presence in Italian cities spread from universities and monasteries to the humanist courts and villas. Lorenzo de' Medici presided over a debate about the sins of Adam, laid at the feet of the Jews. A disputation in Pisa counted in its audience both Lorenzo and the humanist Angelo Poliziano. Another in Genoa reportedly attracted five thousand people. Some of these new participants in the discussion worked actively against Jews: the Venetian aristocrat Ludovico Foscarini likened the presence of Jews in the domain of the Serenessima to "perpetual war."[67] Italians began to see Jews as foreigners, and to display greater bigotry as hatred was translated into fines, stricter regulation, and discrimination. The resulting propaganda was exemplified by Giacomo Ongarelli's *Contra perfidiam modernorum Judeorum* (Against the treachery of today's Jews), which argued both against the Jews and in favor of monti di pietà.

In Florence, though, the early attempt to establish a monte di pietà and to expel the Jews failed. Jews continued to live in the city and to practice the trade of moneylending, yet the undercurrent of anti-Jewish sentiment was building. A moment of danger occurred early in 1488 when the celebrated Franciscan Bernardino da Feltre arrived to deliver a Lenten sermon in which he coupled attacks on Jewish moneylending with advocacy of a monte di pietà.

Trained in philosophy and law at Padua, received into the Francis-

---

66. On the spread of anti-Semitism among humanists, see Gianfranco Fioravanti, "Polemiche antigiudaiche nell'Italia del Quattrocento: Un tentativo di interpretazione globale," *Quaderni storici*, n.s., 64 (1987): 19–37. On the connection between anti-Semitism and the addition of Hebrew to the humanist canon, see Heiko A. Obermann, "Discovery of Hebrew and Discrimination against the Jews: The *Veritas Hebraica* as Double-Edged Sword in Renaissance and Reformation," in Andrew C. Fix and Susan C. Karant-Nunn, eds., *Germania Illustrata: Essays on Early Modern Germany Presented to Gerald Strauss* (Kirksville, Mo., 1992).

67. Fioravanti, "Polemiche," 30.

can order in 1454, Bernardino proved a captivating speaker. Dozens of Italian communes from Milan to Messina wrote to him, his superiors, and even the pope begging that he be sent to preach. Beginning in 1484 he embarked on a one-man crusade against what he perceived as the most pernicious sin of his day—usury. According to Bernardino, those who permitted this practice frequently defended it as useful, convenient, and necessary. But, Bernardino asked rhetorically, useful to whom? The poor were not helped but ruined by the extortionate interest charged by usurers. Convenient? A practice condemned as mortally injurious to the soul could hardly be termed convenient. And necessary? Bernardino hoped to convince his listeners that an effective alternative to usury existed.

He preached about this alternative to an audience in Padua in 1484. The Genoese governor reported that his city's monte di pietà had come about "by means of arguments and advice" of Bernardino. In Mantua his enthusiasm led the duke, Francesco Gonzaga, to complain that the Franciscan had "used strange words, not appropriate for these times, stirring up the people against the Jews, which was a scandalous thing." Preaching along these inflammatory lines, the duke warned, was not to be allowed in public, and if Bernardino wanted to continue, he must confine his sermons to the cloister. Francesco apparently had a change of heart, however, for exactly three months later he wrote to the pope that, through the urging of "zealous and religious men of the order of the Observant Brothers Minor of St. Francis and . . . by consent of the whole people," a monte di pietà had been established in Mantua. A subsequent letter from Lodovico Gonzaga, bishop-elect of Mantua, revealed the importance of the role of Bernardino da Feltre, who "has directed the most praiseworthy monte di pietà." The bishop-elect begged the authorities to allow the Franciscan to extend his stay in Mantua instead of ordering him to move on as planned to Perugia.[68] The Mantuans, from the duke on down, had been converted to the cause. The monte di pietà that they established charged a small fee rather than

68. Agostino Adorigo to the Anziani of Lucca, 12 Jan. 1492, in Meneghin, *Bernardino da Feltre*, 118–19. Also in the same volume: Francesco Gonzaga to Stefano Secco, 27 Sept. 1484, 51–52; Francesco Gonzaga to Pope Innocent VIII, 26 Dec. 1484, 52–53; Lodovico Gonzaga to Angelo da Chivasso, vicar-general of the Osservanza, 29 Dec. 1484, 54–56. Bernardino's role was noted in a letter from Innocent: "quod mons pietatis eius persuasionibus institutus in civitate Mantuae" (63–64).

outright interest on loans. In this way the monte would be assured of retaining enough capital to offset its operating expenses. This detail distinguished the monti founded by Bernardino and met with hard-headed opposition from the Dominicans and others who saw the charge as usurious. The fee at the Mantuan monte was flexible and could be fixed annually according to the monte's needs.[69] In Siena Bernardino offered a series of stirring sermons not long after that city's monte di pietà had begun operation, including one in the Piazza San Martino where he presided over a huge bonfire of vanities.[70]

Other Italian communes, including Assisi, sought out Bernardino as a preacher of and consultant on monti di pietà. His work was regarded by contemporaries as pioneering, and his sermons and written arguments were quickly cited as authoritative for certain practices of monti di pietà. The bishop of Lucca, Nicolò Sandonnino, for example, wrote to his diocesans in 1485 announcing the founding of that city's monte. In defense of the monte's requirement that borrowers pay a small fee on their loans he cited the teachings of Bernardino that it was not usurious for an institution to collect such a fee in order to pay operating expenses. The bishop then wisely sweetened the pill by offering an indulgence to those who supported it, "for indeed the monte di pietà is a most holy thing."[71]

Bernardino preached in Florence in 1482, but though invited by the city to return, received papal license to do so only in March 1488. Speaking at the church of Santa Maria del Fiore, Bernardino declaimed with such vehemence against the Jews and so passionately in favor of a monte di pietà that a number of youths set out on a rampage, and ran to the house of a Jewish moneylender, hoping to kill him and ransack his property.[72] Alarmed, the Otto had the

---

69. Parsons, "Bernardine of Feltre," 27.

70. Diary of Allegretto Allegretti, quoted in Piccolomini, *Monte dei paschi di Siena*, 1:215. As he spread the word, Bernardino also compiled a set of writings on monti di pietà by theologians and canon lawyers. See Meneghin, *Bernardino da Feltre*, 206, n. 3.

71. Bernardino promised the priors of the commune of Assisi that he would accede to their request to preach there in August in his letter of 22 July 1487, in Meneghin, *Bernardino da Feltre*, 64. Nicolò Sandonnino to his diocescans, 25 July 1484, ibid., 105–7.

72. Innocent VIII to Bernardino, 1 Mar. 1488, in Meneghin, *Bernardino da Feltre*, 70–72. Bernardino's opposition to Jews was well known. The remark attributed to one Davit di Dattalo da Tivoli, a Jewish moneylender in Lucca, was classic: "If Fra Bernardino comes here this Lent, I will have to flee." Giovanni Galgani to Bernardino, 28 Feb. 1490, ibid., 122.

crowd dispersed and warned Bernardino against offering sermons in this vein. A day later, for the sake of civic peace, he was escorted from the city. The pious Luca Landucci recorded his dismay at the ousting of the fiery Franciscan.

> This seemed to the people, who wished to live like Christians,
> a bad prognostic for us, because he was considered a saint.
> And it was not long before ill fortune overtook some of these
> Eight: one of them broke his neck by falling from his horse,
> another this thing, another that. Among the others, the one
> who had gone in person to drive Fra Bernardino away . . .
> died insane in the hospital. Thus it seems the matter ended ill.
> God save us![73]

But the matter was not ended. A monte di pietà would be built in Florence. A fiscal crisis, the death of Lorenzo in 1492, the ignominious expulsion of his maladroit son two years later, and the pietistic revival under Savonarola all combined to create the conditions in which those urging a monte would have their way.

73. Luca Landucci, *Diario fiorentino dal 1450 al 1516, continuato da un anonimo fino al 1542* (Florence, 1883; repr. 1985), 51–52. Another incident occurred in August 1493 when a Marrano, "whether out of disrespect for Christians or out of insanity," destroyed images of Mary in the city. A gang of youths stoned him to death. Agostino Lapini, *Diario fiorentino di Agostino Lapini dal 252 al 1596*, ed. Giuseppe Odoardo Corazzini (Florence, 1900), 28.

2 THE CREATION AND OPERATION OF THE MONTE DI PIETÀ OF FLORENCE

THE 1490s IN FLORENCE were characterized by economic and political crises and marked the beginning of a turbulent thirty-year period that John Hale described as "arguably one of the most dislocative and at the same time most formative between the collapse of the Roman empire and the French Revolution."[1] It was in this atmosphere of crisis that the Florentine monte di pietà was born.

The rise of France and Flanders as important centers of commerce, the competition from the growing English textile industry and the concomitant protective measures taken by the English monarchs, as well as changes in the Turkish Empire leading to the worsening of Florentine-Ottoman relations all weakened Florence's economy as did the expenses of the military operations of 1478–80.[2] The monte comune and the monte delle doti entered a period of decline with the former promising only a paltry 1 percent return by 1480. Financing of the public debt, augmented each year by about 116,000 florins, came to devour a substantial portion of the Florentine budget by the second half of the fifteenth century.[3] The uncertainties

1. Hale, *Florence and the Medici*, 79.

2. On the poor economic times see D'Addario, *Formazione*, 24–25. For the fiscal crisis of the 1490s, see L. F. Marks, "La crisi finanziaria a Firenze dal 1494 al 1502," *ASI* 112 (1954): 40–72. Goldthwaite, in *Building of Renaissance Florence*, has challenged this gloomy view of the economy.

3. For the monte delle doti in the fifteenth century see Anthony Molho and Julius Kirshner, "The Dowry Fund and the Marriage Market in Early Quattrocento Florence," *Journal of Modern History* 50 (1978): 403–38.

of foreign policy took a financial and emotional toll too. Marco Parenti, in *Storia fiorentina*, wrote of the populace's exhaustion and of the drain of money the wars had caused, concluding that average citizens, or the *popolo*, "already the traditional enemy of France, [had] not received the least benefit from his Majesty [the French king]."[4]

The settlement reached with the king of France after the disasters of 1494, by which Florence agreed to pay an indemnity to its supposed ally, added another burden to the Florentine economy. By 1500 His Most Christian Majesty was demanding payment of thirty-eight thousand florins owed him for the previous years. Added to this drain on resources were the costly campaign to reconquer Pisa and the threat posed by the ambitious Cesare Borgia. Continued demands for forced loans led to a standoff between the wealthy, who balked at advancing money despite the commune's promises of high rates of interest, and the Great Council, which refused to enact new taxes.[5] Thus the fiscal crisis in Florence persisted.

Into this impasse stepped Fra Girolamo Savonarola, who would play a vital role in establishing a monte di pietà in Florence at a time of uncertainty and crisis. He was not speaking metaphorically when, in the early 1490s, he preached about impending struggle, for he viewed the world "as a battleground between good and evil," and believed the victory of good would bring about a new Eden on earth. Tumult, suffering, and purge were necessary before Florence could throw off the yoke of sinfulness and clothe itself in the robes of spiritual goodness.[6]

Far from looking back to the early Augustinian idea of separation of the spiritual and the temporal, Savonarola preached and worked for the unity of holiness and civic values. His vision was colored by the traditional Florentine feeling that, like the individual, the city could make choices that won God's favor or provoked his wrath. Since the late fourteenth century the commune had become more involved in administering charity, seeing the efficient distribution of

4. Quoted in Nicolai Rubinstein, "Firenze e il problema della politica imperiale in Italia al tempo di Massimiliano I," *ASI* 116 (1958): 14.

5. Marks, "Crisi," 72.

6. Donald Weinstein, *Savonarola and Florence: Prophecy and Patriotism in the Renaissance* (Princeton, N.J., 1970), 32. More recently Weinstein reviewed works published since the appearance of his own book, in "Hagiography, Demonology, Biography: Savonarola Studies Today," *Journal of Modern History* 63 (1991): 483–503.

alms as a civic responsibility. Florentines felt that love of God and love of their city were complementary, and they translated *caritas* into civic philanthropy.[7] The city's controlling elites had other motivations as well, for the wise dispensing of charity served as a political tool by reinforcing the elite's identity.[8] Most of Savonarola's young followers, the *fanciulli*, were under the age of eighteen; the youths set an example that, the friar hoped, would reform their elders and the entire city.[9] His insistence on linking civic and spiritual reform represented the continuation of an old Florentine tradition.

In 1494 Savonarola seized the opportunity that he felt God had offered and became involved in politics, an arena he had avoided outside of an ambassadorial mission. Apparently he went through some type of sudden conversion, for he soon began to preach Florence's destiny as a new Jerusalem.[10] Thus, from the time of the departure of the Medici, Savonarola dreamed of a Florence not only spiritually but constitutionally perfect. In November 1494 a general assembly abolished the One Hundred, the Seventy, the Otto di Pratica, and the Procuratori, all considered instruments of Medici domination. The old republican councils of the Popolo and Comune, whose functions had been usurped after 1458 by the One Hundred, were revived.[11] Counting upon the political capital he had accrued during the French invasion and preaching a message of unity, the Dominican called for a reformed constitution modeled upon that of Venice.[12] In June 1495 Luca Landucci recorded the devotion that Florentines felt for him: "At this time the Frate was held in such

7. Becker, "Aspects of Lay Piety": "It was the concord of the city nurtured by citizen dedication to charity and civic good works that gained for Florence the mercy and love of God" (194).

8. Richard Trexler, "Charity and the Defense of Urban Elites in the Italian Communes," in Frederic C. Jaher, ed., *The Rich, the Wellborn and the Powerful: Elites and Upper Classes in History* (Seacaucus, N.J., 1973), 64–109.

9. Richard Trexler, "Adolescence and Salvation in the Renaissance," in Trinkhaus and Obermann, *Pursuit of Holiness*, 232, 249.

10. Weinstein, *Savonarola*, 56, 128–30. In describing this conversion, Weinstein wrote, "His apocalyptic warnings of tribulation and doom had given way to promises of divine love and favor. . . . [This change] expresses an ever deeper involvement in Florentine life which was now climaxed by his intervention in the constitutional crisis [of 1494]" (147).

11. See L. F. Marks, "The Financial Oligarchy under Lorenzo," in E. F. Jacob, ed., *Italian Renaissance Studies: A Tribute to the Late Cecilia M. Ady* (London, 1966), 123.

12. While the idea of a Venetian-style constitution may not have been his own, Savonarola was in the forefront of this reform and, through his preaching, remained

regard and esteem in Florence that there were many men and women who, if he had said to them, 'Go into the fire,' would actually have obeyed him."[13]

Beginning in December 1494 Savonarola preached that reform of the state was God's command and that all aspects of Florentine life were to be included. The government would be opened to greater participation, civic life would be purified, and sin purged. Especially concerned about the poor, the friar reprimanded Florentines for their lack of charity. In a Lenten sermon delivered in 1496 he told his audience, "If I were to say to you, give me ten ducats to give to a poor man, you would not do it; but if I say to you, spend a hundred on a chapel here in San Marco, you'll do it so that you can put up your coat of arms, and you'll do it, not for the honor of God, but for your own honor."[14]

Savonarola's preaching emphasized the individual's unique responsibility for the care of his or her own soul and forged a strong link between charity, love, and the perfect Christian life. "Do you know why today the good ordering of souls is lacking?" he asked his listeners. "Because charity is dead, annihilated." Love would teach and guide; love could lead to perfect charity. He wrote at length about Christ's command to set aside the things of this world, to seek poverty of the spirit, and, above all, to translate such poverty into meaningful acts.[15]

More than two centuries earlier, another Florentine had set forth

the moving force behind it. Weinstein, *Savonarola*, 151–57. Weinstein suggests that Soderini originated the idea of a Venetian-inspired constitution. In the 1460s many Florentines had rejected the Venetian model as too aristocratic, although some pro-Medici patricians hoped for such a government, dominated by their faction. When the Savonarolans sought reform after the Medici expulsion, they therefore looked to the Venetian constitution as anti-Medicean. Bernardo Rucellai and his Orti Oricellari group worked for such reforms, including creation of a Florentine Pregadi. Piero Capponi's idea of a large council and small senate may have been the origin of post-1494 Florentine interest in Venice as a model. See Felix Gilbert, "The Venetian Constitution in Florentine Political Thought," in Rubinstein, *Florentine Studies*, 463–500. On the Orti Oricellari, see Gilbert, "Bernardo Rucellai and the Orti Oricellari," *Journal of the Warburg and Courtauld Institutes* 12 (1949): 101–31.

13. Landucci, *Diario*, 108.
14. Savonarola, Predica 18, 182, quoted in Ciardini, *Banchieri*, 95–96.
15. From an advent sermon, 1493, "La carità e l'Amore," in Savonarola, *Prediche e scritti*, ed. M. Ferrara (Milan, 1930), 72–74. And from the "Operetta dell'Amor di Gesù": "Thus it appears to me that whoever wishes to attain the love of Jesus, first

the reasons why usury was an odious sin leading those who practiced it to a deep circle of hell. In canto 11 of the *Inferno*, Dante recapitulates Virgil's statement that usury is "an offense against God's goodness" and asks for clarification.[16] Virgil explains that both the law of God and the law of nature prove the sin's evil: "You will see / that in the will of Providence, man was meant / to labor and to prosper. But usurers, / by seeking their increase in other ways, / scorn nature herself and her followers."

Like Dante, Savonarola turned his attention to the question of usury, but he tied it to the Jews. In the Florentine tradition he linked sinfulness to the health of the city as a whole: "Florence, according to whether you do greater or less good, so will your tribulation be greater or less. I have told you many times that you ought to chase out those three sins: first, sodomy: second, luxury: third, usury."[17] For Savonarola the answer was clear: a monte di pietà must be built. He preached its erection and urged the Florentines to "expel the Jews from your land."[18] In so doing, Florentines would approach the ideal of civic and spiritual unity.

At last the time was right for setting up a monte di pietà in Florence. The opposition of the Medici existed no longer. And how could the Dominicans oppose it when the order's most distinguished member had placed himself at the forefront of the campaign? The atmosphere of reform, especially the insistence of Savonarola and his followers that Florentines could construct a new Jerusalem in Tuscany, created the unique moment in which the Florentine monte was born.

By proposing that the Jews be expelled, Savonarola advocated a

---

lifts his heart completely away from earthly things, as [Jesus] says, 'If you wish to be perfect, go and sell all you have and give to the poor, and come follow me'" (75) (Matthew 19:21).

16. *Inferno* 11:95–96, and Virgil's reply, 11:107–11. I am quoting from John Ciardi's translation (New York, 1954). For the original see *Divina Commedia* I, *Inferno*, ed. Natalino Sapegno (Florence, 1955): "diss' io, 'la dove di' ch'usura offende / la divina bontade.'" And the reply (in Sapegno's edition, 106–11): "Da queste due, se tu ti rechi a mente / lo Genesí dal principio, convene / prender sua vita ed avanzar la gente; / e perché l'usuriere altra via tene, / per sé natura e per la sua seguace / dispregia, poi ch'in altro pon la spene."

17. Savonarola, *Prediche*, 96.

18. Quoted in Umberto Mazzone, *"El buon governo": Un progetto di riforma generale nella Firenze savonaroliana* (Florence, 1978), 131.

policy already enacted in several of Europe's nation-states. Spanish reformers under Francisco Jimenes de Cisneros had identified the Jews as the most dangerous enemy of Christian unity and succeeded in convincing the Most Catholic Kings, Ferdinand and Isabella, to expel them in March 1492.[19] England and France had dealt with their Jews earlier; Portugal expelled its Jews in 1496. Incited by sermons now preached by Dominicans like Savonarola and Franciscans like Marco di Matteo Strozzi, the rector of San Miniato fra le Torri, many Florentines clamored for action against the Jews.

For their proponents, monti di pietà constituted part of a broader program of reform. In a letter to Bernardino da Feltre, Bernardino da Ferrara, attached to the church of San Girolamo in Faenza, keenly observed the connections between the erection of that town's monte di pietà and what he perceived as an overall renewal of piety and civic order. A new statute forbade women to parade their vanities; the local confraternity of Corpus Christi "miraculously is increased [in membership]"; the Jews moved out; the shops of three "Jew-loving" citizens had collapsed, though thankfully with no loss of life, incidentally a sign of God's wrath and mercy predicted by Bernardino da Feltre. Many people, Bernardino da Ferrara added, had reformed their morals, "leaving behind their evil ways, men as well as women. Oh, Father," the Ferrarese cleric exclaimed, "you have brought about the greatest results. . . . I write . . . so that you know your effort has not been in vain."[20]

In Florence, Savonarola's desire for reform and his role in tempering the Dominicans' opposition were indispensable in bringing about the legislation creating the monte di pietà. But it was the Franciscan Marco di Matteo Strozzi who breathed life into the fledgling institution and, in the process, set a precedent. For once the monte began operation, its eight officials continued to rely on advice from prominent friars. When in 1503 the eight had to dispose of unforeseen profits, they sought the counsel of both the abbot of San Marco, Ignazio Squarcialupi, and a leading Franciscan, Ilarione Sacchetti.[21]

Several events in Marco di Matteo Strozzi's life held particular im-

19. On the expulsion from Spain see J. H. Elliott, *Imperial Spain, 1469–1716* (New York, 1963; reprint 1966), 103–8.

20. Bernardino of Ferrara to Bernardino of Feltre, 2 Jan. 1492, in Meneghin, *Documenti vari*, 181–83.

21. MP 18, Deliberazioni degli Ufficiali, 5v, 6 July 1503.

portance for him. He knew the precise date of his birth, 30 July 1454, though not of his parents' marriage (which occurred "about the year 1452").[22] An "extraordinary illness" during his youth had left him determined to enter the religious life and, true to his vow, he was ordained subdeacon and then deacon. At the age of twenty-one he was presented by a patron of San Miniato fra le Torri to the archbishop of Florence. In 1477 he accepted his first ecclesiastical office and celebrated his first mass in June 1489. After earning his doctorate in theology at Pisa, he taught for seven years at Florence's cathedral school and later became a canon in Florence and the rector of San Miniato fra le Torri.

Like other Florentine patricians, Strozzi brought a keen business sense to his religious vocation. He advised that the chaplain of San Miniato take care "that he write and keep a good account and record" of the parish's belongings and expenses.[23] When renting land and shops in and around Florence, he made sure that the leases specified rents, obligations, and penalties for late payments or damages. An agreement between Strozzi and the Company of the Men of Santa Maria de' Lombardi, allowing the company to meet at San Miniato fra le Torri, revealed the hand of a man with an innate sense of business: not only was the company to contribute forty lire to the celebration of San Miniato's feast day, but it was to indemnify the church against any damages, excuse it from any obligation to the company, and meet only at particular times. The members were responsible for providing candles and torches at the masses they attended in the church, and for giving alms and wax on feast days. Such a man as Strozzi had the business acumen to appreciate the economic benefits a monte di pietà could offer.

In 1494 Strozzi's cause was aided by the reprinting of the *Tabula della salute*, which put forth examples of the immense profits believed made by Jewish moneylenders through high-interest loans. Its chapter titled "Of the Good and Utility of Creating a Holy Monte di Pietà" urged individuals to place money in the hands of the monte,

22. This and the following information comes from a set of brief autobiographical notes in CS, ser. III, 138, 47r–49v. The notes comprise about six pages, of which two and one-half discuss the Jews and the monte. Records of Strozzi's business dealings as rector of San Miniato fra le Torri are found throughout CS, ser. III, 173, "Raccolta di memorie diverse della famiglia degli Strozzi," especially 72r; and 138, especially 16r.

23. CS, ser. III, 173, 72r. For some of the business dealings noted below, see CS, ser. III, 138, 13r and 15r.

not in the hands of usurers. The spiritual benefits of such generous gifts were enumerated clearly. An analysis of those to be had from a gift of one hundred ducats—the same sum for which the interest received by the Jews over a fifty-year period had been calculated—concluded: "And the highest prize: if in the aforesaid monte one leaves one hundred ducats, more or less, for over fifty years, or in perpetuity, the human mind cannot compute the rewards and the goodness that will result from such alms."[24] Thus the contrast between the bitter sin and misery of Jewish usury and the sweet blessings of Christian charity was made clear in the comparison of the course of a one hundred–ducat investment over a fifty-year span.

Never a man to sit idly by, Marco Strozzi plunged into the campaign to end this usury and the misery he believed it produced. He recognized the economic importance of small loans to the poor and concluded that if a substitute source of such loans could be found, then the Jews could be eliminated along with their usury. Moreover, it is likely that Strozzi or some of his parishioners were already acquainted with the useful services that monti di pietà offered: the institution in nearby Prato permitted Florentine citizens to take out loans against pawns.[25]

By 1494 these ideas seemed to have crystallized in Marco's mind. While serving as vicar of Volterra, Strozzi noted, he "had many discussions with good citizens" about the Jews. Because of their "rites and superstitions," Jews killed animals for consumption in certain ways, he complained, taking those parts they wanted and then selling the remainder of the carcasses to Christians. Repelled by what we must identify as kosher slaughtering and butchering of cattle and other animals, the vicar forbade this practice, "as a result of which the Jews created so much noise and violence that I had to revoke [the order], even though I did right, as far as I was concerned."[26]

Though Jews had lived for some twenty years within his own par-

24. Pampaloni, in "Cenni storici," suggests that this printing was purposely timed to incite anti-Jewish sentiment. This is a credible thesis, given that the same calculation of damages caused by Jewish usury prefaced the provvisione creating the monte. Parts of the *Tabula* have been published by Ciardini (*Banchieri*, 89–92 and xci–c).

25. A.G.B., "Il monte di pietà," in *Pel calendario pratese del 1848: Memorie e studi di cose patrie* (Prato, 1847), 104.

26. CS, ser. III, 138, 103r: "di che feciono li hebrei tanto romore et forza che mi bisognò revocarlo . . . , benchè io lo facessi iustificamente quanto a me."

ish of San Miniato fra le Torri in Florence, "which always displeased me and many others greatly," Stozzi now wrote of his revulsion at their presence, and began a dual campaign of anti-Jewish preaching and of petitioning the authorities "against the Jews and for the foundation of the monte di pietà for the poor." He complained of his own and others' displeasure with the Jews, "those enemies of the cross of Christ," with "their old synagogue, their rites and their usury." The rector approached the Otto di Guardia e Balìa and recalled, "I asked for justice, requesting the removal of the synagogue." Of course he intended not merely to move the Jews from one part of the city to another, but to expel them altogether. Writing to the Signoria in 1499, he complained about the Jews and, despite his own patrician status, identified himself—in typical Franciscan language—with the poor: "Since I was a poor man, I spoke, I knew, I thought as a poor man."[27]

As a member of an old Florentine family that, he proudly claimed, traced its origins back "to the days of the first Roman emperors, as Cornelius Tacitus recounts," Marco enjoyed the social status that allowed him access to the rulers of the city, men who were his social equals.[28] His militant preaching placed him in the camp of the new religious reformers. In his efforts to have the Jews expelled, he noted in his reminiscences, "I approached the Most Reverend Cardinal Giovanni de' Medici, of holy memory, because the supporters of the Hebrews were hindering the justice that I sought." He also tried to convince the *gonfaloniere* (standardbearer) of justice, but, he reported, "It did no good."[29] He turned instead to the populace and, in August 1495, regaled crowds in the Piazza della Signoria with sermons on the evils of the Jews, demanding their expulsion from the city.[30] Four months later, on 26 December 1495, the Council of Eighty approved laws setting up the monte di pietà. Two days later

27. CS, ser. III, 172, 48v and 49v. Cassuto, in *Ebrei*, 36, notes that a synagogue was established in Florence by 1456.

28. CS, ser. III, 173, 72r. Strozzi's claim about his family's roots is fantastic. Richard Goldthwaite notes that the Strozzi's origins, "like that of the other great Florentine families whose roots were not feudal, are completely obscured." *Private Wealth in Renaissance Florence: A Study of Four Families* (Princeton, N.J., 1968), 32.

29. Marco's choice of Cardinal Giovanni may not have been very shrewd; see Cassuto, *Famille des Médicis*, for the generally benevolent attitude of this family toward Jews.

30. Pampaloni, "Cenni storici," 530.

the Great Council confirmed the monte's creation. The same law also called for expulsion of the Jews.

Important as it was, the legislative victory represented only one battle in a longer war. Now that the monte had been created, it needed public support. No government funding had been approved, and the monte was to rely only upon voluntary donations.[31] The rector, describing his contribution to the effort to popularize the new monte, noted that he "took up the cross in order to gain a victory over the Jews." He meant this literally, for he made four crosses out of olive branches to inspire generous charity and was able to report success, for after a procession on Palm Sunday some fourteen hundred florins were pledged to the new monte.[32]

Even before the monte actually began operation on 2 August 1496—an event he called "miraculous before my eyes"—Strozzi worked hard to give it a firm foundation. Between December 1495 when the monte was approved and its opening the following summer, the greatest concern of men like Strozzi was the writing of the monte's bylaws. On 15 April 1496 a group of eight men assembled in the meeting room of the church of Santa Maria del Fiore to draw up the statutes of the Florentine monte di pietà. A complicated electoral process, designed to eliminate nepotism and corruption, assured that the eight selected as formatori of the new "Monte della Carità" would truly be "good men." They were to receive no salary, but would serve "gratis, and for charity and the love of God." As the law required, they retained the services of a notary, whom they duly elected at their first meeting on 4 January 1496.[33] The eight who convened on 15 April—Niccolò de' Nobili, Piero de' Lenzi, Bernardo de' Segni, Niccolò del Nero, Piero de' Guicciardini, Giacopo de' Salviati, Antonio di Sasso di Sasso, and Giacopo Mannucci—had been chosen from the Great Council and included men from Florence's most prominent families.[34] But as was often the case in Florence, concerned citizens, even "good men" like these eight, needed and welcomed the counsel of others who might possess expert knowledge of the problem at hand. One of the men invited to advise

31. MP 1, 8v
32. CS, ser. III, 138, 48v.
33. MP 1. Parts of this document have been published by Piccolomini, *Monte dei paschi di Siena*, 2:271–82.
34. MP 1, 2v.

the eight formatori, and who was present at the final session held in a meeting room in the Opera of Santa Maria del Fiore in April, was the rector of San Miniato fra le Torri, Marco di Matteo Strozzi.[35]

Beginning on 1 January 1496 the eight set to work on a proposal for running the monte. They wielded complete control in drawing up the rules, methods, and organization of the new institution. The Signori and Collegi along with the Consiglio de'Richiesti and the Great Council retained the right to approve or reject the design of the eight.

Earlier attempts to create a monte in Florence had resulted in a set of proposed regulations drawn up by seventeen riformatori. Both the provvisione creating the monte and these regulations would serve as a model for the eight formatori, who were to ensure that the monte's services would allow the city to drive out the Jews. Once the monte actually began operation, the Jews would be given one year "to make good account of the pawns to be found in their hands, and also to satisfy any other debts." After that period, all their old privileges would be revoked and they would be expelled from Florence.[36]

The eight, who convened several times during the late winter of 1496 to draw up the monte's rules, faced a monumental task: creating a functioning institution out of nothing. Indeed, they lacked even a room in which to hold regular meetings and were forced to borrow the premises of other groups. The rules they drew up would have to strike a balance between charitable ideals and the sobering reality of balanced ledgers; between succoring as many of the poor as possible and paying the rent; between trusting unpaid patrician overseers to guide the institution's operation and handing over its day-to-day activities to paid employees; between serving the commune and being served by it. In short, everything from renting a house for the monte to securing its working capital to regulating its acceptance of pawns lay in the hands of the formatori.

The precise role played by Marco Strozzi in guiding the formatori

35. MP 1, 2v. This advisory role may account for Strozzi's statement (CS, ser. III, 138, 49v), "Fecit me procuratorem montis pauperum" (He [or it] made me procurator of the monte of the poor). There was no official of the Florentine monte who bore the title of procurator; Strozzi may have used the word in the generic sense of administrator or advocate. Strozzi's presence is confirmed in MP 4, 119v, which noted the bylaws were confirmed "nell'audienza dell'opera di Santa Maria del Fiore alla presenza del Reverendo Marco di Matteo Strozzi."

36. MP 1, 3r–v.

is impossible to determine, but this most vociferous proponent's participation and influence in drawing up the monte's constitution are undeniable. Among Marco di Matteo Strozzi's papers is a set of guidelines for the monte di pietà that mirrored both his dispassionate sense of business and his passionate hatred of the Jews.[37]

According to the Strozzi guidelines, the monte was above all to avoid any taint of usury. Yet in the exercise of charity, it was both necessary and permissible to expect some small return on loans. Before accepting them, monte employees were to ascertain that all pawns were free, that is, that they were the legitimate property of the persons presenting them and did not fall into one of the categories of objects that the monte was forbidden to receive (such as lengths of unfinished cloth). Limits were set on the amount any customer could borrow, both per item and per year. To redeem the pledge, the borrower had to pay a fee small enough not to burden the borrower but large enough to keep the monte di pietà in the black; the Jews had, after all, charged much higher rates for their usurious loans. These rules also called for the monte's treasurer to keep a careful record of all financial transactions. The cashiers and bookkeepers ought to do their jobs conscientiously and carefully.

This rough sketch for the monte di pietà evinced the writer's familiarity with the operations of other monti in Italy, especially those that owed their creation to the Franciscans. Further, it contained a number of elements that appeared in the final set of rules, approved unanimously in April 1496 by the eight formatori, including the free nature of the pawn, the limit on an individual's credit, the expectation of a small payment—though in the form of low interest rather than a flat fee—in return for its benevolence, and the roles of the several officers named in the guidelines found among Marco Strozzi's papers.

The monte di pietà's statutes were clear about the types of pawns that its employees were forbidden to accept as collateral on loans.[38] No holy items could be pawned, nor could unfinished goods such as bolts of cloth be accepted without the permission of the appropriate guild. This injunction must have seriously impeded the ability of the poorest clothworkers, especially spinners, weavers, and dyers, from

37. CS, ser. III, 138, "La reghola del monte di pietà e di charità," 65r–v.
38. MP 1, chap. 26.

availing themselves of the monte's services, for such people were sometimes paid by wool and silk merchants not in wages, but in kind.[39] Pawning it at the monte would have been one way for the clothworkers to turn cloth into cash, but the eight, perhaps envisioning the monte's rapid decline into a cloth brokerage, forbade the practice. Not until the far-reaching reforms of 1573–74 were monte employees permitted to accept cloth as pawns, and by then the Florentine wool industry was in decline. It is doubtful, however, that the original prohibition was carefully enforced, for at least two lengths of cloth were among the unredeemed pawns sold by the monte in 1504.[40] The statutes also forbade minors and wards (*pupilli*) from pawning items at the monte, even though many of them fell into poverty because, having lost their parents, they were too young to manage their own inheritances, which dwindled in the hands of greedy or incompetent overseers. Despite the exclusion of pupilli, and the effective exclusion of many clothworkers, the monte di pietà's formatori made clear the institution's goal: "to be able to lend against pawns to poor persons with as little interest as possible."[41]

The formatori were above all aware of the need to secure adequate funds for the monte's day-to-day operations. They expressed this foremost concern in the first chapter of the monte's rules. "At the outset," they declared, "all difficulties of a [charitable] institution arise from its not having a [sufficient] quantity of money."[42] From what sources would the monte's operating capital come? Experience told them that several possibilities existed. The state could be asked to lend or give money gratis to the cause. Or the state could direct official or semiofficial organs to deposit money in the monte. Finally, the monte could rely on the generosity of private individuals.

At first, it appeared that the last of these was the least practical. The earlier attempt to create a monte in Florence had called solely upon the charitable instincts of citizens. Despite Lorenzo de' Medici's pledge, this call went largely unheeded. Civic commissions such as the Office of the Pupilli controlled sums of money that might be

39. On this and other tactics used by the wool and silk merchants to avoid paying cash wages to clothworkers, see Spicciani, "'Poveri Vergognosi,'" 58–59. Spicciani's source is Sant'Antonino's acerbic condemnation of these practices as unjust.

40. MP 4, 124v. On the sale in 1504, MP 18, 16r.

41. MP 4, 124v.

42. MP 1, chap. 1.

deposited (at no interest) in the monte to build its capital. This solution apparently received serious consideration, for at a meeting on 1 February 1496, the formatori discussed asking the Signori and Collegi to require the Pupilli officials to appropriate some money for deposit in the monte. Such deposits would be made under the proviso that the monte officials return the deposit upon written notice from their colleagues in the Pupilli. The eight therefore decided to seek formal connections between the Office of the Pupilli and the monte di pietà, and recorded,

> That . . . for the future the camarlingo [head cashier] of the monte della pietà should and will be the *depositario* [treasurer] of the officials of the Pupilli . . . with the authority over and obligation for the payments which the treasurer of said Pupilli officials has held; that the aforesaid camarlingo of the monte della pietà be obliged to pay all sums . . . which are appropriated by the aforesaid officials of the Pupilli according to the regulations of that office.[43]

The camarlingo's assumption of the duties of the depositario meant a formalization of the ties between the monte di pietà and the Office of the Pupilli. This dual position would surely allow the camarlingo access to sums of money under the control of the Pupilli, though the monte did not seek any further legislation forcing that office, or any other state organ, to lend money to the monte. The officials of the monte di pietà were obligated to guard and preserve the funds entrusted to their institution by the Office of the Pupilli, and so the monte di pietà functioned as a treasury for that institution. This action also severed any lingering financial or psychological connections between the exiled Medici and the Pupilli, for during Lorenzo the Magnificent's lifetime the Medici bank had served as the depository for that office.[44]

43. MP 1, notes of a meeting of 1 Feb. 1496. Further, the monte officials were to be held responsible for preserving the resources of the Pupilli. This decision is confirmed in the records of the Office of the Pupilli; see Francesca Morandini, ed., "Statuti e ordinamenti dell'Ufficio dei Pupilli e Adulti nel periodo della Repubblica Fiorentina (1388–1534)," *ASI* 114 (1956): 109: "El Camarlingho degli Uficiali della Pietà sia depositario," 31 Jan. 1496. The councils approved it; ibid., n. 59.

44. This connection was discovered by Richard Goldthwaite, who cites Conventi Soppresi 100, filza 125, no. 2, 5r, as his source. See "The Medici Bank and the World of Florentine Capitalism," *Past and Present* 114 (1987): 26.

Civic support for the new monte di pietà was a two-edged sword, as other monti in Italy discovered. The resources of the state were large, and the few thousand florins needed to set the monte in operation would represent a tiny fraction of a large city's annual operating budget. When the Sienese monte di pietà was established in 1471, the city's council decreed that, in order to give "succor to the poor and needy, and contribute to the capital of the monte, . . . the Magnificent Commune of Siena give over . . . capital to the aforesaid monte."[45] A sum of nine thousand florins was deemed sufficient for the institution's working capital, at least at the outset; income for three years up to that limit might be appropriated for the monte's use. To this end the city fathers called upon the *monte del sale* (salt tax ministry) and the Hospital of Santa Maria della Scala to provide funds for the monte di pietà, "given how useful [this] would be in providing for the poor and needy." Further subvention was to come from the coffers of the cathedral and from the Casa della Sapienza. A statute compelled priests and other religious to collect money from among themselves, the sum to be equitably determined by the archbishop of Siena. The law establishing Siena's monte di pietà emphasized "how much honor and praise befall any republic" that showed compassion for its poor and needy. In Siena the councils left no doubt that the funding of the local monte was primarily a public and civic, rather than a private and personal, responsibility.[46] In other cities, public and private sources combined to fund new monti di pietà. The Pratesi adopted such a plan when, at the urging of an Observant Franciscan preacher, they established one of the first monti in the area near Florence in 1476. They decided to require several pious houses, including the famous Ceppo established by the legacy of Francesco di Marco Datini, to lend the new institution a total of one thousand florins for one year, and they counted on one thousand more from private individuals. With this funding the

45. "Deliberazione del Consiglio della Campana che determina i capitali da assegnarsi al Monte di Pietà," in Piccolomini, ed., *Monte dei paschi di Siena*, 1:302–4. The following discussion of the sources of revenue for the Sienese monte comes from this source.

46. The provvisione establishing the Sienese monte began with the declaration, "Considerato quanto onore e laude si attribuisca a ogni Republica ad provvedere che le povere o miserabili o bisognose persone . . . sian adiutate"; thus, the identification of charity as a communal or "republican" obligation was spelled out. Quoted in Piccolomini, ed., *Monte dei paschi di Siena*, 1:172.

monte of Prato flourished until 1512, when Spanish troops sacked the city.[47]

Communal financing also posed risks. Individuals or corporations that lent money to the various monti di pietà became creditors of the institutions, and while the monti could put this capital to work, they were bound to return it upon demand. Free deposits in the Florentine monte were typically recorded in the ledgers with the stipulation that the creditor "deposits [this sum] in this monte gratis and for the love of God and with the understanding that he may receive it back at his pleasure and as he likes."[48] Because such creditors placed money in the monte freely, the institution had no guarantee that they would not ask for their deposits back at short notice. When the state was a substantial creditor, that possibility not only became more likely, but it also threatened the monte with financial devastation in times of civic fiscal crisis. The Sienese monte would learn this lesson the hard way. It was hopeless for the eight formatori of the Florentine monte to ask the state, already mired in a fiscal crisis, for money. Besides, the formatori reiterated that the monte di pietà was a charity, dependent on the goodwill of more fortunate citizens for its funding.

In the early days of the monte, the city played a supportive role by encouraging the institution's charitable activities and making some carefully designated resources (notably those of the Pupilli) available for its use. But the provvisione of December 1495 that had mandated the monte's creation forbade use of the republic's own funds for the monte. This prohibition was the result of the "adverse circumstances" in which Florence found itself.[49] Unlike their colleagues in some other areas, then, the formatori did not have the option of relying on the commune for support, beyond what might be gleaned

---

47. A.G.B., "Monte di pietà," 98–114. For Francesco Datini's legacy, see Iris Origo, *Merchant of Prato: Francesco di Marco Datini, 1335–1410* (New York, 1957), esp. 347–89.

48. See, e.g., MP 721, Libro di debitori e creditori, 1496–1499: a deposit of thirty florins was made by Donato d'Antonio di Donato Ciani on 30 Aug. 1496, "e' quali . . . depositava in su questo monte grati e amore dei e chon patto che lui gli possa riavere ad ongni suo piacere e volontà."

49. Provvisioni—Reg. 186, 167, 28 Dec. 1495, quoted in Pampaloni, "Cenni storici," noted the "temporali avversi" (534). Note that in 1501, the city councils did agree to assign credits from a tax increase (the *gabella delle porte*) to the monte di pietà. Provvisioni—Reg. 192, 33v–34r, 23 Sept. 1501. I am grateful to Anthony Molho of Brown University for this reference.

from its good wishes and the coffers of the Pupilli. Instead, the eight called upon the monte to rely on the generous sentiments of "inspired persons": those desirous of helping the monte "should voluntarily give aid through free loans of money to the said monte . . . , which we intend to be sufficient."[50] The eight hoped that, regardless of the failure of the first Florentine monte, which too had relied on gifts, and in spite of the economic crisis of the 1490s, the spiritual rebirth of Savonarolan Florence would stimulate Christian generosity, enabling the institution to acquire a mass of wealth, a "monte," to begin operations.

Marco Strozzi had proven that an organized appeal might win pledges of several thousand florins. From a network of pulpits came a call to Florentines to show their support for the new institution by freely depositing money for its use. By 30 July 1496 the monte officials recorded that

alms given to this monte di pietà are credited with 512 gold florins [*d'oro in oro*] and 791 lire, 6 soldi and 4 denari *in grossi* [silver groats] and 6 soldi, 8 denari . . . and 1,384 lire, 11 soldi and 3 denari *di moneta nera* [coins with a high copper content] [all received by] Piero [a monte official] in several installments from 7 March to 5 May 1496, from Francesco di Giovanni Ridolfi, *provveditore* [manager or general overseer] of this monte. And the said Francesco received this sum as alms given on the 27th of March on Palm Sunday from the Church of Santa Maria del Fiore.[51]

The formatori decreed that collection boxes be set up in churches throughout the city so that Florentines, should inspiration come,

---

50. MP 1, 8r.

51. For the amounts collected in alms see MP 721, 1a. N.B.: the figures in the ledger state that 1,389 lire were received, while the words read 1,384 lire. In these notes, references to the ledgers use *a* to refer to the left-hand, or debit page, and *b* to refer to the right-hand, or credit page. The Florentine monetary system was almost hopelessly complicated. Figures are cited in the same currency in which they appeared in the ledgers, unless otherwise noted. Note that lire, soldi, and denari are *always* moneys of account. Florins too could be moneys of account, with subdivisions of soldi and denari. When the preposition *in* or *di* appears, as in the example above, it alludes to coins. Fiorini d'oro in oro, then, refer to real gold florins. See Appendix B for a brief explanation of Florentine money. I am deeply indebted to Richard Goldthwaite for his generous help in these matters.

could easily slip a few coins to the monte. As early as 17 November 1496 the box at the Osservanza yielded 7 lire, 14 soldi, and 4 denari. On 6 March 1497, 2 lire, 18 soldi were removed from the box at San Marco by Giacopo Mannucci, one of the monte officials, in the presence of a notary. Santa Maria del Fiore's collection amounted to 2 lire, 18 soldi. A further 12 lire, 2 soldi, 7 denari came from the Osservanza on 4 April. Boxes placed in Santa Croce and San Salvadore da San Miniato contained similar small donations, given anonymously to the monte by pious souls. Hoping to set a good example, several of the formatori made free deposits of their own in the monte di pietà.[52]

These pittances, however, hardly comprised sufficient operating capital. While it is impossible to ascertain the identities of those who were motivated to slip a soldo or two into a church box, such donors were probably of relatively modest means. One pictures the carpenter's widow, a young apprentice, two clothworkers thinking of the soul of a comrade. Donors of large sums usually wanted to be identified. They also wanted their money back. The first page of the monte's first account book lists nine deposits, some gifts and some only loans, from November 1495 until April 1496. Four of these nine credits came from various collection boxes. Another was a credit of one florin "from a friend." Two came from a private citizen: Giovanni d'Antonio Minerbetti had his banker Tommaso d'Andrea Chelli deliver two separate amounts of L. 5.5.8 and fl. 7, L. 1.7 for his own soul and that of his wife, Lisabetta.[53] Though no doubt welcome, individual loans of this size would no more sustain the monte than would the sums given up by the collection boxes.

The other two entries of the first nine came from corporate groups. The merchants' guild made a generous donation of 59 lire, 5 soldi. On 8 March 1497 the Parte Guelfa agreed to deposit the sum of 150 gold florins to be handed over in two installments, the first of which had been received on 7 November of the previous year. The Parte's bankers had changed the 150 gold florins into a sum in *grossi*, arriving at the total of 176 florins, 6 soldi grossi. This amount was "promised by the captains of the party as alms," which was, the directors noted with gratitude, "quite a great provision."

52. MP 4, 186r.
53. MP 721, 1b–8b, lists the early credits.

The monte's own bookkeeper then changed this sum into lire and recorded a deposit of L. 998.12.8. Though the political power of the corporate bodies in Florence—the guilds, the Guelfs, and others—waned after the late fourteenth century,[54] they still exercised influential roles within strictly delineated spheres. These first nine credits totaled fl. 8, L. 1,089.19.3, giving hope that the provisions made by the eight formatori would allow the monte to flourish, supported by the gifts of individuals, anonymous charity, and corporate gifts.

Even with sufficient funding, the monte di pietà might still founder if its organization were not carefully and conscientiously drawn up. Thus its constitution called for the city's councils to appoint as overseers eight citizens "of sufficient faith and ability, and of good name and reputation."[55] With a three-year term of office, these eight officials were granted authority "in effect, over the care and general governance of the said monte." The officials ought to be at least thirty-three years old and had to be Florentine citizens eligible for communal office. They were required to meet at least once per week. Two months before the end of their term of office, the appropriate civic councils would elect successors, with no man allowed to succeed himself. Those chosen were to receive "no salary or emoluments, other than the ordinary perquisites of all other officials," leading to the possibility that, in the troubled 1490s, Florentines eligible for office would urge their colleagues, as did their counterparts in Venice, "Do not elect me! Do not want me!"[56] The duties of elective office often left little time to attend to one's business. The monte's statutes, therefore, forbade anyone duly elected from refusing to serve.

Though they delegated to others the task of keeping the day-to-day account books, the monte's eight officials bore ultimate responsibility for its finances. Each group of eight delegated one member to keep a ledger (*libro di debitori e creditori*), though by the mid-six-

54. See, e.g., John Najemy, "Guild Republicanism in Trecento Florence: The Successes and Ultimate Failures of Corporate Politics," *American Historical Review* 84 (1979): 53–71; and Gene Brucker, *The Civic World of Renaissance Florence* (Princeton, N.J., 1977).

55. See MP 1, chap. 1 for the following discussion.

56. Donald Queller, "The Civic Irresponsibility of the Venetian Nobility," in Robert Lopez, Vsevolod Slessarev, and David Herlihy, eds., *Economy, Society and Government in Medieval Italy: Essays in Memory of Robert L. Reynolds* (Kent, Ohio, 1969), 224–26: "'Non me eleze, non me voie!'"

teenth century the sheer volume of transactions led them to appoint a notary, and later a chancellor, to do it. Whenever an official entered into any financial transactions on the monte's behalf, he and his seven colleagues were collectively obligated to see that debts were paid and bargains kept. All such transactions had to be approved by the majority. The commune and the officials of the monte comune agreed "to preserve without loss the said officials of the [monte di] pietà."[57] Reluctant to support the monte di pietà with funds, the city at least threw its moral support behind the monte's officials.

The monte di pietà shared with other Florentine institutions the need to attract capital and to reassure prospective donors that their money was safe in its hands. The Florentine dowry fund had faced similar challenges. At the time of its creation in 1425, the dowry fund began to accept deposits in girls' names for terms of either seven and a half or fifteen years. The city fathers hoped that the resulting accumulation of deposits could help offset the communal debt. But the shrewd Florentines, fearful of losing their deposits, did not rush to invest despite the fund's generous rates of return (either 11.33 percent or 12.99 percent, depending on the term) because the death of an enrolled girl meant the loss of the investment.[58] During its first seven years, despite hikes in its interest rates, the dowry fund attracted total investments of less than six thousand florins. Not till 1433, when changes in its statutes allowed it to accept deposits under conditions that assured Florentines that their money was safe, did many citizens invest.[59]

If the dowry fund's rates of 12 or 13 percent failed to attract capital, consider the far greater disadvantage under which the monte di pietà labored. Unlike its sister institution, it could not pay interest on deposits. Its only attraction lay in its claim to perform a charitable exercise: the care of the poor undertaken without the stigma of usury. The only returns donors might expect were God's grace, which came to those who practiced the virtue of charity, and the personal satisfaction of helping a civic institution to perform a vital service.

These were, however, powerful beliefs with deep roots. In the early fifteenth century, a provvisione noted approvingly that a

57. MP 1, chap. 4.
58. See Molho, *Public Finances*, for the crisis of the 1420s.
59. See Molho and Kirshner, "Dowry Fund."

foundling home for abandoned and orphaned infants had recently opened in the city. "One may firmly believe," it declared, "that through these [foundlings] . . . who shine in purity, our most high and omnipotent God in his . . . mercy will not only deign to conserve this his city, and state, but will allow it to grow daily."[60] Following in the footsteps of Sant'Antonino, whose pious spirituality and interest in charitable foundations presaged the events of the 1490s, the Savonarolan reformer Domenico Cecchi pointed out that "everyone [is] obliged to help [address] the needs of his country," adding that the goals of civic reform should be "the salvation, the enrichment, and the health of each person."[61]

In Florence, however, the spiritual rewards heralded by the monte's promoters were never spelled out as clearly as in some other cities. A friar preaching in Bologna was shrewd enough to obtain from Pope Julius II license to dispense a plenary indulgence to those who supported the monte di pietà. If a contemporary record is to be believed, the prospect of receiving this indulgence played a decisive role in convincing the citizenry to contribute. One Jacopo Melocchi recorded, "To better supply [the monte di pietà] with money [Fra Bartolomeo] got from Pope Julius II a plenary indulgence and *jubileo* [jubilee year indulgence] for all those who offered something for that pious work. And thus I took this jubileo and absolution . . . for all my sins, and . . . committed myself to pay three ducats within one month."[62]

Florentines did, however, expect a collective spiritual benefit to accrue from the pious activities of the monte di pietà. Though this theme was often implicit, it received clear articulation in the opening page of the debtors and creditors ledger of 1506–9. After invoking the three persons of the Trinity, the eight called on a long list of saints beginning with Mary and John the Baptist, "all the saints and apostles," and, for good measure, many more, including the three great monastic saints, "the most holy virgins and widows . . . and

60. From a provvisione of December 1456, quoted in Trexler, "Foundlings of Florence," 260.

61. See Arnaldo D'Addario, "Note di storia della religiosità e della carità dei fiorentini nel secolo XVI," *ASI* 126 (1968), esp. 62–74. On Savonarola and reform, see Domenico Cecchi, "Riforma Sancta et Pretiosa," in Mazzone, *"Governo,"* 181–206.

62. Acquisti e Doni, 8, Libro di ricordi di Jacopo Melocchi, 32r, 13 Jan. 1505. (Note that the Bolognese started the new year on 1 Jan.) I am grateful to William Connell of Rutgers University for this reference.

most glorious angels and saints of the celestial choir of paradise."
They concluded this preamble by asking these saints to aid "this holy
work of piety" for "the poor, with the health of our souls, and
theirs."[63]

All the righteousness on the peninsula would not help the monte
were it to mishandle or neglect its day-to-day affairs. The eight officials were to appoint a Florentine citizen of good character as *massaro*
(or *massaio*), charged with looking after the pawns brought in by the
needy poor. This employee oversaw the actual transaction, which
had to be undertaken in a prescribed way. The massaro and his two
assistants (*scrivani*) accepted the pawn from its owner after the latter
swore that the object was rightfully his or hers; perjury was punish-
able by loss of the pawn. Having examined and noted the quality
and condition of the object, they handed it over to two assessors
(*stimatori*) who would determine its value. The massaro then wrote
out a numbered receipt in three copies, recording the owner's name
in such a way as to make him or her easily distinguishable. He noted
on the receipt the type of object pawned, its condition, and its assessed value. Finally, the amount of money to be lent—usually two-
thirds of the pawn's value—was appended in gold florins (*fiorini
larghi d'oro*), soldi, denari. An entry was made in the massaro's account book. The employee then made out the second receipt, which
he attached to the pawn itself. A third copy was given to the owner.
On this last copy appeared the date on which the monte had accepted the object, cross-references to its entry in the books, and the
amount lent out. The owner then received his loan in cash from the
head cashier (*camarlingo*). This employee was responsible for keeping his own records of all money paid out and taken in, including
interest (*interessi, meriti,* or *avanzi*) on pawns. He was also charged
with holding a second book of "Debtors and Creditors" in which
deposits were recorded; a running account for each deposit recorded withdrawals or additions.

Throughout its history the monte di pietà regularly employed in
the most important and best-paid positions men whose surnames
identified them as patricians. The first set of employees included
Lorenzo Guidotti as massaro, Francesco Ridolfi as provveditore, and
Adovardo Canigiani as camarlingo. Even the lesser posts sometimes

63. MP 728, Libro di debitori e creditori, 1b.

fell to patricians, though it is likely these must have been the ne'er-do-wells of their families, the relatively young, or members of cadet branches: no banker or merchant would have had the time or the volition to serve, as did Cardinale di Nicola Rucellai, as scrivano in 1496 at a salary of two and a half florins—L. 14.19.2—per month. In 1503 the provveditore was Niccolò Serragli; Cosimo Strozzi served as a massaro along with Neri Compagni and Giovanni Mazzei.[64] In 1518 Serragli was once again named provveditore. Giovanni Scolari, Giovanni Neri, and Alessandro Rinuccini acted as massari, and one of the cashiers was Filippo Arrigucci.[65] Often fathers were succeeded by sons, especially in the job of massaro: Alessandro Rinuccini, who held the post at the second branch from 1521 through 1530, gave way during the next triennium to his son Francesco. Neri Compagni, serving as massaro from 1527 through 1533, was followed by his son Dino, who served through the mid-1540s. For a three-year period, Girolamo Cioni held this position at the first branch, and a dozen years later his son Nicolaio was appointed massaro at the third branch.

The tendency to place patricians in the more important paid positions, which, it must be added, demanded considerable financial expertise, became even more pronounced during Duke Cosimo's reign. He wisely moderated his own kinsmen's employment in the monte, though Chiarissimo de' Medici did serve as provveditore. In 1560 the same post fell to Antonio degli Albizzi, while the massari were men from families of the first rank: Vincenzio Rucellai, Francesco da Filicaia, and Baldo Taddei.[66] The presence of such men among the paid employees is evidence of ducal favor, and also points to the eagerness with which members of the patriciate served as ducal functionaries.[67] There are also frequent examples of men from patrician families seeking lower-level employment. One Carlo Spini, "needy . . . and desiring to serve Your Most Illustrious Excellency," sought a post of scrivano in a Florentine magistracy; Bene-

64. MP 727, Libro di debitori e creditori, 1, 2a–b.
65. MP 734, Libro di debitori e creditori, 1, 59a–b.
66. See MP 756, Libro di debitori e creditori, 1, and MP 764, Libro di debitori e creditori, 306a.
67. See Litchfield, *Emergence of a Bureaucracy*, for patricians serving as functionaries.

detto di Tommaso Rucellai, "finding himself extremely poor," sought a similar position.[68]

The matter at hand for the men who were entrusted with setting up the structures of the monte di pietà was rather different. The eight were keenly aware that the monte's limited resources had to be carefully husbanded. The massaro was accordingly forbidden during the monte's first year of operation to authorize payments exceeding twenty-five lire to individual city inhabitants (*cittadini*), or ten lire to country dwellers (*contadini*) living within five miles of the city. These limits were necessary "because the monte at present finds itself with a small sum of money."[69] Of course the monte was expected to attract ever greater sums of money as word spread of its benevolence. In that case the officials were given the latitude to raise the maximum loans to fifty lire for citizens, fifteen for country dwellers. These limits on loans were similar to those of other nearby monti di pietà. At about the same time as Florence's monte began operation, Prato's fixed the limit on an individual loan to four florins.[70]

Careful provisions were made for redeeming pledges, for it was in this process that the monte would make enough profit to offset its expenses. A borrower who wished to redeem his pawn had to appear with his receipt before the massaro. This employee wrote out a new receipt for the cashier, stating how much money had originally been paid out against the pawn as well as the extra amount due the monte in interest, or, as the institution preferred it, "for payment of salaries and rents." The formatori had waxed philosophical on this point. "Because every effort desires a reward," they declared, "it is appropriate that he who receives the benefit of the effort contribute something to that effort."[71] Thus, they ruled, those who pawned items should pay a low interest rate. This rate might fluctuate from one to one and a half denari per lira per month (or 5 to 7½ percent per annum), depending on the state of the monte's fiscal health. In practice borrowers paid 5 percent interest on their loans, with rare

68. MP 721, 2a–b. For the cases of Spini and Rucellai, see Magistrato Supremo 1119, Filza seconda di suppliche e lettere dall'anno 1545 al 1560, Magistrato Supremo to Cosimo de' Medici, n.d., but from early 1561.

69. MP 1.

70. A.G.B., "Monte di pietà," 104.

71. MP 1.

exceptions, until late in the reign of Cosimo I (1537–74), when graduated rates were introduced. The interest rates of the Florentine
establishment compared favorably to those of some of the other
monti di pietà in the area. In Prato, for example, the poor had to
pay a relatively high 10 percent per annum, a rate that the reforms
of 1494 cut in half. The same rate prevailed at Pistoia.[72]

The monte's employees held positions of great responsibility, having to keep track of pawns and loans, maintain several different sets
of records, watch over interest rates and expenses, and handle sizable amounts of cash. The institution's charter, taking this into account, clearly delineated rules for its employees' public, and in some
cases private, behavior. They had to swear before a notary that they
would conscientiously discharge the duties of their offices. To insure
the honesty and impartiality of the assessors, penalties were to be
applied to indemnify the monte from any losses incurred from improper estimates of the values of pawns. And like many Florentine
officials, they had to find guarantors (mallevadori) before accepting
office. The amounts for which guarantors were responsible varied.
The massaro, who exercised the greatest responsibility (and, though
this was not bluntly stated, therefore had the greatest opportunity to
steal or mismanage the monte's money), had to find eight men who
trusted enough in his integrity to pledge one thousand florins each.
The head cashier needed the backing of four fellow citizens who
could pledge one thousand florins. Other employees—assessors, servants, and so on—had to find guarantors for smaller sums. Besides
serving to guard the monte against damages and to keep these officials honest, the bondsmen assured that only men of high social
standing would hold the higher offices, since only they were likely to
have acquaintances willing and able to wager hundreds of florins on
their honesty. Further controls on the monte's employees included
fines for improper or dishonest behavior. Finally, the massaro and
one other employee were required to "live civilly and honestly" in
the monte's quarters, "as befits a pious and religious house." The
two permanent inhabitants of the monte's premises were forbidden
to stage plays, dances, games, or other festivities there.[73]

72. On Prato, see A.G.B., "Monte di pietà," 104; and E. Stumpo, "Le istituzioni e la
società," in Fasano Guarini, *Prato*, 323–27. For Pistoia, see Capecchi and Gai, *Monte
della pietà a Pistoia*, 74.
73. MP 1, chaps. 34–35.

The employees' rather liberal salaries came from the income generated by interest payments on loans. The massaro was allocated 120 florins per year, payable in fiorini larghi. The cashier was paid 80, the massaro's two assistants 30 each, the assessors 40 each, and the two servants 24 each. Total salaries in the first year of operation thus totaled 388 fiorini larghi.

To avoid any incentive for profit making, the formatori limited the monte's expenses to 600 florins per annum. Salaries accounted for nearly two-thirds of this sum, leaving 210 florins for rent, provisions, and sundries. The cashier was instructed to keep a tight hold on the pursestrings in order to hold the monte to this figure. After all, the lower its expenses, the lower the rate of interest to be levied on loans.

Finally, the eight formatori turned their wary attention to the future. Living in the tumultuous 1490s, they were keenly conscious of the vicissitudes of Florentine fortunes. It would be a tragedy indeed if bad luck or political adversity overturned their careful efforts. Having designed a program for the monte's acquisition of capital and a detailed, practical set of bylaws for its operation, the eight tried to safeguard the monte di pietà against all foreseeable perils. Therefore, they stated that

> this new monte di pietà shall endure in perpetuity, and no one, for any person, magistrate, official, rector, or anyone else whomsoever, either directly or indirectly, under any pretext, may impede or remove or seize, spend or divert the money belonging to the said charitable institution; and anything which contradicts this ordinance is null and void. . . . The only use for the new monte's funds is in the care for the poor needy in the manner hereabove prescribed, as is the intention of the entire people. This [is] so that we will not have to turn anew to the Jews, with injury and prejudice to our souls.[74]

The formatori knew that the inclusion of this provision amounted to a statement of principle rather than a realistic policy. More practical and farsighted was the breadth allowed to future monte officials to change the bylaws with the approval of the Signori and Collegi. They recognized that "experience proves many things that could not

74. MP 1, chap. 40.

earlier have been foreseen" and thus opened the way for the evolution of the monte's operation and structures. They were in fact hopeful that, as its resources increased, the monte would be able to raise the limits placed on loans, open additional branches in the city, and, in short, adapt to meet the needs of the poor.

In the statutes of 1496, the eight formatori addressed in pragmatic terms the biggest problems facing the monte: its financing, its relationship to the state, its day-to-day operations, and its future. The reforming ideals of Savonarolan Florence met and were tempered by the hard-nosed Florentine sense of sound business. The extent to which the early monte succeeded in addressing the needs of the city and in attracting capital remains to be seen.

3 DEBTORS AND CREDITORS, 1496–1499

THE MONTE DI PIETÀ'S debtors and creditors ledgers—the libri di debitori e creditori—provide an almost unbroken record from 1496 on. The single lacuna spans the years 1551–57, overlapping the period of the war with Siena.[1] This gap notwithstanding, the ledgers along with other records allow a detailed examination of the monte's sources of income and its expenses. It was also during these early years that the monte began to develop its modes of operation, its clientele, and its core of benefactors.

In July 1496 the eight directors of the Florentine monte di pietà reached an agreement with Francesco d'Antonio Nori to rent a house in Piazza San Remigio in Santa Croce. This dwelling would be the monte's headquarters: it would house two employees, serve as the center where the poor would come to pawn and redeem their valuables, and store both records and pawned objects. On 11 February 1496 the monte paid Nori the first installment of 46 florins d'oro in oro (or fl. 54, L. –.10 di grossi) toward the total rent of 102 florins di grossi for the period 1 August 1496 through 30 April 1499. Improvements to the house required a further outlay of 11 florins d'oro in oro and L. 490.1.2., paid out to carpenters for alterations

---

1. In the inventory of the monte di pietà file at the Archivio di Stato di Firenze, two each of the ledgers and of the income/outgo books are listed as missing. These comprise MP 758–61. Fortunately, the compiler of MP 4 of 1667 had access to the missing books, for he cited some figures and accounts from those years.

and improvements.[2] Other expenses, including a little more than 7 florins for rental of a shop in Piazza Sant'Andrea in which to sell unredeemed pledges, totaled fl. 70, L. 918.13.5. Initial expenses, excluding salaries, amounted to fl. 148, L. 1,608.6.7; normal yearly expenses, however, were limited by statute to 600 florins larghi di grossi.[3]

The monte di pietà's employees and officials kept a hierarchy of records, with only those at the top of the hierarchy still extant. At the base was the first written record of every loan against pawns: the receipt, in three copies, written by the massaro, whose job included caring for the pawns. On this receipt he noted the type of pawn he had accepted, its condition, quality, and estimated value, its assigned number and the amount and currency paid out (florins larghi d'oro, lire, soldi, and denari). The massaro took this information and made "an individual entry of the receipt in a master book (*libro grande*)."[4] A copy of the receipt was given to the client and contained additional information: the day, month, and year of the transaction and a reference to the page of the libro grande, held by the massaro, where it had been entered. Neither the receipts nor the libri grandi survive.

The transaction was continued by the camarlingo, the chief cashier, whose job it was to pay out the money to the borrower. This employee kept a book of income and outgo (*entrata e uscita*) divided into two halves. The first half recorded "all money from those who redeem the pawns" along with a marginal note of the receipt, entry by entry, of the interest collected on the loan. The second listed money lent against pawns day by day in the order and amount of the receipts handed to him by the massaro and containing the same information, including a cross-reference to the massaro's entry in his libro grande. Each page of the camarlingo's book was to be tallied so as to make clear the state of the monte's income and outgo on loans at a glimpse. He was to keep the accounts in florins larghi, lire, soldi, and denari *di moneta vecchia* (old money). These books are no longer extant.

When a client came to redeem a pawn, the process was repeated. The massaro first drew up a receipt, which noted not only the

2. MP 721, 15a–b, 19a.
3. MP 1, chap. 36; and Piccolomini, ed., *Monte dei paschi di Siena*, 2:281.
4. The following discussion is based on MP 1, also published in Piccolomini, ed., *Monte dei paschi di Siena*, 2:271–82.

money repaid on the loan itself but also the interest. The monte's statutes, still not quite comfortable with the idea of collecting interest, referred to this sum as "the cost of salaries and rent." The camarlingo took the receipt and collected the borrower's cash "in the same money as was lent out" and entered the figures in the entrata section of his books, signed the receipt, and handed over the redeemed pawn. He recorded in the margins alongside the entry the amount taken in interest, "such that quickly and clearly one can see how much money the camarlingo has in his hands through the said entrata." The aim of this marginal entry was to allow the monte di pietà to repay any profit to those who had paid interest on loans; in practice this policy turned out to be unworkable.

The camarlingo kept a second set of books of entrata e uscita, tracking, on a day-by-day basis, money deposited in or donated to the monte or spent by the institution.[5] These books served as the source for the ledgers (libri di debitori e creditori) held by the eight officials, in which all debtors and creditors appear. Both sets—the books of income and outgo held by the camarlingo and the ledgers held by one of the eight officials—are extant, though with a six-year lacuna in the 1550s.

The busy camarlingo held a third book. Every time he needed cash, he would proceed to the monte's strongbox in the Badia, bringing with him one of the eight officials and a representative of the gonfaloniere of justice, each of whom held one of the keys needed to open the box. He removed an amount which he then entered in a cash book (*quaderno* or *libro di cassa*) "wherein is written all that [money] that is placed there [in the box] and all that is drawn out occasion by occasion." The three then locked the box with the book inside. These libri di cassa no longer exist. A second strongbox, to be kept "wherever it will be judged to be most convenient," held cash on hand at the monte di pietà's premises, and the camarlingo was obliged to lock up this money at the close of business every evening. He could remove money from this box only by order of the eight officials.[6]

5. MP 1, chap. 16; or Piccolomini, ed., *Monte dei paschi di Siena*, 2:277: "tutta l'entrata dell'assegnamenti pervenuti e che perverano a detto monte per qualunche altro denaio che avessi a servire a detto monte, e così l'uscita di quello accadessi pagarsi dì per dì per cagione del monte detto, la quale entrata e uscita si ragguagli a un libro debitori e creditori da tenersi per uno delli offitiali di decto monte."

6. MP 1, chaps. 17–18.

The sale of pawns that were never redeemed might sometimes bring in more money than their owners owed on their loans plus the accrued interest. For such cases the camarlingo kept a quaderno in which the owners of these pawns were made creditors for the excess they had paid. These books have disappeared, but the balances appear in the ledgers under the rubric "creditors of the remainder of the pawns" (creditori di resto de'pegni).

At the apex of the hierarchy stood the ledgers, or libri di debitori e creditori, kept by the eight officials, one of whom they designated bookkeeper, until in the mid-sixteenth century the eight appointed a notary to handle the task. In these ledgers the different activities of the institution come together: its charitable lending; its search for capital in the form of donations or deposits; its salaries, operating costs, and other sundry expenses. The ledger had to be balanced at the end of the officials' three-year term, with the debits and credits then posted forward to the next ledger of the new eight. These ledgers reveal the ways benefactors and, after 1537, investors viewed the monte and used it for their own financial purposes. They also bring into sharp focus the relationship between the state and the monte, a relationship that often carried advantages for both parties and that would, especially during the reign of Cosimo I, have a great impact on the institution.

The founders of the monte di pietà anticipated two kinds of financial support for it. These were either outright gifts or free loans that would be given out of purely pious considerations by "inspired persons." Spurred on by an aggressive campaign of preaching by men such as Savonarola and Marco Strozzi, citizens responded by donating or pledging money to the monte during a special Palm Sunday appeal. From 27 March through 25 May 1496, these efforts yielded a total of fl. 640, L. 1,389.17.6 in alms.[7] These donations were made anonymously, having been placed in special almsboxes by the faithful. Among the first category of outright donations were those made by individuals as testamentary bequests and gifts in memory of a

---

7. MP 721, 1a–b. Almsboxes were placed in the Duomo and other churches. The money collected included "several false florins largo d'oro, some florins *leggieri* and some filed down French scudi . . . and some false grossi," which would be reckoned up separately. Because the sum collected came from outright gifts, it formed the core of the monte's permanent endowment. The figures that follow for contributions and gifts all come from MP 721, 1–15. The sum of alms is found on 36b.

departed loved one. The rector of San Miniato fra le Torri brought in fl. 1, L. 3.–.5 that came from an unnamed "friend" who offered the gift to the monte simply "for God." Ser Giacomo Alessi, a priest at San Pier Maggiore, donated fl. 1, L. 2.7 "for the love of God to serve the poor," although the wording of the entry suggests that the priest may have removed this sum from a collection box in his church. Corporations too took up the task of building the monte's capital. The Parte Guelfa made good on its pledge of Palm Sunday, paying L. 998.12.8.[8] The wool guild pledged and paid L. 300, and the merchants' guild fulfilled a promise to hand over fl. 10 di grossi (or L. 59.9). Strikingly ironic was a gift of alms to the monte, an institution that must have appeared to Florentine Jews as a monument to intolerance, from the testament of Manuello di Buonaiuto da Camerino, himself a Jew.[9] These and other entries listed as alms were combined in a single account in the monte's ledgers. When the books were balanced in 1499, alms donated to the institution as part of its permanent capital came to fl. 893, L. 3,758.19.4.

The ledgers were kept in double entry. Accounts in the ledgers (by 1557 sometimes called the libri grandi) were kept in the "Venetian style," with debits always entered on the left-hand page and credits on the right.[10] When a deposit was placed in the monte, the officials made an entry on the credit side (referred to herein as *b*) in the current ledger. Each entry included the benefactor's name, the date, and the amount, expressed either in actual money deposited or in lire/soldi/denari. Some entries listed detailed restrictions that the creditor placed on the deposit or extraordinary circumstances surrounding the deposit. Where space permitted, additional deposits by the same party were added below the first, a practice that allowed officials to view the account at a glance. On the debit side (referred to herein as *a*), an entry was made for each withdrawal. The bookkeeper gave cross-references for both sides of the account to other monte di pietà books, particularly the entrata e uscita (income and outgo) books, which listed these entries as they occurred, as well as

8. This and other sums in lire/soldi/denari represent the value of coins (often of a type or types not specified) as expressed in a money of account.

9. MP 721, 26b.

10. For double entry and the "Venetian system," see Florence Edler, *Glossary of Medieval Terms of Business: Italian Series, 1200–1600* (Cambridge, Mass., 1934), Appendix 2 ("Medici Methods of Bookkeeping"), 352.

to other notations for the same account within the ledger. Such cross-referencing is a sign of mature double-entry bookkeeping. At the end of the three-year period of each ledger, the accounts were balanced. In the event that the debits equaled the credits, the account was closed and it disappeared entirely from future records. When credits exceeded debits or vice versa, the account was closed with a transfer entry and reopened by being posted forward to the next ledger. Responsibility for all accounts shifted from the outgoing officials to their successors.

The monte's activities at its inception, then, fell into separate categories and were recorded in distinct sets of books. First, it lent money to its poor clientele and took in money from the same persons when they redeemed their pledges. Second, it accepted deposits from individuals or groups and paid out money in withdrawals or expenses. There follows a sample account.

On the credit side:

Donato d'Antonio di Donato Ciani is credited [*dè avere*] on August 30 1496 30 florins larghi d'oro in oro that he deposited in this monte freely and for the love of God, with the agreement that he may have them back at his every pleasure and wish, and under the condition that whenever he wants them back, he must let us know at least one month before, and . . . he wishes that, in the event that he has passed away, the said money be made good to his sons or heirs. —30 florins[11]

On the debit side:

1498. Donato on the page opposite is debited [*dè dare*] on June 19, 1498 30 florins d'oro in oro. —30 florins

The record of Donato Ciani's account in the monte consisted of one entry for his deposit in August 1496 and a second one for his withdrawal, nearly two years later, of the entire thirty florins. Because Donato's account balanced, it was closed.[12]

11. MP 721, 6a–b. This example contains cross-references omitted here.
12. The monte di pietà's bookkeepers borrowed language in common use among Florence's local bankers. By the late fifteenth century, local banks were accepting short-term, interest-paying deposits (though the interest was disguised to evade the

Most of the conditions Ciani placed on his deposit were typical, though the one-month withdrawal notice required by the monte was somewhat out of the ordinary. The institution, trying to safeguard its limited resources against sudden withdrawal, obviously wanted depositors to agree to give notice.[13] To avoid any danger of losing this patrimony in the event of his death, Ciani made it clear that his heirs were to receive the payment.

Deposit institutions, whether banks or charities, needed enough cash on hand to satisfy depositors seeking withdrawals and other creditors, but they also wanted to use their accumulated capital. Venetian banks, for example, probably as a matter of course had less than 100 percent of their cash in reserve. In Florence the records of the local banks of the Strozzi, Cerchi, and Datini show that, at least half the time, they had less than 100 percent. Such bankers kept a cash book (quaderno di cassa) that held accounts of those debtors and creditors who agreed to pay in cash. These cash books, according to Richard Goldthwaite, were not part of a "hierarchy of accounts but an independent record of a separate activity." To disguise any evidence of usury, local banks avoided keeping a tally of cash on hand; the amount instead had to be determined by taking inventory of the banker's strongbox.[14]

Like some banks, the monte di pietà appears to have kept no tally of its cash reserves. It too held a set of records called quaderni di cassa, which no longer exists, but cross-references in surviving books suggest that these quaderni kept track of a "separate activity" from deposits and withdrawals: moneys paid on loans against pawns, and taken in on redemptions. As such these quaderni are different from the books of the same name kept by private banks. The monte's statutes made access to its cash on hand complicated. As

---

usury code) that were payable on demand ("we have to pay at [the depositor's] plea-sure" ["abbiamo a paghare a ongni suo piacere"]). Richard Goldthwaite, "Local Banking in Renaissance Florence," *Journal of European Economic History* 14 (1985): 19.

13. Some creditors spelled out the term of their deposits. Monna Selvaggia, widow of Filippo di Matteo di Simone degli Strozzi, opened an account on 28 November 1496 in "the amount of 1,000 fiorini larghi di grossi, which money she gives to the monte di pietà for its use for one year from that date, freely and for the love of God." As it happened, she generously waited nearly two years—until 17 September 1498—to withdraw any of this money. MP 721, 10a–b.

14. Goldthwaite, "Local Banking," 14, and *passim*.

noted earlier, the eight officials could open the strongbox in the
Badia only in conjunction with a representative of the gonfaloniere
of justice and the camarlingo. The monte di pietà was liable to have
a good amount of liquid capital, but the complexity of gaining access
to it was meant to discourage its casual use and to win the monte a
reputation as a safe repository. Finally, though some monti di pietà
in Italy evolved into banks, these early modern institutions were
charities at heart. They did not extend capital in order to make
money, but to offer low-interest loans to the poor.

Many accounts were more active than Donato Ciani's.[15] A few examples follow.

On the credit side:

Francesco di Filippo d'Agnolo, tailor or rather cloth merchant
[*panaiolo*] beyond the gates of San Niccolò of Florence, is credited on 15 December 1496 the sum of 15 florins.

And on 3 January 1497, 25 florins.

TOTAL   40 florins.

On the debit side:

Francesco di Filippo opposite is debited on 15 February 1497
20 florins.

And on 18 April 1497 20 florins.

Francesco made four transactions over four months, depositing
and then withdrawing his forty florins. The monte had the use of his
capital for only a limited time. Cross-references were, as always,
made in the appropriate places, but this account, like Ciani's, disappeared from the succeeding records since it had been closed out.

Many accounts remained active for longer periods of time.[16]

On the credit side:

Caterina of Montecatini is credited on 28 February 1496 [O.S.]
fl. 20 d'oro in oro [the entry stipulated that she might with-

15. MP 721, 11a–b.
16. MP 721, 14a–b, 15a–b.

draw half this sum freely at her pleasure, and that half was to be paid to a second party].

Note that Monna Caterina has another account here . . . 10 florins.

On the debit side:

Caterina of Montecatini opposite is debited [n.d.] 10 florins.

And on 30 April 1499 she is debited 20 florins, posted forward as creditor to our successors.

Caterina's account had not been closed out. On 30 April 1499, when the departing directors balanced the ledger for their successors, Monna Caterina's remaining credit of twenty florins was posted forward to the end of the current ledger, debited from that book, and credited to her in the beginning of the next ledger.

All told, in April 1499 the ledger listed twenty-three accounts, including a generic category of alms as well as one for "profits from the cash box" (*avanzi di cassa*) that were reported by the camarlingo. This list obscures the help offered to the monte by persons who deposited money there during the three years but who had withdrawn it prior to the balancing of the books. Twenty-one deposits, including a few large ones from patricians, were all withdrawn.

During its first three years of operation, most supporters of the monte were private individuals. Corporate groups such as the guilds or the Parte Guelfa made up a second though numerically small category. Yet another included accounts where the state had intervened in one way or another, as in cases where it directed individuals or groups to deposit money in the monte. Such accounts illustrate the early involvement of the city despite its determination not to allow its own revenues to serve the monte. The last category consisted of anonymous gifts of charity such as those taken from church collection boxes. The following list shows the number and percentage of lenders to the monte during 1496–99.

Category	Number	Percent
Private individuals	42	61
Corporate groups	4	6

Category	Number	Percent
State	5	7
Anonymous	18	26
TOTAL	69	100

As its founders had expected, private individuals, presumably motivated by pious and charitable instincts, deposited money in the monte di pietà. Of the 69 accounts, they held 42, or 61 percent. The other three groups, in comparison, accounted for only 27 entries.

Among private deposits, the amount of money placed in the monte ranged from less than a florin to over a thousand florins. The mean of the total amount in all forty-two private accounts was about 167 florins,[17] an impressive sum at first glance. But a more meaningful figure is the median deposit, about 40 florins, a sizable figure in relation to the average Florentine's income. The mean of total amounts, 167 florins, is skewed by a small number of relatively large private donations. The following list shows the twenty-one largest deposits by private individuals.

Range of deposit	Number (and amount of deposits)
Over fl. 1,000	1 (fl. 1,100)
500–999	4 (903, 893, 881, 539)
200–499	4 (480, 450, 232, 200)
100–199	6 (166, 150, 100, 100, 100, 100)
40–99	6 (67, 50, 44, 44, 40, 40)
TOTAL	fl. 6,679

Omitting the five highest and five lowest deposits, the mean of the remaining thirty-two deposits drops to 82.6 florins, a difference of 84.4 florins. The effect of the several largest donations on the statistics makes clear the monte's heavy dependence upon a few generous persons.

The twenty-one largest deposits constituted over 95 percent of all private deposits, whose sum reached only about 7,008 florins. The five largest private donations totaled about 4,316 florins, or about 62

---

17. The amount in each account has been rounded off to the nearest florin.

percent of all private deposits. Not one of the five largest accounts remained on the books on 30 April 1499 when the first ledger was closed. Many of those who had deposited money freely in the monte must have seen it as deserving temporary but not permanent help. The following list shows the five largest private accounts during 1496–99 and their duration of deposit.

Name	Deposit	Withdrawal
Selvaggia, widow of Filippo Strozzi	fl. 1,000 larghi di grossi 28 Nov. 1498	by 30 Apr. 1499
"A secret friend"	fl. 1,100 larghi d'oro in oro 30 July 1496	by 17 Sept. 1498
Niccolò del Nero (a monte official)	fl. 482, L. 2,465 18 July 1497	28 Nov. 1497
Lisabetta, widow of Braccio de' Medici	fl. 881, L. 1.13 30 July 1496	by 26 Jan. 1498
Piero Lenzi (a monte official)	fl. 390, L. 896.6 8 July 1497	28 Nov. 1498

The constant movement of money made the monte's quest for capital a continuing one. In the case of significant private deposits, no sooner would one account be opened than another would be closed. In fact, the monte di pietà offered Florentines the chance to support a charity and still get their money back.

Some individuals seemed intent upon setting a good example for their fellow Florentines. Several of the monte's own officials, such as Niccolò del Nero and Piero Lenzi, maintained accounts, albeit rather briefly. The del Nero bank was involved in handling other monte business.[18] At least one employee followed the officials' lead: Paolo Velandini, an appraiser (stimatore) for the monte, became a creditor in the amount of twenty florins on 8 October 1496.[19]

18. MP 721, 13b and 2b; the bank of Simone del Nero is mentioned.
19. This sum represented half his yearly salary. On 4 September 1496 Paolo had been paid his monthly salary in moneta nera amounting to L. 19.18.10. In effect, he pledged to work for the monte for six months gratis, or more accurately, he deferred payment of his salary because he was at liberty to withdraw his twenty florins at a later date, and he did. MP 721, 2a–b.

Foremost among those who set a good example was the enthusiastic Marco di Matteo Strozzi. As early as 2 August 1496, the rector of San Miniato fra le Torri deposited one hundred florins in the new institution for whose creation he had worked so passionately. Strozzi's act of charity seems to have influenced at least one of his friends or parishioners, for on the same day he brought along a small deposit (fl. 1, L. 3.5.) from "a friend." With further deposits, the priest lent fl. 330, L. 121.11.[20] One of the most substantial loans came from the widow of another Strozzi, Monna Selvaggia, who lent the monte fl. 1,000 larghi di grossi, though her relationship to Marco is unclear, as is any role he might have played in convincing her of the worthiness of the monte's cause. The entry shows only that the family bank arranged for the deposit.[21]

In the final analysis, the monte's advocates were at best only marginally successful in convincing wealthy Florentines to support it. Of the individuals who gave or lent money to the institution during its first three years, few represented wealthy, well-known patrician families, although the eagerness with which such families invested in the monte comune and monte delle doti during their profitable years has been well documented.[22] Similarly, their fondness for lavishing patronage on selected charities is understood. Of course some of these families had been forced to flee Florence as a result of the civil strife of 1494 and its aftermath. Many had been hurt by the economic troubles of the decade, which were serious enough to compel the city to rescind its order that the Jews wind up their affairs and leave. Seeking to "alleviate the needs of our republic without spending any money," the councils decided that the Jews would after all "be tolerated" for three more years in the Florentine domain; in exchange for that policy the Jews would lend the city nine thousand florins.[23] But the Florentine patriciate was remarkable for its resilience and obstinately maintained its leading economic and political position well beyond the fifteenth century.[24] Why was it so conspicuously absent from the monte di pietà's ledgers? Simply put, unless

20. MP 721, 1b, 4b.
21. MP 721, 10b.
22. See Molho, *Public Finances*, and Molho and Kirshner, "Dowry Fund."
23. Misc. Rep., busta I, ins. 37.
24. See Litchfield, *Emergence of a Bureaucracy*.

the monte could offer an attractive return on investments, the patriciate en masse was not interested.

There were some exceptions. One of the largest private accounts was that of Monna Lisabetta, widow of Braccio de' Medici. The motivation behind this largesse must have been genuine piety, especially in light of the traditional Medici hostility to monti di pietà. A small sum was deposited by Giovanni Minerbetti. The daughter of Antonio di Ridolfo de' Bardi deposited one hundred florins, and Monna Alessandra, a widow and the daughter of Giorgio di Giovanni Antinori, lent the monte forty-four florins. Ridolfo de' Bardi's daughter Maria deposited, through her uncle Ser Tommaso, one hundred florins. Maddelena, the daughter of one of the Falconieri, was creditor for a thousand lire. Messer Giorgiantonio di Ser Amerigo Vespucci, the *proposto* (head of the chapter) of the Duomo, deposited one hundred florins, apparently influenced by Marco Strozzi, who later added ten florins to Vespucci's original deposit. The three monte directors who lent money to their own institution were surnamed Lenzi, del Nero, and Guicciardini.

Even though women in Renaissance Florence had only limited control of wealth, they were important contributors to the monte. Among the forty-two individual accounts, eleven belonged to women and twenty-seven to men, with four either shared or anonymous. Two of the five most important depositors were Monna Lisabetta, the widow of Braccio de' Medici, and Monna Selvaggia, the widow of Filippo Strozzi. These patrician women must have had greater access to money through their families' general wealth or their own dowries, which reverted to them upon the deaths of their husbands.

Such creditors were exceeded in number by middling tradesmen, unknown widows, and others of their ilk. Though their deposits were almost always small, these middle-class people were more representative of the monte's early supporters than were those named Medici or Bardi. Cristoforo di Manozzo, a spice merchant (*speziale*) who deposited forty florins; Franco di Filippo, a tailor, who presented the monte with a total of forty florins; Caterina, the daughter of Luca of Montecatini di Valdinievole in whose name the monte held thirty florins; Mariotto di Franco, a tailor who with his wife pledged nine florins; a Third-Order Franciscan offering the generous sum of fifty florins; and an Observant Franciscan from Pistoia who favored the monte with two hundred florins—all these were

typical of the persons who helped the monte in its early years of
need. The wealthy found better things to do with their money.

Florentine corporate bodies represented another potential source
of income. The wealthy guilds, like wealthy patricians, all had their
favorite charities. The Calimala, for instance, supported well over a
dozen monasteries in Florence and the environs, including those of
the Carmine and Santo Spirito, not to mention a like number of
hospitals such as Santa Maria Nuova, San Gallo, and the Bigallo.
The Hospital of Santa Maria degli Innocenti was a pet concern of
the silk guild. In some cases the Signoria delegated the administration of charities or benevolent companies to selected guild members,
many of whom worked without compensation.[25]

Two guilds came to the aid of the monte di pietà. The Arte et
Università de'Mercanti, also known as the Calimala or international
merchants' guild, and the Lana, or wool guild, deposited money in
the charitable pawnshop. Just as quick was the Parte Guelfa, whose
gift of alms was recorded in the monte in March 1497. Most impressive of all was the size of each deposit, as seen in this list of corporate
loans to the monte during 1496–99.

Corporation	Date of deposit	Amount
Parte Guelfa	8 Mar. 1497	L. 998.12.8
Arte de'Mercanti	11 Apr. 1497	L. 59.5
Arte della Lana	3 Jan. 1497	L. 5,984.7.2
Arte de'Mercanti	n.d.	fl. 148, L. 1,105.1.4

The monte calculated the Arte della Lana's account as equivalent to
the original deposit of fl. 1,000 larghi di grossi.

These four corporate groups provided the monte with considerable capital during its earliest days. The first two listed deposits, offered in the spring of 1497, together accounted for L. 1,057.17.8.
This sum represented over 20 percent of the early total that the
monte reckoned at fl. 640, L. 1,389.17.7.[26] The Guelfs had appar-

25. See Edgcumbe Staley, *The Guilds of Florence* (Chicago, 1906), 535–53; Howard
Saalman, *The Bigallo: The Oratory and Residence of the Compagnia del Bigallo e della Misericordia in Florence* (New York, 1969); and Luigi Passerini, *La storia degli stabilmenti di
beneficenza e d'istruzione elementare gratuita della città di Firenze* (Florence, 1853). On the
Signoria's delegation of authority see Saalman, *The Bigallo*, 4.
26. MP 721, 1a–b.

ently been moved by the Palm Sunday processions whose theme had been charity to the monte.

Corporate gifts and loans totaled fl. 148, L. 2,162.19 plus fl. 1,000 larghi di grossi. But for how long would the guilds allow the monte to use this money gratis? The ledgers show that by the end of the three-year period, only part of this total remained in the guilds' accounts. For instance, of the Lana's deposit of fl. 1,000, fl. 900 larghi di grossi (or fl. 831 d'oro in oro, by the monte's reckoning) were withdrawn on 29 January 1499. The remaining fl. 50 (or L. 300, according to the ledger), were donated to the monte in perpetuity as alms.[27] The fl. 50 were carried over into an account for general alms received from many different sources. Such alms were outright gifts and would therefore enlarge the monte's small patrimony.

The merchants' guild withdrew its L. 59.5 prior to April 1499, temporarily leaving the larger sum of fl. 148, L. 1,105.1.4 on deposit for the monte's use. Long before the triennial balancing of the books, however, every last denaro had been withdrawn. Of the original corporate deposits, only fl. 148, L. 1,405.1.4 remained.

Though few in number, corporate deposits lent significant support to the early monte di pietà. There is little reason to doubt that the long association between corporations and charity came into play. At the same time, both guilds and Guelfs were evidently reluctant to commit large sums for an extended period, and most of the funds they offered were withdrawn by spring 1499.

The third source of support for the monte was the state. The city of Florence steadfastly refused to make any direct fiscal commitment to the monte, and in fact forbade any state funds to be appropriated either as a gift or as a loan. Yet at the same time it was a civic law, or provvisione, that had brought the monte into being, and the monte's success, especially in the Savonarolan climate of anti-Semitism and pietistic revival, was in the city's interest. The city therefore placed its prestige behind the monte, and prestige was backed up by deed when the city decreed that the monte take over some of the fiscal administration of the Pupilli.

Indirect means abounded for the state to aid the monte. Individuals in Florence were constantly seeking redress of wrongs in the

---

27. MP 721, 12a and 26b. An entry made on the same date noted that a receipt written by the guild's provveditore ordered this gift to be made.

city's courts, which often levied fines against the liable party. In the early years of the monte di pietà, the courts of the Mercanzia and the Otto di Guardia e Balìa handed down four sentences ordering the offenders to pay sums into the monte in the name of the vindicated plaintiffs. In the first case, a certain Margherita di Francesco and her daughter Marietta sued the former's employer Bernardo di Stefano Porcellini, a spice merchant, for L. 102 "in back wages for the eight years that Margherita served in his house."[28] The judges rendered their verdict in her favor for seventy lire, ordering Bernardo "to deposit this sum in the monte di pietà . . . with the condition that it will be paid freely to Marietta or her future husband as part of her dowry."[29]

Similar sentences were handed down by the Otto di Guardia e Balìa. In compliance with one such sentence, on 3 January 1497 one Agnolo di Rinieri del Pace deposited forty lire in the name of Margherita, daughter of Piero di Giovanni da Poppi. The sum was to be paid upon Margherita's marriage. Should she die, the money would remain permanently in the monte. In March of the same year, their provveditore opened an account on behalf of two women to whom the Otto had awarded a settlement of five florins, the sum to be paid to one of them upon her marriage as part of her dowry.[30] In April the Otto judged Antonio di Checcho da San Giovanni Alavena to be the aggrieved party in a dispute with Donato di Bonifazio Fazi and ordered the latter to deposit ninety florins in his name.[31]

The presence of such credits in the monte helps unravel a problem that has spurred debate in the historiography of monti di pietà, namely, the apparent support that the lower middle classes offered the institutions.[32] But how could the poorest persons—"individuals

---

28. Mercanzia—Sentenzie de' Sei 7372. Tribunale. 30 Aug. 1496.

29. On 3 January 1497 the money was deposited in Marietta's name under the proviso that, should she die or never marry, the money would go to her mother or to some other individual named by Marietta. MP 721, 11b.

30. MP 721, 14b.

31. MP 721, 16b. Each of these four awards remained on deposit in April 1499 when all accounts were balanced. MP 721, 36b, 37b.

32. In examining the first ledger, that is, MP 721, Guido Pampaloni noted the paucity of patrician benefactors of the new monte di pietà and concluded that the city's elites did not heed the cry for alms and Christian generosity and that Florentines from completely unknown lower- and middle-class families formed the monte's core of support. Pampaloni, "Cenni storici," 536.

placed in the lowest grades of society," as Guido Pampaloni put it—
find even small sums of money in the difficult 1490s? The plague
struck Florence in 1496, bringing along with it a grain shortage. The
crisis persisted for several years, leading the desperate citizens to
bring to Florence the famous Madonna of Impruneta; she, however,
rendered no help.[33] That these poor souls, no matter how worthy
their intentions, were among the patrons rather than the clientele of
the monte di pietà during years of plague and famine is hard to
imagine, despite the evidence of the ledger, with dozens of deposits
(and not only in the first book, but also in the subsequent ones) attributed to unknowns, widows, and provincials.

The ledger for the years 1548–51 proves, however, that many of
the persons credited with deposits were not the persons who had
provided the funds for them. For example, we have seen that beginning in 1496, Monna Margherita da Poppi enjoyed a credit in the
monte as the result of a "condemnation" handed down by the Otto.
Because it was intended as a dowry, this was not a free deposit but a
conditional one payable only under certain circumstances (in her
case, to her future husband as part of her dowry). The 1496–99
ledger listed her as a creditor but gave little information about her
or the circumstances of her account. But half a century later the
bookkeepers noted the origins of her credit and explained its continued existence with the words "she not having married, it stays with
us."[34] An anonymous "friend" identified only by the initials F.G.B
who had placed a small sum in the monte (fl. 1, L. 3.6.4 by the
exchange rate of 1548) apparently was troubled by a fraudulent
business deal wherein he had purchased a pendant as fake while
knowing it was really genuine. Perhaps to compensate for his illicit
gain at another's expense, F.G.B. never withdrew his money. Marco
Strozzi's name, hidden for fifty years, lay behind the accounts of
three obscure creditors whose small deposits came not from their
own resources, but from the rector's testamentary bequest to them.

The list continues. The daughter of a carpenter claimed fl. 7, L. 4,
deposited in 1503 when the Otto condemned one Bartolomeo, a
woodworker, to pay this sum into the monte as a potential dowry for

---

33. Mano. 117, "Diario istorico di quello ch'è seguito nella città di Firenze comin-
ciando l'anno 1435 a tutto il 1522," 72v–8or.

34. MP 756, Libro di debitori e creditori, 2b. Her deposit had been changed into
florins and was worth fl. 5, L. 5. It earned no interest.

the girl. A similar judgment had resulted in a deposit of fl. 5, L. 5 for Gostanza di Francesco da Empoli, to be paid when she married or entered the convent. In 1508 the Otto ordered an account opened for Domenica di Francesco da Buggiano, to be paid when she married or took vows. In 1527 the Otto told Alesso Baldovinetti to hand over fl. 7, L. 1 "to give to two girls." Several other deposits, intended as dowries, had reverted to the institution when their creditors died, for virtually all these entries specifically stated that, should the girl die, the monte would keep the money. The Commission for Poor Mendicants ordered one Tommaso di Bartolomeo, described as a *paternostraio*, to pay the monte two florins for some unnamed offense.[35] The Signori themselves ordered the priest Ser Giusto di Santi to put over fourteen florins in the monte, and called on Paolo Davanzati to place over thirteen florins there in 1506, "and it has to be paid as the standard-bearer of justice shall direct."[36] Giovanni Mori had, in 1529, deposited over twenty-one florins "by order of the officials of the health board (Sanità), to pay to the heirs of Maddalena, former servant of Leonardo Manucelli."[37]

Although most deposits that dated from the early decades of the monte's life had long since been withdrawn, twenty-nine deposits entered prior to 1530, including the ones noted above, still stood on the books in 1548. Thirteen of them had judicial or testamentary origins and had been provided not by the persons in whose names they were entered, but by losers in legal cases or by patrons or employers concerned with providing a girl with a dowry that would remain safe until needed. Four more of these old deposits had been furnished by persons other than the females in whose names they were opened. Evidence from the more descriptive ledger of 1548 shows that many of the deposits belonging to people apparently of the "lowest grades of society" had not in fact been offered to the monte for the "love of God," but had been placed there by others in compliance with orders from a state organ. It is likely that many of the other deposits, long since closed out by 1548 (and whose origins remain unknown) also fell into these categories. This evidence up-

35. MP 756, 10b. I have been unable to determine the precise meaning of "paternostraio"; it may refer to a cleric or possibly a beggar, perhaps one who promised to pray in exchange for charity.

36. MP 756, 2b.

37. MP 756, 11b.

holds the thesis that the poor were beneficiaries rather than patrons of the monte di pietà.

Far more useful than small deposits were large benefactions that reverted to the monte from the state, despite its avowed intention not to provide funds for the institution. Such deposits might come from taxes or duties. The *decima* on priests and on the Studio of Pisa yielded, in 1502 and again in 1506, two deposits totaling ninety-nine florins. Because the Signoria had ordered this sum paid into the monte, it was credited to "our magnificent Signori" (magnifici signori nostri). The officials of the monte comune had, in 1508, allotted fl. 283, L. 4.8 to the monte di pietà, and the commune itself had, at the same time, handed over fl. 1,205, L. 3.15. The old Pupilli account, from which ordinary expenses were appropriated, still contained fl. 80, L. 3.15.8 in 1548.[38] In 1501 the city also allocated income from an increase in the *gabella delle porte* (a tax on certain imports and exports) to the monte, but noted that this money was intended only to supplement the generosity of "good and pious persons" in aiding the "popolo minuto."[39]

The largest benefaction to the monte came from the state, though in a manner no one could have anticipated. In 1494, taking advantage of the changing political alignments and the diplomatic confusion brought about by Charles VIII's invasion of Italy, Pisans rose against the hated domination of Florence. Though Charles promised to deliver the rebellious city to Florence in exchange for Florentine diplomatic and financial support, his failure to do so caused the Florentines to abandon their exuberant cry of "Viva Francia!" and gave rise to bitter disappointment and disillusion.[40] During the course of the campaign, the French king's betrayal was revealed, culminating on 1 January 1496 when word came that Charles had handed over the Pisan forts to the Pisans and withdrawn his own troops to Lucca. Florence's long struggle to reconquer the city ended only in June 1509, when "a horseman bearing the olive branch arrived with the surrender of Pisa."[41]

38. MP 756, 5b, 9b.
39. Prov.—Reg. 192, 33v–34r, 23 Oct. 1501. I am grateful to Anthony Molho of Brown University for this reference.
40. Landucci, *Diario*, 17 Nov. 1494. See also Rubinstein, "Firenze e il problema della politica imperiale," esp. 14–15.
41. Landucci, *Diario*, 8 June 1509.

In the spring of 1498, a provvisione designated the monte as the depository for proceeds from the sale of goods seized from the Pisan rebels.[42] More than private donations and deposits, anonymous charity, or corporate gifts and loans, the sale of these confiscated goods helped put the monte di pietà on a sound financial footing. In a series of deposits beginning in July 1498 and continuing through March of the following year, a total of fl. 5,893 d'oro in oro and L. 2,086.2.8 *di moneta nera* came into the monte. Several withdrawals by the provveditore of the officials delegated to oversee the disposition of the rebels' property reduced the sum, as of the balancing of 30 April 1499, to the still substantial figure of fl. 5,496, L. 1,941.13.14. By 1502 this account had increased to fl. 13,253, L. 2.19.2.[43]

How much this income meant to the monte was made clear by an anonymous writer who, in 1667, pored over the financial records. The deposits made by the officials overseeing the disposition of the goods of the Pisan rebels constituted a turning point for the monte di pietà, for from 1497 on, said the author, the monte enjoyed improved fiscal health. By 1506, after paying its expenses and debts, it ended its triennial accounting period with a surplus of L. 3,202.[44]

With the opening of this account came the early signs of the monte di pietà's usefulness to the state as a kind of honest broker. While all moneys received from this source were theoretically available for helping the poor, the officials in charge of the confiscated goods occasionally directed the monte to debit their account and send the amount specified to one of their own creditors. Such was the case, for example, in 1501 when the monte paid an official from Montepulciano L. 150 from the account of the Pisan rebels at the behest of the overseers.[45] Here the monte di pietà behaved much like a local bank. The deposit by the officials was a free corporate deposit, payable on their demand. From this practice, Richard Goldthwaite noted, "it is only a short step [for] . . . the client to order payments to third parties."[46] Just as local banks made this "short step," so did the monte di pietà—and quickly. Though their deposits

42. Prov.—Reg. 186, 136.
43. MP 724, Libro di debitori e creditori, 25a–b, 47b.
44. MP 4, 185r–187v.
45. Cited by Pampaloni, "Cenni storici," 536; also see MP 4, 146, and MP 721, 21 a–b.
46. Goldthwaite, "Local Banking," 19–20.

earned no interest, the monte's creditors could regard their accounts as active capital, safely stored in the monte's coffers and available for its benevolent purposes, but ultimately to be used for their own debts and expenses.

Willingness to see the potential of the monte's financial services was present in some depositors from the institution's inception. It has already been shown that some individual accounts were quite active: sums flowed into and from them continually. Occasionally ledgers hinted at the reason for withdrawal. Chimenti di Berto Ciardi from Castel Fiorentino, for example, was credited with the amount of forty-four florins. His father-in-law, Ser Stefano di Giovanni da Ponte a Sieve, had deposited this sum in Chimenti's name on 23 August 1496, stipulating that it serve as part of the dowry for his daughter Lucrezia, Chimenti's wife. Only three days later Chimenti removed all his money from the monte, revealing that Ser Stefano had had no charitable motives in making this deposit. Rather, he saw the monte as a convenient way to transact part of his daughter's dowry. We cannot know how the majority of creditors used the funds they withdrew from the monte, but no doubt many individuals permitted the institution to make use of their private funds only until they were needed for other purposes, at which time they were conveniently withdrawn in cash.

For those individuals who wished to make benevolent donations upon their deaths, the monte was a very suitable charity. Dino di Giovanni, a master weaver, agreed to deposit sixty-seven florins larghi d'oro in oro "freely and for the love of God, under the condition that he can have them back whenever he likes." Dino agreed that, should he die before withdrawing his money, "half would go to the monte, and the other half to Santa Maria Nuova for his soul."[47] How convenient and salutary for Dino's soul! Not only could he deposit money in the monte and reap the spiritual benefits that charity bestowed, but he could be sure that, in the unfortunate event of his death, his soul would automatically win the grace befitting his pious bequest, for unlike unscrupulous heirs or scheming lawyers or priests, the monte could be trusted to carry out his will.[48]

47. MP 721, 7b. As it turned out, the weaver withdrew his money in three installments by 28 November 1498.

48. Richard Trexler, in "The Bishop's Portion: Generic Pious Legacies in the Late Middle Ages in Italy," *Traditio* 28 (1972): 397–450, noted that, well into the fifteenth

Some historians, studying cases like these, have argued that monti di pietà in fifteenth-century Italy were little more than banks that had repudiated the principle of making money through interest. Monti di pietà, they noted, held both long-term and short-term deposits, were generally trustworthy, and offered convenient banking services to the middle classes. This argument states that the early monti preached by the Franciscans derived their structures from private pawn banks (*a pegno*), particularly those run by the Lombards and the Jews, omitting only the collection of interest.[49] In fact, the monti di pietà performed one important service that most commercial banks usually did not: they accepted deposits from individuals, although Florence's monte did so without paying interest to creditors until the late 1530s. Banks like that of the Medici of the fifteenth century made their money not on deposits or private loans but in foreign exchange and other international commercial services. Monti di pietà did not become involved in such services. Some local banks did accept deposits, though rarely fixed deposits (*a discrezione*), in order to raise operating capital; the local firm of the Cerchi held two such accounts. This kind of service was not, however, ordinarily available to the general public.[50]

In fact, the early Florentine monte di pietà was not structured like a bank, nor did it behave like one most of the time. Many of the traits that characterized fifteenth-century banking either did not appear at all in the monti or appeared only much later. The monte's charitable purposes and its belief that profits must be returned to the poor set limits on its nascent banklike nature. Because it was not out to earn a profit, it did not seek financial diversification, a trait that characterized Italian banks of the period.[51] Serving the poor

century, bishops tried to appropriate a portion of bequests to confraternities, hospitals, and other charities under the pretext that a bishop, as "father of the poor" (*pater pauperum*), had a right to one-quarter of such legacies. This phenomenon may account for the development, traced by Marvin Becker, of a growing preference in Trecento and Quattrocento Florence for lay rather than ecclesiastical control over charities. See Becker, "Aspects of Lay Piety."

49. Garrani, *Carattere bancario*, 11, 21.

50. Recent scholarship has revised some of the assertions in R. de Roover, *Medici Bank.* See especially Goldthwaite, "Medici Bank." For local banking services, see Goldthwaite, "Local Banking," 27–28.

51. See R. de Roover, *Medici Bank*, 108: "During the Middle Ages, the Renaissance, and the Age of Mercantilism, merchants and merchant bankers did not specialize in

took precedence over all of the monte's other activities. It is correct that monti di pietà offered cheap credit, but that credit was designed as a form of charity and as a result brought theoretical and theological problems subtly different from those that banks faced. Moreover, the Florentine monte di pietà's original structures, that is, its organization, bylaws, mode of operation and goals, served it poorly as a bank, and it did not attract many depositors as long as it offered no interest on deposits. Only when Duke Alessandro de' Medici changed its rules to allow it to pay interest to depositors did the monte undertake this recognizable function of a modern deposit bank. As for its structures, they remained almost unchanged until the broad administrative reforms of the early 1570s. The institution's banking functions slowly evolved despite its structures, which had been designed after all to cope with the demands of the charitable pawnshop business. The roots of some of the monte's future banking functions may be found instead in the principle of taking interest on loans made to the poor.[52]

To suggest that monti di pietà were more interested in distributing credit rather than charity[53] ignores the fact that extending credit at a very low interest rate to those who otherwise would have no source of credit is a form of charity. The men who founded the Italian monti di pietà, both laymen and religious, concurred in and emphasized the benevolent and charitable nature of the institution, designed "to be able to lend to poor persons against pawns with as low an interest rate as possible consistent with the maintenance of the place, salaries, . . . and other expenses."[54] Monti were to serve a poor clientele, and extending credit to such persons was an act of charity whose roots surely reached back to the powerful Italian communal idea of civic charitable responsibility.

The eight formatori designed the organization of the monte to provide efficient service to those who wanted to pawn items at low

---

one line of business but in general diversified their activities and neglected no profit opportunities."

52. On 25 February 1497 the bookkeepers reckoned the interest accumulated from 1 August 1496 through 31 January 1497 "from many persons who have redeemed their pawns" as L. 162.5. MP 721, 136.

53. See Garrani, *Carattere bancario*, 29: "The activity of the monti di pietà thus consisted in extending credit and not in offering charity."

54. Acquisti e Doni 281, 2, Memorie sull'erezione del Monte di Pietà.

interest. By the end of the reign of Duke Cosimo I (1574), the institution regularly made large loans at interest, paid interest on deposits, and handled ducal finance. Only then did it undergo a thorough reorganization. It needed extensive reforms because its changed functions had evolved despite its structures, and its staff as constituted could not easily handle these evolving responsibilities.

While lamenting the shortage of individuals willing to help the monte "in the recent times of need," the eight officials could, after its first three years, claim modest success. The institution remained active and operating, apparently unaffected by the fall and execution of Fra Girolamo Savonarola, under whose sweeping reform program it had been created. When the ledger was balanced on 30 April 1499, its creditors held fl. 7,887 d'oro in oro and L. 9,906.11.1 in moneta nera.[55] In April 1499 the camarlingo and massaro agreed that the monte had lent out a total of fl. 14,818 and L. 41,388.15, all duly entered in the outgo section of the book of pawns (*libro de'pegni*). Against this sum they they placed credits of fl. 8,439, L. 25,550.14 realized from the redemption of pawns, leaving a debit of fl. 6,379, L. 15,838.1, which represented the difference between what the monte had lent out and what it had recouped on those loans.[56] The massaro, Lorenzo di Francesco Guidotti, was responsible for this sum and was posted as a debtor in that amount when the ledger was balanced. The debt charged to Lorenzo proved that the monte's path to fiscal independence and to operating in the black would be paved with difficulties. All its debtors taken together, including Guidotti, owed fl. 7,002, L. 16,044.18.8.[57] Receipts from creditors along with other profits (including nearly fl. 1,350 received as interest paid on loans it had made) came to fl. 7,887, L. 9,906.11.1.[58] At the prevailing rate of six lire per florin, moneys paid out came to L. 58,056.18.8, while those taken in reached L. 57,228.11.1, a deficit of L. 828.7.7, or about fl. 138.

This deficit could be seen as either reassuring or alarming, de-

55. MP 721, 36b. At six lire per florin, these L. 9,906 would come to fl. 1,651; thus the total translates to fl. 9,538.11.1. For this exchange rate, see, e.g., MP 721, 2a–b, where employees' salaries were changed from florins to lire: 6⅔ fl. came to L. 39.17.9, etc.

56. MP 721, 34a–b.

57. MP 721, 36a.

58. On the fl. 1,350, see MP 4, 146v.

pending on whether one was an optimist or a pessimist. On the one hand, given the fiscal crisis and the difficulties inherent in setting up such an enterprise as the monte di pietà, the surprising thing was not that the institution had run a deficit, but that the deficit was not much larger than fl. 138. With the advent of better times, the monte could hope to pull itself into the black and even make a modest profit, which eventually would create a new set of moral problems.

On the other hand, the monte's eight officials had to take drastic measures to keep the deficit so low and had to rely on extraordinary subsidies from unusual sources. They borrowed "60 florins grossi and 10 soldi, 3 denari [L. 361.11.6] . . . to have to lend to the poor in the recent times of need, that is, during the dearth of bread . . . and the war." The monte's directors emphasized that this measure was extraordinary and that they did not intend the institution in their charge "to deviate from such a praiseworthy work" as aiding the poor. But they despaired of "finding anyone these days who, freely and without [receiving] interest, was willing to serve or help the monte, as used to be the case."[59]

Further, much of its income had come from alms offered in the course of an aggressive and well-planned campaign to build the start-up capital for the new institution; the directors could not expect such an outpouring of generosity to remain constant in the future. The monte's proponents had vigorously announced that all the charitable institution required was start-up money, a "monte," and that the laws of mathematics would guarantee that money's increase as the poor paid their 5 percent. The largest and most important loans offered the monte came from the proceeds realized from the sale of goods confiscated from Pisan rebels, and although Florentine history was, and would continue to be for the foreseeable future, replete with the connivings of rebels and exiles, the monte could not count on regular support from such a source. The amount that came from the rebels' goods was great: fl. 5,496, L. 1,941.13.4, or about 61 percent of all income in the ledger as of the triennial balancing in April 1499.

Given the difficulties of the 1490s, it is remarkable that the monte survived at all. It owed its continued existence partly to those "inspired persons" who gave it alms or lent it money gratis. But its

59. MP 721, 13a–b.

directors should, above all, have been grateful to the Florentine republic, which had ordered the rebel officials to deposit their proceeds in the monte, and whose several courts ordered, in an unsystematic but helpful way, a set of deposits (stemming from legal cases) to be placed in its coffers.

Equally disquieting was the institution's failure to exploit the charitable instincts of Florence's wealthier classes. But until it had something concrete to offer, the monte could not convince large numbers of the wealthy to part with substantial sums of money. It could only hope that, having demonstrated its reliability and its willingness to repay creditors fully and promptly, it could change the minds of some who might have hesitated to place deposits there.

4 GROWTH AND CRISIS, 1500–1530

THE PERIOD 1500–1530 proved that the monte di pietà could not exist in happy isolation from the vicissitudes of Florentine politics. This thirty-year span saw the Medici return in 1512 only to be exiled again in 1527, the subsequent establishment of a radical republic, and the terrible siege of the city which, in 1530, culminated in the Medici family's triumphant reentry as lords. These events profoundly affected the functions and governance of the monte di pietà. The early sixteenth century also saw the expansion of the charitable activities of the Florentine monte di pietà as well as its growing integration into civic and political affairs.

In December 1502, recognizing the usefulness of the monte di pietà in meeting the growing needs of the poor, the Great Council approved legislation allowing the eight officials to open new branches at their discretion. The monte quickly rented a second house, belonging to Neri Acciaiuoli, located in Borgo Santi Apostoli in the quarter of Santa Maria Novella. A year later, another branch opened in a house leased from the Portinari, permitting the monte to serve the public from three convenient locations: one in Piazza San Felice in Santo Spirito, one near the Lungarno, and one in the Canto de' Pazzi.[1]

1. Pampaloni, "Cenni storici," 537. The locations of the branches are mentioned periodically in the monte's records; see, e.g., MP 22, Deliberazioni (1525–28), which lists the employees of "the first monte in Santo Spirito," "the second monte on the

In May 1503 the eight new officials calculated that altogether the monte held fl. 19,757, L. 121,753.13.10 from a total of thirty-eight accounts. Among the monte di pietà's creditors was Marco Strozzi, whose fl. 94, L. 12.11 had remained on deposit for nearly eight years. The rector also shared two accounts, totaling fl. 30, L. 21.2, with unidentified "others." The sizable credit of fl. 148, L. 1,105.1.4 of the merchants' guild still rested in the monte, as did Monna Margherita da Poppi's modest L. 40. Sixty florins, left over from the original deposit of fl. 70 on 30 May 1502, had come from "our most exalted Signori."[2] This deposit was augmented in 1506 to fl. 99 and remained on deposit through the lifetime of Cosimo I. In 1548, recording the origins of this and several old deposits, the monte's bookkeeper noted that the fl. 99 represented "the profits of the decima levied on the priests and the Studio of Pisa."[3] The fl. 99 were more symbolic than substantive: they demonstrated the government's approval without committing large sums from its own resources.[4]

The first surviving evidence for the sale of unredeemed pawns dates from 1504, when one Monna Piera, widow of Niccolò di Sandro de' Baroncelli, purchased a number of items.[5] Because the libri de'pegni of the Florentine monte no longer exist, the list of

Lungarno," and "the third monte in the Canto de' Pazzi." For the law of 1502, see Misc. Rep. 7, 218, Notizie del monte di pietà. The first branch, originally situated in Via de' Neri in Piazza San Remigio in the quarter of Santa Croce, moved to a more central location south of the Arno in Piazza San Felice. The third branch remained in its original place not far from the Duomo until midcentury when it transferred its operations to a house owned by Gianbattista di Jacopo Pandolfini. The building was situated in the present-day Via Santa Margherita near the Chapel of Santa Margherita de' Cerchi, the church of Dante's Beatrice and the Portinari family. MP 762, Libro Grande, 8a–b; Touring Club Italiano, *Firenze e dintorni*, 6th ed. (Milan, 1974), 170.

2. See MP 725, Entrata e uscita segreta, 2r; and MP 726, Libro di debitori e creditori, 1a–b, 56b.

3. MP 756, 3b. The decima, enacted by the republic in 1494, was levied on the possessions (*beni stabili*) of citizens, contadini, and other inhabitants. Its existence continued during the duchy. For a discussion of the decima in Florence, see Giovan Francesco Pagnini del Ventura, *Della decima*, 2 vols. (Bologna, 1967; orig. pub. Lucca, 1765), esp. 1:37–108.

4. Arnaldo D'Addario reaches a similar conclusion about the origins and early years of the monte: the provvisione that created it demonstrated that "the authority of the state was placed at the service of the most miserable." From "Note di storia della religiosità," 126.

5. According to MP 4, 189r, public auctions of unsold pawns began only in 1506. This early sale may have been undertaken by private agreement between the widow

items that the monte sold to Monna Piera gives a rare glimpse into the kinds of items pawned:

one black frock in the name of Gianfrancesco, son of the said Niccolò, pawned on 3 October 1503 for fl. 1, L. 5

one gown in the same name pawned on 17 February 1504 for L. 4.10

one black cloak in the same name pawned on 6 March 1504 for fl. 1, L. 7

one tablecloth in the same name pawned on 10 February 1503 for L. 2

one small knife in the same name pawned on 1 March 1503 for L. 5.10

one lined gown in the same name pawned on 10 February 1503 for L. 10

one dress in the same name pawned on 23 March 1503 for L. 7

two tin saucers in the name of Giovanni Simone di Serrino pawned on 24 February 1504 for L. 3

one basin in the name of Cosimo di Marco di Nofri pawned on 7 February 1504 for L. 2

one box in the name of Matteo di Giovanni d'Antonio pawned on 7 October 1504 for L. 1

one gray Flemish cloth in the name of the said Giovanfrancesco di Niccolò pawned on 4 January 1504 for L. 8

1-1/6 *braccia* of red velvet in the same name pawned on 29 February 1504 for fl. 1, L. 1.10

one new twill gown and a pair of small knives [*coltellini*] in the same name pawned on 29 December 1503 for L. 5

one small white jacket in the same name pawned on 9 March 1504 for fl. 1, L. 7.[6]

Some of the libri de'pegni from Siena's monte di pietà still exist, and they confirm that its clients pawned similar items.[7] Some bor-

---

and the monte since several of the pawns had belonged to her son. See also MP 19, Deliberazioni (1506–12), 4v, for discussions of the details of the sale of pawns.

6. MP 18, 16r.

7. For this and the following discussion of books pawned in Siena, see Duccio Balestracci, "I libri impegnati al monte di pietà senese: Una fonte indiretta per la storia dell'alfabetismo nel xv secolo," *Alfabetismo e cultura scritta. Seminario permanente. Notizie,* Nov. 1982: 14–16.

rowers, possibly those in the direst straits, even sacrificed tools and other items necessary for practicing a trade. A few (forty-four among the thousands who pawned at the Sienese charitable pawnshop from 1483 through 1511) left books as collateral for their loans. Among these forty-four were a tailor, a book publisher, a stationer, members of the Sienese patriciate, priests, doctors, and lawyers. Eleven of the group were women, including a nun and the daughter of a dyer. Some of the books were ornate and valuable, constructed of vellum and leather and decorated with precious metals. Others were inexpensive editions. The books themselves included devotional literature, especially saints' lives and marianist works (often referred to as a "little book of Our Lady"—"libriciulo di Nostra Donna"). Some of these titles were among those known to be exchanged among an informal book-lending circle of women. A canon lawyer brought a commentary by Antonio di Butrio on a book of decretals. Priests even left their breviaries as pawns. Other works pawned included a book by Cino da Pistoia, a pair of books called "Digesto nuovo e vechio" and the *Infortiatum*. A tailor who inexplicably owned a medical text took a loan of one and a half lire on it. A printer left five unfinished and unbound books. The records of the monte di pietà of Siena offer some insight into book ownership and literacy. They also reveal that those who took advantage of the monte's services were not always from groups we would consider the poor, but rather they represented a wide spectrum of social classes. For some, monti di pietà surely proved preferable alternatives to secondhand shops, for the monti would take any item of value—regardless whether an actual buyer could be found for the item—store it safely, and offer the owner a low-interest loan. And it is highly unlikely that all owners actually intended to redeem their pledges.

The Florentine monte di pietà's ledger for 1503 listed only thirty accounts belonging to individuals, and these represented relatively little of the monte's resources. In fact, the weightiest deposits did not come from individuals at all. One of the most important accounts was still that of the officials in charge of the goods confiscated from the Pisan rebels; it contained fl. 13,253, L. 2.19.2 in 1503. The huge sum of fl. 1,039, L. 105,094.15.11 fell under the generic category "alms and copper money" and comprised all outright gifts including anonymous charity.[8] A third large account, named "interest and

8. MP 725, 1r.

profits," totaled L. 12,723.18. This category included the payments of principal plus interest made on loans by borrowers. In 1506 the outgoing officials of the monte reported a respectable increase in its capital: it held fl. 20,328, L. 162,888.9.4.[9] Such modest but steady increases characterized the monte's record books during the first thirty years of its operations. These modest increases, however, were not always sufficient for the institution's needs.

It is important to realize that the monte di pietà listed as its debtors those to whom it had paid out money and not only those who owed it money. Therefore, the total amount attributed to debtors was more than what the monte could actually hope to collect. For example, in 1512 the ledger showed Giovanbattista Giovanni as a debtor for fl. 113, L. 6.1.8 "to balance [the account of] the house" that the monte rented from him. But this sum was money the monte had paid Giovanbattista in rent, not an amount it expected to collect from him. He was a debtor only in the sense that the sum attached to his name had to be counted as money the monte had paid out. The monte also listed the monte di pietà of Castel San Giovanni as a debtor for L. 329.3, a sum it had granted its poor relative in credits. In theory the institution in Castel San Giovanni owed this money to the Florentine monte, but in fact the Florentine monte seemed to consider it a permanent gift.[10]

Its debtors were, then, individuals or groups who had actually received money or credit from the monte di pietà. They also included the monte's own employees when these men's books showed more debtors than creditors. For example, the records of the three massari, Giovanni Scolari, Domenico Lapaccini, and Dionigi Nasi, and three camarlinghi, Cosimo Strozzi, Neri Compagni, and Giovanni Mazzei, all showed more debtors than creditors in 1512, so the six were listed as debtors of the monte di pietà. In other words, at the moment the books were balanced, these employees had lent out more money than they had taken in at the branches where they worked. The debtors and the creditors columns also allowed the monte's bookkeepers to rectify errors: thus, fl. 4, L. 29.14.1 previously credited in error appeared as a debit.[11]

Similarly, creditors were not only those who had deposited money in the monte and could demand this money back, but also those who

9. MP 726, Libro di debitori e creditori, 3b, 69b.
10. MP 732, Libro di debitori e creditori, 2b.
11. MP 732, 2b; 48a.

had given money outright and did not expect its return. The institution's permanent endowment was really only what it held under "alms," outright gifts from the pious, often made anonymously through collection boxes in churches, which in 1512 amounted to fl. 1,540, L. 152,581.8.6. Although the monte di pietà did not have to pay back these creditors, alms were entered in the credit side of the ledger since they represented sums actually received. Contrast this kind of credit with that of Messer Cosimo Pazzi, archbishop of Florence, who freely placed fl. 833, L. 4.6.4 in the monte and who not only expected his money back on his demand, but who did in fact remove it in March 1515.[12] In the monte di pietà's ledgers, debtors were those who had received money whether or not that money could be called in as a debt by the monte, and creditors were those who had paid money to the monte, regardless of whether the monte had an obligation to repay it.

On the one hand, the monte di pietà had failed to capture the attention (and the money) of wealthy Florentines, depending more and more heavily on small anonymous acts of charity, its position as repository for the goods of the Pisan rebels, and the interest it collected from loans. This repository role grew, for beginning on 11 January 1504 the monte became the custodian of profits from goods confiscated from another source. The officials and auditors (ufficiali e sindaci) of the estate seized from the exiled heirs of Lorenzo de' Medici were credited with fl. 26, L. 2.19.6. Three more deposits soon brought the total to fl. 214, L. 12.17.6. This sum remained on deposit at the time of the triennial balancing of the ledgers on 20 May 1506 and made the Medici, albeit unwillingly, supporters of the Florentine monte di pietà.[13] Not until 23 March 1509 did the monte di pietà receive an order from the Signori to pay this sum to Monna Lucrezia, wife of Jacopo di Giovanni Salviati, and to Antonio di Lorenzo de' Ricci, procurator of Alfonsina Orsini, the widow of Piero di Lorenzo de' Medici, for her dowry.[14]

---

12. MP 732, 1a, 20a–b.

13. MP 726, 4b, 69b. The reasons for the delay in the city's attaching this property are unclear. Perhaps the cumulative effects of the 1501 threat of a takeover by the Medici aided by Cesare Borgia and the death of Piero de' Medici in 1503 sparked the regime to act. See Sergio Bertelli, "La crisi del 1501: Firenze e Cesare Borgia," in S. Bertelli and G. Ramakus, eds., *Essays Presented to Myron C. Gilmore* (Florence, 1978), vol. 1, especially 4–13; and Hale, *Florence and the Medici*, 87–94.

14. MP 728, Libro di debitori e creditori, 16a. Lucrezia was Lorenzo's daughter

The monte's biggest worry was its own liquidity, taxed by a heavy demand on its resources even though the maximum amount allowed per pledge was fixed at two florins.[15] In May 1505 the eight officials authorized several of their fellows to seek four loans of one thousand florins each "in order to be able to satisfy all poor persons."[16] The need for these loans attests to the heavy demand borrowers placed on the institution and its inability to meet this demand with capital on hand.

On the other hand, on several occasions beginning in the sixteenth century, the monte discovered that after covering all its own expenses and balancing its books it had more capital on hand than it needed to carry out its charitable functions. It had accrued this surplus despite having to bear the added expenses of setting up its two new branch offices.[17] Its bylaws were clear about this eventuality: under no circumstances was the monte di pietà to retain any profits. Instead, any money remaining after payment of expenses was to be given away, preferably to those who had originally paid this interest on what they had borrowed. A seventeenth-century examination of the institution's old records noted that, even in the monte's early years, "it was the custom to return all the profits to the owners of the pawned items." The monte officials would notify several of the city's preachers, who in turn would announce from their pulpits the

---

and the future mother of Maria Salviati, who married Giovanni delle Bande Nere. The result of that marriage would be the future duke and grand duke, Cosimo I.

15. MP 18, 4r–v, 22 May 1503: "non possit mutuari . . . super aliquo pignore ultra florinos duos," and reiterated on 21 Feb. 1504, 19v, and in MP 19, Deliberazoni, 1v, 21 May 1509.

16. MP 18, 21v, 8 May 1505: "ut omnibus pauperibus personis satisferi possit. . . . Deliberaverunt et deliberando elegerunt et deputaverunt Nicolaim olim Bernardi del Nero et Alexandrum olim Leonardi de Mannellis ambos eorum collegas in dicto officio ad acquirendum mutuo et seu ut vulgo dicitur a cambio nomine eorum officii predicti fl. mille . . . per auxilio dicti montis et pro subventione dictorum pauperum." Also delegated over the next few days were Jacopo Salviati ("ad acquirendum mutuo pro dicto monte et ad cambium . . . fl. 1,000"), and Giovanni Bardi and Piero Guicciardini (fl. 1,000).

17. MP 725, 70v–71r. In May 1502 the directors authorized payments of fl. 72, L. 283.14.6 "for repairs made in the house [rented from the Portinari] in order to be able to offer loans there," fl. 4, L. 27.28.8 for general household expenses, L. 16.3.8 for "household goods" at the same location, fl. 83, L. 87.1.2 for furnishings at the house rented from the Acciaiuoli, and fl. 32, L. 114.15.8 for books, charcoal, and other sundries.

monte's surplus so that all who had paid interest on loans could go to their branch offices to receive at least partial reimbursement. Admirable as this practice might have been, it effectively limited the accrual of a permanent cash reserve by forcing the monte to give away excess funds and to borrow in times of great need, as it had to do in May 1505 and would consider doing again in the future.

The ledgers for 1500–1503 reveal that the institution occasionally gave alms, including customary gratuities offered on saints' days and other holidays. When it rented a house in which to sell unredeemed pawns from the guild of used-clothing merchants, for example, the monte not only paid rent of twenty-five florins per year, but also offered Christmas gratuities of two florins to be divided among the guild's retainers. A more substantial act of charity was the credit of L. 329.3 given to the monte di pietà of Castel San Giovanni di Valdarno. The entry in the ledger pitiably noted that "they are poor and have great need."[18]

The monte's officials, however, saw the need for a better defined policy on distributing profits. In 1503, when they consulted the city's leading Franciscans and Dominicans, the officials were advised that while restitution to the individuals who had paid interest was preferable to generic restitution, it was not always possible. Distribution of alms to others among the city's poor, the clerics suggested, was a reasonable alternative.[19] So in August 1505 the eight appointed a new commission consisting of the priors of the monasteries of San Marco, the Badia, and San Francesco to resolve the problem. The commission concluded that all profits be given to the Company of the Good Men of San Martino.[20]

The commission made an interesting choice in designating the Company of San Martino as the recipient of the monte's charity. The company had been created in 1442, apparently at the urging of Fra Antonino, the future archbishop of Florence, to serve the needs

18. MP 725, 67v, 68v, and 45v.

19. MP 18, 5v–6v, 6 July 1503.

20. Pampaloni, "Cenni storici," 537; MP 4, 185r. MP 18, 18r, states that the monte's directors called in advisers to settle the question "of the distribution of interest left in the hands of the camarlingo . . . of the said monte." On 1 July 1504 they approved the recommendation to give the money to the Company of San Martino (18v): "sufficiat distributio dicti frumenti . . . pauperibus personis," who turned out to be the "shamed poor" of San Martino (5v).

of the "shamed poor" (*poveri vergognosi*),[21] including persons who had been accustomed to earning their own living but who had been beset by misfortune. Too ashamed to beg, they were reduced to poverty. By the mid-to-late fifteenth century, financial reverses, exile, and other misfortunes had greatly enlarged their numbers.[22]

Contemporary Florentine observers drew a clear connection between the miserable descent into poverty of the "shamed poor" and the resulting humiliation of the individual, his or her family, and the commune. This group deserved to be pitied and, along with poor widows, foundlings, and the ill, comprised the "worthy poor." From the point of view of the Florentines, the dishonor and shame that fell on the poveri vergognosi cast a shadow not only over themselves, but also over the entire city. The humanist notion of the dignity of man (*dignitas hominis*) reinforced this view, as it implied a sense of responsibility for the unfortunate of all social strata, the impoverished among the middle classes included.[23]

The vast majority of those who received charity, either in the form of money or symbolic white bread, from the Company of the Good Men of San Martino during the fifteenth century were not impoverished patricians. Instead, most were craftsmen from the minor guilds or else simply unskilled or semiskilled workers. The shame of these persons lay not in their fall from patrician status into poverty but in their inability, through illness or misfortune, to care for them-

21. The *poveri vergognosi*, too proud to admit their need, were first contrasted with the *poveri pubblici*, who openly sought alms, by Sant'Antonino himself. For a brief discussion of the company, see Passerini, *Storia degli stabilmenti*, 501–15, and documents T and V, 929–33. For an even briefer one, see Gennaro Maria Monti, *Le confraternite medievali dell'alta e media Italia* (Venice, 1927), 1:185. The recent article by Spicciani, "'Poveri Vergognosi,'" closely examines this charity's first thirty years of operation. Giovanni Ricci, in "Povertà, vergogna, e 'povertà vergognosa,'" *Società e storia* 5 (1979): 305–37, points out the existence of a company of the shamed poor as early as 1248 in Modena. The role of Sant'Antonino in the Florentine company's foundation is still debated. Trexler, in "Charity," found no connection between the saint and the Company of the Good Men of San Martino. Vespasiano da Bisticci's life of Antonino, however, insists that the archbishop began the distribution of bread to the "shamed poor" and founded the company of the shamed poor. On this point, Spicciani's informative article is confusing: note 11 (162) states that the author found no sign of Antonino's "personal" involvement in the charity's foundation, but later he cites two contemporary sources that credit Antonino with precisely that role.

22. See Staley, *Guilds of Florence*, 551–52; Trexler, "Charity"; and Passerini, *Storia degli stabilmenti*, 506 and 932.

23. See Trexler, "Charity"; and Becker, "Aspects of Lay Piety," 196–200.

selves or their families despite having a trade and a willingness to work. Not until the sixteenth century do we find some patrician families on the rolls of the company. Even then, however, at least fragmentary evidence suggests that most of those who received help from this charitable institution were truly poor. In 1545 the duke's Magistrato Supremo heard a petition on behalf of one Meo, an assistant at a local barber shop who had been thrown into prison over a debt of twenty-six lire to his own employer. Meo had fallen sick and, unable to care for his family, had "frequently been supported by the Good Men of San Martino." The petition noted the "dishonor" Meo and his family suffered. In a similar case, a letter to the duke on behalf of the Magistrato Supremo in 1548 described a woman in dire straits: "The poor petitioner . . . finds herself today in great poverty and misery . . . and nursing a son." She had to beg her bread from her neighbors and, having sold off her belongings, "has in her house neither bed nor furniture." She also, the letter concluded, "receives alms from the Good Men of San Martino."[24]

Although its charity was cloaked in secrecy to preserve the honor of those it served, the company seems to have given out about fourteen thousand gold florins per year in the mid-fifteenth century, ample evidence of its financial security. But it soon became corrupt, and its officers apparently altered and destroyed some of its ledgers.[25] It may have suspended its operations during 1455–66 when a tithe was collected by Antonino to finance a crusade against the Turks.[26]

Because it had retained strong connections with the Dominicans

24. On the shamed poor and the Good Men, see Spicciani, "'Poveri Vergognosi,'" 120–21, 129. Staley's notion of the shamed poor as the "wealthy" poor (*Guilds of Florence*, 551) is badly dated, for the company's records show that until the sixteenth century, the recipients of its aid were artisans and clothworkers. Ricci agrees that they were of neither high nor extremely low status ("Povertà," 308). On the case of Meo, Magistrato Supremo (MS) 1119, Filza seconda di suppliche e lettere dall'anno 1546 al 1560, Jacopo Polverini to Cosimo de' Medici, 31 Dec. 1545. On the second case, MS 1121, Suppliche, Jacopo Polverini to Cosimo de' Medici, 13 Feb. 1548 (O.S.). Note that Meo "spesso è stato subvento da' buonhuomini di Santo Martino" as well as the present-tense verb Polverini used in the second case ("ella ha la helemosina da'buoni huomini di San Martino"). They make clear that the Good Men offered ongoing charity rather than one-time relief.

25. Passerini, *Storia degli stabilmenti*, 505–8.

26. Spicciani, "'Poveri vergognosi,'" 128, 165, n. 36.

and Savonarola, the company fell under the suspicious scrutiny of the new Florentine government after the execution of the Frate in 1498. The Signoria, reiterating the importance and utility of the help offered the "shamed poor" by the company, delegated eight citizens to direct it.[27] Despite these measures, in 1502 a provvisione noted that "the company has fallen into serious decline" and no longer drew the support it formerly enjoyed. This state of affairs was especially lamentable since "the number of poor has increased greatly, given these difficult and adverse times."[28] By the time of the canonization of Antonino in 1516, the company had begun to assist impoverished patricians, especially by providing young girls with dowries. As many as six hundred such families received charity from the company.[29] The decision to hand over profits from the monte di pietà was, then, a timely one: it helped strengthen the company morally and fiscally during a period of reorganization and reform when, moreover, it seems to have included aid to impoverished patricians among its tasks, and permitted the monte di pietà to divest itself of gains its own statutes prohibited it from keeping.

Yet the relationship between the two charities was paradoxical. The provvisione that had created the monte di pietà had envisioned its clientele as primarily the "needy poor" of the city and countryside. With its tie to the Company of the Good Men of San Martino, the monte extended its charity to a new social group, the "shamed poor," including, by the sixteenth century, at least a few impoverished patricians. Ironically, the money to subsidize the shamed poor came from the unredeemed pawns and interest payments on the loans of the monte's own needy clientele.

The credits granted by the monte di pietà to the Company of the Good Men of San Martino reflected the monte's own fiscal health. After twenty-five years of operation (1496–1521), it had provided the company nearly fourteen thousand florins in credits. But the 1520s brought a turnaround, as the list below of monte di pietà credits granted to the Company of San Martino shows.[30]

---

27. Provvisione of 18 May 1498, published by Passerini, *Storia degli stabilmenti*, 929–31, Document T.
28. Provvisione of 11 Feb. 1502 (N.S.), ibid., 932–33, Document V.
29. Spicciani, "'Poveri Vergognosi,'" 129.
30. MP 4, 187r–188r.

Years	Amount (rounded to nearest florin)
1496–1521	13,994
1521–1524	2,121
1524–1527	879
1527–1530	290
1530–1533	0

The monte di pietà's practice of supporting the Company of the Good Men of San Martino was, then, already well established when it received papal approbation during the reign of the first Medici pope, Leo X (Giovanni di Lorenzo de' Medici). In 1519 the pontiff sent the officials of the monte a letter demonstrating his familiarity with both of these Florentine institutions. Leo praised those works of charity devoted to succoring the shamed poor, "those who, because of their status or for some other reason, cannot work, and who are ashamed to go begging."[31] He noted that the statutes of the monte di pietà of Florence expressly prohibited profit making, instead requiring divestiture of any funds remaining after payment of salaries and expenses. Therefore, the pope observed, the officials of the monte customarily had not distributed such money directly to the poor, but had instead given it to the overseers of the Company of San Martino, "to be distributed only to those needy noble persons of the city, whose shame would have them sooner die of hunger." The pope added that he issued this decree "not at the urging of the aforementioned Officials and Overseers . . . but by our own decision," and declared that, by "apostolic authority, . . . henceforth and in perpetuity" the monte was obliged to credit "the money remaining as profits every year" to the company. The pope made it clear that the overseers of the Company of San Martino were forbidden to use their monte credit for any purpose other than aiding the shamed poor.

During the ducal regime the monte di pietà sometimes found itself able to help the shamed poor of San Martino, sometimes not. In 1539, for instance, profits from the pawnshop business (the *conto de' meriti*) reached 8,788 florins, of which 706 went to the company and

31. For this discussion of Leo's role, see MP 4, copy of letter from Leo X, 1r–2r. Leo concluded his letter with a mild pontifical malediction that threatened violators of his decree with the "indignazione d'Iddio omnipotente, e de'Santi Apostoli San Pietro e San Paolo."

the rest into a credit account in the monte itself.[32] The durability of the relationship between the company and the monte is proven by the existence during the reign of Cosimo II (1609–21) of a huge, interest-paying deposit in the grand duke's name, "the fruits of which are paid to the Good Men of San Martino." By 1669 this account held 107,900 florins. The grand duke's successors saw this procedure as a good way of giving to charities, for they also deposited over one hundred thousand florins in the monte, with the interest to be "distributed as dowries for the anniversary of the Most Serene Grand Duke . . . on February [1670]."[33]

From the beginning, the company's overseers regarded their relationship to the monte as that of account holder to banker. Through their proposto (chairman of the board of directors), Domenico Mazzinghi, they ordered twenty-five withdrawals from February 1504 to May 1506, all duly noted in the books of income and outgo. Theirs was an extraordinarily active account that highlights the willingness of some contemporary Florentines to use the monte di pietà as a bank.[34]

The Company of San Martino had long received special attention and important financial support from the Medici.[35] Leo X was keenly interested in all Florentine institutions and his interest in the monte di pietà went beyond the monte's role as a charitable foundation. Leo knew that some questioned the propriety of a monte collecting interest from Christians, even for a good cause. Tied to this issue were the relationship between Christians and Jews and the problem of licitly restoring any profit made to those who had shouldered the costs.

These questions were raised periodically, especially by the Dominicans, who continued to challenge the legality of any interest taken in by monti di pietà.[36] The battle had been rejoined in the 1490s, its acerbity seen in the sarcastic title of the Augustinian Nicholas Bar-

32. MP 4, 189r.

33. MP 4, unnumbered folios, accounts of Grand Duke Cosimo II, 1669.

34. MP 725, 31 a–b; MP 726 *passim*.

35. Spicciani, "'Poveri Vergognosi,'" 123. "After 1472, ties with the Medici became very close, so much so that . . . the Buonomini appear to have been the almoners of this powerful family." Up to 1455, when the records leave an eleven-year hiatus, Cosimo de' Medici's alms to the company accounted for about half of all the charity it dispensed. Leo's attention to the company continued a family tradition.

36. See Monaco, "Questione dei monte di pietà," 115–17.

ianus's tract of 1494, "De monte impietatis." This pamphlet raised old objections anew, particularly the question of whether even a pope could authorize the collection of interest. It also attacked the stories of miracles and revelations that allegedly prompted the founding of some monti di pietà, which the institution's proponents happily used to persuade people to give money for the cause. The Franciscans hastened to the defense of their pet institution, with Bernardino de' Busti replying in 1497 with a tract citing sixty points in favor of the monte di pietà. Thomas de Vio, the Dominican who, as Cajetan, would later become famous in the debate with Luther, reiterated his order's complaint that the monte di pietà lived by usury. In areas where Dominicans ran the Inquisition, they declared that anyone who excused the practice of usury was a probable heretic, thus putting Franciscan proponents of the monte di pietà on the defensive. Where the Franciscans held the upper hand, they returned the favor by accusing the Dominicans of heresy for having defied papal pronouncements in favor of the charitable pawnshops.[37] And so the battle went on.

Finally, at the Fifth Lateran Council, in his bull *Inter Multiplices*, Leo X formalized for all Christendom what his predecessors Paul II, Sixtus IV, Innocent VIII, Alexander VI, and Julius II had done for individual monti di pietà in particular circumstances: he gave papal approval to the practice of charging interest on loans against pawns. Centuries later this bull would served as the basis for Pius X's canon 1543, the Catholic church's clear modern statement on usury, another sign that the debate over the monte di pietà had far-reaching economic significance.[38]

His charitable concerns aside, Leo never forgot that he was a Florentine and now, as pope, the patriarch of the Medici family. Having spearheaded the attempts to restore his exiled family to dominance in Florence, he hoped to use his influence to make the Medici more secure,[39] and his high church position presented him with almost

37. See Nelson, *Idea of Usury*, 20, on the claim that "not everything the Pope tolerates is *ipso facto* licit." On the content of Barianus's work and the replies to it, see Parsons, "Economic Significance," 11–12, and Monaco, "Questione dei monti di pietà," 117–18.

38. On Leo's role, see Monaco, "Questione dei monte di pietà," 121–27. On Pius X's use of *Inter Multiplices*, see Parsons, "Economic Significance," 16.

39. See Stephens, *Fall*, 74–75. Giorgio Spini emphasizes the central role played by the Medici popes in winning control of Florence for their family: "The Medici regime

innumerable means to do so. Upon his election, this Medici son was reputed to have remarked that the papacy had been given to him and he was now going to enjoy it. Indeed, his nepotism has been amply demonstrated, and the reigns of both Medici popes have been seen as distasteful proof of the High Renaissance papacy's corrupt extravagance.[40] But as an advocate of his family's interests, Leo proved tireless, innovative, and shrewd. He arranged politically useful marriages for his sisters and niece to the Salviati, Ridolfi and Strozzi, thus tying these important Florentine families to the Medici destiny.[41]

Before he became Pope Leo, Cardinal Giovanni achieved one of his dearest goals: he arranged for his young nephew Lorenzo de' Medici to be made *signore* of the city. Giovanni sent Lorenzo a letter of advice "to remind you of all that which, in my opinion, is useful and necessary to govern . . . and to give you a means to be able to think better and more carefully of the well-being and the preservation of our homeland."[42] He quickly pointed to three magistracies—

---

in Florence was nothing more than the product of the tenacious and often intelligent will of popes and princes of the house to build a state." For this reason, Spini insists that ducal politics in Florence are best understood as dynastic ("la politica della casa"). Spini, "Questioni e problemi di metodo per la storia del principato mediceo e degli stati toscani del Cinquecento," *Rivista storica italiana* 58 (1941): 76–93. Eugenio Dupré Theseider comes to a similar conclusion in "I papi medicei e la loro politica domestica," in *Studi fiorentini* (Florence, 1963), 7:271–324.

40. Ludwig Pastor speaks of the apocryphal nature of this anecdote, but insists that its sense is correct, in *History of the Popes* (London, 1908), 8:76.

41. Cecil Roth, *The Last Florentine Republic* (London, 1925), 5.

42. Giovanni de' Medici (Leo X), "Tre documenti: Instructione al Magnifico Lorenzo," ed. Tommaso Gar, *ASI* App., 1 (1842–44): 299–306. There is disagreement on what Giovanni de' Medici meant when he wrote, "The monte is the heart of the city" (305). Cecil Roth in *Last Florentine Republic* and Guido Pampaloni in "Cenni storici" thought "the monte" referred to the monte di pietà, and Pampaloni even called the monte di pietà "the heart of the city," a phrase taken directly from Giovanni's letter. But L. F. Marks ("Financial Oligarchy," 127) cited the same phrase used in reference to the monte comune as early as 1470. Marks's view is supported by a correct reading of the letter of instruction: "Li Offitiali del Monte, quando prestano danari, bisogna che sieno apti a quello exercitio, cioè ricchi e benestanti. . . . è necessario tenere ministri al Monte secreti e fidati, i quali sieno tui, et sieno apti a simile exercitio, . . . perchè il Monte è il core de la Città." Anecdotal evidence shows the continuing association between Leo X and the monte di pietà. Today, one can purchase in the souvenir shops near the Vatican a poster titled "I sommi pontefici romani." Beneath the tiny portrait of each pope is a brief account of what the poster's anonymous creators felt were that pope's most memorable accomplishments. We

the Signori and standardbearer of justice, the Dieci di Balìa, and the Otto di Guardia e Balìa—as being of the utmost importance. "In all three of these magistracies," he wrote, "you should place men as friendly to yourself as possible." Other offices such as the Captains of the Guelfs were "not important to the state," but could be very useful to Lorenzo as they were honorable posts that, if awarded thoughtfully, could secure him the friendship of men who aspired to importance. Giovanni probably saw the monte di pietà as belonging to this category.

The monte di pietà was a focal point of charity and benevolence that extended credit to those who had no other source, and for Giovanni this function had frankly political as well as pious effects. In words that ring of Machiavelli, the prelate pointed out to his nephew the importance of appearances and of mollifying persons of all classes. "You must not refuse to hear out all citizens whomsoever, woman, peasant or pauper, all of whom will make infinite requests of you and pester you; rather you must take care to make few promises to them but to listen to them liberally." Furthermore, Florence contained "more poor people than you believe," and it was essential to care for them in a compassionate way that did not demean or insult them.[43] They too deserved quick justice and protection from those who, through superior wealth and power, sought to exploit or injure them.

There is no evidence that Lorenzo de' Medici cared very much one way or the other about the monte di pietà or that he took to heart his uncle's political advice. Disdaining Leo's suggestions about whom to appoint to the re-created Council of Seventy and rejecting the pope's anti-French policy by marrying into the French nobility, the young signore sought to establish a more powerful, almost regal position for himself and his posterity. Unlike his namesake, Lorenzo was a warrior rather than a statesman; it is no accident that he is better known for his conquest of Urbino in 1516 than for any sensitive appreciation of the workings of Florentine institutions.

---

learn two basic facts about Leo: he failed to understand or to arrest the spread of Lutheran ideas, and "he contributed to the institution of the pawnbroker's activity seen as a work of charity for the assistance of the less fortunate." This passage refers, of course, to his support of monti di pietà.

43. Giovanni de' Medici, "Tre documenti," 305.

The interest in Florentine institutions expressed in Cardinal Giovanni's letter, however, was more typical of subsequent Medici behavior than were Lorenzo's policies. The Medici "pattern of control" required steady and careful watchfulness over all Florentine institutions. Even the anti-Medicean leaders of the last republic of 1527–30 quickly discovered the usefulness of the monte di pietà as a source of cash in times of emergency; henceforth, whether republicans, oligarchs or signori, Florence's masters saw the monte not simply as a charitable foundation or even as a bank, but as an institution with political and economic potential. Once installed as ruler in Florence in 1530, Alessandro de' Medici turned his attention to the Florentine constitution and to those institutions that kept the city functioning, including the monte di pietà. But the man who most clearly saw the political uses of the monte was Duke Cosimo I, whose adroit manipulation of the monte closely mirrored his skillful handling of other Florentine institutions.

We saw in the previous chapter that, from 1496 to 1499, the monte held 69 accounts ranging from loans offered it by private individuals, by court order, and by Florentine corporations, to gifts of alms. The following list shows the number of creditors between 1496 and 1530.[44]

Year	Number of creditors
1499	69
1502	37
1506	65
1509	62
1512	69
1515	64
1518	64
1521	67
1524	68
1527	68
1530	83

44. MP 721–44, Libri di debitori e creditori, *passim*. The number of creditors reflects the number of accounts on the credit side of the ledger at the beginning and end of each triennium.

Except for the drop in 1502 when the monte's books showed only 37 credit accounts and the surge in 1530, the number remained stable over the first three decades of the sixteenth century.[45] Omitting those two years, the institution averaged about 66 such accounts. Of the 65 credits in 1506, 22 (about 33.8 percent) had been on the books in 1503 (including generic categories like alms as well as individual or corporate accounts). In 1509, however, 35 (or 53.8 percent) remained on the books. Thus began a trend: of the 83 accounts from 1530, 47 (56.6 percent) remained on the books in 1533. In a sense, then, 1506 represented for the monte di pietà the beginning of a stable period that ran until the late 1520s, during which time the monte developed a core of creditors and deposits. A smaller core of these deposits gradually became part of the monte's permanent endowment and was never withdrawn. In the period 1506–30 the monte di pietà was able to replace withdrawn credits with new credits, but was unable to realize much of an increase in the number of creditors until 1530, a year of uncertainty and instability.

The several dozen deposits that made up what we have called the core of the monte's capital included three important accounts listed below. Closely examined, these accounts yield a finer picture of its fiscal health. The first such account contained all outright gifts of alms that pious Florentines made to the institution. Funds placed in the monte from sale of the Pisan rebels' goods constituted a second. The monte's bookkeepers called a third account "creditors of the remainders of the pawns" (creditori di loro resti di pegni), broken down for each of the three branches. These sums showed the "profit" the monte made "from pawns sold . . . bringing in more profit than money lent plus interest charges, which profit had to be returned to those persons who came with the receipts."[46] Never did the monte's officials recognize any irony in the fact that the monte, like the Jewish pawnbrokers it sought to replace, could sell unredeemed pawns at a profit. Such money, however, was supposed to pay overhead costs, with any remainder going back to the poor or to some other worthy recipient of charity, often the Good Men of San

---

45. The 22 percent increase in 1530 may be explained by the turmoils of the last republic and its thorough search for revenue. People may have tried to protect cash by placing it freely in the monte di pietà, which kept cash reserves under lock and key.

46. MP 4, 9r–10r.

Martino. The amounts in the three accounts given for 1499–1530 are in florins, lire, soldi, denari.

Date	Account	Amount
May 1499	Alms	fl. 893, L. 3,758.19.4
	Pisan rebels	fl. 5,496, L. 1,941.13.4
	Creditors of pawns	—
May 1503	Alms	fl. 1,093, L. 105,094.15.11
	Pisan rebels	fl. 13,253, L. 2.19.2
	Creditors of pawns	fl. 77, L. 1,731.9.4
May 1506	Alms	fl. 1,169, L. 152,243.19.9
	Pisan rebels	fl. 15,556, L. 26.4.10
	Creditors of pawns	fl. 83, L. 1,920.2
May 1509	Alms	fl. 1,438, L. 152,425.14.3
	Pisan rebels	fl. 15,571, L. 88.18.10
	Creditors of pawns	fl. 204, L. 4,739.6.4
May 1512	Alms	fl. 1,540, L. 152,581.8.6
	Pisan rebels	fl. 14,394, L. 57.11.5
	Creditors of pawns	
	First branch	fl. 117, L. 2,717.15.5
	Second branch	fl. 107, L. 2,132.12.7
	Third branch	fl. 95, L. 1,622.–.10
	Total	fl. 319, L. 6,472.8.10
May 1515	Alms	fl. 1,540, L. 152,607.8.6
	Pisan rebels	fl. 14,394, L. 57.11.5
	Creditors of pawns	
	First branch	fl. 197, L. 3,108.8.11
	Second branch	fl. 120, L. 3,089.4.2
	Third branch	fl. 160, L. 2,186.10.1
	Total	fl. 477, L. 8,384.3.2
May 1518	Alms	fl. 1,546, L. 152,861.14.8
	Pisan rebels	fl. 14,394, L. 57.11.5
	Creditors of pawns	
	First branch	fl. 254, L. 3,688.7.8
	Second branch	fl. 192, L. 3,405.18.10
	Third branch	fl. 160, L. 2,974.14.1
	Total	fl. 606, L. 10,069.–.7
May 1521	Alms	fl. 1,546, L. 152,874.1.4
	Pisan rebels	fl. 14,394, L. 57.11.5

	Creditors of pawns	
	First branch	fl. 293, L. 4,023.6.7
	Second branch	fl. 241, L. 3,803.14.7
	Third branch	fl. 178, L. 3,504.10
	Total	fl. 712, L. 11,331.11.2
May 1524	Alms	fl. 1,546, L. 152,874.1.4
	Pisan rebels	fl. 14,394, L. 57.11.5
	Creditors of pawns	
	First branch	fl. 331, L. 4,709.18.1
	Second branch	fl. 251, L. 4,329.11.5
	Third branch	fl. 178, L. 4,113.7.5
	Total	fl. 760, L. 13,152.16.11
May 1527	Alms	fl. 1,546, L. 152,874.1.4
	Pisan rebels	fl. 14,394, L. 57.11.5
	Creditors of pawns	
	First branch	fl. 317, L. 4,576.8.11
	Second branch	fl. 309, L. 4,906.10.7
	Third branch	fl. 178, L. 4,976.18.3
	Total	fl. 804, L. 14,459.17.9
May 1530	Alms	fl. 1,546, L.153,430.8.10
	Pisan rebels	fl. 14,793, L. 57.11
	Creditors of pawns	
	First branch	fl. 317, L. 6,695.7.8
	Second branch	fl. 309, L. 6,313.12.11
	Third branch	fl. 167, L. 7,862.11.1
	Total	fl. 793, L. 20,871.11.8

After a period of steady growth, the credits in the alms account reached their height in 1521 and then leveled off. The same thing happened even earlier to the account held by the overseers of the goods confiscated from Pisan rebels. This account reached its height in 1509, declined slightly by 1512, and remained steady thereafter.

The only category to increase in value through this period was the account holding the proceeds from the sale of pawns. A notable jump occurred in 1530, a year of war, famine, and surrender, when the value of the lire portion (the florins remained virtually constant) of these accounts increased by about 46 percent at the first branch, 29 percent at the second, and 58 percent at the third over the amounts from three years earlier. Such an increase did not signify good times for Florence's poor, however. In the terrible siege of

Florence and the dire last days of the last republic, the monte either took in more pawns from those in desperate need or auctioned off more pawns when their owners were unwilling or unable to redeem them. These profits represented the debris of a violent storm rather than the fruits of a rich harvest.

This development meant that the steadiest contributor to the monte's surplus was its own clientele, the group the institution was supposed to be saving from the usury of the Jews. At the same time, the poor's demand on the monte's resources and the crises of the late 1520s tested the institution's ability to contribute to its own favorite charity, the Good Men of San Martino. By 1530 its contribution dwindled to nothing. The monte di pietà had failed to attract a growing circle of depositors; instead, its books carried many of the same accounts triennium after triennium. The deposits of the Pisan rebels and other involuntary contributors had leveled off. Florentines had stopped giving alms to the monte di pietà in significant amounts by the middle of the second decade of the sixteenth century.

The last Florentine republic (1527–30) faced political, economic, and moral crises that spilled over into almost all phases of civic life. These crises had a profound effect on the monte di pietà and in fact threatened to bring about its destruction. The sack of Rome in 1527 and the subsequent humiliation of Clement VII gave impetus to an anti-Medicean uprising in Florence. On 17 May the Medici left the city peacefully and a new republican government was formed. In these troubled times, the old answers of the ancient past no longer seemed as immune to challenge as they once had, and many of the new answers betrayed a dangerous lack of political pragmatism. Such was the case when the Great Council declared Jesus Christ king of the city in February 1528. More practically, the Medicean balìa was terminated, a new Great Council and Council of 120 formed, and the Otto di Pratica reappointed.[47]

Hand in hand with these problems and attempted solutions came a series of strict sumptuary laws designed to reform the city. The beloved horse race, the *palio*, was suppressed, the celebration of the carnival ended. The Great Council approved taxes aimed at punishing Medici supporters, thereby deepening civic dissension. So fierce

---

47. Roth, *Last Florentine Republic*, 76. See also Stephens, *Fall*, chap. 6.

did factional rivalries become that the moderate gonfaloniere Niccolò Capponi found himself isolated and ultimately impotent against
the surge of pro-French, anti-Medicean feeling. Accused of secretly
negotiating with the pope, Capponi was dismissed and sent into exile. His successor, the radical anti-palleschi Francesco Carducci,
fared little better. While Francis I, the king of France and Carducci's
would-be ally, assured the gonfaloniere of his fidelity, at the same
time he secretly negotiated peace with the emperor. In early August
1529 the king blithely abandoned his Florentine allies, leaving the
city with no choice but to prepare for war against papal and imperial
armies.[48]

In Florence the desperate regime took drastic measures to pay
mercenaries and *condottieri* and to feed the population. Heavy taxes
fell on the wealthy, especially those Mediceans (*palleschi*) who remained within the walls, and the *decima scalata* was levied. The militia
was revived and reorganized. In mid-1527 the plague struck. The
Great Council, without papal approval, placed a decima on the Florentine clergy, a provocative move that elicited condemnation from
the pope, Clement VII, the former Giulio di Giuliano de' Medici.[49]

Once it became clear that the enemy planned to lay siege to their
city, Florentines turned to God in the hope that a sincere demonstra-
tion of civic piety might win his favor. The Signori called for a public
oration where a youth would speak "in commemoration of the holy
invocation of the only Son of God, Christ Jesus, as our King." Pious
processions would wind through the streets, moving slowly from
church to church, and the Signori themselves would go about "pray-

---

48. Hale, *Florence and the Medici*, 117–18; Roth, *Last Florentine Republic*, chaps. 3–
4; and D'Addario, *Formazione*, 134–35.

49. Bernardo Segni claimed that military expenses during Capponi's twenty-two
month gonfalonierate reached 350,000 ducats, 500,000 ducats during Carducci's
eight months in office, and 450,000 under the last republican gonfaloniere, Raffaello
Girolami. All expenses during these three terms ran to the astounding total of
1,650,000 scudi, "without taking into account," Segni added, "the private losses, the
ruin of crops, the slaughter of livestock, the devastation of fields, and the effort spent
on the poor." Manoscritti e Codici Litterari—Bardi, *Historia da fiorentina di Bernardo
Segni*," bk. 4, published as Bernardo Segni, *Storie fiorentine di Messer Bernardo Segni,
gentiluomo fiorentiono, dall'anno MDXXVII al MDLV colla vita di Niccolò Capponi*, 3 vols.
(Milan, 1805), 1:228. See also Roth, *Last Florentine Republic*, 74–76; and D'Addario,
Formazione, 134–35. On the decima, "Historia da fiorentina di Segni," bk. 1, or *Storie
fiorentine*, 1:110–15.

ing God that he might deign to preserve his city, work of his most holy hands, in liberty." These festivals and rituals were aimed at reminding the populace of the importance of the virtues of obedience, strength, and loyalty.[50]

The battle of Florence began with shots fired at San Miniato on 29 October 1529. Abandoned by its allies, its commerce shut off, besieged Florence was in desperate need of money for provisions that might be smuggled through the lines. The chronicler Bernardo Segni later wrote that the regime quickly realized the war had to be financed by means other than "infinite taxes," which constituted "an unbearable expense" for the populace. The dire straits in which Florence found itself, Segni complained, led the councils to pass a provvisione

> by which could be put up for sale all the goods of the guilds
> of Florence and Prato, as well as of all pious houses, which
> have been left by ancient legacies for the pious cause of alms,
> and which had been preserved untouched up to that time. Not
> content with that, they passed another law that authorized the
> sale of ecclesiastical goods belonging to religious and friars, . . .
> doing this, they said, in order to save the liberty of our home-
> land. . . . The income from these sales totaled more than
> 250,000 scudi.[51]

These provvisioni signaled the regime's willingness to support its defense of "liberty" by the seizure and sale of pious bequests controlled by the city's religious and of ecclesiastical and guild property. The Signori promised repayment to both guilds and church from the funds realized by the sale of goods to be confiscated from Medicean rebels,[52] but who knew, in the charged atmosphere of war, whether such recompense would ever be forthcoming? And how long would it take before the idea occurred to some enterprising republican to take advantage of the resources of the monte di pietà? The government continued this policy of exploiting whatever assets remained in the city, attaching next the deposits, "wherever they

50. On the preparations of the last republic, see Archivio della Repubblica—Signori e Collegi, Deliberazioni fatte in forza di speciale autorità 42 (1529), 42r.

51. "Historia da fiorentina di Segni," bk. 3; or *Storie fiorentine*, 1:110–15.

52. Roth, *Last Florentine Republic*, 269.

could be found" according to Segni's accusation, "of widows and wards, . . . and many were ruined by this stroke."[53] In an attempt to bring in still more money for the defense of the republic, the Signori announced a compromise that they hoped would encourage communal debtors to pay what they owed. Anyone who possessed worked silver that he or she wished to use to offset debts could bring it to the mint, where an official would appraise its worth at the rate of nine florins per pound of silver.[54] The city also imposed emergency measures on its domain. The pious establishments of Prato, for example, were forced to sell off much of their property, with the proceeds going to the central government and repaid late if at all. So severe was the resulting fiscal damage that, in the late 1530s, Duke Cosimo de' Medici had to order some Pratese hospitals temporarily closed pending reform and reorganization.[55]

As always in time of war, the needs of the poor increased as work became scarce, pious donations dried up, and the price of provisions rose. The same regime that had defiantly called upon Christ to reign as its king began, by 1529, to discuss the possibility of sending away the useless poor.[56] In its desperate search for revenue in the fall of 1529 the regime commanded the officials of the monte di pietà to assign it credits from the monte's resources. At the time the monte listed its gross assets at more than forty-eight thousand florins. By receiving credits the Signori became debtors of the monte, for this money amounted to an interest-free loan to the regime. There is no record that collateral was offered. Altogether the monte credited the regime with fl. 16,408, L. 20.5.6, which went directly to the shops of Florentine goldsmiths where it was exchanged for its value in gold,

53. "Historia da fiorentina di Segni," bk. 3, or *Storie fiorentine*, 1:222–23.

54. Arch. della Rep.–Signori e Collegi, Deliberazioni, Ordinaria autorità 133, 28 May 1530, 27r–v. This measure was apparently ineffectual, for on 8 June the Signori and Collegi ordered all churches and persons, except for foreign soldiers, to turn over all silver to the mint. The only items excluded were medals designed to be worn on caps, antique medallions, and the firing mechanisms of harquebuses. The penalty for noncompliance was fifty gold florins. Ibid., 30 June 1530, 44r. According to Roth, *Last Florentine Republic*, 269–71, the plate of ecclesiastical establishments was forcibly collected, and special coins were struck from the melted-down metals.

55. Enrico Stumpa, "Le istituzioni e la società," in Fasano Guarini, *Prato*, 2:318–19.

56. From the pratica of 7 December 1529, cited by Roth, *Last Florentine Republic*, 267.

which in turn went to the mint to be melted down and struck into coins.[57]

Summer 1530 brought a worsening shortage of victuals. On 6 June the Signori appointed sixteen officers to search all houses and religious establishments for grain, flour, wine, and oil and to inventory what they found. This law was strengthened only a day later when the Signoria ordered all houses, convents, monasteries, hospitals, shops, and churches to supply complete information on all grain in their possession, under penalty of a fifty-florin fine. But the spate of threats and warnings issued over the next several weeks merely proved the ineffectiveness of these laws. On 19 July the Signori, "wanting to arm the rest of the city," took desperate steps to reinforce the militia, calling upon all men, whether citizens or only inhabitants of the city, to meet the following Friday at the Duomo with whatever arms they possessed; failure to appear would result in a two-florin fine.[58]

The diversion of capital from the Florentine monte to causes only tangentially connected to charitable purposes was shared by several other Italian monti.[59] The civic pawnshop of Udine lent money to the commune for various purposes, usually for public works like the purchase of grain in times of shortage. Castellarano was able to hire a physician to care for the poor who were ill by having its monte di pietà subsidize his salary. Other monti supported existing hospitals: the monte di pietà of Badia Polesine gave one-sixth of its profits to a hospital. As early as 1471 Perugia's monte set aside one thousand

57. MP 742, Libro di debitori e creditori, 79a. It must be pointed out, however, that the final two transactions, amounting to fl. 2,465, L. 8.4.16, date from 22 December 1530, four months after the fall of the republic. Since the sum was charged to the old regime's account (under the entry "Magnifici signori nostri"), it is possible the transaction had occurred during the siege and only entered later on, perhaps when the accounts were balanced. On the other hand, it is also possible that the new Medici regime simply pillaged the monte of almost twenty-five hundred florins and tacked the debit on to the account of its predecessor. There is, however, no corroboration of this latter possibility, and in any case all these credits were paid to goldsmiths for bullion to be minted into coins. MP 744, Libro di debitori e creditori, 18a–b; and Archivio della Repubblica—Signori e Collegi, Deliberazioni, Ord. aut. 133, 33v.

58. Arch. della Rep.—Signori e Collegi, Deliberazioni, Ord. aut. 133, 41v, 44r, and 89v. For other measures, including those intended to shore up patriotism, see Arch. della Rep.—Signori e Collegi, Deliberazioni fatte in forza di speciale autorità 42, 42r.

59. For this discussion, see Meneghin, *Monti di pietà*, 44–47.

florins from its available capital to provide needy students with loans for clothes or books. Busseto's monte di pietà helped endow the public library, paid for a librarian, and supported four students. Monti in Castelfranco Veneto and Feltre helped construct or rebuild their cities' duomo. All these causes were at least concerned with public health, safety, spirituality, or education. Further removed from such concerns and closer in spirit to the frankly political forced loans made by Florence's pawnshop during the siege was a loan extended by the monte di pietà of Faenza in 1501 to the city's lord, Astorgio III, to oppose the armies of Duke Valentino. Later, in 1531, the same monte di pietà lent a thousand scudi to the commune of Faenza. The loan of sixteen thousand florins made in 1529–30 in Florence, therefore, was unprecedented in scope but not in type.

In June 1530 the new ledger showed that the Florentine monte still held about thirty-two thousand florins in credits even after paying out large sums to the state.[60] Yet the institution's health was shaky at best. The new account book, notable for its brevity, indicates that there were few substantial transactions, few new deposits, and little movement within extant accounts. While the monte had enjoyed relative fiscal stability prior to 1529, the loss of over sixteen thousand florins and the lingering malaise of war and destruction left it greatly weakened. And with the appointment of Alessandro de' Medici as head (*capo*) and later as duke of Florence, the monte di pietà's fate rested, for the first time, in the hands of the Medici.

Medici involvement in the monte di pietà, however, predated Alessandro's appointment. In 1500 a Medici first sat as one of the eight. This prominent Medici was Lorenzo di Pierfrancesco, a second cousin of Lorenzo the Magnificent and, like his cousin, a great-grandson of Giovanni di Bicci and a member of the Cafaggiolo branch of the family. Remaining quietly in Florence even though his kinsmen had been subjected to the humiliation of exile and confiscation of their property, Lorenzo di Pierfrancesco held office in Florence and patronized artists. Along with Piero Guicciardini, Piero Soderini, and Bernardo Rucellai, he was one of a group of *ottimati*, or leading citizens, who in a *pratica* (where invited citizens addressed important issues before the city's councils) in January 1501 proposed the creation of a council of eighty, thus placing power in the hands

60. MP 744, 1a–2b; MP 4, 188r.

of an elite.[61] Little is known of the state of his health, and so no explanation can be advanced for his death on 20 May 1503, by coincidence the last day of his term on the board of directors of the monte di pietà. Less than a year earlier he had been robust enough to leave the city suddenly for a trip of several months' duration. The first resolution reached by the new eight who met for the first time on 21 May sadly noted that this "worthy man" had "passed from this life yesterday." They decided to attend the funeral services out of respect for Lorenzo's work on the monte's behalf.[62]

As a group, the men who served on the monte de pietà's governing board through 1512, when the Medici returned to the city, cannot be identified as especially anti-Medicean. Serving along with Lorenzo di Pierfrancesco de' Medici, for example, were Alamanno di Averardo Salviati, Piero di Antonio Taddei, and Agnolo di Bernardo de' Bardi, all from pro-Medici families. The last two had kin with connections to the Medici bank, and the Salviati Company had survived the threat of bankruptcy in the mid-fifteenth century only when infused with Medici funds. Though several Salviati had been deeply involved in the conspiracy of 1478, Lorenzo sought, in the words of Filippo Nerli, to "win back for himself the house of Salviati" by marrying his eldest daughter Lucrezia to Jacopo di Giovanni Salviati. Piero di Antonio Taddei acted as a kind of troubleshooter for the Medici bank and had been entrusted with closing out its Venetian operations in 1481.[63]

The sole common trait of those who served on the monte di pietà's board at any time in its history was patrician status. With the possible exception of the directors appointed at the end of the last republic in 1530, the character of men appointed to the eight was notable more for its continuity than its discontinuity. The nonpatricians elected to the eight can almost literally be counted on the fingers on one

61. Bertelli, "Crisi del 1501," 3.

62. On Lorenzo, see Gaetano Pieraccini, *La stirpe de' Medici di Cafaggiolo* (Florence, 1924), 1:353–57. For his presence among the eight and the decision to honor his memory, see MP 18, 2r–v, 21 May 1503.

63. Filippo de' Nerli, *Commentarj de'fatti civili occorsi dentro la città di Firenze dall'anno MCCXV al MDXXXVII* (Augusta [Florence], 1728), 57; and R. de Roover, *Medici Bank*, 359–60, 378. Sometime in the 1550s Filippo de' Nerli received a loan, at Cosimo de' Medici's orders, for which the duke agreed to pay the 5 percent interest due the monte di pietà. As of the opening of the new triennium in 1560, the loan came to fl. 138, L. 5. MP 764, Libro di debitori e creditori, 8a–b, 301a.

hand, and Medici domination did nothing to change this pattern. Perhaps those who served after 1512 were somewhat more Medicean than those who served earlier, and in 1515 this characteristic was emphasized by the appointment of Galeotto di Lorenzo de' Medici, the first of his family to serve since Lorenzo di Pierfrancesco.

The appointment of patricians served three purposes. During both the republics and the duchy, patricians pursued offices as their birthright with a tenacity remarkable for its consistency and vigor. Competition for offices was a natural outlet for their energy and ambitions. Second, the Medici dukes used the eight seats to further their own ambitions through the exercise of patronage. Finally, the monte di pietà relied on the expertise, acquired from business, politics, family affairs and education, that men of this stature had to offer. Considerable familiarity with bookkeeping techniques was necessary to maintain the ledger, a task the eight delegated to one of themselves until the middle of the century when the sheer volume of transactions made the task too onerous. Appointing men who had already served once meant that the monte benefited from their knowledge and experience. Piero de' Lenzi, for instance, served as one of the first eight directors in 1496–99 and held a second appointment during 1506–9. Piero Guicciardini sat on the board with Lenzi in 1496 and was selected again in 1503. Both men's frequent presence at the pratica attests to their status.[64] Niccolò del Nero actually succeeded himself when he served a second, consecutive term in 1499, even though the monte's rules forbade this practice.

Even while the siege of Florence tightened in 1530 and the republic sought desperately to prevent a Medici victory, the last eight to serve under a republican government took office in mid-June 1530. They were Zanobi di Leonardo Bartolini, Luigi di Giovanfrancesco de' Pazzi, Luigi Soderini, Larione Martelli, Lorenzo di Filippo Strozzi, Tanai di Piero de' Nerli, Vittorio d'Antonio Landi, and Filippo di Bartolomeo Baroncini.[65] Among these surnames are several virulent anti-Medici republican families, especially the Pazzi, Strozzi, and Nerli. Yet at least one traditionally palleschi family, the Bartolini, was represented, perhaps in hope that its presence among the

---

64. Denis Fachard, ed., *Consulte e pratiche, 1505–1512* (Geneva, 1988), *passim.*
65. MP 744, 1b.

monte's directors might soften the vindictiveness of the Medici should their forces win, an increasing possibility in the summer of 1530. For a list of all monte di pietà directors from 1530–1575, see Appendix A, Table 1.

The appointment of Lorenzo di Filippo Strozzi was especially intriguing. Strozzi's ancestors, from an ancient, wealthy and respected *popolano* (commoner, as opposed to magnate) family, had been excluded from political power under Lorenzo the Magnificent. François Rabelais, writing in 1535 from Rome, noted Duke Alessandro's fear of Filippo Strozzi: "[Filippo's] possessions, which are not inconsiderable, the duke wanted to confiscate, for after the Fuggers of Augsburg in Germany, he is estimated to be the wealthiest merchant in Christendom and had placed men in that city to capture or kill [the duke]."[66] Though their feelings about the Medici ranged from heated antipathy to indifference, Rubinstein tells us that "no Strozzi could be found among the ranks of the Palleschi."[67] Two of them made anti-Medicean marriages: Fiammetta married into the Soderini family, and her sister Alessandra wed Niccolò Capponi, who served as gonfaloniere after the expulsion of the Medici in 1527. Their brother, Filippo di Filippo (son of the builder of the family's elegant palazzo), broke with his clan's tradition of anti-pallescianism through his risky and controversial marriage in 1508 to Lorenzo the Magnificent's daughter Clarice.[68] Filippo's brother Lorenzo, who became a director of the monte di pietà in 1530, had shown himself much warier of the Medici: when the gonfaloniere for life fell from power in 1512 and the Medici prepared to enter the city, Lorenzo found it prudent to flee to Lucca.[69] Lorenzo di Filippo also repre-

---

66. Rabelais to Geoffroy D'Estissac, 30 Dec. 1535, in François Rabelais, *Oeuvres complètes*, ed. Guy Demerson (Paris, 1973), 961. It was on the pretext of this alleged conspiracy, Rabelais added, that Alessandro had received permission from the pope to go about armed and with a thirty-man guard.

67. Nicolai Rubinstein, *The Government of Florence under the Medici, 1434–94* (Oxford, 1966), 213–15, cites the account of the 1484 scrutiny by Piero Guicciardini.

68. This Filippo became an important Medici supporter until near the end of his life when he lost favor after the death of Clement VII. The Soderini family's divided loyalties have been studied by Paula C. Clarke, *The Soderini and the Medici: Power and Patronage in Fifteenth-Century Florence* (Oxford, 1991). Although Tommaso Soderini remained a friend (*amico*) of the Medici, his brother Niccolò, presaging the family's position in the sixteenth century, became an enemy.

69. On the Strozzi marriages and family members mentioned here, see Bullard, *Filippo Strozzi*, 3–4, 45–46, 50–51, 66.

sented the last republican regime as a member of the delegation sent in August 1530 to the imperial forces encamped outside Florence "to conclude a peace agreement [*concordia*], or rather a surrender [*capitolazione*]."[70]

The Pazzi family had an even more anti-Medicean history, most clearly seen in the famous attempted coup of 1478 that resulted in the assassination of Lorenzo de' Medici's younger brother, Giuliano. The bloodbath that resulted as the Mediceans took their revenge brought about the deaths of three Pazzi. Many more were exiled, and the family was shamed publicly by frescoes painted by Botticelli depicting the Pazzi as traitors. In the early sixteenth century, as part of his policy of placating some prominent Florentine families traditionally hostile to the Medici, Leo X bestowed a treasurership on a Pazzi. Despite such symbolic olive branches, the Medici in the sixteenth century did not consider the Pazzi to be "very reliable" (*molto sicuri*)."[71] However, no Florentine family could force every member to toe a single political line. In the Pazzi clan, Cardinal Alessandro de' Pazzi composed an oration lauding the virtues of Cardinal Giulio de' Medici. Still, Alessandro, though advocating a return to one-man rule either by a prince or a lifetime gonfaloniere, typified the oligarchism of his family in his call for a senate composed of lifetime members empowered to choose their own successors.[72]

Members of the Nerli family, including Tanai himself, rivaled the Pazzi as anti-Medicean. A family of wealth and stature, the Nerli were marked for attack in 1497 by a conspiracy, which ultimately failed, to restore Piero de' Medici, for the conspirators considered the Nerli among the most avid anti-pallescians. Some of the family exhibited Savonarolan (*piagnone*) sympathies, at least insofar as this policy was politically expedient, for Tanai de' Nerli accompanied Sa-

70. Jacopo Nardi, *Istorie della città di Firenze* (Florence, 1858), 2:214, esp. n. 2. Despite the marriage of Filippo and Clarice, the Medici continued to distrust the Strozzi and consequently were slow in granting them political favors; for example, Lorenzo was not added to the balìa until 1522. Ibid., 6n.

71. Cecilia Ady, *Lorenzo dei Medici and Renaissance Italy* (New York, 1962), 68–70; Hale, *Florence and the Medici*, 85; and, for the quotation, Bullard, *Filippo Strozzi*, 34.

72. See Nardi, *Istorie della città di Firenze*, 2:70, esp. n. 2. On the difficulty of determining political allegiances among family members, see the discussion in Roslyn Pesman Cooper, "The Florentine Ruling Groups under the 'Governo Popolare,' 1494–1512," *Studies in Medieval and Renaissance History* 7 (old series 17): 71–181, esp. 128, n. 260.

vonarola on an ambassadorial mission to Charles VIII. The anti-Medici plot of 1522 called for a new government to be dominated by a council of eight, among whom a Nerli was to have been included.[73]

At the same time, the Nerli illustrated the ways in which prominent families could be politically divided. Filippo de' Nerli, author of the pro-Medicean *Commentarj de'fatti civili occorsi dentro la città di Firenze*, was arrested as a Medici supporter in 1512. After the restoration he served the ruling family as, successively, chief Florentine administrator, or *podestà*, of Prato, governor of Modena, and Florentine captain in several cities. In his commentary Nerli emphasized the bloody and bitter struggles that the firm government of the Medici put to an end, and concluded that the peace and stability Cosimo created were themselves justification for his rule.[74]

At first glance the Soderini seemed to have dangerously pallescian roots, for the family had enjoyed the friendship of the Medici since the early fifteenth century. One of them, Niccolò Soderini, had been tried for plotting the assassination of Cosimo de' Medici's enemy Niccolò da Uzzano. Piero the Gouty's friends included Tommaso Soderini, who considered Lorenzo almost a nephew, and, until their falling out, Niccolò Soderini, who had served as gonfaloniere.[75] Several other family members, notably Francesco, a distinguished lawyer and humanist, and his brother Paolantonio, rector of the University of Florence, belonged to the circle of intellectuals that surrounded the Medici. Lorenzo's friend Marsilio Ficino maintained an intimate correspondence with these men, lending them books and flooding them with advice.[76]

73. Bullard, *Filippo Strozzi*, 45–46. Jacopo di Tanai de' Nerli was one of Piero's chief opponents in the collegi in 1494. When Piero returned to Florence after treating with the French forces, he found the palace guarded against his entry by Jacopo di Tanai. According to one account, Nerli told Piero that he could come inside only if he came alone through the gate's small doorway (*sportello*). Hearing this, Piero "bit his fingers in spite." Nardi, *Istorie della città di Firenze*, 1:32–33, esp. n. 2. On Tanai, see Weinstein, *Savonarola*, 115n. For the anti-Medici plot, see Stephens, *Fall*, 120.

74. For Filippo de' Nerli and his *Commentarj* see Rudolf von Albertini, *Firenze dalla repubblica al principato* (Turin, 1970; orig. pub. Bern, 1955), 320–29.

75. See Dale Kent, *Rise of the Medici: Faction in Florence, 1426–1434* (Oxford, 1978), 236–39. Niccolò Soderini was acquitted, but one of his conspirators was found guilty. On the Soderini see also Niccolò Machiavelli, *History of Florence and the Affairs of Italy* (New York, 1960), 327–28, Ady, *Lorenzo dei Medici*, 47; and Clarke, *Soderini and the Medici*, 20–21.

76. See, e.g., letters 127 and 131 (vol. 1) and 35 (vol. 2) in Ficino, *Letters*.

The Soderini were not immune to the attractiveness of Savonarola's call to reform or to the political opportunity his regime offered the elite. Paolantonio Soderini, disillusioned with Lorenzo de' Medici's tight hold on Florentine politics, fell under the mystical Dominican's influence. After Lorenzo de' Medici's death the rector called for more moderate Medicean authority. Under Savonarola, as one of the Ten of Liberty, he helped draw up a proposed constitution. As an advocate of a government based on that of Venice with its hereditary aristocracy, an idea later embraced by Savonarola, Paolantonio was motivated in part by the desire to insert men like himself into the power structure.[77]

The family's political fortune reached its zenith in 1502 when Piero Soderini was chosen gonfaloniere for life. Considered a moderate and a republican, he could be counted on to oppose any attempt by the palleschi to reinstate their own regime.[78] Indeed, when in 1512 the siege by imperial troops threatened Florence with the possibility of a new Medici takeover, the gonfaloniere reportedly sought "an agreement with the Spaniards for any sum of money whatsoever, if only the Medici were kept out."[79] By the time of the last Florentine republic, the Soderini were defenders of oligarchy and opponents of Medici rule.

The Martelli became enthusiastic Medici supporters after 1434 and were rewarded as more of their members passed the scrutiny, thus becoming eligible for civic office. Several held important positions in the Medici bank. A namesake of the monte director, Ilarione di Bartolomeo Martelli, served as a partner of Lorenzo the Magnificent in the Medici bank's Pisan branch from 1486 to about 1488 and

77. For a discussion of Soderini's role in the piagnone government, see Weinstein, *Savonarola*, 121, 150–51, 258, 274. Soderini seems to have been one of the few Florentines conversant with the actual workings of the Venetian constitution, which he had had the chance to observe during his ambassadorship to Venice. See Gilbert, "Venetian Constitution," 203.

78. Weinstein, *Savonarola*, 324. See also D'Addario, *Formazione*. The piagnone Luca Landucci rejoiced in Soderini's election, calling it "truly a work of God." Landucci, *Diario*, 22 Sept. 1502.

79. Machiavelli to an unidentified lady, Sept. 1512, in Niccolò Machiavelli, *Lettere*, ed. Franco Gaeta (Milan, 1961), no. 118, pp. 222–28. Stephens, *Fall*, 27, unequivocally refers to the Strozzi and Soderini as "families which were famous for their hostility to the Medici." This hostility was manifested by the ultimate sign of anti-pallescianism: in 1509 Luigi Soderini purchased a house and shop from the overseers of the confiscated Medici estates.

was listed as a creditor in the amount of fl. 972.5.5 in 1486. Bartolomeo Scala warned Lorenzo that men like Martelli were oligarchs at heart and consequently posed a threat to the Medici.[80] Yet Francesco di Ruberto Martelli was among a handful of men found to have conspired to return Piero di Lorenzo de' Medici to power in Florence in 1497. While the family's record of support for the Medici was strong, evidence shows a lessening of support by the late fifteenth century.[81] Other members of the family would demonstrate their affection for the Medici in different ways: Camilla Martelli became Cosimo I's mistress in the 1560s.

Alone among the eight, Zanobi di Leonardo Bartolini belonged to a palleschi family of uncompromising loyalty. The Medici-Bartolini friendship dated back to the second half of the fifteenth century when the Medici invested in the Bartolini bank. This association continued into the sixteenth century as Leonardo Bartolini, a "devoted confidant" of the Medici, became gonfaloniere in 1516 and served as a banker to Leo X. Zanobi Bartolini provided loans to Lorenzo de' Medici for his conquest of Urbino. Originally a supporter of the republic, Zanobi came to be suspected by that regime of collaborating with the enemy during the siege of 1529–30.[82] Zanobi's friendship with the Medici was revealed by his selection as one of the Eleven of Balìa upon the Medici triumph of 1530. Bernardo Segni called these eleven "the foremost among the palleschi faction."[83]

80. Rubinstein, *Government of Florence*, 9n., 4, and 178–79; Dale Kent, *Rise of the Medici*, 34n. 4; and R. de Roover, *Medici Bank*, 277–78. There is some evidence, however, that the partnership with Ilarione Martelli was abruptly terminated, and the branch failed to show a profit.

81. On Francesco, see Nerli, *Commentarj*, 70. The father of one Piero Martelli had been a member of an anti-Medicean group prior to 1494 (Bullard, *Filippo Strozzi*, 49), and a certain Niccolò Martelli was captured in Siena in 1514 and implicated in an anti-Medicean plot. The conspiracy of 1522 to murder Cardinal Giulio and restore Piero Soderini was hatched, at least in part, by one Niccolò Martelli. Stephens, *Fall*, 120; D'Addario, *Formazione*, 119–20; and Nardi, *Istorie della città di Firenze*, 2:76.

82. Bullard, *Filippo Strozzi*, 34, 73–74, 127n.; and Albertini, *Firenze*, 151.

83. "Historia da fiorentina di Segni," bk. 5, or *Storie Fiorentine*, 1:295. The other members were Baccio Valori, Messer Ormanozzo Deti, Messer Matteo Niccolini, Messer Luigi della Stufa, Leonardo Ridolfi, Antonio Gualterotti, Andrea Minerbetti, Ottaviano de' Medici, Filippo Machiavelli, Raffaello Girolami, and Niccolò del Croscia. The Bartolini friendship with the Medici was richly rewarded after 1512 when one Gherardo won the lucrative position of treasurer to Lorenzo and later served as proctor to Giulio. The cardinal chose this same Gherardo for the honor of traveling to France to receive a knightly insignia that the French monarch had bestowed upon the Duke of Urbino. Stephens, *Fall*, 110.

Of the eight, two surnames, Landi and Baroncini, have left few traces. Of the remaining six, one, the Bartolini, was staunchly pro-Medicean. Another, the Martelli, had a history of Medici sympathy but wavered in the sixteenth century. A third, the Strozzi, had little affection for the Medici but included some members like Filippo, who made their political compromises. The remaining three families—the Pazzi, Soderini, and Nerli—were anti-Medicean.

On 15 October 1530 the Signori and councils ordered the Madonna of Impruneta, traditionally carried down to Florence in times of crisis, to be returned to the church in her hilltop village. Brought in before the siege and then, like the citizens who revered her, caught inside the walls by the papal-imperial forces, her departure signaled an end to the crisis. Consolidation of the new regime was about to begin.[84]

Once installed as lords after the fall of the republic in 1530, the Medici restored the constitutional status quo ante 1527 and placated the patriciate by abolishing the Great Council, whose middle-class membership they detested. Most city officials, including the eight directors of the monte di pietà, were dismissed, and the Signori and councils chose new ones who could be counted on to support the new regime.[85] Unlike his predecessor of 1512, when the Medici had

84. On the Madonna of Impruneta see Arch. della Rep.—Signori e Collegi, Deliberazioni fatte in forza di speciale autorità 42, 138r, 15 Oct. 1530.

85. Roberto Ridolfi, ed., "Diario fiorentino di anonimo delle cose occorse l'anno 1537," *ASI* 116 (1958): 544–70, gives valuable details on the new officers appointed upon Cosimo's accession in 1537. On constitutional change see Felix Gilbert, *Machiavelli and Guicciardini: Politics and History in Sixteenth Century Florence* (Princeton, 1965), 49–104; and Francesco Guicciardini, *History of Italy*, trans. Sidney Alexander (New York, 1969), bk. 20, 431. See also "Historia da fiorentina di Segni," or *Storie fiorentine*, 1:294–96. Segni noted that the first move of the palleschi was to call a *parlamento*. He then found it necessary to explain what a *parlamento* was! The Mediceans, he continued, announced their intention to "return" to this custom. Albertini (*Firenze*, 328–34) notes that Segni's career typified that of many anti-Medicean patricians. Having rejoiced at the Medici's expulsion in 1527, Segni found himself and his family in serious financial difficulty when property seized from the exiles of 1527 was forcibly restored to its former owners. After making a financially advantageous marriage to a Ridolfi, Segni entered the service of the Medici, and later produced his "Historia da fiorentina," which Albertini judged to have been more balanced and cautious than those of Varchi and Nerli. The judgment would have pleased Segni, who wrote that most contemporary histories were too partisan and that he, "detached from the many causes of passion," would try to be objective; bk. 1; or *Storie fiorentine*, 1:3. On the new officials, see Arch. della Rep.—Signori e Collegi, Deliberazioni fatte in forza di speciale autorità 42, 15 Nov. 1530.

made "no clean sweep of offices,"[86] Alessandro proved a more thorough housekeeper.

In the peace treaty Charles V guaranteed Florence its "liberty," which many citizens took to mean that the republic would survive.[87] Clement VII and Alessandro de' Medici could afford to bide their time, accepting for the present the government dictated to them by Charles as well as Alessandro's position as capo. Clement enjoyed advantages that he might gradually press: his family still had a network of supporters in the city, an asset the emperor lacked, and the pope understood better than Charles the nature of Florentine politics. From Rome Clement could respond more quickly to events in Florence than could the Habsburg ruler, for whom Florence was but one of a dozen concerns. The pope also trusted in the inability of the patriciate to develop a viable regime comprising pro-Mediceans and anti-Mediceans alike. This lesson had been demonstrated only a year earlier, when the moderate gonfaloniere Niccolò Capponi had tried to include former Medici supporters and ultimately had been overthrown for his trouble.[88]

Contemporary accounts of the events of 1530 exhude a feeling of relief at the end of the siege and at the entry of the Medici. Francesco Guicciardini criticized the blindness of those who "were driven by ultimate desperation unwilling lest their own downfall should occur without the slaughter of their country. . . . And . . . the magistrates shared that stubbornness."[89] In retrospect he saw the age of the Medici as a golden time of Florentine peace, power, and wealth. The Medici exile in 1494, Guicciardini now realized, marked "the beginning of . . . years of misfortune." He and men like him, viewing with horror the disastrous history of the republic after 1494, began to turn their backs on the old Florentine humanist belief in the sanctity of the republican form of government, with Guicciardini himself offering the extraordinary conclusion that "the ancient times of the

86. Stephens, *Fall*, 141–42.

87. Hale, *Florence and the Medici*, 118. In addition, the city would be allowed to retain possession of its *dominio* in exchange for a pledge of obedience, fortified by a payment of eighty thousand ducats, to the emperor. The citizens would receive a general pardon. D'Addario, *Formazione*, 149–52; and Guicciardini, *History*, bk. 20, 430–31.

88. Guicciardini, *History*, bk. 19. See also Albertini's discussion of the almost impossible task facing Capponi (*Firenze*, 107–19).

89. For Guicciardini's remarks, see *History*, bk. 20, 430, and bk. 1, 32.

Romans and the Greeks are no longer."[90] Thus the ottimati resigned themselves to domination by one of their own, the Medici—an outcome they saw as preferable to domination by the despised middle classes.

The reforms that affected the monte di pietà beginning in November 1530 must be seen against this backdrop. The old republican charitable foundation was not singled out by the Medici, nor did they view it as a peculiarly Savonarolan—hence, dangerous—creation. Rather, Alessandro and his successor Cosimo I closely scrutinized all Florentine institutions, seeking to discover how such establishments could best serve the needs of the dynasty and the state. Consciously or not, they followed the advice of Machiavelli, who told his prince that one way to keep a newly acquired state, formerly free, was to create a "government composed of a few who will keep it friendly to you."[91]

The monte di pietà's books are laconic about the effects of the Medici victory, noting only that "on 17 November 1530, new officials were created" by the Signori and councils. Their identities reveal the political tact the Medici would have to exercise if they hoped to secure their power without provoking the opposition of the wary patriciate. While all eight republican officials of the monte di pietà were dismissed, its regular employees were not: the provveditore, Giovanbattista Primerani, and the chancellor (*cancelliere*), Ser Bartolomeo d'Antonio Mei, may represent a new professional class of functionaries who carried on their duties from regime to regime while their superiors suffered the consequences of the city's political vicissitudes.[92]

From the 1530s on, the patrician air surrounding the men chosen to sit on the monte's board of officials became even purer. Begin-

---

90. Quoted by Gilbert, *Machiavelli and Guicciardini*, 101. See also Guicciardini's remarks in *Ricordi*, ed. Raffaele Spongano (Florence, 1951), on government in Florence: "Just as a private citizen errs against the prince and commits *crimen lese maiestatis* . . . so does a prince err and commit *crimen lesi populi* [*sic*], doing that which is the prerogative of the people and citizens" (104).

91. Niccolò Machiavelli, *Il principe*, ed. Luigi Fiorentino (Milan, 1969), 41. The translation is from Machiavelli, *Prince and the Discourses*, ed. Max Lerner (New York, 1959), 18.

92. See MP 744, first page (unnumbered); and Arch. della Rep—Signori e Collegi, Deliberazioni fatte in forza di speciale autorità 42, 162r for the naming of the monte's new directors and the retention of salaried employees.

ning with the 8 appointed by Alessandro in 1530 and continuing through the appointments made in 1572, Alessandro and Cosimo named fifteen boards of 8 men each, for a total of 120 nominees, plus 3 replacements for men who died in office. Of these 123 appointees, 8 served twice and 1 served three times, leaving 113 different individuals appointed to the board by the dukes and subsequently approved by the senate. The majority of these men—74, or nearly two-thirds—served as senators themselves, and most of the rest belonged to families with members in the senate, proof that the dukes considered the monte's directorship important enough to fill it with men of senatorial rank and patrician standing. At least four of those appointed held a knightly rank, and many more had kinsmen who did. Although a seat in the senate was the most common appointment among this group, a number of them held other positions, including posts on the Nine Conservatori, the Sanità (or health board), and, in the case of Francesco Rinuccini, as massaro of the monte itself.[93] At least eight Florentine banking families—the Capponi, Ricci, Salviati, Antinori-Alamanni, Rinuccini, Pandolfini, and del Nero—were represented one or more times among the eight. It was probably no coincidence that a lot of monte business came the way of these banks, especially to the Ricci and Salviati firms, and that men from each of these two banking families were named four times to the monte di pietà's eight-man board during the reigns of Alessandro and Cosimo.[94]

The eight new monte officials of 1530 were handpicked by the new regime. The record books list the age of each man, thereby adding dignity to their names as well as recognizing the worthiness of their experience. First among the eight, though by virtue of his position, not his age, was none other than Bartolomeo Valori, "at the present time commissioner of the pope," a man with a long history of rash pro-Mediceanism.[95] His presence among the eight revealed

---

93. See Giuliano de' Ricci, *Cronaca (1532–1606)*, ed. Giuliana Sapori (Milan, 1971), *passim*, for the appointments mentioned.

94. See Appendix A, Table 2, Families with More than One Appointment to Monte di Pietà Board, 1530–75, and Table 3, Families with One Appointment to Monte di Pietà Board, 1530–75.

95. MP 744, first page (unnumbered). In 1512 Valori had been brought into a plot by several young patricians to oust the gonfaloniere and to restore the Medici; Guicciardini, *History*, bk. 11, 263. In the shaky years 1524–27 he had been a well-known member of an extremely pro-Medicean circle of young patricians, including

the importance Alessandro placed on control of the monte di pietà. Leo X would have been pleased.

The oldest among the eight, Filippo d'Alessandro Machiavelli, was a different man altogether. At a pratica in 1529 he advised against capitulation to the Medici, asserting that "one must risk life for the defense of liberty."[96] Like his better-known kinsman Niccolò, Filippo sought a republic dominated by the patriciate. The family also represented a group that the Medici would have to handle with delicacy —the old ottimati who demanded a place in government. Alessandro's recognition of this fact may account for Filippo's appearance among the eight. His election to a second important post, the Eleven of Balìa, shows he was considered unthreatening, perhaps because at nearly seventy years of age he was too old to possess the energy to oppose Medici policy.[97]

Averardo d'Alamanno Salviati, born in 1489, was the youngest of the eight. The links between the Medici and the Salviati, forged in the mid-fifteenth century through political, business, and matrimonial deals, were occasionally rattled but never broken in the sixteenth. The Medici rescued the Salviati bank from collapse in 1465 with an infusion of twelve thousand badly needed florins.[98] The participation of Francesco Salviati in the Pazzi conspiracy created a serious though temporary rift that was mended by a Medici-Salviati marriage alliance, or *parentado*, in 1488. Giovanni delle Bande Nere de' Medici's marriage to Maria Salviati—who herself had Medici blood—cemented the bond and, even more important, produced Cosimo, Alessandro's successor. Both Averardo and Piero Salviati were known to favor Alessandro's return to Florence, even his elevation to capo, though their support stopped short of a Medici ducal appointment.[99] Averardo Salviati had, in 1511, sided with Julius II against those Florentines who favored holding a church council at

---

Ottaviano de' Medici, Palla Rucellai, Roberto Pucci, and Lorenzo Martelli (Stephens, *Fall*, 172; Stephens's source is Benedetto Varchi). After the surrender of the city in 1530 but before the reentry of the Medici, Valori had been, along with Malatesta Baglioni, virtual boss of Florence; D'Addario, *Formazione*, 152: "After 12 August, the real bosses of the city became Baglioni . . . and Valori."

96. Quoted in Stephens, *Fall*, 252, from Consulte e pratiche 71, 76v.

97. "Historia da fiorentina di Segni," bk. 5, or *Storie fiorentine*, 1:295.

98. R. de Roover, *Medici Bank*, 359–60.

99. Gilbert, *Machiavelli and Guicciardini*, 125, 128; Ady, *Lorenzo dei Medici*, 47; Stephens, *Fall*, 172–73.

Florence; his party comprised the city's Mediceans. His father, Al-amanno, married into the Medici family when he took as his wife a sister of the same Lorenzino who later murdered Alessandro.[100] The family's high social standing in the city, however, meant that it shared the view of its peers that a place in government must be re-served for the ottimati. Occasionally, republican sympathies led to trouble: Jacopo Salviati, for instance, was exiled for his republican-ism. Yet by and large the Salviati were pro-Medicean and after 1512 stood, as John Stephens put it, "first in the pecking order."[101]

The Gondi too fell into this category. Like most of the other men appointed to the monte board of officials (and to other offices), Ber-nardo di Carlo Gondi, nearly seventy years old in 1530, belonged to an ancient, respected, and wealthy family with a background of close, if not overly warm, relations to the Medici. The Gondi also had ties to the Salviati, and in fact acted as their agents in Florence. One of them, Giuliano, had spoken out in a pratica against Sa-vonarola, suggesting that the friar intended to make himself pope over his flock.[102]

One of the two youngest of the eight, born in 1488, was Filippo di Filippo Strozzi. His presence on the board is a surprise since, as has been seen, the Strozzi were generally anti-pallescian, and one of Fi-lippo's kinsmen, Lorenzo di Filippo, had served the monte under the last republic and was forced, along with his colleagues, to leave his post. The appointment of Filippo may have represented an at-tempt by the Medici to placate the powerful Strozzi: one anti-Medi-cean in the clan was dismissed, but in compensation a young mem-ber was chosen to replace him. It did not take much political acumen to read these signals: cooperation with the Medici would lead to

---

100. Rosemary Devonshire Jones, *Francesco Vettori, Florentine Citizen and Medici Servant* (London, 1972), 40–41, 56–57, 70.

101. Stephens, *Fall*, 126.

102. For the Gondi-Salviati tie, see Stephens, *Fall*, 245. On the anti-Savonarolan statement, see Weinstein, *Savonarola*, 230. One Giuliano Gondi was captured, tortured brutally, and implicated in the assassination of Alessandro de' Medici (D'Addario, *Formazione*, 206), a bloody act that cannot be seen as anti-Medicean as much as anti-Alexandrine. Segni expressed horror at the murder of Luisa Strozzi, wife of the patri-cian Luigi Capponi; "it is said," Segni wrote, "that the duke, indignant with her, had her poisoned." Segni concluded that the conspiracy to murder the duke succeeded because its victim was "universally hated." "Historia da fiorentina di Segni," bks. 6, 8, or *Storie fiorentine*, 2:66 and 2:129.

honors and offices. Two years later both Filippo di Filippo and Matteo di Lorenzo Strozzi would sit in the Senate of Forty-Eight.[103]

Two of the monte's eight, Giuliano di Francesco del Zacheria, born in 1479, and Luigi di Francesco Pieri, a year younger, have left few traces. It would not be surprising to discover that they were newcomers, for the Medici strategy included introducing "new men" into the ruling circles. Some of these newcomers came from the dominion, some from more distant cities.

The presence of the "old patriciate" (*vecchio patriziato*, in Diaz's words) in positions of authority under the first Medici dukes is testament to their resilience, persistance, and importance in the city. While outspoken critics of the new regime were kept out of office or even sent into exile, the Medici sought to co-opt as many of the old families as possible. Thus among the eight of the monte di pietà sat men like Filippo d'Alessandro Machiavelli, Bernardo di Carlo Gondi, Giovanfrancesco d'Antonio de' Nobili, and Averardo d'Alamanno Salviati. The first three of these garnered appointments from Clement VII to serve in the Senate of Forty-Eight even while they sat on the monte's board, and Salviati served in the senate under Cosimo in 1537.[104]

Further, the established, powerful families felt a growing dismay toward the old popular regime. As Guicciardini noted, "When men of bad faith and the ignorant govern, it is not surprising that virtue and goodness are not valued, because the first hold them in disdain, and the second don't know them."[105] Even before 1512, he observed, wealthy and distinguished Florentines—in other words, those of his own social standing—had begun to complain of the constant demands made on their personal resources by the government of Piero Soderini. They were so weary of this burden, Guicciardini continued, that they might be willing to support any alternate regime, provided they were left alone to enjoy, conserve, and increase their wealth.[106] As discussed earlier, the last republic levied high extraordinary taxes to meet the costs of defense. By late 1528 the patriciate and the regime were at loggerheads, a position exacerbated by the

103. Ricci, *Cronaca*, 5–6. Several writers urged the Medici to promote young men from patrician families, arguing that these *giovani* were more flexible and pragmatic than their elders. See Federico Chabod's preface to Albertini's *Firenze*, ix–xiii, for Lodovico Alamanni's advice to the Medici in 1517.

104. Ricci, *Cronaca*, 6–7.

105. Guicciardini, *Ricordi*, 254.

106. Guicciardini, *History*, xxiii.

regime's demand of uncompromising obedience from all citizens. Beginning in 1529 a number of important men and women were tried, often in absentia, and sentenced to exile or death for treasonable activities ranging from leaving the beleaguered city without permission to criticizing the government to plotting its downfall. Those on whom the government's condemnation fell included Lucrezia Salviati, Piero d'Alamanno Salviati, Messer Onofrio di Lionardo Bartolini, the archbishop of Pisa, and Giuliano di Niccolò Strozzi—all from families who, in November 1530, were represented among the monte's eight officials. In short, members of the "old patriciate" had become disillusioned with the republican regime. By subsequently including such men in office, the Medici offered them an alternative to the radical republicanism of men like Francesco Carducci, during whose gonfalonierate these denunciations had flourished.[107]

The treatment the monte di pietà received at the hands of the Medici reflects their handling of other Florentine institutions and lends insight into their gradual establishment of control over Florence. Alessandro and Clement VII displayed political finesse in their choice of ministers. The sweeping dismissal of the last eight to serve under the republic—a move paralleled in other offices—threatened to antagonize the families who suddenly found themselves, once again, under the thumb of a Medici ruler. The Medici, shrewdly understanding the importance to the regime of broad ottimati support, smoothed ruffled feathers by distributing some of the spoils to carefully chosen patricians. The political energies and ambitions of these men thus flowed into safe channels carefully carved by the Medici. The truly important jobs were reserved for close friends; "new men," loyal to the dynasty and covetous of office, were also well rewarded. In this way potential discontent was contained, the patriciate was kept occupied, and a loyal proto-bureaucracy began to take form.

Chapter 7 of Machiavelli's *Prince*, "Of New Dominions Acquired by the Powers of Others or by Fortune," might have been written for

---

107. See Stephens, *Fall*, 249–50. Stephens identifies the other dominant families as the Canigiani, Altoviti, Acciaiuoli, Antella, Albizzi, Pitti, Corbinelli, Capponi, Filicaia, Alberti, Corsini, Mancini, Giugni, Medici, Ricci, Guicciardini, Rucellai, and Carnesecchi. Of these all but the Canigiani, Pitti, Corbinelli, Corsini, Mancini, and Giugni were represented among the monte's eight at least once between 1530 and 1575. All had been represented in the priorate, itself a creation of 1282, by 1302. Ibid., 8–9. For the remarkable staying power of the Florentine patriciate, see Litchfield, *Emergence of a Bureaucracy*.

Alessandro, who rode to power on the coattails—or rather, pontifical robes—of Clement VII. Machiavelli advised such a prince to
"take immediate steps for maintaining what fortune has thrown into
his lap, and lay afterwards those foundations which others make before becoming princes." Alessandro was not the man Machiavelli
had in mind, for his dissolute life and offensive treatment of those
around him disgusted even his kinsmen, one of whom killed him.
Alessandro, with Clement's advice, began to "lay the foundations,"
but his successor, Cosimo, was the master builder for whom Machiavelli might have written chapter 9, "Of the Civic Principality." This
young duke maintained his position, as Machiavelli suggested, by
"cunning assisted by fortune, . . . by help of popular favor or by the
favor of the aristocracy."[108] Both rulers conformed to Machiavelli's
advice to make use of the nobles in order to hold their loyalty.
Among the officials of the monte di pietà was the pope's commissioner, Bartolomeo Valori, whose presence assured that Medicean
wishes would be carried out. Along with him, pallescians like Gondi,
Salviati, and Nobili assured a Medici majority. Filippo Strozzi's appointment might have helped assuage the resentments of at least
part of this powerful family. Filippo Machiavelli represented the important old republicans who would have to be soothed and carefully
included in government. Finally, the two unknowns, Giuliano del
Zacheria and Luigi Pieri, may have been newcomers who threw their
lot in with the duke. The eight-man board was a microcosm of Florentine politics as the Medici consolidated power.[109]

  The monte di pietà's board of eight officials provided eight slots
for patronage. This fact alone insured its usefulness and atoned for
the monte's connections to the Savonarolan and the last republics.
Far more important was the monte's potential usefulness as a source
of cash to the new Medicean state. Florence's new rulers had only to
study the republic's own examples of how the monte might be used
to serve the regime. In time, the dukes showed themselves to be
brilliant pupils who far outshone their old masters.

  108. Machiavelli, *Principe*, 48 and 60; in the Lerner edition, 24 and 35.
  109. The analysis proffered by Stephens of Medici policy in 1512 is illuminating
for 1530: "Of course, the unquestioning supporters of the Medici were themselves a
minority, but the Medici now enjoyed new opportunities to fix the positions of leading
Florentines in their following. [The Medici] could offer them first of all, as they had
before, a share in their political estate. But leading Florentines expected a large share
of the honours whatever the government of the city." Stephens, *Fall*, 124.

5 REVOLUTION AND EVOLUTION, 1530–1569

THE RESTORATION OF 1530 marked the beginning of over two centuries of Medici rule, brought to an end only by the extinction of their line in 1737. The impressive length of the dynasty's reign resulted from the efficiency of the Medicean consolidation during the mid-sixteenth century. In Guicciardini's view, "the power of the Medici remained freer and more absolute and practically regal" after 1530 and resulted from the impoverishment of "so long and dreadful a war."[1] Their devotion to the task of insinuating their supporters into every arm of government, including the monte di pietà beginning in November 1530, eliminated once and for all the possibility of unpleasant reversals in the councils or other institutions, and allowed them to placate the patriciate—even former enemies—by carefully doling out offices and honors. Since the Medici intended to gain control of all Florentine institutions, especially those dealing with lawmaking and finance, the monte di pietà did not escape their scrutiny.

The monte's record keepers in the Savonarolan and post-Savonarolan republics had carefully detailed the constitutional processes that led to the selection of the monte di pietà's officials. One bookkeeper, the camarlingo Adovardo Canigiani, wrote that he himself had been "elected and appointed by the respected officials of the

---

1. Francesco Guicciardini, *Storia d'Italia*, ed. Costantino Panigada (Bari, 1929), 5:299. The historian saw a direct link between both the "dire necessity" and "all this poverty" that the war had brought, and the increased power of the Medici.

monte di pietà and then approved by our magnificant Signori and their venerable Collegi and by the Council of the Richiesti of the city of Florence." The last monte officials of the last republic had been elected by the Great Council. The officials named in 1533, during Alessandro's rule, were "elected in the Senate of Forty-Eight," a Medicean creature that nonetheless maintained the facade of constitutionality. In 1548 the monte's officials selected Piero Velluti to keep their records, the first person to hold this position who was neither an employee of the monte nor one of its eight overseers. Velluti recorded that the men who had chosen him were "elected from the Council of Forty-Eight by order of His Excellency for the governance of the monte . . . for the next three years."[2] In consultation with Florence's highest magistracy, the Magistrato Supremo, Cosimo simply chose whomever he liked from a list of candidates proposed by the secretary of the Tratte. By 1566, four of the eight were elected from the Senate of Forty-Eight, four from the Council of Two Hundred.[3] By Cosimo's reign the salaried employees of the monte di pietà served at the pleasure of the duke, whereas in the early years some had, like the eight officials, been drawn for their posts through the Tratte. The employees thus were a permanent staff, and Medici control over them went a long way toward establishing control over the institution as a whole. The census of 1551–52 shows that the monte di pietà employed twenty people, from the notary Bartolomeo Mei who served as chancellor to the scribes and assessors. By 1604 the number of permanent employees had reached thirty-two. With its three branches, the monte di pietà had become one of Florence's large institutions.[4]

Alessandro de' Medici was single-minded when it came to finance.

2. On Canigiani, MP 723, first (unnumbered) folio. On the last republic, MP 744, first (unnumbered) folio. On Alessandro's appointments, MP 746, first (unnumbered) folio: "li ufiziali eletti nel Consiglio de' xlviii." On Piero Velluti, MP 756, first (unnumbered) folio. See also, e.g., MP 762, first (unnumbered) folio, where "His Excellency" has been embellished into "the Most Illustrious and Excellent Lord Duke." The Velluti family served Cosimo well: one of them received an ambassadorial appointment in 1548. See letter 6 of Giovambattista Busini, 29 Dec. 1548, in *Lettere di Giovambattista Busini a Benedetto Varchi sopra l'assedio di Firenze*, ed. G. Milanesi (Florence, 1860), 60.
3. MP 768, first (unnumbered) folio.
4. Biblioteca Nazionale di Firenze, Palatino 756, Census of 1551. I am grateful to R. Burr Litchfield of Brown University for helping to clarify these procedures and for sharing his data from the censuses of 1551–52 and 1604. See also Litchfield, *Emergence of a Bureaucracy*, Appendix A.i.

Working through the Otto di Pratica, he and his advisers ordered the monte comune to pay the salaries of members of his household staff and demanded even greater sums to pay for those arms upon which, early in his rule, he depended.[5] In demanding payment from the monte comune, the duke gave notice that these accoutrements of princely authority were the fiscal responsibility of the state, not its head, and this assumption established a precedent.[6] A far greater drain on Florentine taxpayers was the expense of maintaining the army of occupation. The Otto di Practica dutifully told Girolamo Morelli, treasurer of the monte comune, to make available to the duke the large sum of fl. 10,055, of which fl. 55 represented the rectification of a bookkeeping error against Alessandro, and fl. 10,000 were meant to pay "for the provisions and relief of His Excellency for six months, from last September 25 through the twenty-fifth of this month [March 1531]." This money went to pay for the horses, lances, and other military expenses "of this most happy state."[7]

Raiding the monte comune was one way to make state institutions underwrite ducal finance, but no matter how efficiently done, it was not enough. Even though men like Guicciardini believed that dire poverty sapped the Florentine will to resist and facilitated the Medici quest for control, a city that remained impoverished would not be content but would, sooner or later, rise against its masters. The Medici would have to prove themselves capable of restoring the prosperity of the city after the long siege, and Alessandro and his advisers set about this task almost at once. The last republic had almost ruined the monte di pietà when the regime ordered the withdrawal of

5. On these payments, see Pratica Segreta, Otto di Pratica (Principato), Deliberazioni 155, Stanziamenti, 23 June 1532. Apparently the salaries were overdue, for the order, dated 23 June 1532, was effective retroactive to April 18.

6. Unlike their contemporaries the Tudors, who were supposed to "live of their own," the Medici had made their money in trade and banking rather than from landed estates and did not, in the mid-sixteenth century, have vast wealth to draw on as they had had a century earlier. Cosimo I especially lacked money. Shortly after his accession he was obliged to admit that he was unable "at present because of the difficulty of [acquiring] money to satisfy in cash the third part of the tribute of 25,000 scudi." He promised to pay the outstanding balance of sc. 8,600 within three months. Mediceo 657, Cosimo de' Medici to Lopez Urtado di Mendoza, 20 June 1538, 11r.

7. Otto di Pratica (Principato), Stanziamenti, 167, filza 2, 21 Mar.–23 Oct. [1531]. This file provides rich detail on the finances of both the ducal household and the state.

over fl. 16,400 and the institution's officials would have to face the reality that the debt would never be paid. The monte's situation was in some ways reminiscent of its first days in 1496: it needed to begin again, to attract new deposits, but in 1530 there was no one to preach as Savonarola or Marco di Matteo Strozzi had done.

In June 1530 the monte di pietà's ledgers held eighty-three deposits for a total of fl. 19,964, L. 202,012.4.6. Of these eighty-three, several represented "internal" accounts, that is, money taken in from redemptions, interest payments, and sales of pawns left behind by their owners. The following list shows the amounts in these "internal" accounts at that time (amounts are in florins, lire, soldi, denari).

Entry	*Amount*
Creditors from sales of pledges, first monte	fl. 317, L. 6,695.7.8
Creditors from sales of pledges, second monte	fl. 309, L. 6,313.17.11
More creditors than debtors, second monte	fl. 2,473, L. 8,488.18.10
Creditors from sales of pledges, third monte	fl. 167, L. 7,862.11.1
Pledges remaining at the third monte	fl. 2, L. 10.16
Interest	fl. 58, L. 851.13.11
TOTAL	fl. 3,326, L. 30,223.5.5

These accounts held nearly 16 percent of all monte credits. While this figure may seem small, its importance emerges once the origins of the other seventy-seven credits are traced. Of the seventy-seven, forty-one were already on the books in June 1527, and many of these dated back even further. More important, they included the largest deposits, such as the fl. 14,394 placed in the monte by the officials in charge of the goods confiscated from the Pisan rebels. Money already on deposit as of 1527 and still listed as credits in 1533 amounted to about fl. 16,073, L. 165,934. These old deposits comprised over 81 percent of the total credits listed in 1530. Of new accounts opened between 1527 and 1530 and still on the books as of the latter date, of which there were fewer than three dozen, among the few significant ones were two deposits of over L. 680 each. The average deposit was L. 166, or about fl. 23, L. 5. But the standard deviation is high, about L. 214.10, or fl. 30, L. 4.10, because of the two large deposits mentioned earlier, plus another of L. 525 placed by the innkeepers' guild, a deposit that was withdrawn completely before the ledger was balanced in 1533. These figures show that few Florentines supported the monte di pietà with voluntary deposits during the turbulent years 1527–30. Instead, most of the monte's remaining assets after the fall of the last republic had accrued prior to the Medici exile in 1527, and the only meaningful increases in capital came not from new deposits but from income taken in on loans, redemptions, and sales of pawns at the three branches.[8]

Through the 1530s the institution's financial position remained weak. Lack of new deposits was reflected in the brevity of the ledger covering those years. Only fifty-seven pages of the book bear accounts, and the rest are blank. (By way of comparison, the preceding book used ninety-eight pages.) Also, only about half a dozen new deposits were made. A number of deposits were reduced in amount. Of the two large significant new depositors noted earlier, the Otto di Guardia, which had monte di pietà credits of L. 687.9 in 1530, held only L. 407.9 three years later. The other account, containing L. 682.10 in 1530, was withdrawn in full by November 1533. Another depositor withdrew some L. 50 so that his account went from over L. 150 to just over L. 100.[9] As a result, total credits listed in 1533 came to fl. 19,442, L. 213,998.8.9, or L. 350,092.8.9. The total for 1530 came to L. 341,760.4.6, so 1533 brought an increase of only L. 8,332.4.2 (or just over fl. 1,190), a meager gain of about 2.4 percent over 1530.

The monte's inability to regain the sound financial standing it had enjoyed before 1530 discouraged deposits; lack of an infusion of new capital in turn kept it weak. The totals held by all creditors rose slightly from 1533 to 1539, but declined slightly from 1539 to 1542. This situation was concurrent with continued demand on the monte's resources as Florentines tried to cope with what might be called ducal normalization and the hard times that often follow war, especially a war of siege. From 1530 to 1533 the second branch alone realized fl. 721, L. 3,347.4.3 from the sale of "pawns of various

8. MP 742, 1a–2b; MP 738, 80a–81b.
9. MP 744, 1530, 1b and 57b; these last two accounts belonged to Domenico di Lorenzo da San Cervagio, and to Giovanni di Messer Niccolò d'Anghiari and others.

kinds."[10] The records do not state the number of pawns auctioned off, but this large sum, which accrued from the sale of pawns remaining unredeemed after a year, implies that many Florentines found it impossible to accumulate both the interest and principal to buy back their pledges from the monte. During the same period, the second monte had to meet "ordinary expenses" not including salaries of L. 1,804.13.6. Such costs for all three branches amounted to L. 3,444.3.8.[11] To make things worse, fire struck the third branch in 1533, with the resulting loss entered in the ledgers as "burnt pawns" valued at L. 100.6.[12] Finally, through its first three decades of operation the monte had suffered serious losses from inept or even dishonest officials, and it was only partially successful in repairing those damages.[13]

It is not difficult to read, between the neat lines of the ledgers, a sense of uncertainty and crisis. From January 1531 through 17 November 1533 when the books were balanced, the monte collected L. 8,275.13.3 in interest alone (*meriti*) on a total of fifty-five hundred pawns. Redemptions brought in L. 24,889.3.7.11.[14] The institution remained true to its charitable goal by keeping the pawn shop up and running, but the lack of new deposits ruled out any expansion of its lending activities.

A new scheme was needed to restore the monte's capital and to recapture the stability of the years prior to the siege of Florence. To meet this need Alessandro decided to increase the cost of borrowing money on secured loans from the monte di pietà. This strategy meant that those in need would be asked to increase the subsidy of their own relief. A provvisione of 23 July 1532 noted the concern of the duke and his advisers for all facets of civic life, "but especially for the care of the poor." Furthermore, His Excellency was aware "of the disorder into which the monte [di pietà] fell from the year 1529 to 1530," and—aiming a blow at the last republic—placed the blame for this sad outcome on "those who used to govern the city then." The withdrawal of "some seventeen thousand florins" had left the monte di pietà "virtually exhausted" of funds, yet the institution,

10. MP 744, 1530, 30b. This amount, added to the current account for "resti di pegni venduti di più sorte" of 30 June 1530, came to fl. 1,030, L. 9,661.2.2.

11. MP 744, 49a.

12. MP 744, 2b, 57a. A previous fire had caused lesser damages.

13. The serious losses resulting from fraud and theft are treated in Chapter 7.

14. MP 744, 1530, 49b.

"with no little difficulty, and no little effort," had struggled "to keep open [its] doors for the care of the poor needy." Heroic as this effort had been, some other means of increasing the monte's capital was called for. With the approval of the Senate of Forty-Eight, in July 1532 Alessandro licensed the monte to collect, for a period not to exceed five years, two denari per month for each lira borrowed on secured loans, thus doubling the per annum interest rate from 5 to 10 percent.[15] If at the end of five years the institution's fiscal health improved, the profit made should be returned to those persons "who had borne this interest."[16] During the prescribed five-year period the monte di pietà collected L. 60,824.15.1, proof that its small loan business was booming despite the greater cost of taking a loan. When the five-year term expired in 1537, the eight then placed a surcharge of four denari, equal to one quattrino, on each loan.[17]

Flat taxes fall hardest on the poor, and this charge on each loan was no exception. In October 1539 the eight monte officials, lamenting the "indigence and the need of poor persons . . . and the exhaustion and lack of funds," declared a return for one year to the original interest rate of 5 percent, or one denaro per lira per month. Presumably this decision meant that the monte would forego collecting the four-denari surcharge on loans for this period.[18]

15. Senato de'Quarantotto 1, 22v; also available in MP 2, Parte degli Statuti, 12v–14r.

16. MP 4, 188v. The compiler of this collection, which dates from 1667, made particular reference to the hardship this provvisione brought. The insistence on restoring the excess interest to those who had paid it was an old theme: the monte's original statutes had called for such restitution. The practice was ended by Leo X's bull ordering the monte to aid the Company of the Good Men of San Martino instead.

17. On income realized at 10 percent, see MP 752, 124a. The sum was posted as a credit under the rubric "meriti dell'anno '32 al '37 a 10 per cento." On the four-denari surcharge in addition to the regular interest, see MP 2, Parte degli Statuti, 14r, 27 Feb. 1537 (O.S.): "si provvede che i Kamarlinghi de'Monti . . . siano obbligati e devino ritenere a qualunque impegnerà a' detti Monti cosa alcuna danari quattro per ciascuna partita oltre all'ordinario, dovendo annotare in margine . . . tale ritenzione e tenerne diligente conto." Later sources suggest that the fee might have been collected when the pawn was redeemed, rather than off the top when it was presented as collateral for a loan. See the addendum to Pratica Segreta (PS) 4, no. 44, whose title suggests that the money was paid only by those who actually redeemed their items: "Informatione del provveditore de'monti di pietà sopra denari quattro per pegno, che si ritiene a' poveri che risquotono i pegni" (that is, the four denari came from "the poor who redeem their pawns").

18. MP 26, Deliberazioni, 28 Oct. 1539: giving consideration "ad indigentiam et necessitatem pauperum personarum et indigentiam maxime de presentis . . . et ad

The surcharge, however, became a fixture, but not because of any benefit it brought to the monte di pietà. The eight officials who originally approved it wanted the resulting income handed over to "pious works" other than the monte di pietà. Many years later, reviewing the circumstance of the decision to levy this fee as well as its effects, Cosimo's Pratica Segreta noted, "It was ordered that one quattrino per pawn be kept . . . in order to give it to pious houses. . . , and in the year 1538, [the monte began], and Your Excellency ordered the provveditore of the monti, to pay it to the Chapter of San Lorenzo, and thus it was done." In 1558 the monte di pietà's officials claimed that over a period of some nineteen years San Lorenzo had benefited to the tune of 2,323 ducats. Thus the monte di pietà's poor clientele was put by Cosimo into the position of subsidizing a favorite Medicean institution, the church of San Lorenzo, though the money was intended for relief of the poor. In 1557 over fl. 250, raised by the surcharge and authorized by the Pratica Segreta, were used to defray the costs of cleaning the second monte branch after the terrible flood of that year.[19]

In June 1533 the Senate of Forty-Eight, seeking a way to help the monte di pietà recover its financial stability, passed a law allowing the monte to accept deposits on which it would pay interest of 5 percent. The statute was strengthened by a clause that backed up the monte's fiscal credibility by placing both its property and that of the commune behind it.[20] Although the implementation of this change was delayed (the first instance of payment of interest on a deposit in the monte appears only in November 1539), its eventual impact on the monte di pietà was revolutionary.

The decision to accept deposits on which it would pay interest was not unique to the Florentine monte, for other monti di pietà in Italy had found it necessary to offer interest as an incentive to potential

---

exhaustatem et . . . penuriam pecuniarum . . . deliberaverunt. . . . Quod in futurem pro tempore et termino unius anni . . . incipiendi die prima mensis decembris commodatur et commodari possit et debeat ad rationem Denarii unus . . . pro libram."

19. PS 4, no. 44. See also MP 762, 219a–b: "Ritentione di danari quattro per pegno in virtù di partito della praticha segreta di Sua Excellentia Illustrissima dè dare fiorini 252, L. 5.12. . . . per pagarli a più persone per spese fatte nel secondo monte per causa della piena l'anno 1557."

20. Acquisti e Doni 281, 2, "Memorie sull'erezione del monte di pietà"; MP 4, 188v; and Senato de'Quarantotto 1, 61r–v (10 June 1533).

depositors. As early as 1475, for example, the Pistoian monte di pietà, founded only two years earlier, paid between 1 and 7 1/2 percent interest on deposits.[21] Scanty evidence also suggests that Prato's monte di pietà accepted money at interest from individuals; it expected to "take in at interest" one thousand florins from private persons.[22]

One Pietropagolo di Mariotto, known as Il Perugino, received the first recorded payment of interest on a deposit in the Florentine monte di pietà. On 3 January 1538 he deposited L. 402.10,[23] and with his account accruing interest at the rate of 5 percent, the bookkeepers noted on 6 November 1539 that "We made good to him L. 78.2 as interest from 3 January 1538 through the 17th of this month on the sum of money above."[24] Pietropagolo withdrew this payment for his own unstated purposes, leaving the principal on deposit, and was posted forward as a creditor of the monte in the amount of L. 402.10. See Appendix A, Table 4, Accounts of the First Eighteen Depositors with Interest-Bearing Accounts, 1539–1542.

Why the delay between the authorization of interest payments on deposits and the first payment? The provvisione itself offers no clues, for it simply stated that the eight could authorize the monte to give 5 percent "for the future." The likely explanation is that the officials expected the increases in interest and the surcharge, measures that would not cost the monte money, to solve its problems, restoring the capital lost during the siege of the last republic without necessitating the payment of interest. The five-year period of 10 percent interest on loans ended in mid-1537; Pietropagolo's deposit began earning interest in early 1538.

This change in policy was not an instant solution, however, and in 1539 the monte's inability to reverse its declining fortunes led to drastic measures. From 14 May through 17 November the officials found it necessary to borrow nearly a thousand florins "for the needs of the monte." This sign of distress meant that the monte di pietà was unable to provide adequate help from its own assets dur-

21. Capecchi and Gai, *Monte della pietà a Pistoia*, xi, 74.

22. From the "Quaderno di memorie" of the monte di pietà of Prato, quoted in A.G.B., "Monte di pietà," 99–100.

23. MP 748, 55a–b, 64b.

24. MP 750, 18b. A little later the eight agreed to pay Monna Gostanza, the widow of Cipriano, a used-clothing dealer, 5 percent on a deposit of seventy florins; MP 26, Deliberazioni, 24 Feb. 1539 (O.S.): "Quod in futurem solvatur: pro deposito fl. 70 ad rationem quinque pro cento."

ing the late 1530s. However, the plan to attract capital by paying interest on deposits worked. By the time the account books for the years 1542–45 closed, deposits at interest had begun to flood into the institution.[25]

These changes of the late 1530s and early 1540s took place in a time of trouble. In 1537 Florentines were shocked by the assassination of Alessandro and the insecurity that always accompanies political turmoil. The early years of his successor Cosimo's rule were not made easier by the famine and economic stagnation that affected many levels of society. The officers of Por Santa Maria, the master wool-weavers' guild, received permission from the Magistrato Supremo in September 1539 to "recall and bring back" into the city a number of master weavers whose flight from Florence "because of debt" was largely responsible, in the eyes of the Magistrato, for the hard times in the cloth industry.[26] The same magistracy became alarmed at the departure of debt-ridden contadini from the land and deplored the resulting waste of arable land and the effect on the Florentine food supply. The peasants had fallen into "calamity and misery" because of the "universal sterility and penury of the present year 1540," and so the Magistrato went to the unusual length of declaring an eight-month moratorium on the private debts of contadini in an effort to entice those who had left to return, and to persuade those who were wavering to remain on their lands. Any creditor who pestered them for repayment would be subject to a fine of one hundred lire.[27]

Florence's poor needed relief from "the misery and poverty which today are found in the city." Unheard of numbers of poor, the Magistrato observed, could no longer provide themselves and their dependents with life's necessities and had no recourse but begging. Here Duke Cosimo, playing the role of universal father to his sub-

25. MP 748, 62b, 56a, 57a–b, and 64a–b. "Giuliano Capponi e Averardo Salviati, dua de' nostri ufitiali deputati dal'ufitio nostro a trarre a' cambio certa somma di danari debbono havere [here follows a list of sixteen entries from May through Oct. 1539] e addì 17 novembre 1539 debbono havere [L. 10] per resto di fiorini 995.8.6 presi a cambio per noi che del resto ne sono in credito Niccolò Cioni nostro cassiere." The rate of exchange was exactly seven lire per florin.

26. MS 5, Protocolli de'deliberationi, 11r, 4 Sept. 1539.

27. MS 5, 48r–v, 9 Jan. 1539 (O.S.).

jects, had to take action. It was proper for "any good, discreet and just prince . . . to provide for the nurturing and maintenance of his poor people with an act of charity; nor should he tolerate their dying of hunger in his city." The duke thus consented to the creation of the Commessari Sopra i Poveri Mendicanti, charged with looking after the needs of beggars.[28]

Cosimo was only a teenager when he became ruler of Florence in 1537, but he harbored no illusions about the realities of the European political arena. He would have to deal with the French king and the Holy Roman emperor, who at the time of Alessandro's death were engaged in their third war. When the Truce of Nice of 18 June 1538 ended the latest stage of the hostilities between the Most Christian King and His Catholic Majesty, the relieved Magistrato Supremo ordered celebrations and closed shops on 1 August because God had "liberated [Florence] various times from many . . . dangers." The magistracy noted the announcement of the reconciliation of the two monarchs, particularly the "many and diverse signs of reciprocal love and exuberant affection" that meant that the two were now "true and good brothers and sincere friends." With presumably unintended irony, the Magistrato Supremo recorded that while Francis and Charles had agreed to "perpetual friendship," they had signed only a ten-year truce.[29] Truly Cosimo's political world would know little permanence, which in the 1540s made the search for stability in Florence all the more important.

In such a world the importance of the security offered by the monte should not be underestimated.[30] First, unlike banks, the monte did not invest deposits in ventures, because their failure could send it into bankruptcy. Instead, it lent out the money in secured loans. Second, since the monte di pietà handled its paperwork conscientiously, questions about the deposit—amount, date, rightful creditor—could easily be answered by referring to the ledgers or other books. Third, its surplus cash was, by statute, kept under lock and key, or rather, under locks and keys, to prevent theft. The importance of security was also revealed later when Cosimo's Pratica

28. MS 5, 62r–v, 13 Feb. 1539 (O.S.).
29. MS 4, 29 July 1538, 81v, and 31 July 1538, 87v.
30. I am grateful to Richard Goldthwaite for his most helpful comments on this issue.

Segreta took up the issue of reform of monti elsewhere in Tuscany. The Pratica ignored the advice of the Florentine captain in Prato, who had argued that the Pratese monte, protected by "extremely strong walls" and located "under the palace of the Podestà," would be wasting its money if it hired a guard to sleep on the premises. Paying a guard, the Pratica concluded, would be "reasonable . . . for satisfaction and security." It showed similar concerns when reviewing the proposed reforms of the monte di pietà of Arezzo.[31]

From November 1539 through 17 November 1542, when the ledger was balanced, eighteen new deposits accrued interest (see Appendix A, Table 4). While this number may not seem substantial, it becomes significant against the background of the monte's lackluster history of attracting donors since the days of Marco Strozzi's enthusiastic fund-raising in the 1490s. His goal had been to acquire, quite literally, the initial monte, a "mass" of capital with which the institution could begin its operations. Once this "mass" was collected, the institution was expected to use and reuse it to lend to the poor. But this process was hardly designed to turn a profit and as a result was a limited means of increasing capital. Paying interest on deposits, however, would lead to an increase in the monte di pietà's business and its capital as new deposits came in. By midcentury the monte would enjoy an influx of deposits, some of them substantial, at interest. With this change the establishment adopted a policy that guaranteed a profit to anyone willing to subsidize its charitable activities, and whatever pretenses it chose to maintain, it recognized it could no longer rely on "gratis" deposits and individual generosity.

Examination of these first eighteen depositors yields a rough group portrait. Of the eighteen, one was a corporation, the Capitani del Bigallo. Only five men, of whom one was a religious, made deposits, perhaps because men generally exploited other entrepreneurial outlets available to them. Twelve of the accounts were held by women. The following list shows the average amount of interest earned by these groups during 1539–42.[32] Amounts are rounded to the nearest lira.

31. On Prato, PS 9, no. 12, 28 June 1571. On Arezzo, PS 5, no. 56, 12 Sept. 1562, 558r. Lelio Torelli approved the Pratica's resolutions on both occasions.
    32. MP 752.

Group (no. of depositors)	Average interest
Men (5)	L. 40
Women (12)	L. 50
Corporation (1)	L. 36
All depositors (18)	L. 47

The average value of the accounts by group as of 17 November 1542 is as follows. Note that two depositors had closed their accounts by this date.

Group (no. of depositors)	Average account
Men (4)	L. 296
Women (11)	L. 639
Corporation (1)	L. 386
All depositors (16)	L. 538

These figures show not only that, during 1539–42, nearly two-thirds of those setting up deposits at interest were women, but that women also held much larger average deposits in the monte di pietà than did males. This had been a trend throughout the monte's history, since more women than men had been creditors of the monte di pietà in its early years. In many cases the money these women invested came from their dowries, and they were contractually obliged to place the money only in land or in secured investments.

Equally noteworthy is the absence of the patriciate from the ranks of depositors during the first years interest was paid on deposits. Men in the highest social and political echelons could find ways of making greater profits than the 5 percent offered by the monte di pietà on deposits. A classic example of the tie between more lucrative investments and public service may be found in the appointment, in 1539, of the eight new officials of the monte comune, the funded public debt. Ottaviano di Lorenzo de' Medici, Jacopo di Ulivieri Guadagni, Jacopo di Messer Bongianni Gianfigliazzi, Filippo di Alessandro Machiavelli, Raffaello di Luca Torrigiani, Luigi di Francesco Pieri, Averardo di Alessandro Salviati, and Matteo di Lorenzo Strozzi took office on the condition that they lend the commune sums ranging from one thousand to over three thousand florins, "with those emoluments or, truly, interest that in one or more occasions will be declared by their magistracy." The Magistrato Supremo stated that these eight were to receive 12 percent per annum, a healthy return on such a secure investment by any standard, and certainly in comparison to the monte di pietà's 5 percent. Because these sums were not sufficient for the commune's needs, Gherardo di Bartolomeo Bartolini was allowed into the profitable scheme in return for a loan of two thousand florins. A lack of capital was no bar to participation: two-thirds of Ottaviano de' Medici's three thousand florins were provided by six other patricians.[33] As this investment was open only to these officeholders (and, apparently, to friends of Ottaviano de' Medici), it was by definition closed to women.

More evidence suggests that men with money to lend could expect to find a borrower willing to pay 12 percent. In the early 1550s as he prepared secretly for war with Siena, Cosimo de' Medici had to turn to private lenders, including at least one who had provided funds at 12 percent to the monte comune as noted above. The records of the General Treasury, the Depositeria Generale, show a series of such loans.[34]

Lender	Amount lent	Amount repaid
Francesco da Mugnale	fl. 1,000	fl. 1,020
Girolamo da Sommaia	2,000	2,040
Giovanni and Piero Dini	1,000	1,020
Calandro Calandri	500	510
Duchess Eleonora	3,000	3,060
Girolamo Guicciardini	1,000	1,020
TOTAL	fl. 8,500	fl. 8,670

All six loans were for a duration of two months at 12 percent per annum, and the same terms prevailed in these loans to the duke as had prevailed in the loans to the commune. First, the interest rate was attractive, far more than that of the monte di pietà. Second, the

33. MS 4, 6 June 1539, 173r–v. Ottaviano's co-investors were Agnolo Strozzi, Simone and Niccolò del Nero, Ruberto Acciaiuoli, Andreuolo Zati, and Girolamo da Sommaia.

34. Depositeria Generale (DG), Parte antica 948, nos. 104–7, 111.

investment was secure, as the prestige of the duke in one case and the commune in the other was at stake. Finally, except for the duchess, who obviously occupied a privileged position, the lenders were patrician men. Eleonora had access to more liquid cash than most people in Florence, men or women. On the other hand, in February 1556 she took a ten-day loan from her husband of three thousand scudi d'oro in oro and was charged no interest.[35]

Of the first eighteen interest-accruing accounts in the monte di pietà, both the principal and interest of fourteen were left untouched during 1539–42. The bookkeepers credited these accounts with interest, but did not actually pay money out to the accounts' bearers. Income from all redemptions of pawns during this three-year period came to L. 44,023.15.1; after subtracting the monte's debits, the accountants recorded a surplus of fl. 23, L. 103.4.11.[36]

The first signs, after about three years of deposits at interest, were encouraging. The commencement of interest payments on deposits not only added to the monte's functions by allowing it to serve as a savings bank, but also widened its circle of depositors. The institution had long attracted occasional small depositors from both within and without the city, but it now offered a sound, if conservative, investment that enabled it to compete successfully with other enterprises. Most notable among these new depositors was the Compagnia della Misericordia of Pisa, which in 1545 earned a total of L. 1,989.17.10 in interest on a deposit of L. 37,500. The company withdrew the interest but left the principal on deposit. From Florence the Compagnia di Santa Felicità made a deposit of L. 70.12 on which it earned L. 3.13 in interest.[37] Individuals too began to place sums in the monte. These persons had made the leap from viewing the monte di pietà as a charitable holding company that kept their money safe, intact but unaugmented, to a bank offering a sound opportunity for investment.

Through the mid-1530s the monte had enjoyed the use of money placed in it for safekeeping by patrons who made a contractual

35. DG, Parte antica 950, no. 795 6 Feb. 1555 (O.S.).

36. MP 750, 74a–b. About a third of the total of L. 44,023.15.1, received from redemptions, had been brought forward from old accounts ("Recò meriti di contro deono havere per tanti posti dare L. 15,093.1.5"). The remainder came from the current operations of the three monte branches ("per tanti messi . . . a entrate . . . e per meriti di pegni riscossi").

37. On the Misericordia, MP 752, 123a, 125b; on the Compagnia, MP 752, 122a.

agreement with the institution that it would pay the sums as dowries upon the marriage of the woman in whose name the account had been opened.[38] But this practice had not become widespread, for although the monte was a safe place to keep money, deposits placed there did not accrue interest. Now that this shortcoming had been remedied, the monte di pietà caught the eye of Florentines once again. In 1546 the provveditore Chiarissimo de' Medici received a deposit of fl. 14, L. 2 from Lorenzo di Matteo Strozzi through the Salviati bank on behalf of one Benedetta di Giovanni di Lanzotto. Her benefactor was a member of a family distinguished as old friends of the monte di pietà. The relationship between the two was not spelled out, but she was most likely his servant, and Lorenzo was named as her heir. The money was to earn interest while it remained on deposit until such time as the girl married or entered the convent. Over one and one third years, interest of fl. 1, L. 1.6.8 accrued, and Benedetta was forwarded as a creditor in the amount of fl. 15, L. 3.6.8.[39] With the extinction of the dowry fund during this period, the monte di pietà began to attract more deposits specifically intended for dowries.

The convenience of a monte account appealed to another group of Florentines, namely, those who wanted or needed to place their capital in real estate or secured investments like bonds. Florentines were keenly aware of the importance of preserving their family's patrimony and by the mid-sixteenth century resorted to the legal devices of primogeniture and, in Goldthwaite's words, "ties of inalienability" of their property to do so.[40] Thus in March 1546 Felice

---

38. There seems to have been an attempt to encourage in the minds of Florentines a link between the monte di pietà and dowries. Not only did the monte willingly accept deposits earmarked for this purpose, but its directors had, in 1507, appropriated one hundred florins of the monte's "profits" to endower poor girls. MP 19, 14v. At least one translation of Niccolò Machiavelli's will of 1511 claims that Machiavelli specified that some of his possessions should be sold to the monte di pietà's creditors so that his widow might live off the proceeds. However, this translation is mistaken; the will refers to the sale of some of Machiavelli's goods, with the proceeds used to acquire either real estate or *credits* (not creditors) in "the monte," a clear reference to the monte comune ("converti debeat in emptionem, sive acquisitionem creditorum Montis vel bonorum immobilium"). The incorrect English translation comes from Anthony J. Pansani, ed., *Niccolò Machiavelli and the United States of America* (Greenvale, N.Y., 1969), 1227–28. For the will in the original, see Niccolò Machiavelli, *Opere complete di Niccolò Machiavelli* (Palermo, 1868), xxxiii–xxxiv.

39. MP 754, 97a–b.

40. Goldthwaite, "Medici Bank," 9.

di Zanobi Brunacci was credited with thirty-seven florins, which he had to place in secured investments, this sum representing some of the proceeds from the sale of a house. The money did not remain in the monte long, for Felice withdrew it about two months later. But his money was safe and could at least accrue 5 percent interest while he looked for the right investment.

The monte also attracted the attention of legal guardians of minors, who sought a safe investment for their charges' inheritances. The survivors of Matteo Vannegli had an account that, accruing interest, came to L. 1,072.17 by November 1545. The heirs of one Matteo, a master tanner, saw their principal increase to L. 2,288.4.6 as of the same date. Roberto Alamaneschi's heirs enjoyed credits of L. 5,699.11.7.[41] Similarly, minors whose affairs were in the hands of the Office of the Pupilli sometimes received monte accounts, and their inheritances, placed in the monte, earned a safe 5 percent annually. In one case, Filippo Calandri, provveditore of the Pupilli, opened an account of one hundred florins for the heirs of Giovanni, called Carnescale, da Scarperia.[42]

Occasionally, religious who found no other place to invest or who perhaps believed in the monte's charitable purposes placed money there, showing no overt qualms about the interest their deposits earned. One Fra Pietro, an Observant of Santa Maria del Monte Ortone then serving as subprior of the convent of Santo Spirito in Florence, placed one hundred florins in the monte di pietà in January 1546. Until the brother closed the account in September of that year, it earned fl. 3, L. 1.6.9 in interest.[43]

When the triennial ledger was closed on 17 November 1545, the monte counted 133 creditors, by far the largest number in its history to that point. Nine creditors held "internal" credits (interest the monte had collected on loans and so on). Forty-four held old deposits that did not earn interest (such as the fl. 99 placed in the monte by "Magnifici signori nostri" back in the 1490s). But 80 new deposits, all dating from 1538 or later and some very substantial, earned interest. The average value of these 80 interest-earning ac-

41. MP 752, 125a–b.
42. MP 754, 100a–b. These heirs were posted forward as creditors of the monte for a total of fl. 107, L. 4.10 on 17 Nov. 1548.
43. MP 754, 91a–b.

counts was about L. 1,878,[44] which at seven lire per florin would come to about fl. 268. An average account left on deposit would earn about fl. 13, L. 3.10 in interest annually.

In addition to balancing the income and outgo books and the ledgers at the beginning of each three-year period and posting the accounts forward into the new ledger, periodically during each triennium the bookkeepers balanced all current accounts in order to keep track of the monte's financial condition at a given moment in time. When the officials whose terms began on 18 November 1557 rendered such an interim balancing of accounts, they listed numerous debtors and creditors who had been consigned to them by their predecessors.

Two pages chosen at random from the book of debtors and creditors of 1557–60 list 88 accounts.[45] Of these, 38 belonged to women, many of whose hopes for marriage rested in these deposits, which represented their future dowries. A number of them were placed in the monte by the officials of the Pupilli or by other male guardians. Fourteen accounts were credited to unspecified heirs, who, however, must have been predominantly if not exclusively male, for the simple reason that female heirs usually enjoyed credits in their own names because it was so very important to provide for their dowries. Five different corporate groups held accounts: the church of San Martino al Colle Alemite, the nuns of the Cross of Empoli, the workers of Santa Brigida, the provveditore of the abandoned poor, and the ducal Camera Fiscale (these accounts are examined below). The remaining 31 depositors were men, but a good number of their credits were dotal payments received from their wives and could be removed only for investment in securities or property.

Of the 83 accounts held by private individuals, only 5 mention the creditor's occupation, making the monte's records a poor source for the occupations of its creditors. Of the five occupations listed, only one was ascribed to a male, a cook, presumably practicing that trade. The others—two shoemakers, a poultryman, and a messenger (*procaccio*)—actually described the late husbands of widows, and were probably included in the entry for identification of the account

---

44. Sums have been rounded to the nearest lira in this computation. One account, that of the Florentine Misericordia, old but continuously active, did not earn interest.

45. MP 762, 19a–b; these two pages list creditors only. Most of these deposits dated from before 1557, but the books for 1551–57 are missing.

holder: Maria, widow of Giovanni the shoemaker, as opposed to Maria, widow of Giovanni from Pistoia. In all, 47 individuals were identified by surname, and another 10 by place of origin or nationality (da Prato, Tedesco, and so on). Of those creditors identified by surname, nearly 40 percent belonged to families in the politically active classes. While at this time generally the Florentine patriciate did not hold deposits in the monte di pietà, the ledgers contain some notable exceptions. The following list gives a sample of identifiable patrician depositors during 1557–60.

Depositor	*Amount*
Piero di Giovanni Arrigucci	1,400
Heirs of Giovanni Doffi	40, 4.15
Jacopo di Lazzero de' Medici	405, 3.19.8
Alessandra di Ms. Antonio Guidotti	500
Monna Ginevra di Giovanni Corbinelli	6, 5
Monna Piera di Francesco Galilei	204, 3.1
Camilla di Battista de' Nerli	105, 5.6
Monna Pippa di Francesco Becchi	59
Giovanni del Buono Busini	908, 5.1.8
Caterina di Stefano Betti	224, 2.1.8
Giovanni di Pandolfo Rucellai	4,206, 2.10
Heirs of Andrea Alamanni	39, 4.10
Francesco di Federigo Benintendi	301, 2.8
Maddalena di Matteo Martini	644, 4.15
Maria di Bindaccio Rucellai	52, 3
Gabriele di Gabriele Strozzi	384, 1.6
Monna Fiammetta di Piero Capponi	188, 2
Monna Ippolita di Gherardo Taddei	191, 2
Bartolomeo and Benedetto Doffi	21
Messer Sforzo di Vincenzio Almeni	5,946, 5.8
Heirs of Filippo Frescobaldi	651
Diamante d'Antonio Guicciardini	32, 3.3
Heirs of Jacopo Nucci	247, 6.15
TOTAL	fl. 16,762, L. 4

Altogether, these twenty-three depositors held about 26 percent of all accounts in the sample and deposited over fl. 16,762, L. 4 out of a total of fl. 30,192, L. 4.–.2. Thus these patricians held a disproportionate 55.5 percent of all money in the sample. The average amount of money held by each patrician was about fl. 728.[46]

As patrician deposits in the monte grew, some members of the middle class discovered in the monte di pietà a unique opportunity. In fact it may be argued that without deposits from this middle-class collective, the institution could not have functioned at all. But the many nonpatricians who together held an important stake in the monte di pietà are much harder to identify. Who was the obscure Giuliano di Domenico di Giusto, whose interest-bearing account amounted to fl. 40, L.–.14, in November 1557?[47] The heirs of Croce d'Antonio, former procaccio in Venice, might have belonged to a family of functionaries about whom really nothing of importance is known. Their credits of over fl. 473 earned interest to be paid to Monna Nannina, the widow of the deceased and guardian (*tutrice*) of the estate, though all withdrawals had to be authorized by Croce's brother Ser Giovanni. There can be no doubt that these depositors, largely unidentifiable, found the monte every bit as convenient and useful as did the duke or the patricians.

Like most Florentine institutions, the monte di pietà in the ducal period was dominated by the interests of the duke and the politically active classes, who not only ran it, oversaw its operations, and held the best paid positions in it but also invested in it more heavily than their small numbers alone might predict. Nevertheless, in contrast to the monte delle doti, the preponderance of whose shares were owned by about half of the wealthiest households in the city,[48] a much smaller percentage of Florentine aristocrats invested in the monte di pietà, and they invested along with tradesmen and middle-class widows. The monte di pietà, designed to address the needs of the poor in a dignified Christian way, was the most populist of the three great Florentine monti. And unlike other institutions, it carried out a valuable charitable purpose, and many of the beneficiaries of that charity remained persons of the lower and middle classes.

46. Figures have been rounded to the nearest florin. Of course with the smallest deposit amounting to less than fl. 7 and the largest to nearly fl. 1,000, the standard deviation is high. All these depositors belonged to families Litchfield identified as patrician; *Emergence of a Bureaucracy*, App. B, 362–82.

47. MP 762, 39a–b. The account accumulated interest until it reached fl. 542, when it was withdrawn to pay to her new husband.

48. Anthony Molho, "Investimenti nel monte delle doti di Firenze: Un'analisi sociale e geografica," *Quaderni storici* 4 (1986): 147–70.

In the 1560s the monte matured as a financial institution. Tuscans flocked to it to make deposits, for they viewed monte di pietà credits as a safe and sound investment. Borrowers took out large loans on which they paid interest and which they sometimes secured by pawning valuable items like jewels.[49] The monte began to figure prominently in the financial strategies of many Tuscans, both as an investment and as a source of loans.

An examination of deposits made in the 1550s and 1560s shows that deposits at interest fell into two broad categories—free deposits and conditional deposits—whose parameters had existed earlier but which became clearer as time went on. The first group included deposits fully redeemable at the pleasure of the depositor and over which no outside authority exercised control. Regardless of whether the entry specified the motive behind it, all free deposits were identifiable by their formulaic language: the money placed in them, along with interest it earned, could be withdrawn "at the pleasure" of the depositor. Conditional deposits were identified by language in the ledger stating that certain restrictions governed the deposit: in some cases it was payable to a second party or could be withdrawn only for certain purposes.

Free deposits found their way into the monte di pietà for various reasons. The monte could be counted on to carry out testamentary bequests, particularly those made to charity, so persons with charitable designs often left money there. In a typical arrangement, the widow Francesca di Mariotto Casini of Santa Maria Impruneta deposited thirty florins in the monte, "which she may withdraw together with the interest at her pleasure." When Francesca made her deposit, she expressed her desire that, in the event of her death, any money remaining in the account be paid "to a poor and good girl" to be selected by a designated agent in consultation with the monte di pietà's provveditore.[50] Francesca knew that while she lived she could make use of the interest that accrued and withdraw the principal at her pleasure, but if she died, her soul would enjoy the grace that redounded from an act of benevolence.

Free deposits might also earn interest which the depositor could order to be paid regularly to a second party. When exercised by the Medici, this practice became a useful form of patronage. Duke Co-

49. This is the subject of Chapter 6.
50. MP 762, 18a–b.

simo himself, acting through his Camera Fiscale, opened a monte account that, though its principal remained redeemable at his pleasure, accrued 5 percent interest payable to Alessandro di Gherardo Corsini as long as the beneficiary lived. Alessandro must have been getting along in years, for he had been among the first group of forty-eight senators named by Clement VII in 1532. The Corsini were frequently represented on the powerful four-man Magistrato Supremo and also served on the Otto di Guardia e Balìa, unmistakable signs of their patrician rank and of ducal favor. The family had not only preserved but increased its wealth and status during the duchy, as evinced by its construction of a fabulous palace on the Lungarno in the late sixteenth century.[51] Cosimo de' Medici did not make explicit his motive for granting this small subsidy to Alessandro Corsini, but it is most plausible that this was patronage, albeit more symbolic than substantive, for the ruler often granted pensions to men who had served him well.

A rare case of an identifiable Florentine working woman who was probably supporting herself by her trade after the death of her shoemaker husband emerges from the records of the free deposits. Prior to 1557 this widow, a warper (*orditura*), invested a modest sum of about thirty florins, with both principal and interest redeemable at her pleasure, in the monte di pietà.[52] She made occasional small withdrawals—three florins one month, twelve another—but the account still earned fl. 3, L. 3 in interest and contained twenty-three florins when the ledger was balanced in November 1560.[53] The monte di pietà attracted her deposit because it allowed her money to earn interest while not hindering its liquidity in times of need.

The second category of deposit was the conditional deposit, so

51. During the course of the sixteenth century, several of Corsini's relatives became senators, and one was an important courtier who held the position of steward (*sottomaggiordomo*) in the late 1570s. Ricci, *Cronaca*, 295v, 446v. Busini noted that Alessandro's father, Gherardo, had been an ardent republican, but switched his allegiance to the Medici in hopes of avenging the murder of his son in Naples. Thereafter, "Gherardo rose so much in stature that he was more Medicean than the others." Busini, *Lettere*, x, Jan. 1550, 98. For offices and appointments held by the Corsini, see Diaz, *Granducato*, 176–77, 246. On the palace, see Hale, *Florence and the Medici*, 190.

52. Because the two preceding ledgers are missing, it is impossible to know exactly when she made this deposit or for how much. When it was carried forward to the 1557–60 ledger, it amounted to fl. 34, L. 4 with accrued interest.

53. MP 762, 9a–b.

named because the ledger listed various conditions that the creditor had to meet before the monte di pietà would allow him or her to withdraw the deposit. Because the Florentine dowry fund had been absorbed into the ducal treasury in the 1540s (the last deposit placed in it was entered in 1569), Florentines were faced with the task of finding a new place to invest money set aside for their daughters' dowries. They turned in growing numbers to the monte di pietà.

Deposits in the monte di pietà which came from dowries were considered conditional because husbands could withdraw them only as long as they invested the cash in ways agreed upon in writing by the families involved. Usually—and this was a big advantage in placing dowries in the monte di pietà, at least in the short run—any interest that accrued could be withdrawn without restriction. In this way, families hoped to protect their patrimony. The dowry, though at least partly controlled by her husband, represented a woman's share of her father's estate, and her family usually insisted on written restrictions on its disposal. Many deposits in the monte di pietà came from dowries, and any conditions to which the contracting partners had agreed were carefully summarized in the monte's records. The monte di pietà became a safe and popular investment for husbands who had received some cash as a dowry. Jacopo di Lazzero de' Medici deposited four hundred florins, noted in the list of patrician deposits above, that had formed part of the dowry of his wife, Alessandra. The deposit earned the customary 5 percent, which Jacopo could use as he liked. The entry in the ledger stipulated that the principal might be withdrawn only if he planned to invest it in real goods or in monte comune credits. He was able, in 1560, to withdraw over eighty florins in accrued interest. For her part, Alessandra was concerned with a different dowry, that of her niece, also named Alessandra, for whom she provided a five hundred–florin credit in the monte di pietà. The niece's husband, Galeotto Pazzi, could spend the money only in the secured ways usually agreed upon for dowries.[54]

Often benefactors deposited funds in the names of girls to whose future husbands or convents the deposits and their accrued interest would be paid. The officials of the Pupilli made a number of such

54. MP 762, 22a–b. Alessandra and Galeotto withdrew interest of fl. 68, L. 2.6.8. In February 1560 the wife died; the account was made over to Galeotto and later closed out.

deposits on behalf of their female charges. By placing money earmarked for a dowry in the reliable monte di pietà, the officials could watch the deposit earn interest, protect the girl's future by insuring the survival of some of the family's patrimony, and exercise control over it themselves. Piero di Luca Guicciardini, for instance, died before his daughters Gostanza and Maddalena were married. But the two girls were assured of their upkeep as well as their dowries, for the Pupilli officials ordered fl. 900 deposited for them in the monte di pietà. The girls were not free to withdraw any of the money, not only because they were minors but because their guardians exercised complete discretion over it. Even small payments for the girls' everyday needs had to be authorized by the Pupilli officers: for example, they approved the expenditure of fl. 10 to buy clothes for one of the girls. Later they agreed to pay fl. 100 as part of Gostanza's dowry, and fl. 130 for Maddalena's. By November 1560 only fl. 5 remained of the principal of fl. 900 plus accrued interest of fl. 51.[55] In other cases the interest was allowed to accrue in order to make for a larger dowry. An example was the fl. 500 left to his daughter Maria by Niccolò di Ser Piero Martini. With her marriage prospects in mind, the officials of the Pupilli deposited this money in the monte di pietà, where at 5 percent it increased to fl. 542 by the time they released it to pay her dowry.[56]

Occasionally, conditional deposits represented sums given by a court. The Otto di Pratica decided that the priory of San Piero Scheraggi had suffered damages of 986 florins "for certain houses ruined in order to build the street along the Arno." Of this sum, fl. 54 were placed on deposit (the rest having presumably been reinvested in property) and could be withdrawn by the monks "on their declaration" and only if they intended to reinvest it in real goods for the priory. They evidently preferred to let their money collect interest, for in 1560 they were carried forward as creditors for fl. 77.[57]

Charitable instincts drove some Tuscans to leave conditional deposits, often with detailed restrictions, in the monte di pietà. A large deposit was entered in the name of Bartolomeo di Girolamo Buonagratia in the mid-1550s. He had left a legacy of four thousand florins that he had requested be paid to the Hospital of Santa Maria

55. MP 762, 46a–b.
56. MP 762, 39a–b.
57. MP 762, 15a–b.

Nuova. Because the monte di pietà's ledgers for that span of time are missing, it is impossible to know how part of this sum became lost; perhaps his heirs or the officials of the Pupilli made poor investments. In order to recover the several hundred florins that had been alienated, the city officials stepped in and ordered the remaining principal placed on deposit in the monte di pietà until it had increased to four thousand florins. Thereafter accrued interest could be withdrawn only on order of the Pupilli's officials. As it turned out, the principal of Buonagratia's deposit never reached four thousand florins again. In February 1559 it had, however, increased to fl. 3,997, L. 4.-.10, which apparently was close enough for the money to be withdrawn and handed over to Santa Maria Nuova.[58]

These several types of deposits reveal that Tuscans who used the monte as a savings bank did so for different purposes that are often clearly identifiable as parts of larger financial schemes. In thinking through the problem of how to provide for a dowry, a father or guardian often concluded that the monte di pietà offered the safety that such an important investment demanded. Scholars of the Florentine monte delle doti have uncovered the complexity and sophistication of the dotal strategies devised by Florentines of different social classes.[59] If these strategies grew in importance as dowries became inflated in the late fifteenth and sixteenth centuries, it is certain that, given their growing disappointment in the dowry fund, Florentines found it desirable to diversify investments intended to provide future dowries. In most cases of a deposit intended for or paid as a dowry, the entry in the monte di pietà's books noted that the deposit represented only a part of the endowment. A wise planner would consider placing part of the principal intended for the dowry in a conservative but dependable investment like the monte di pietà, and the rest elsewhere. The reliability of the monte di pietà made it, by the mid-sixteenth century, a consideration in the dotal planning of many fathers.

58. MP 762, 45a–b: "Bartolomeo di Girolamo Buonagratia dè avere fiorini 3,876, L. 4.10 . . . i quali fecono dipositare e magnifici signori consiglieri per seguire quel-tanto che per il testamento di Buonagratia dispone, . . . de'quali danari non s'à paghare alimenti sino a tanti non anno rifatto la somma di fiorini 4,000 come fu l'origine del deposito."

59. See Molho, "Investimenti," for, e.g., the case of Antonio di Francesco *legnaiolo*.

Even the first ledger, covering the period 1496–99, shows that some persons placed money on deposit freely and with no conditions except that they be able to withdraw it at their pleasure. Others placed detailed conditions on the deposit. But not until the reforms of 1573–74 did the monte's eight officials decide to reorganize the bookkeeping to accommodate these two kinds of deposits, suggesting once again that the monte's structures evolved to meet new demands on its services and not the reverse, and that those structures had to be amended in accord with the public's and the prince's requirements. In a brief prologue to a ledger that he began in 1574, the monte di pietà's provveditore, Giovanni Bizzeri, explained that this particular book would record "conditional deposits [*depositi condizionati*] according to the recently published reforms." At that time the monte held conditional deposits worth about fl. 230,000. Seventeen months later, in December 1575, when Bizzeri closed out the book, the total of conditional deposits had jumped to fl. 284,000, an increase of some fl. 54,000, or about 23 percent.[60] The conditional-deposit business was booming.

As in earlier years, the Medici had their hands in other people's deposits, one of which represented the largest deposit in the book. The Spaniard Baldassare Suares, husband of Signora Maria Martelli, daughter of a knight of Santo Stefano, owed his wife's original deposit of six thousand florins to the duke. To remove the money, Suares had to "invest it in secured investments for the security of the said dowry and [by] declaration of the Lord Officials of the monte or by His Highness [Don Francesco de' Medici], and give to him the interest of five percent." It had already earned fl. 91 in interest and remained as a credit when the ledger closed on the last day of December 1575, by which time it had grown to fl. 6,166. However, this credit remained only through the magic of creative bookkeeping, for in October, Baldassare Suares, with the duke's permission, had received fl. 6,000 in cash, "having promised to put them back into this monte within four years, and having provided guarantors."[61] In effect Suares received a loan against his own deposit.

A sample of creditors during 1557–60 shows only half the story, for the monte had debtors as well, as the following list shows. Be-

---

60. MP 1360, Libro di depositi condizionati, first folio (unnumbered), and 5b, 238a–b.
61. MP 1360, 74a–b.

cause the prior six years remain a blank thanks to the two missing ledgers, it is impossible to pursue the motives and authorization of all these loans and other debits, but at the opening of the 1557–60 triennium, the debits stood as follows.

The [monte di pietà] officials, our predecessors, should have from the debtors listed below, now assigned to us:[62]

Debtor	*Amount (fl., L., s., d.)*
Baldassare (former assistant)	fl. 179, L. 4.13.11
Raffaello (former assistant)	183, 2.4.7
Several bad and worthless debtors	473, 4.15.10
Our magnificent Signori	16,410, 6.5.6
Monastery of Santa Chiara	200, —
Agnolo Mannucci (former assessor)	27, 5
Giovanbattista Primerani (former employee)	624, 1.7.10
Francesco Peccotti (former assessor)	127, 1.19.8
Company of the Good Men of San Martino	474, 3.14
Giovanbattista de' Nobili (rent payments)	143, 2.2.6
Heirs of Niccolò Becchi	4, 4
Ms. Jacopo Polverini	1,400, —
Filippo Nerli	283, 1.17
Monna Margarita di Luca	55, 3
Giovanbattista Pandolfini	500, —
Ms. Donato Acciaiuoli	8, 5.8.4
Giovanbattista Pandolfini	153, 4
Giovanbattista di Giovanni	13,–.10.4
Bartolomeo Baroncelli	59, 5.3
Fiumi (river) officials	1,152, —
Giuliano Ricasoli	1,000, —
Duke Cosimo de' Medici	5,775, 6.4.10
Nicolaio Cioni	3,949, 1.18.6
Ser Agnolo del Favilla	112, 2
Monna Maria Mei	60, 1.3
Monna Nannina de' Medici	110, —

62. MP 762, 1b.

Chapter of San Lorenzo	219, 1.3
Alfonso della Casa	106, 1.15
Bartolomeo Rigolini	346,–.13.4
Wool guild	175, —
Lorenzo Tanini et al.	260, —
Alessandro di Jacopo de' Medici	252, 4.5
Ms. Marco degli Asini	222, —
Caterina di Pagolo, barber[63]	30, 5
TOTAL DEBITS	fl. 35,094, L. 3.5.2
And to balance this account	fl. 30,243, L. 2.16.5
TOTAL	fl. 65,338, L.–.1.7

Some of these entries were simply old, bad debts that the monte had no hope of collecting, such as the losses caused by Raffaello and other former employees. The two hundred owed by the Convent of Santa Chiara dated back to the first decade of the monte's existence. In 1506 a monte official, Jacopo Buongianni, was charged with a debt of two hundred florins, "which money he promises and obliges himself . . . to pay us as soon as he is able, and if he passes away before he has paid, he wishes and obliges his heirs to pay." Jacopo was to use this sum to purchase grain whenever that commodity reached forty-five soldi per *staio* (Florentine bushel). In this event the nuns of Santa Chiara were to request a loan, and they could then distribute the grain to the poor.[64] Jacopo died in 1508, praised for his good work while serving the monte but without having repaid this sum.[65] The largest single debt, after the uncollectible fortune lent out to the last republic in 1529–30 (to "our magnificent Signori"), was incurred by none other than Cosimo de' Medici, who in taking out this loan revived the practice of asking the monte to subsidize the expenses of ruling.[66]

In November 1563 the monte's bookkeepers balanced the institution's books. The impressive success of the campaign to attract de-

---

63. "She is made a creditor in the book because she was made a debtor here, which should not have been done." MP 762, 1b.

64. MP 727, 31a; MP 19, 3r–v.

65. MP 19, 11v.

66. This is the subject of the next chapter.

posits at 5 percent fairly jumps from the pages of the triennial ledger for 1560–63. In the years when deposits earned no interest, the monte had fewer than a hundred depositors at any given time. Now, 330 accounts had already earned some interest, with another handful deposited too close to the end of the triennium to have accumulated calculable earnings. The average account earned just under fl. 20 in interest during its term of deposit. Some were much more substantial: Tommaso di Jacopo de' Medici's deposit of fl. 1,610 had earned fl. 203, making it the largest account to that point in both interest and principal. Eleven other accounts earned more than fl. 100 in interest.

One striking development represented the fulfillment of a trend begun in the monte's earliest days: minors' inheritances placed in the monte, accruing interest until the heirs came of age and found a suitable use for the money. (See Appendix A, Table 5, Accounts of Heirs.) When all accounts were balanced in 1563, fifty-one were found to belong to heirs, many of whom were wards (*pupilli*). These accounts contained together fl. 13,981, L. 1.17.11, representing about 15 percent of the total credits of fl. 92,963, L. –.4.2.[67] The old connection between the monte di pietà and the Office of the Pupilli grew stronger once deposits began to earn interest.

Of these fifty-one accounts, several belonged to patrician families like the Strozzi, Pitti, and Villani. Many depositors, however, could not claim descent from the Florentine patriciate; the legacies of Domenico di Parente, or of Captain Bartolomeo Greco, for instance, fell into this category. The money that belonged to these heirs lay on deposit in the monte di pietà, accounting for a sizable chunk of the excess capital that allowed the institution to make large loans to the duke and his friends.

It did not take the Medici, always looking for economic opportunities, especially ones that offered the chance for patronage or other forms of political control, very long to infiltrate the institution. Alessandro had taken a big step when he removed the institution's eight governors elected during the last republic and appointed men he favored. He and his successors made sure that each group of eight included men on whom they could rely. In 1536, for example, Raffaello di Francesco de' Medici sat among the eight, along with

67. MP 764, 301b, 302a–306b.

other Medici supporters such as Lapo del Tovaglia and Averardo Salviati. Even more important, at the same time Chiarissimo di Bernardo de' Medici became *provveditore* of the monte; unlike the eight with their finite three-year term, he served at the duke's pleasure.[68] And Cosimo, while taking a page from Alessandro's book, wrote new volumes on the subject of the usefulness of the monte di pietà to the governance of his state.

It is tempting to suppose that, once the monte began to offer 5 percent interest on deposits, the hundreds of middle-class creditors who hastened to the monte made it their investment of choice, influenced by its reliable return of interest on deposits. No doubt many did open accounts solely to enjoy the fruits of their deposits. But by the 1560s most ledger entries noted any unusual reasons behind the opening of accounts, and most of these reasons belie the alleged attractiveness of the 5 percent interest rate on deposits. A random sampling of deposits made during 1566–69 reveals the particular motivations that typically lay behind deposits.[69] See Appendix A, Table 6, Sample of Creditors, 1566–1569.

The total of all credits, including interest and capital, in the names of a sample of forty-five depositors came to fl. 8,643, L. 5.18.6. Of this total, fl. 4,466, L. 2.8 remained at the triennium's end. In other words, nearly half—about 48.3 percent of the capital along with accrued interest—in the sample had been removed from the monte before the end of the three years, leaving just over half, 51.7 percent, on deposit. The flight of nearly half the capital in this sample brings home powerfully the constant state of flux in the monte, which depended on hundreds of depositors who placed money in it at 5 percent interest. These depositors did not see their deposits as long-term savings accounts the way today we might open a savings account at our local bank and keep some funds in it for decades.

Only eleven of the monte's forty-five creditors allowed their capi-

---

68. MP 748, first folio (unnumbered). Chiarissimo did not hold this position for life. In 1573 he was appointed to an important magistracy, the Nove Conservatori del Dominio e della Giurisdizione Fiorentina, the chief administrative body for the Florentine dominion. Diaz, *Granducato*, 177–78. Ricci (*Cronaca*, 2v, 418 and 29r, 478) mentioned that on his death in November 1587 he was *luogotenente* (lieutenant) in the Magistrato Supremo and that he had been named to the Senate of Forty-Eight in March 1587.

69. Three five-page samples have been taken at random from MP 768: 212a–216b, 285a–289b, and 349a–354b. See Appendix A, Table 6, Sample of Creditors.

tal and the accrued interest to remain untouched. These eleven
break down into several categories. One deposit represented a charitable bequest to a convent; apparently, the repair of the convent's
walls, the purpose for which the bequest had been intended, had not
yet been undertaken. Only one untouched free deposit belonged to
a male. Four were the property of widows, and although the monte's
records mention no restrictions on these four, it is likely these
women were investing all or part of their returned dowries. In such
cases, there may have been conditions placed on the disposition of
these funds. Further, the opportunities for investment for widows
were few, and the return of 5 percent on a monte deposit as well as
the security of the investment must have been attractive to them.
Three untouched deposits had been made as dowries and were,
therefore, conditional. Two had been placed in the monte in the
names of heirs by the officials of the Pupilli, so these two deposits
were conditional, not freely redeemable by the persons in whose
names they had been opened. Out of the eleven deposits in this sample that were allowed to accrue interest untouched, five were un-
questionably not free deposits, and the four belonging to widows
were probably conditional. Thus few persons, and almost no men,
voluntarily placed free deposits in the monte as long-term investments. Deposits whose principal remained untouched tended to belong to persons, like widows and wards, who were not free to remove them at their pleasure. Such a conclusion requires that the
argument for the monte as a bank of choice for the Tuscan middle
classes be revised. In many cases, it was the only choice available, the
only financial institution suitable for their purposes.

In nine cases depositors withdrew only an amount equal to or less
than the interest their accounts accrued. Among these was Monna
Ippolita d'Alessandro Rinuccini, the wife of Bernardo Machiavelli
(and incidentally from a family that provided two monte di pietà
massari in the sixteenth century). Her account stands out for two
reasons. First, she belonged to the city's patriciate, and second, the
ledger went into revealing if repetitive detail about her deposit, insist-
ing upon its free nature and her autonomous control over it. Hers
was a *conto a parte*, that is, a separate account belonging to her, earning 5 percent interest, and redeemable at her pleasure. As if this
were not enough, as if it were scarcely credible that a married
woman have under unsupervised control some six hundred florins,
the entry noted reassuringly that "at such deposit her husband Ber-

nardo Machiavelli was present and consenting, and affirmed such
money belonged to the said Monna Ippolita."[70] It is extremely rare
to find a woman in unequivocal and independent personal control
over a large free deposit in the monte di pietà. The very detail of the
entry testifies to the rarity of such cases and leads to the speculation
that many other monte di pietà credits belonging to women must
have been under the control of husbands, fathers, brothers, or sons,
even though this fact might not be explicit in the ledgers.

In several other accounts in which the interest alone was withdrawn, the depositors were constrained from removing the principal
except for placing it in secured investments or property. Francesco
Anichini, having deposited 450 florins from his wife's dowry in a
monte account, removed most of the interest his money had earned
but apparently had not happened upon a suitable investment for the
principal. Marietta Ruchetti, while enjoying usufruct of the interest
of her deposit, could not touch the capital, which was to be settled
on her nephew's two daughters as part of their dowries. Andrea del
Garbo and Niccolò Boni had both deposited proceeds from the sale
of houses or real goods and were allowed to use the interest as they
pleased, but were restricted when it came to use of the principal.
Several widows, living at least in part off the income from their deposits, withdrew interest only.

All told, in twenty cases, or about 44.4 percent of the sample, depositors withdrew no money at all or removed only an amount equal
to or less than the accumulated interest. Many of these deposits have
proven to be accounts restricted by clearly stated conditions.

On the other hand, twenty deposits were closed out by the end of
the period, the same number as those left untouched or reduced
only by withdrawal of interest. Ten of these were completely free
deposits. The remaining ten were conditional: four were to be reinvested only in property or secured investments; five provided dowries for women who had married or entered a convent; one was a
legacy controlled by the mother of a boy. In every case withdrawal of
the capital signaled either compliance with the conditions for removal or, in two cases, a change of heart about the investment. Five
more depositors removed their accrued interest plus part of the
principal for unstated reasons.

70. MP 768, 349b.

A challenge faced the monte when as many creditors withdrew every last soldo of their accounts as kept all the principal on deposit. Added to those who withdrew at least some of the principal, the former accounted for about 55.6 percent of all depositors in the sample. At a time when the monte was offering large and small loans at 5 percent and paying more in interest to depositors than it was collecting in interest payments on loans, the institution's fiscal stability rested on its ability to attract new depositors. The ideal client placed a generous deposit in its coffers and left both deposit and interest untouched as long as possible. But during the years 1566–69 almost half the deposits placed in the monte in this sample were withdrawn before the end of that period. Most deposits that could be removed were removed. The majority of those still remaining in November 1569 could be removed only for carefully stated purposes or belonged to women, whose entrepreneurial opportunities did not range far beyond the 5 percent offered by the monte and who, in the case of widows living off the interest, must have had to abide by the rules of fiscal conservatism.

The importance of not simply maintaining but of increasing the monte's capital becomes clear once the vast extent of the institution's pawnbroking activities is understood. The ledger for 1545–48 offers a glimpse into these activities, for unlike most of the other ledgers, it contains a detailed month-by-month account of pawns accepted and redeemed at each of the three branches. See Appendix A, Table 7, Number of Pawns Pledged by Branch, December 1545–November 1548, Table 8, Number of Pawns Redeemed by Branch, December 1545–November 1548, and Table 9, Debts Charged to Each Massaro. Figures for the second monte in Borgo Santi Apostoli, for example, depict a bustling office with the massaro Francesco Rinuccini straining to keep track of so many transactions.[71] Indeed, assuming twenty working days per month—by statute, the monte closed on *feste*, which would include Sundays and important feast days—monte officials at the second branch alone had to note, assess, and record in

---

71. The Rinuccini, like so many other monte officials of the ducal period, became important courtiers. Francesco's son Alessandro was made a senator in 1615. Ricci, *Cronaca*, 455, n. 1. Some family members, heads of an important bank, had the technical expertise required to help run the monte di pietà. Unfortunately the rich information of the ledger of 1545–48 does not extend to a listing of the names of individuals who borrowed against pawns. In fact, no such records exist.

triplicate the quality, nature, description, and owner of an average of seventy-five items each day.[72]

The sheer numbers involved at this single branch of the monte are astounding. At any given moment, each of the three massari was likely to have on his hands well over 16,000 pawns. For example, subtracting the number redeemed from the total on hand, we find that the second monte held 16,189 pawns on 18 November 1545 (when a new group of eight took office), against which it had made loans worth fl. 22,059, L. 2.15.[73] Ten months later the accumulation of pawns in that branch had grown by 857 to 17,046 and their total value in loans had increased by more than fl. 1,500 to fl. 23,604. When the totals were reckoned in November 1548, Francesco Rinuccini was responsible for 19,403 pawns, securing loans worth fl. 25,020, L. 4.18, that remained unclaimed at the second branch. Tripling these figures gives an idea of the activity at all three branches combined and shows a steady increase in demand during the three-year period.[74]

On the average, a person pawning an item at the second branch from December 1545 through September 1546 received about 1 1/4 florins per pawn. This is only an average, however, and monthly fluctuations occurred. The average loan against a pawn rose sharply from June through November 1546, dropping sharply in December.

The pattern of the number of pawns pledged is less definitive than that of their average value, but nonetheless yields several conclusions. The summer, fall, and winter months display a clear trend. Clients pawned a high number of items at the second monte during winter 1545–46, but the number fell off steadily toward the warmer summer months. Fewest pawns were taken in during the fall. The

72. The estimate of twenty days is just that—an estimate. In 1570 the duke's Pratica Segreta, reviewing the statutes for a new monte di pietà in Pescia, authorized the institution to lend "two or three days" per week (or about eight to fourteen days per month). However, Pescia was a small town compared to Florence, and these same deliberations called for a limit on its "monte"—its lending capital—to eight thousand scudi, a tiny sum in light of the total lent by the Florentine monte. No such formal restrictions governed the Florentine institution. It is likely that the three branches of the monte in the capital city were open more often to meet the demands of their clientele. On Prato, PS 9, no. 12, 28 June 1571.

73. As customers were to receive only two-thirds of the appraised value in loans, the assessed value of the pawns is 50 percent higher than this figure, or about fl. 33,089.

74. MP 754, 51a–b, 147a–b.

warmth of the summer and fall in Florence coupled with even the temporary abundance of harvest and postharvest months may explain this trend. In December, with the return of cold weather, pledges shot up again by a factor of about 3.75. This increase in numbers, however, was accompanied by a decrease in the average worth of each pawn pledged. This pattern continued until December 1546, when the average worth of loans against pawns declined from fl. 2.24 in November to fl. 1.18. Persons leaving pledges in this bleak month left items of far less value and were probably less well off.[75]

This trend is, for the most part, confirmed by the incidence of pawns redeemed. During the hard winter months in 1545–46, few persons came to the second branch to pay off their loans plus interest. By April more clients redeemed pawned items than came to the monte seeking secured loans. After a slight dip in late spring, the summer brought a high frequency of redemption that dropped precipitously in the fall, a season that appears to mark a point of equilibrium where few needed to pawn items for cash, but relatively few retrieved their pledges. Thus while the disappearance of the daily record books from each branch precludes definitive conclusions, these data nonetheless indicate seasonal changes in the well-being of the average Tuscan as well as a pattern of vigorous activity in the monte di pietà's pawnshop business.

Of course in any medieval or early modern city, seasonal fluctuations were to be expected. Winter and early spring brought an increased need for clothing and fuel, and coincided with the time when stores or cash put away to tide the least wealthy over the winter were liable to run short. In a city regulated, in effect, by the sun (in Renaissance Florence, sundown meant the closing of the gates and the imposition of the evening curfew), winter's brief span of daylight limited the hours during which one could earn a living or, in the case of the poorest, beg for bread. Conversely, summer and fall normally offered greater opportunities and were the time of harvest.[76]

75. The figures for November reveal the general failure to adhere to the legal limit of two florins per pawn.

76. See Gene A. Brucker, *Renaissance Florence* (New York, 1969; reprint with supplements, Berkeley, 1983), esp. 38–39, for seasonal fluctuations. Brucker notes that in winter, Florentines "curtailed their activities and, whenever possible, remained in-

The pattern of more pledges being made at the second branch in the hard months of winter and fewer in the prosperous months of summer generally held throughout 1547, though the trend is not as unmistakable as it had been a year earlier. Pledges reached a peak of 2,081 in January 1547 and stayed high through May when 1,956 were pawned. July (1,633), August (1,382) and September (1,597) marked a decline, followed by a sharp rise in October (1,882) and November (1,923), with a perplexing drop lasting from December through May 1548 (in these months 1,061, 1,332, 1,164, 797, 369, and 954 pawns were left as security for loans). But in June, the cittadini and contadini who came to the monte di pietà for aid brought 2,914 pawns. The numbers remained high throughout the summer (July, 2,474; Aug., 2,286; Sept., 2,562; Oct., 2,849; Nov., 2,785).[77] Redemptions, however, followed a predictable pattern: they tended to decline during periods when many items were pawned, and to increase during periods when the demand for loans went down.

A poor harvest in fall 1547, followed by a mild winter and a cold spring, might help account for these trends. In fact, one natural disaster alone could account for the pattern of the years 1547–48. In August 1547 heavy rains brought the worst floods in years to Florence and its contado. The entire quarter of Santa Croce was under water, and damage in both city and countryside was extensive. Groves of trees and even the very soil in the countryside were washed away as the waters receded. One writer estimated the losses at three hundred thousand scudi.[78] Workers in the city suffered first from the damages high water brought and second from the high bread prices damages to crops caused. Contadini watched helplessly as their grain was destroyed. The suffering of both groups accounts for the increased use of the monte di pietà for loans against pawns.

---

doors. The coming of the celebrated Tuscan spring brought a revival of energy and spirits, and also an influx of foreign visitors" (43). Fernand Braudel, in *Capitalism and Material Life, 1400–1800*, trans. M. Kochan (New York, 1973), describes the increasing dependence of early modern society on "the sequence of good and bad harvests" (19).

77. All statistics are from MP 754, 117a–b, 147a–b.

78. Mano. e Cod. Litt.—Bardi III, cod. 3, "Historia da fiorentina di Segni," bk. 2. The writer suggests that poor engineering of the Arno's bed had contributed to the devastation, the worst in two hundred fifty years. There may be truth to this explanation, for Cosimo later engaged engineers, at great expense, to make improvements.

Through February 1547 relatively few Florentines redeemed their pawns: only 981 pledges were retrieved by their owners that month. The pattern was broken in March when an astounding 2,525 pawns were redeemed. In the late spring and summer, redemptions leveled off but, in contrast to expectations, rose dramatically in November and December. The pattern of few redemptions in the spring, more in the late summer, and a precipitous drop in October then reappeared.

These patterns appear, with a few exceptions, in the records of redemptions at all three branches. The unexpectedly high number of redemptions at the second branch in March 1547 stands out in contrast to redemptions at the other branches (1,241 at the first, 877 at the third). Except for the 137 pawns redeemed in August 1548 at the third branch—the lowest number recovered from any branch during the three-year period under scrutiny—the patterns of redemption at the three branches are less notable for their discrepancies than for their similarities.

It must have taken a good deal of luck and intuition, not to mention a dash of wizardry, for the massari or camarlinghi to predict how much money the monte branches ought to keep on hand to meet the needs of their clientele. The number of pawns pledged ranged from a low of only 137 during March 1547 at the third branch, to just under 3,000 pledged during several months of summer and fall 1548. On several occasions two of the three branches labored under comparable levels of demand, as in the parallels between pledges at the first and third monti from January until May 1548. The third monte lent the smallest amount in one month of the three-year period when in March 1547 its outlay came to fewer than five hundred florins; less than a year earlier it had to meet demands for loans surpassing thirty-one hundred florins. The first and second branches were not subject to such wild fluctuations, but they too found that their clients' needs varied greatly from month to month and year to year.

One correlation that appears in the analysis of the activity of the second branch over the ten months from December 1545 through September 1546 is borne out by all branches over the three-year period. As a rule, if the average loan taken on a pawn increased, the number of pawns pledged declined. With only one exception, whenever during a given month the average loan exceeded 1 3/4 florins, fewer than nine hundred pawns were received for that month. Cor-

respondingly, when the average loan declined to less than 1.1 florins, the number of pledges skyrocketed to over two thousand per
month (again, with one exception). It is unlikely that the assessors at
each branch inflated their estimates of the value of pawns since they
and their guarantors were responsible for any resulting shortfalls.
Instead, the estimates most likely reflected the nature, quality, and
condition of the pawns themselves. Those who brought pawns into
the monte di pietà in exchange for loans during months when loans
averaged over 2.6 florins (as they did, for example, at the third
monte in February 1547) must have brought items of better quality
that were assessed at higher rates.

Though patterns of pawning and redeeming surely bear some relation to natural disasters, harshness of winters, success of harvests,
prices of bread, and so on, such influences offer only a partial explanation for the fluctuations evident from the tables in Appendix A.
Another explanation relies on differences in prosperity among
neighborhoods throughout the city. Persons seeking a loan from the
monte di pietà probably patronized the branch closest to their
homes, with the result that different branches reflected the character of the neighborhoods they served. By the mid-sixteenth century
the first branch occupied rooms rented from the Corbinelli in Via
Maggio in Santo Spirito.[79] The second was housed in premises
rented from the Acciaiuoli in Borgo Santi Apostoli on the right bank
of the Arno and parallel to the Lungarno that bears the landlords'
name. The third, originally located in a house leased from the Portinari not far from Santa Maria Nuova, east of the Duomo, moved
about two blocks south to a house owned by Giovanbattista di Jacopo
Pandolfini near Santa Margherita de' Cerchi. One would then expect to find, for example, that the first monte in Santo Spirito would
become extremely busy during times of depression—seasonal or
otherwise—in the cloth industry, for its clients would have included
the clothworkers of San Frediano.

---

79. The first branch had been located in a house near the small church of San
Remigio in the quarter of Santa Croce, but in 1503 the lease expired and the officials
decided to find a "more convenient" house. The document claims that this monte
branch was located near the church of Santa Felicità. That establishment, however,
was located not in Via Maggio but in (present-day) Via Guicciardini. A likely explanation is scribal error: the Corbinelli church was San Felice, not Santa Felicità, and the
church is situated at the southern end of Via Maggio where it meets Via Romana. MP
18, 8r.

Held responsible for the loans granted against pledges and credited for money taken in on redemptions and interest, each massaro had periodically to balance his accounts and keep a careful record of his debits and credits. An examination of the accounts of Francesco d'Alessandro Rinuccini, massaro at the second branch, shows how the accounts worked over each three-year period. At the opening of the triennium on 18 November 1533 the massaro's debits came to fl. 37, L. 67,248.12.

Periodically the accounts were brought up to date and balanced:

And on 6 August 1535 [he is debited] fl. 17, L. 155,642.6 for so much paid out, and entered in [the book of] outgo "Z" from 18 November 1533 through April of 1535 against 20,326 pawns.

And on 30 September [1535, he is debited] L. 50,726.1 for so much lent out against 5,235 pawns, as can be seen in detail in [the book of] outgo "Q."

And on 17 November 1536 [he is debited] L. 139,945.1 for so much paid out and entered in [the book of] outgo "A" from 20 September 1535 up to this day against 13,934 pawns. . . .

Total pawns accepted: 39,495
Total lent: fl. 17, L. 346,313.8
Total debit: fl. 54, L. 413,562.

Balanced against debits and entered on the page opposite them were the moneys Francesco took in on the monte's behalf from redemptions and interest on loans.

Francesco Rinuccini . . . is credited on 17 March 1534 [O.S.] fl. 21, L. 67,309.14 for the accounts of the capital of 7,712 pawns [*per conti di capitali di pegni* 7,712].

And on 20 September 1535, [he is credited] fl. 12, L. 120,170.7 for redemptions in [the book of] income "Z" from 18 November 1533 through this day. . . .

And on said day, [he is credited] L. 10,878.12 redeemed in [the book of] income "A" on 1,203 pledges. . . .

And on 16 November 1536 [he is credited] fl. 5, L. 35,471 for so much [in] redemptions in [the book of] income "Z" re-

deemed from 20 September 1535 through this day. . . on
4,203 pledges. . . .

And on the 17th of this month [he is credited] L. 95,533.7 for
so much in redemptions for capital on 9,730 pawns redeemed
from 20 September 1535 through this day.

TOTAL REDEEMED: fl. 38, L. 329,363

These credits, the total that Rinuccini's branch took in from redemptions and interest, were struck off from the total lent out, leaving a
debit of fl. 16, L. 84,199. On 17 November 1536 Francesco was
posted forward to the next triennial ledger as a debtor in this
amount.[80]

During the same period the account of Dino di Neri Compagni,
massaro at the third branch, showed that in November 1535 he was
responsible for a total of fl. 4, L. 72,165.1 lent out in unredeemed
pawns. In March the bookkeepers added the sum of fl. 3, L. 5,426.2
still outstanding on 555 pawns, technically the responsibility of
Dino's father Neri, who had preceded his son in this post. Another
figure—fl. 2, L. 41,709.9—joined the current account, given in
loans on 5,241 pawns in late 1534–35. Finally, loans on items
pawned during the past six and a half months of the triennium
brought the total amount pawned to fl. 9, L. 324,838.17.6.

During this period redemptions too came in and were struck from
the amount for which the massaro was responsible. This income reduced Dino's "debit" to fl. 9, L. 290,955.–.6, the amount still outstanding on loans made from the third branch when the books were
balanced on 17 November 1536.[81] At the same time Giovanni Cioni
at the first branch still held an unstated number of pledges against
which he had, on the monte's behalf, authorized loans of fl. 6, L.
166,692.13. Income from redemptions, however, reduced this
amount to fl. 6, L. 70,480.[82]

In November 1560 when the books were balanced, the book-

80. MP 746, 2b, 32a–b, 88a. The sums reported by the massaro were double-
checked by at least one other employee at his branch. Bartolomeo Baroncelli, cashier
at the second branch, kept track of redemptions and concurred in Rinuccini's tabula-
tions. The cashier also kept a list of his own debits and credits. See, e.g., Baroncelli's
accounts on 85a–b.
81. MP 746, 54a–b, 88a–b.
82. MP 746, 80a–b, 89a–b.

keepers received from the massaro of each branch his report of money currently outstanding in loans against pawns.

1st monte, Bernardo Miniati, massaro: fl. 20,572, L. 2.10, on 17,153 pawns

2d monte, Francesco da Filicaia, massaro: fl. 26,278, L. 6.10 [pawns not listed]

3d monte, Alfonso della Casa, former massaro: fl. 7,375, L. 2.6.8 [pawns not listed]

Baldo Tedaldi, new massaro: fl. 22,714, L. 2.18 [pawns not listed]

TOTAL fl. 76,940, L. –.4.8

Thus, nearly fl. 77,000 were outstanding at this given moment in loans against pawns.

In sum, from December 1545 through November 1548 the three branches of the monte di pietà accepted a total of 162,585 pawns. During the same period its clients redeemed only 146,950 pawns, a difference of 15,635. About 9.6 percent of all pawns, then, were left unredeemed by their owners during this period. To recoup these loans, the monte di pietà auctioned the pawns publicly, hoping that the prices fetched would cover the capital lent on the pawn as well as 5 percent interest.

The period from the mid-1540s through the late 1560s brought important changes to the monte as it accepted increasing numbers of deposits at interest and as it began to offer large loans at the duke's command. Its pawnshop activities, however, remained its raison d'être. Table 10, Number of Pawns Pledged by Branch, 1567–1569, and Table 11, Number of Pawns Redeemed by Branch, 1567–1569 (in Appendix A) show that from January 1567 through December 1569 all three branches together offered about fl. 370,150 in loans against 170,899 pawns. This last figure represents an increase of about 5 percent over the number of pawns in the late 1540s. As the number of loans increased, so did the percentage of pawns left unredeemed. During the same period 153,110 pawns were redeemed by their owners, leaving 17,789 pawns or 10.4 percent up for auction.

The second and third branches realized more income than outgo during 1567–69, although the first branch took in fl. 11,809 less than it expended. Overall, the monte di pietà had a shortfall of just over fl. 5,800 as a result. The first branch, the source of the short-fall, made by far the greatest number of loans. The 65,748 pawns it accepted amounted to 38.5 percent of all pawns the institution accepted during this three-year period. Redemptions at the first branch, however, were proportionally lower—about 36 percent. In addition, the average size of each loan (and by extrapolation, the average value of each pawn) made by the first branch, located in Santo Spirito, was small. On average each pawn was worth a loan of 1.64 florins at the first branch; in contrast, the second branch lent out an average of 2.95 florins on each pawn, and the third branch 1.96. The items pawned at the first branch were assessed as significantly less valuable than those accepted at the other two and probably came from poorer persons who were less able to redeem their pawns at the end of the loan's term.

Offering small loans to the poor remained the heart of the monte's mission, but from the mid-1540s comprised only part of its activities. It also accepted deposits at interest. At the same time, the monte had taken up, at Cosimo's command, the practice of making large loans to ducal clients. This activity rounded out the monte's growing identity as a banking institution. However, attempts to characterize the monte di pietà as merely the forerunner of the modern bank sidestep the most interesting and important facet of its development in the mid-sixteenth century: its integration into the machinery of ducal finance.

6 PATRONAGE, LOANS, AND THE EXERCISE OF DUCAL CONTROL

ON 4 MARCH 1545 Bartolomeo Gualterotti, "agent of his Excellency," borrowed L. 37,500 (or about fl. 5,357) from the monte di pietà. The ledger, recounting the circumstances of a loan far exceeding the amount the monte di pietà was allowed to lend against pawns, noted that "the above-mentioned money has been paid by order of his Excellency . . . and is payable on our demand with interest of five percent." From the inception of the loan until the closing of the books some seven months later, Gualterotti paid all the interest, which came to L. 1,317.13.8. He paid none of the principal, however, and so was posted forward as a debtor of the monte di pietà in the amount of L. 37,500.[1] This was the first of many large loans that the Medici dukes would authorize.

---

1. MP 752, Libro di debitori e creditori, 92a–b, 125a: "Nota come li sopradetti danari [L. 37,500] si sono paghati per hordine di Sua Excellentia . . . e per riavergli a ogni nostro piacere con alimento di cinque percento." The Gualterotti enjoyed Medici patronage throughout the sixteenth century. Antonio di Piero Gualterotti was among the first Forty-Eight created by Clement VII in April 1532, a sure sign of his Medicean sympathies. Ricci, *Cronaca*, 295v, 5. Giovanni d'Alberto was among one hundred gentlemen "dressed in brown with long capes and caps with veils" who made up an impressive courtly delegation at Cosimo's funeral. Ricci, 358r, 105. The total lent by the monte di pietà in large amounts during the five years of 1564–69 is over fl. 205,078 (the amount of one loan is illegible). For large loans, see my article "Loans and Favors, Kin and Clients: Cosimo I de' Medici and the Monte di Pietà," *Journal of Modern History* 61 (1989): 487–511. Since the publication of this article, I have discovered additional loans made by the monte at ducal command; these loans are included in Table 12 in Appendix A.

Small at first, by the mid-1560s the big loan business became an important part of the monte di pietà's activities: during 1564–74 it lent out more than 427,000 scudi (sc.) in 249 loans on ducal orders (see Appendix A, Table 12, Documented Large Loans, 1564–1574) and would lend even greater amounts in the following years. About sc. 185,000 of that sum were loans to the Medici themselves.

The records do not state the purpose of Gualterotti's loan, but the careful association in the records of Gualterotti with the duke and the precise notation of the authorization of the loan suggest that in obtaining it he acted in his official capacity. Moreover, it is a notable coincidence that the amount of this loan equaled precisely the amount deposited, at interest, by the Misericordia of Pisa at about the same time, pointing to the strong possibility that the loan was designed to take advantage of the Misericordia's deposit.[2]

Deepening Medici interest in the monte di pietà is evident from the 1540s on. The ledger covering the years 1545–48 contains the first account held by the duke. Furthermore, Attilio de' Medici was appointed *cassiere* (cashier) at the second monte as soon as that office fell vacant, and Chiarissimo de' Medici continued to perform his duties as provveditore. The reason for this intensified Medici interest is simple: instead of seeing the monte di pietà as merely a worthwhile charitable institution, Cosimo was beginning to realize what a rich source of support it was for himself, his friends, and his state. Until 1568 the monte di pietà asked only 5 percent interest even on large loans, an extremely attractive rate, as the usual cost of borrowing money in the mid-sixteenth century ranged from 10 percent to as much as 60 or 70 percent.[3]

2. This deposit remained on account on 17 November 1545, when the company was posted forward as a creditor in the next record book. The principal of the ducal agent's loan remained static at the same time. By 17 November 1548 Gualterotti had reduced the loan by about 60 percent (to fl. 2,112, L. 6). MP 754, Libro di debitori e creditori, 164a.

3. Raymond de Roover (*Medici Bank*, 268) noted that in the early fifteenth century the Milanese branch of the Medici bank lent at about 15 percent. Florence de Roover ("Restitution in Renaissance Florence," 788) corroborated those rates for the late part of the century. Rates do not seem to have declined in the sixteenth century, and for royalty they could be much higher. Genoese bankers who lent to Charles V made average profits of 15 percent during 1520–32, but during 1552–56 they profited by as much as 67 percent on loans secured by monopolies, taxes, and so on. See Giorgio Doria, "Conoscenza del mercato e sistema informativo: Il know-how dei mercanti-finanzieri genovesi nei secoli xvi e xvii," in Aldo De Maddalena and Hermann Kellen-

Besides the remaining fl. 2,112, L. 6 charged to Gualterotti, more sums were soon lent to Medici friends and kinsmen. Captain Giuliano di Giovanni de' Medici and some of his friends took a loan of fl. 1,200 that the duke ordered the monte to make available to them. Giuliano was to have use of the money for a period of twenty months and ten days beginning on 29 May 1546, paying the same 5 percent interest (or fl. 60 per annum) that others paid on small loans against pawns. On 17 November 1548, by order of the duke, the loan's term was extended another two years, with Giuliano obliged to "pay the interest as he has done in the past."[4]

In this way Cosimo began to make use of the monte to exercise patronage. Money might be paid out by his order in loans to his kinsmen aimed to bring different branches of his family closer together (important after the divisions wrought by the murder of Alessandro by Lorenzino). When he authorized a loan to a man like Giovanni Capponi, he emphasized his own position as the font of such patronage while quietly signaling that the Capponi were his esteemed courtiers but no longer his equals. Even more important, timely loans to those outside his family could earn him the goodwill of men he wished to cultivate. On 23 July 1546 he ordered the institution to lend to Messer Bernardetto d'Andrea di Messer Tommaso Minerbetti, bishop of Arezzo, along with his father and nephew, the sum of one thousand scudi d'Italia. The Minerbetti were to pay 5 percent interest for the term of the loan and, every six months, two-thirds of the remaining principal. The bishop, however, felt no hurry to pay off the interest, which by 17 November 1548 amounted to fl. 124, L. 2, nor did he abide by the provision to begin repayment in six months: the monte's bookkeepers posted him forward as a debtor for fl. 1,134, L. 4.10, an amount larger (because of accrued interest) than the original loan.[5] "By the word of His Excellency," another loan was offered to one Monna Margherita, called La Infolina, of Pistoia; by late 1548, fl. 114, L. 2 were still outstanding.[6]

benz, eds., *La repubblica internazionale del denaro tra XV e XVII secolo* (Bologna, 1986), 68.

    4. MP 754, 69a–b.

    5. MP 754, 76a–b. The contract for the loan, recorded by the monte's chancellor Ser Bartolomeo Mei, stated that Minerbetti might enjoy the loan "by commission of the magnificent lord officials and by the word of our excellent lord duke."

    6. MP 754, 164a.

The Medici talent for using a wide variety of sources of patronage thus began to emerge clearly with their growing involvement in the monte di pietà beginning in the 1540s. The Minerbetti were an old and powerful family, and Arezzo itself was a strategic city from Florence's point of view.[7] Only in 1543 had Cosimo succeeded in recapturing all of Florence's old fortresses and freeing himself from Spanish influence, and that same year the duke turned his attention to refining and controlling the institutions of the state. It was important that he be able to rely on the vicar of Rome in Arezzo, and behooved him to do whatever favors were within his reach to cement this alliance. He was successful, for the bishop became an important and trusted friend of Cosimo, as did several of his family. An intellectual in the humanist tradition who translated Virgil and helped found the Accademia degli Umidi, Bernardetto held the most sensitive diplomatic post of his day, that of ambassador at the court of Philip II. He represented Cosimo at the splendid funeral of Charles V, and published an elaborate account of the event that popularized it throughout Europe and set the standard for princely funerals thereafter. He was one of the first men informed by Cosimo's successor of the grand duke's demise in 1574.[8] His kinsman Alessandro best exhibited the closeness of the Medici-Minerbetti relationship when, upon the death of Don Francesco de' Medici in 1614, he published a eulogy, "Delle lodi dell'Illustrissimo et Excellentissimo Signore Principe Don Francesco Medici."

The evolution of the duke's interest in the monte di pietà must be placed against the background of reform and change that characterized ducal government in the 1540s. In November 1543 Cosimo decreed the creation of the *auditore fiscale* (secretary of the fisc), who wielded broad financial authority, sat on the Pratica Segreta, and

7. Roth, in *Last Florentine Republic*, notes that Arezzo was "the centre of the Florentine system of defence towards the south" (166). One of Bernardetto's kinsmen was described by Busini in these revealing if unflattering terms: "Andrea Minerbetti was . . . a gutless pallesco, with little brains and little honesty." *Lettere*, Busini to Varchi, letter 9, 23 Jan. 1550, 87. Cosimo's plans for consolidating Medici power depended in part on limiting the power and influence of the Church within his domain. See, e.g., D'Addario, *Formazione*, 216 and 244. Cosimo especially feared the ambitions of Paul III, a Farnese, vis-à-vis Tuscany.

8. See Eve Borsook, "Art and Politics at the Medici Court, 1: The Funeral of Cosimo I de' Medici," *Mitteilungen des Kunsthistorischen Institutes in Florenz* 12 (1965): 32, 34, 36.

bore responsibility for overseeing the fisc.[9] Finance was at the fore-front of Cosimo's mind, for control of finance and control of his state were closely linked. The large, newly acquired liquidity of the monte made it even more attractive to a duke seeking to solidify his power and, moreover, to one not having come to office a wealthy man.

These concerns led him to the monte di pietà. On 30 December 1547 he ordered the charitable institution to grant him a loan for the large sum of seventy-five hundred ducats to be paid over to his majordomo Pierfrancesco Ricci.[10] Cosimo promised to pay the usual interest of 5 percent, but unlike the agreements for the other loans he ordered, his contract with the monte placed no conditions (such as deadlines for repayment) on this loan. The duke paid not a soldo of interest or principal and so, on 17 November 1548, was forwarded as a debtor of the monte for the amount of fl. 7,831, L. 1.15, which comprised the principal plus 5 percent interest over ten and a third months, amounting to fl. 331, L. 1.15.[11]

This was the duke's first loan from the monte, but it was hardly the first time that Florence's rulers had ordered the monte to make them a loan on the basis of dire need. The precedent for Cosimo's act was the forced loan of some sixteen thousand florins to the last republic during the siege of 1529–30. That early loan was never repaid, though at the beginning and end of each ledger the hopeful and dogged bookkeeper listed it as a debit. Nor did Cosimo invent the tactic of using funds held in communal institutions for his own purposes: Alessandro had earlier ordered the monte comune to deliver sums of money to finance various activities. This practice illustrates what Diaz called "the confusion between the patrimony of the prince and the public treasury" and complicates the task of untangling state finance.[12]

9. Diaz, *Granducato*, 93–94. On the auditore fiscale, see Litchfield, *Emergence of a Bureaucracy*, 78–79.

10. The Ricci family remained loyal to the Medici dukes and reaped advantages from that loyalty. A namesake of Pierfrancesco became a senator and received offices under Gian Gastone. Diaz, *Granducato*, 525. See also Ricci's gossipy *Cronaca, passim*.

11. MP 754, 130a–b, 164a.

12. Diaz, in *Granducato*, 160, addresses this difficulty: "The confusion between the prince's patrimony and the public treasury . . . is such that the reports of income and expenses found here and there in contemporary documents are always incomplete

The extent of these loans and their effects on the monte di pietà may be seen against the background of average lending against pawns at the branches. The loans authorized by the duke to Miner-betti, Monna Margherita, Gualterotti, Giuliano de' Medici, and to himself totaled over fl. 15,242. In an average month during 1546, the second branch of the monte lent about fl. 1,750 against pawns; loans from December 1545 through September of the following year (when the monte's bookkeeper balanced these accounts) reached about fl. 16,425. The duke's patronage had eaten up a sum close to the total amount lent by one monte branch over a ten-month period. Such patronage could imperil the monte's charitable mission, and in fact a warning sign to this effect appeared at the end of the decade, even though there is no evidence that the monte was forced to cur-tail its lending against pawns because of depletion of its capital. Rather, the deposits it attracted at 5 percent interest allowed it to accommodate both its traditional clientele and the duke's interests, at least for the next two decades.

In summer 1549 the monte di pietà's provveditore, Chiarissimo de' Medici, wrote to the duke that the institution's deposits, amount-ing to some forty thousand scudi, were insufficient to meet the de-mands of borrowers. The shortfall compelled the monte's eight to borrow "about three thousand scudi. . . . We will be forced," Chia-rissimo continued, "in order to satisfy the needs of the monte and the poor to make some new provision for money." Borrowing "a cambio"—from a bank at the prevailing interest rates—had already proven harmful. The provveditore proposed several remedies; on behalf of the duke, his first secretary, Lelio Torelli, wrote, "Let the counselors issue an order that the camarlingo of the [Office of the] Pupilli put his money in the monte and the treasurer of the Mer-canzia do the same."[13] These measures, along with the growing num-ber of deposits at 5 percent interest, were sufficient to alleviate the problem.

Who were the lucky recipients of large loans from the monte di pietà authorized by ducal patronage? Their most striking trait was, not surprisingly, close political and familial ties to the Medici. Sev-

---

and approximate." The monte's receipt of money from the Magona at Cosimo's order illustrates Diaz's point; see below.

13. Magistrato Supremo (MS) 1122, undated, but from July–Sept. 1549.

eral, such as Giovanni Capponi, belonged to patrician families who had welcomed the return of the Medici after the disasters of the republic and who had become reconciled to the duchy so long as their own social positions were not harmed.[14] Others were relative newcomers or outsiders who under the dukes became courtiers, captains, or functionaries. Signor Mario Sforza dei Conti di Santa Fiore, for example, spent much of his life at the Medici court, becoming particularly close to Francesco and serving him as general of infantry. A contemporary account called him "one of the most prominent gentlemen of the court."[15] The Tartaglia family was one of the petty noble families that took up military commands under the dukes; Andrea himself held the military title of *capitano delle bande*.[16]

A great many of these loans went to men who served in the senate or whose kin had done so. Cammillo Pazzi, Giovanni Capponi, Andrea Minerbetti (whose family had, as we have seen, already enjoyed a loan from the monte), Antonio Lanfredini, Donato Tornabuoni, Lucrezia Pucci-Panciatichi, and Niccolò Baldovinetti all came from senatorial stock.[17] The men of these patrician families had easily made the adjustment from republic to duchy with their positions intact. Two men, recipients of large loans, might be accused of conflict of interest: Carlo di Roberto Acciaiuoli, who received fourteen hundred scudi at 6 percent, was elected an official of the monte in 1566, and Lorenzo Ridolfi, who enjoyed four thousand at the same rate, had served two successive terms during 1560–66.[18]

14. See Hale, *Florence and the Medici*, 85. This pro-Medicean attitude demonstrated the pragmatic nature of the family: Niccolò Capponi had been an ardent republican. See Roth, *Last Florentine Republic*, 319.

15. Ricci, *Cronaca*, 421r-v, 1577. In 1581 Francesco and Mario had a falling out when the latter's son broke his engagement to Virginia de' Medici, daughter of Cosimo, in order to seek a cardinal's hat. Mario left the court "dissatisfied" (473r).

16. Diaz, *Granducato*, 269, n. 5.

17. Ricci, *Cronaca*, 57v, 58r, 313r, 295v, 55v, 57r, 297r, 302r; and Diaz, *Granducato*, 176.

18. It is only fair to point out that loans to members or former members of the eight were rare. These two loans may be found in MP 266, Atti di Cancelleria, Suppliche e mandati, a volume compiled in 1584 by Francesco di Guglielmo Ciacchi, provveditore of the monte di pietà. This file contains petitions to and mandates from the duke regarding the monte di pietà from 1564 on. Petitions are generally in the third person and written on behalf of an individual or group. For convenience's sake, these notes identify the petitions as from a petitioner to the duke, even though some were sent through other officials. Perusal of this file shows that it contains petitions that were granted, but none that were refused.

Several belonged, or would soon belong, to a more exclusive club, the Order of the Knights of Santo Stefano, founded in 1562 by Cosimo "to the honor and glory of God's majesty, and for the defense and growth of the most true faith."[19] Membership in this quasi-religious order was awarded solely by the duke, and its conferral signaled one's "arrival" among court gentlemen. Cosimo, "with license and most ample privileges obtained from Pius IV," created this knightly order "and endowed it with many, many privileges, dedicating it to Saint Stephen the Pope, in memory of the victory he [Cosimo] won on the day of that saint on 2 August [1554] against the rebel Piero Strozzi."[20] Modeled after the great medieval crusading orders, the Order of Santo Stefano demanded that candidates for membership prove their "nobility" on both sides of their families and, according to the order's statutes, that they be eligible for "those grand dignities and ranks that only the most noble gentlemen" could enjoy. Members were forbidden to exercise any trade. Forty individuals enjoyed both monte di pietà loans and admission of a family member to the knighthood. Ciro Alidosio, Traiano Bobba, Luigi Dovara, Giovanni Gori, Cammillo Malespina, Pierfrancesco de' Conti di Montedoglio, Jacopo Offredo, Postumio Placidi, Lorenzo Ridolfi, Mario Sforza, and Raffaello, Francesco, and Duke Cosimo de' Medici were all knights as well as borrowers of large sums from the monte. Borrowers who had relatives admitted to the order came from the Acciaiuoli, Manni, Bardi, Ricasoli, Bonsi, Albizzi, Pazzi, Nobili, Strozzi, Antinori, Busini, del Caccia, Caprini, Chieli d'Anghiara, Gianfigliazzi, Gondi, Mannelli, Martini, Minerbetti, Miniati, Conti di Montauto, Marchesi del Monte, Naldini, Panciatichi, Salviati, Spini, and Vannucci da Cortona.[21] Clearly membership in this neofeudal elite, with its close ties to the Medici, could confer benefits beyond spiritual ones. Moreover, the men who tended to become members were prominent at court and in Tuscan society.

We can with certainty place fifty monte di pietà borrowers from a

---

19. Auditore delle Riformagioni 307, "Statuti originali della religione di Santo Stefano," 2.

20. Ricci, *Cronaca*, 305v. The knights were supposed to follow the rule of Saint Benedict, but it is difficult to imagine that the order's patrician members took this requirement very seriously. Lists of members may be found in Mano. 652 and 659; the latter also contains a copy of the order's statutes. See also Aud. delle Rif. 307, 62–86, for membership categories and requirements.

21. Ricci, *Cronaca*, 57v, 58r, 357v, 59v, 317r, 305v, 298v, 302r.

sample five-year period, 1564–69, into the Florentine patriciate.[22] In addition to these fifty, twenty more borrowers were socially prominent through association with the Order of Santo Stefano or through their military or administrative posts. Three more were important churchmen, and nine had lesser connections to the ducal court (barber, sculptor, and so on). These groups total eighty-two borrowers who can be seen as having important connections to the duke. Of the remaining twenty-eight individuals who borrowed money with the duke's permission from the monte during 1564–69, several more were important foreigners (like Marchese Carlo Trolio). Here Cosimo continued an important Medici tactic by allowing selected foreigners access to Florentine financial institutions. Lorenzo the Magnificent, for instance, had permitted the Bentivogli of Bologna to enroll three daughters in the monte delle doti, normally open to Florentines only;[23] Cosimo permitted some foreigners to tap the cheap credit available through the monte di pietà, thus displaying his own ability to offer patronage.

Borrowers of large sums represented both the true cream of the crop and close ducal favorites. Donato Tornabuoni was not a knight, but had served as senator in 1547, as an official of the Sanità, and on the Six of the Mercanzia, among other offices. So trusted was he that the duke sent him to hold the outpost of Monte San Savino, near Arezzo, in 1569; perhaps his loan was meant to reconcile him to his stay in the provinces. Luigi Dovara served as ambassador to Venice in the same year as he received his loan.[24] Lionardo de' Nobili's loan of four hundred scudi at 5 percent was granted to help him meet expenses during his upcoming ambassadorship to Spain.[25] Lucrezia Pucci's late husband, Bartolomeo Panciatichi, held several offices and his family owned a bank. Don Ernando di Toledo represented the Spanish influence in Florence after the Habsburgs' departure from Tuscany and served the dukes as squire (*castellano*). The social standing of Giusto Bono, a Sicilian, is uncertain, but another Bono,

---

22. That is, by using the standards set by Litchfield, *Emergence of a Bureaucracy,* App. B, 362–82. Litchfield suggests that patrician families were those who had been represented among the Priors at least four times during the fifteenth century or entered in the Libri di Oro in the late eighteenth century.

23. This and similar cases are cited by Molho, "Investimenti."

24. Ricci, *Cronaca,* 297r, 2r, 383r, 301v, 305v.

25. MP 266, 17 Oct. 1565.

Giuseppe, received from Cosimo lucrative privileges and in 1571 himself enjoyed a loan from the monte di pietà.[26]

Several loan recipients were foreigners living in the city, including some already in the service of the duke, especially in the army. The loyalty of the German Guard had above all to be insured, which may have played a role in the duke's approval of a loan to the German captain Giovanni Fierenberger for 1,000 ducats for five years.[27] Bartolomeo Volterra, a Greek who served as a cavalry captain, took out a loan for sc. 600 at 6 percent. Even more important was conciliation of the Spaniards who remained in Florence. The duke approved a loan of sc. 120 to Michele di Giache, a Spanish bombardier, who pledged "one of his houses that he has in Florence in Via Maffia, which pays eleven scudi per year, and a little house [*casetta*] that he has near the Badia that pays three scudi per year, . . . and in addition, the yield of eight *staiore* of vines." The loan of sc. 2,000 to Don Ernardo di Toledo also belongs in this category. Another Spaniard, writing to the duke, complained that he had been assessed (or, as he put it, "condemned") by the officials of the salt tax (*gabella*) to pay sc. 15. Unable to find this sum, he persuaded the duke to allow him to withdraw a monte di pietà deposit of sc. 200 that, because it was a dowry deposit with stipulations about how it could be reinvested, ought to have been inalienable for such a purpose. Other foreigners who did business with Cosimo might convince him to order the monte di pietà to arrange a loan for them: thus Cornelio Merman', a German jeweler, borrowed sc. 1,500. Two Genoese merchants took the large sum of sc. 12,500.[28]

Cosimo's approval of these requests for loans served a single purpose: he exercised his power of patronage, placating the borrowers and placing them in his debt. Beginning in the late 1560s, foreigners

26. On Giuseppe, see Diaz, *Granducato*, 145, esp. n. 2.

27. MP 266, Cosimo de' Medici to monte di pietà, 9 May 1569. Fierenberger was obliged to repay one hundred scudi every six months and to hand over pledges or else find guarantors for principal plus interest.

28. All from MP 266: Cosimo de' Medici to monte di pietà, 18 Sept. 1569; Cosimo de' Medici to monte di pietà, 7 June 1569; Bartolome Romero to Cosimo de' Medici. The last must have been in dire straits, for his petition insisted that "no tiene de otra cosa con que pagarlos [i.e., the 15 sc.] humilmente supplica a V.A. se a servido demandas le denari por libra de la dicha condenacion"; Cosimo de' Medici to monte di pietà, 1 Feb. 1569 (O.S.). The rate of exchange had climbed to L. 7.16 per scudo; Cosimo de' Medici to monte di pietà, 21 Nov. 1567.

of more impressive stature began to approach the Tuscan ruler for loans as they became aware of the liquidity and compliance of the Florentine monte di pietà. Cosimo and his successors granted their requests because they wished to cultivate the good wishes of such foreigners and to cement political bonds. As the source for the money for such loans, the monte di pietà had, by the end of Cosimo's reign, become an instrument for furthering certain foreign policy aims.

Just as he had done when allowing his friends to withdraw otherwise inalienable funds, Cosimo bent the rules for those whose favor he wished to cultivate. When the Most Reverend Cristofano Mandruzo, cardinal of Trent, asked to borrow ten thousand scudi for a term of eighteen months, Cosimo ordered the monte to accept a number of luxury items as pledges and to forego its usual procedures.

> We command you to lend . . . to the cardinal of Trent, and for his Highest Reverence to Messer Massimo Grotta his procurator, the sum of ten thousand scudi against pledges . . . for a term of eighteen months with the usual interest. . . . And this which we command, you will do by virtue of our plenipotence, other laws and statutes or other orders to the contrary notwithstanding; because if within the eighteen months the said pawns are not redeemed, and if after the eighteen months they have not been sold for the amount lent along with interest and expenses, according to the statutes of the monte, in this case we will preserve the monte without loss, we ourselves taking care of this loan and pledge.[29]

So important did Cosimo consider this loan that he himself promised to indemnify the monte from any losses resulting from the transaction. He therefore made it clear that the monte was to submit to his wishes in this matter, disregarding any laws, including its own, to the contrary.[30]

29. MP 266, Cosimo de' Medici to monte di pietà, 3 Oct. 1566.
30. The cardinal could invoke a special relationship with the duke: the year before he had escorted Barbara, a daughter of Ferdinand I (and the sister of Johanna, who married Francesco de' Medici), to Ferrara on the occasion of her marriage to Alfonso d'Este. Mary G. Steegman, *Bianca Cappello* (London, 1913), 61, 64.

The cultivation of prelates, however, could be expensive. Antonio Angeli, bishop-elect of Massa, wanted to borrow eight hundred scudi from the monte, but had trouble securing guarantors for the loan, the in-law of his brother (who was the grand-ducal physician) not having been approved. He complained about this refusal to the duke, suggesting that the duke himself might guarantee the loan ("if [Antonio] merits such favor"). But Cosimo wanted no part of the responsibility and instead ordered the monte di pietà to "accept the father-in-law [as guarantor] on the word of His Majesty."[31]

Cosimo also approved requests for loans on behalf of other charitable and religious institutions. Officers of the hospital of San Paolo, "in the greatest disorder due to various circumstances, and particularly many debts," wrote the duke that they could no longer put off their creditors. In debt for more than four thousand scudi, they asked to be allowed to borrow half that sum, "with that interest and those conditions by which you have, at other times, accommodated several pious establishments." The hospital would reimburse the monte "as soon as it can." Cosimo approved this request along with several others. The prior of the Innocenti asked for eight hundred scudi, paid in eight equal weekly installments, "for the expenses of the walls of the new monastery." When the church of Santa Maria Novella sought to make improvements, it took an advance of one hundred scudi "to remake the door that goes into the church below the organ in the cloister."[32]

Cosimo's devotion to charity was no mere facade, and any attempt to portray his use of the monte di pietà as exclusively a cynical subverting of the monte's charitable functions in favor of his own needs fails to take this fact into account. Recent scholarship on charity and religion in ducal Florence has described the state of well-being enjoyed by the city's institutions of beneficence during Cosimo's rule.[33] During the war to conquer Siena, a time of special hardship for many Tuscans, Cosimo sent word to his treasurer that he wished to subsidize two hospitals that cared for "the needs of the soldiers of

31. MP 266, Antonio Angeli to Cosimo de' Medici, and Cosimo's reply, 1 Oct. 1570.

32. MP 266, Constantino Antinori, administrator (*spedalingo*) of the hospital of San Paolo, to Cosimo de' Medici, 14 Feb. 1568 (O.S.), and Cosimo de' Medici to monte di pietà, 31 Jan. 1569 (O.S.). Some of the eight payments were made through the Ricci bank; MP 266, Cosimo de' Medici to monte di pietà, 30 Mar. 1569. The loan was given to the "opera et operai di Santa Maria Novella."

33. See D'Addario, "Note di storia."

Spanish nationality [who have been] injured or wounded." Every month, for the duration of the conflict, the treasurer was to see that the hospital of San Bonifazio receive twenty scudi from the ducal treasury, and the hospital of Lemmo fifteen scudi. The Company of the Good Men of San Martino, which earlier in the century had received subsidies from the monte di pietà, now received two hundred scudi per month from the duke himself, "so that alms may be given at their discretion." By October 1555 the overseers of the company acknowledged receipt of twelve hundred scudi, paid them from 23 January through 5 October 1555.[34] Cosimo did not quite live up to his promise, for this eight-month period should have netted the company sixteen hundred scudi. His gift nonetheless compares favorably with the charity the monte di pietà had been able to offer the same institution in the pre-ducal period.

The duke's concern for charity and piety extended to the reform of those establishments that had become corrupt. He sternly ordered the Overseers of the Monasteries (Deputati sopra i Monasteri) to proceed at once to reform the "disorder" of the monastery of Santa Chiara fuori di Castelfiorentino. "Proceed," he instructed them, "with all those remedies that you judge opportune and necessary for the honor of God and for the well-being of that place." Should their efforts fall short, they were to write to the Holy See for authority to do more.[35]

The duke cared passionately about charity and was willing to support it with the full force of his authority. Charity, however, ought to uphold the ideals of the state, and Cosimo shared the old Florentine belief that the recipients of charity ought to be deserving and that those who claimed to practice piety ought to be truly devoted. In no case should the control of charity be allowed to slip out of the ruler's hands. The hospital of Santa Maria Nuova was a revealing case. It already had links to the monte di pietà, for it rented to the monte several rooms in which the third branch auctioned unclaimed pawns. This hospital was situated in the neighborhood of the Portinari family, who owned the house in which the third branch originally operated and who also, as the hospital's chief patrons, exercised influ-

---

34. Depositeria Generale (DG), Parte antica, Rec. di Cassa, filza 949, no. 475, 25 Aug. 1554, and no. 543, 16 Jan. 1555 (O.S.).

35. Mediceo (Med.) 236, Cosimo de' Medici to Deputati sopra i Monasteri, 24 May 1572, 121r.

ence over it. The papacy under Clement VII had managed to wrest control from the Portinari, a desirable development from the Medici point of view as long as a Medici was pope. Beginning in 1544 Cosimo felt powerful enough to nominate his own overseer for the hospital. Shortly thereafter, the last of the Portinari in Florence died, and the papacy pushed its claim to regain control of Santa Maria Nuova. Cosimo averted this danger by finding a Portinari from outside the city and naming him overseer.[36] By 1561 all lay charities and pious groups in the domain were subject to audits by the Nine Conservatori under the watchful eye of the Pratica Segreta.[37]

His concern for social reform led the duke to. create a body to oversee Florence's many charitable organizations. The Magistracy of the Buonomini, founded in 1542, was charged with assisting the jobless poor, housing homeless and parentless children, and feeding beggars. The duke pushed for paternalistic measures aimed at providing the able-bodied poor with jobs, a typically Cosiminian solution intended to remove such persons from the welfare rolls and increase the number of taxpayers. He also outlawed certain forms of begging.[38] When the flood of 1557 damaged the monti branches and some pawns housed in them, the charitable institution recouped its losses—and covered the costs of paying the religious who cleaned over fourteen thousand pawns—by imposing a surcharge of four denari on each pawn pledged. It is significant that this decision was made not by the monte's governing board but by Cosimo's Pratica Segreta. The tendency begun by Alessandro to retain control over important decisions thus continued under Cosimo.[39] The duke's de-

36. D'Addario, "Note di storia," 105, 118, 120–21.

37. Pratica Segreta (PS) 5, no. 95, 817r, 27 Mar. 1563. The Pratica found a total of 1,108 such establishments.

38. D'Addario, *Formazione*, 243–44.

39. MP 762, 219a–b: "Ritentione di danari quattro per pegno in virtù di partito della praticha segreta di Sua Excellentia Illustrissima dè dare fiorini 253.5.12 per pagarli a più persone per spese fatte nel secondo monte per causa della piena l'anno 1557." Despite its name, this "libro grande" is actually a libro di debitori e creditori—a ledger. See also PS 4, no. 44, 15 Mar. 1557 (O.S.), which shows repairs and damages costing L. 5245.12. The monte di pietà of Milan has published its "Ordinazioni capitolari" of 1497–1580; these records of the meetings of its governing board show that important changes in the Milanese institution, like those in Florence, were not ordered by this board. The records contain mostly mundane decisions, such as the election of the board and of its prior (the equivalent, apparently, of the Florentine board's *praepositus*), but little of real interest. Monte di Pietà di Milano, *Libro giornale (1506–1535) e ordinazioni capitolari (1497–1580)* (Milan, 1973).

sire to encourage charity and to streamline its operations coincided with his desire to control it as closely as possible. As D'Addario observed, charitable institutions "became an instrument of political power. . . . The greatest institutions of charity and benevolence were considered as integral parts of the bureaucratic structure of the state."[40]

Loans to friends, clients, charitable institutions, and foreigners represented an important part of Cosimo's financial and political schemes. Loans to his own kin were equally important. The duke, since he determined who received loans and in what amounts, was free to authorize his own government and his own kin to borrow as much money as he wished from the monte di pietà. Only his good sense exercised restraint upon this self-designed carte blanche.

Toward the end of Cosimo's reign, the Medici authorized a number of large loans to themselves. From 1565 through 1574 (O.S.) members of the Medici family borrowed over fl. 185,000, about 43 percent of the total granted in large loans. Such loans served many purposes, but the documents tend to be silent—perhaps tactfully so—about the intentions of the borrowers. Typical was a large loan in 1566 of sc. 10,000 to Don Francesco "for certain needs of ours."[41] Not long thereafter Francesco found himself again having to turn to the monte for a loan whose scope dwarfed the first one. For reasons he did not care to make clear, and "finding the monte abounding in wealth," he ordered the institution to lend him "about forty thousand florins." The monte's officials were to "pay into our General Treasury whatever Agnolo Biffoli, our treasurer, shall ask of you." The treasury would diligently meet the schedule of interest payments of 5 percent, and the prince promised that "in a short period of time the capital will be returned to you."[42]

Though the ledger is laconic, Francesco had good reason to need money, for in 1566 he married Johanna of Austria, the daughter of

---

40. D'Addario, "Note di storia," 119.

41. MP 266, Don Francesco de' Medici to Giovanni Bizzeri at the MP, 24 Sept. 1566.

42. MP 266, Francesco de' Medici to Giovanni Bizzeri, 8 Mar. 1567 (O.S.): "atteso che ci ocorre pigliare a interesse per servizio di una persona a cui non possiamo mancare circa di fiorini quarantamila, e trovandosi cotesto monte abondante di danari . . . pagherete in la nostra Depositeria generale quel tanto vi domanderà Agnolo Biffoli nostro depositario e da essa depositeria vi saranno pagate le discretioni per quel tempo si terranno a cinque per cento a ragione hanno e in breve termine vi si restituirà il capitale."

the late emperor Ferdinand I and sister of the present emperor Maximilian II. This daughter of the house of Habsburg brought with her a dowry of one hundred thousand German florins, to be invested in real property at 5 percent, as well as unprecedented prestige for the Medici, who had finally married one of their offspring to a legitimate member of the imperial family. But as was often the case in the Renaissance, the new husband was also expected to bring some wealth to the marriage. This gift usually took the form of a trousseau, sometimes paid for at least in part by the dowry itself. In keeping with this custom, Cosimo and his son Francesco promised Johanna an income of ten thousand scudi skimmed from the revenues of the salt or customs taxes. Cosimo also pledged to the new bride jewels worth forty thousand scudi.[43] These two amounts—ten thousand and forty thousand—coincided with the amounts Francesco sought in loans during the same time period from the monte di pietà. It is as tempting as it is plausible to suppose that he used the loans to bridge a gap in liquidity, paying the institution back once other revenues had come in. Even if the transaction occurred in a different fashion, there is no doubt the marriage was expensive. Francesco and his retinue had set out for Innsbruck in October 1565 in order to wait for his betrothed's arrival, a sojourn that involved considerable expense.[44]

The monte's alleged good times, however, were not as good as Francesco thought, and the huge sums it lent out to him and others burdened it to the point where its officials foresaw trouble if it were not allowed to raise its interest rate to 6 percent on loans over one hundred scudi. Still, loans to the patriciate and to Medici kin continued: Isabella de' Medici took two thousand scudi against some jewels in 1569.[45] She received two more loans totaling sixteen thousand scudi. Chiarissimo de' Medici borrowed money. Raffaello de' Medici and other Medici kin did the same. Cosimo himself took the huge sum of fifty thousand scudi in 1568.[46]

43. On the trousseau and dowry, see Christiane Klapisch-Zuber, "The Griselda Complex: Dowry and Marriage Gifts in the Quattrocento," in Christiane Klapisch-Zuber, ed., *Women, Family and Ritual in Renaissance Italy* (Chicago, 1985), 213–46; for the details of the transaction, see Steegman, *Bianca Cappello*, 62.

44. On the departure for Innsbruck, see Steegman, *Bianca Cappello*, 64.

45. MP 266, Cosimo de' Medici to Giovanni Bizzeri, 26 July 1569.

46. MP 768, Libro di debitori e creditori, 333a–b. See Chapter 8 below for this loan. This transaction is found in MP 266, petition on behalf of Bongianni Gianfigliazzi, 20

Both Cosimo and Francesco were willing to order the monte to circumvent its own laws, as in the case of Antonio Angeli, the needy bishop, and such actions would prove significant for the monte di pietà. The treatment the monte received at their hands could only have occurred in a state whose ruler had a clear vision of his power and was comfortable setting aside the rules as he liked. Even the contracts that governed the payment and disposition of dowries could be put aside by Cosimo. A remarkable example may be found in a petition of November 1564 from Bongianni Gianfigliazzi to the duke. Bongianni had deposited three thousand florins in the monte di pietà. The deposit was designated as a dowry for his daughter Ginevra, who had since married Roberto Pucci. Both Roberto and his father-in-law wanted to liquefy the deposit without the limitations placed on them by the dotal contract. Therefore the duke ordered the monte di pietà to disregard the law: "We are content that you have [fifteen hundred scudi] paid out to the husband of Ginevra . . . without making other reinvestments, the conditions of the deposit notwithstanding, in that way asked of you by the said Bongianni, because we wish it to be paid at his pleasure."[47]

The plan called for the remaining fifteen hundred to be invested in monte comune credits at 7 percent, with the monte di pietà obliged to hand over "at every request" of Bongianni and his son-in-law all interest accrued "up to the sum of the 1,500 florins that remain to be paid." This scheme allowed these men to gain access to money that, coming from a dowry, was governed by a dotal contract calling for its investment only in real estate or securities. Still Cosimo intended to indemnify the lending institution against any loss resulting from the transactions. He concurrently ordered the hospital of Santa Maria Nuova to deposit in the monte di pietà fifteen hundred florins in payments to be determined by the monte's needs.[48] The case is notable for Cosimo's willingness to intercede on behalf of

June 1564; Cosimo de' Medici to monte di pietà, 27 Nov. 1564; and Cosimo de' Medici to monte di pietà, 14 Feb. 1564 (O.S.).

47. The Gianfigliazzi had become important courtiers. Two named Bongianni were appointed senators; another Bongianni became a knight of Malta, fought at Lepanto, and served as ambassador to the sultan. At least two of the family became knights of Santo Stefano, and Orazio Gianfigliazzi served the monte di pietà as provveditore beginning in 1604. Ricci, *Cronaca*, 279r, 317r, 433v, 306r, 57v, 60r.

48. MP 266, Cosimo de' Medici to Tommaso de' Medici, 27 Nov. 1564 and 14 Feb.

courtier-friends, even to the point of finding a way around dowry
contracts, and for his concern in protecting the monte di pietà's interests—a concern he displayed on several other occasions—for
these interests were his own as well.

Cosimo willingly went to similar lengths to accommodate other
friends and clients. One courtier reminded him of his purchase
from the petitioner for fl. 1,300 of a house "in the name of your
Excellency." Apparently this house, located in the Piazza del Grano,
had been part of the dowry the courtier had received, for he was
required to deposit the proceeds in the monte di pietà and could
withdraw them only if he intended to reinvest in real property or
secured investments. Of this sum, all but fl. 170 had been withdrawn
by the time of the petition in 1565. The courtier asked to be freed
from the legal restrictions on the removal of this remainder, for he
had good reason to need liquid cash: he had just been nominated a
knight of Santo Stefano and had to come up with one hundred scudi
for his initiation fee.⁴⁹

Cosimo would also order that the law be ignored to accommodate
groups deserving of charity. Girolamo da Sommaia, appointed a senator in 1554, had bequeathed a house in Borgo Ogni Santi to the
Fanciulle della Pietà, a group of poor orphaned and abandoned
girls. His will stipulated that the house and the goods therein must
not be alienated under penalty of the reversion of the property to
Girolamo's heirs. But the location was not convenient, and unable
legally to sell the house, the girls' overseers appealed to the duke. He
granted the request on the condition that the proceeds from the sale
be placed in the monte di pietà until reinvested in a different house,
and that permission from Girolamo's heir Giovanni be secured. Giovanni agreed to the sale, for 1,710 scudi, of the house and its gardens to the Observant Franciscans, and the ducal chancery duly informed the monte di pietà of the circumstances of the case.⁵⁰

1564 (O.S). Bongianni Gianfigliazzi to Cosimo de' Medici, forwarded to Tommaso de'
Medici, 20 June 1564.

49. MP 266, Constantino Talani to Cosimo de' Medici, n.d., but from early 1565.
The new knight was Constantino di Giovanni Filipetri Talani, a Florentine admitted
to this elite order in October 1564. Ricci, *Cronaca*, 307v. This request proves, incidentally, that those selected for this distinction were not always wealthy. It also shows that
hard-up nobles were willing to scramble to pay the fee, whether they could afford it
or not, because they appreciated the benefits of belonging to the order.

50. Ricci, *Cronaca*, 297v; and MP 266, Act from chancery, 19 Aug. 1563. The will

In the 1560s the monte di pietà became ever more tightly bound to ducal patronage. Late in 1564, for example, Signor Ciro Alidosio (or Alidosi), at the time serving as a gentleman-butler in the duke's household (*cameriere*), needed money "for certain important matters of his." He appealed to the duke, who ordered the monte di pietà to lend Ciro three thousand scudi for the term of four years. The institution was to hold from the borrower whatever pledges seemed appropriate and could collect from him 5 percent interest.[51] Just a little over a year later, Ciro again requested Cosimo's intervention and received yet another loan from the monte di pietà. This time he borrowed two thousand scudi for one year at 5 percent, with the institution holding some of his belongings as security.[52]

In the course of about a year, then, Ciro enjoyed five thousand scudi in loans from the charitable pawnshop. There is only one explanation for this good fortune. Ciro was extremely close to Cosimo and to his successor Francesco, who had already begun to take over some of the duke's responsibilities by the early 1560s. By the time of the first loan Ciro had been inducted into the exclusive knighthood of Santo Stefano; in fact he was one of the original group of 310 knights named by the duke in spring 1562. Two of his sons attained special prominence: one, Giulio Cesare (how fashions in given names could change!), became head of the German Guard, and the other succeeded to his father's knighthood upon the older man's death in 1589. To Ciro Alidosio fell two high honors that testified to his status even within the elite circle of important courtiers. First, he served as ambassador to Philip II in 1574 and again in 1577. Second, while at the Spanish court in 1575 he was chosen to bear to Cosimo's successor Francesco the news of his imperial appointment as grand duke of Tuscany.[53]

---

had been quite specific: the chancery document related that Girolamo "volle quelli [i.e., casa, orto, e beni] sempre restare in dette fanciulle, et collegio, et in caso di contrafactione, volse i medesimi beni ricadere, et ritornare ne'sua heredi." The duke's meddling in the last wishes of a subject illustrates the extent of his power.

51. MP 266, Cosimo de' Medici to Tommaso de' Medici, 8 Mar. 1564 (O.S.).

52. MP 266, Cosimo de' Medici to Giovanni Bizzeri, 20 Mar. 1565 (O.S.).

53. Ricci, *Cronaca*, 305v, 510r. Ricci relates Alidosio's involvement in a feud and a lawsuit—indulgences of leisure time for the late-sixteenth-century courtier—which resulted from one of his sons attacking Roberto Ridolfi. When the conflict escalated with Jacopo Bartoli's entry into it, the duke himself intervened, sending Bartoli out of the city (510r).

The duke authorized a similar loan "on our word" to Antonio di Bernardo degli Albizzi for twelve hundred scudi. Though his recipient's political importance could not match Ciro Alidosio's (although Antonio had been named a senator in 1559),[54] his family name shone with much brighter distinction in Florentine patrician society than that of the newcomer Alidosi. Family prestige notwithstanding, Antonio had in common with Ciro a need for quick cash, in his case "to satisfy several of his creditors." The duke obliged by ordering a loan for him, secured by suitable pledges, at 5 percent.[55]

An intriguing case of patronage was exercised by Prince Don Francesco de' Medici. As a youth Don Francesco was placed under the tutelage of Fabrizio Arazzivola, the marquess of Mondragone, a Neapolitan Spaniard in Duchess Eleonora's retinue.[56] Contemporary chroniclers noted, perhaps a little jealously, Fabrizio's special talent for staying in the highest favor of the young prince, and contemporaries recounted that the Spaniard received countless favors and gifts from Francesco and his friends. This assessment was seconded by Don Francesco's intercession on his tutor's behalf in the monte di pietà.

Fabrizio had two daughters, Violante and Maria, and he was anxious to provide a dowry to marry off at least one of them. He was less concerned about which daughter married: the contract summarized in the monte di pietà's records simply stated that the prospective husband, Signor Giovanni da Montalvo, must marry one or the other.[57] The girls were made joint creditors of a deposit of two thousand florins in the monte di pietà in 1564. The money was to accrue interest that would be plowed back into the capital to earn more interest until it reached the sum of four thousand florins, which sum "should be paid to the said Violante, or truly to the said Maria, that is, to the one who marries the said Signor Giovanni." This equivocal

---

54. Ibid., 298r. Several Albizzi joined the knighthood of Santo Stefano. See, e.g., 446v.

55. MP 266, Cosimo de' Medici to Giovanni Bizzeri, 21 July 1565.

56. Steegman, *Bianca Cappello*, 34, 45. The Mondragone palace supposedly later served as a meeting place for Francesco and Bianca Cappello during their love affair (46–47, 53).

57. This restriction of patrimony to provide a huge dowry for only one daughter derived from the vast inflation of dowries (noted by Anthony Molho in his work on the monte delle doti) and from the consequent changes in dotal strategies in the late sixteenth century.

document assured that the payment would reach the husband only upon fulfillment of this contract and upon declaration that the marriage had been consummated. Fabrizio need not fear that the whole arrangement would collapse if Giovanni died prior to this happy occasion, for the dowry would be paid upon the marriage of one of the girls to any one of Giovanni's brothers in case of his untimely demise. This scheme was designed to join two families in parentado and payment to any husband other than one of the Montalvo was contingent upon the approval of Don Francesco himself. This was only fitting since the prince was responsible for providing the two thousand florins in the first place. He instructed the monte di pietà to list him as its debtor in that amount and stipulated that, should the dowry be unpaid for any reason, it would revert to him.[58] These schemes proved the truth of Guicciardini's observation just a few years earlier that "nothing is more difficult in our civil life today than marrying our daughters properly."[59]

By the 1560s, then, orders to the monte di pietà came not only from Cosimo but also from his heir apparent, Don Francesco. The prince wished to reward his old friend and tutor Fabrizio by helping him acquire a substantial dowry for one of his daughters. The prospective husband was carefully chosen, and the entire affair must have been arranged long in advance. Given that the average upper-class Florentine woman who remained unmarried beyond her early twenties was considered an old maid, the two daughters must have been no older than five, for the time span in which two thousand florins would double at 5 percent is just over fifteen years. In this case, the monte di pietà served precisely the same function that the now-defunct monte delle doti had served.

Fabrizio, furthermore, was an extremely ambitious man who milked princely patronage in every way he could. Ricci stated that Fabrizio's boundless greed led him to abuse his privileges and that he tried to compete with Bianca Cappello and Jacopo Salviati, two princely favorites, for Francesco's attention. Giving voice to the sentiments of the typical Florentine patrician toward the Neapolitan Spaniards at court, Ricci sniffed that Fabrizio was born "in a vile and

58. MP 266, Don Francesco to Giovanni Bizzeri, n.d., but from early 1565.
59. Guicciardini, *Ricordi*, 117. Guicciardini then added maliciously, "But this advice is not meant to suggest one degrade oneself so that, like Francesco Vettori, one gives [one's daughter] to the first who asks for her."

base condition." Using wile and cunning, profiting from the gossip
that filled the corridors of the palace, Fabrizio hoped to climb the
social ladder to a rung of importance in ducal Florence. Francesco's
patronage, exercised through the monte di pietà, not only allowed
him to reap the honor that redounded upon a generous prince, but
also helped Fabrizio to forward his social ambitions. His choice of
Giovanni da Montalvo as the prospective spouse for his daughter
was no accident and aimed to contribute to this strategy. Giovanni's
father, like Fabrizio himself, was a Spaniard, and one who set an
example of the type of man Fabrizio hoped to become: he and two
of his kinsmen were knights of Santo Stefano.[60] In 1575 Fabrizio fell
out of favor for reasons that remain unclear, a reversal of fortune
much gossiped about by his courtly contemporaries.[61]

The cases of loans authorized and circumventions of ordinary law
and contracts—in other words, of ducal patronage—continued.
Piero Arrigucci and his nephews asked Cosimo to free up for a set
period of time fl. 1,400 in dotal deposits in the monte di pietà; Cosimo concurred, and Arrigucci promised to repay the cash on a set
schedule. The monte lent, at ducal order, sc. 500 to Signor Montauto de' Conti di Montauto for a two-year term at 5 percent, secured by appropriate pawns. Traiano Bobba, the duke's cameriere,
received a loan. Bartolomeo Ammannati, court sculptor and archi-
tect, borrowed sc. 450 that the duke himself guaranteed. Monna
Nannina de' Talani and her sons requested that Cosimo free up sc.
100 in the monte so that they might satisfy some creditors who had
begun to harass them. Ducal employees were apt to receive the favor
of a loan. Thus, Filippo Giannetti, a ducal almoner (*nostro spenditore*),
borrowed sc. 700, secured for him by others. A ducal cashier was
lent 500 sc.[62]

60. Ricci, *Cronaca*, 305v, 308r, 309v. Signor Antonio Ramires de Montalvo, Signor
della Sassetta and cameriere of the duke, had extensive holdings in the monte di
pietà, and was thus acquainted with its usefulness as a place of safe deposit. In 1558
he opened an account there with a deposit fl. 6,200. With further deposits and accrued interest on this and another account, he possessed credits of over fl. 9,600 in
1569; interest alone had amounted to nearly fl. 900. MP 768, 355a–b.

61. Ricci, *Cronaca*, 393r–v. See esp. n. 1, where the editor cites the historian G. E.
Saltini, who called the tutor a "a duplicitous Spaniard." The Lapini diary suggests that
Fabrizio's fall from favor resulted from his betrayal of diplomatic secrets to the Span-
iards. He was finally expelled from the state. Agostino Lapini, *Diario fiorentino*, 158.

62. All these loans are found in MP 266. Officials of MP to Cosimo de' Medici, 30
June 1564, including the duke's affirmative reply: "Così si faccia." Cosimo de' Medici

As a result of this new demand among Florentine patricians for loans, the institution began to require that pledges cover not only the principal of these large loans but the interest as well. Alternatively, borrowers were allowed to find others who would serve as guarantors (mallevadori) of the loan plus interest. Thus, two knights of Santo Stefano had to hand over items of sufficient value to cover principal plus interest, or to provide acceptable guarantors for the loan: Raffaello de' Medici had to find mallevadori to cover a loan of one thousand scudi plus 6 percent, and Jacopo Offredo, who held a high post in the Knights of Santo Stefano (*gran priore del convento*), offered security for six hundred scudi for three years.[63]

Even subjects of obscure, if any, importance to the duke might approach him out of desperation and, throwing themselves on his mercy, implore his aid in obtaining a loan. One Barbara Geralda found herself involved in a lawsuit over a house that, she claimed, was rightfully hers. To pursue the case, she needed to round up one hundred scudi in cash; otherwise, "not paying it, I will lose the house and all my goods." She seemed to know that the monte di pietà could most easily provide the help she needed, and she knew to go to the duke for his authorization.[64]

In 1562 Cosimo approved a small change in the monte's operation that underscored the evolution of the institution. The process by which the monte sold off unredeemed pawns was streamlined and the institution became the prime creditor, freed from the obligation to satisfy earlier creditors of the defaulter. Only where another creditor claimed a dowry would exceptions be made. The catalyst behind this change was the case of Bernardo Miniati, a debtor of the monte di pietà whose goods had been confiscated by the institution for sale. Once again, Cosimo intervened to protect the fiscal interests of an institution that had become valuable to him.[65]

---

to MP, 5 July 1567. Monna Nannina to Cosimo de' Medici, 31 Dec. 1567. Cosimo de' Medici to MP, 22 Aug. 1567. Cosimo de' Medici to MP, 28 Aug. 1567. Cosimo de' Medici to MP, 15 Aug. 1568. Cosimo de' Medici to MP, 18 Nov. 1568.

63. MP 266, Cosimo de' Medici to MP, two letters of 11 Dec. 1568. The monte officials were to lend Raffaello one thousand scudi for two years at 6 percent.

64. MP 266, Barbara Geralda to Cosimo de' Medici, n.d.

65. Misc. Rep., busta vii, ins. 218, "Notizie del monte di pietà." In October 1562, "essendo seguita la confiscazione de'beni di Bernardo Miniati debitore del Monte, il Duca Cosimo de' Medici concede il privilegio al Monte, tanto in detto caso, quanto in

Nearly all the individuals who received loans were courtiers and bureaucrats, many from patrician families and a few from new or provincial families. As a group they were deeply immersed in politics, prominent at court, and prime components in the duke's network of friends. A more convincing example of the ruler's use of monte resources to help himself could not be imagined, for in the world of Renaissance patronage, favors to one's friends redounded, in the end, to one's own honor, security, and prestige. In making themselves masters over patronage, the Medici seemed to have achieved what Guicciardini had feared: in his *Ricordi*, he wrote, "Whoever depends on the favor of princes hangs on every gesture, on the least of their signs, such that he quickly jumps at their every whim."[66]

In October 1568 Tommaso de' Medici, the camarlingo of the monte di pietà, told the duke the monte was now losing six hundred ducats per year, "expenses being higher than earnings," and noted the causes of this shortfall: rents were escalating, and the monte was paying the same rate of interest on deposits as it took in on loans. In November of that same year, taking their cue from Tommaso de' Medici, the eight officials repeated the complaint that too much money was being spent in interest payments to depositors and not enough was being taken in from interest paid on loans. They were not referring to small loans given to the poor: this unfortunate group should not have to bear oppressive interest rates so that the more fortunate might enjoy the fruits of 5 percent. Instead, they had in mind large loans—that is, those the institution was forbidden to grant except by authorization from the duke—to individuals who could easily afford higher rates (and would undoubtedly be charged such rates if they sought loans elsewhere). They voiced this complaint in a letter: "We write to inform his Excellency of the losses the monte has suffered, and suffers daily, in paying interest on deposits at 5 percent, and in lending at the same rate. . . . This evil, still inconsiderable today, [should] not go on increasing, which would cause disorder." They suggested a solution. The loans given to the poor should still be offered at 5 percent; in fact, all loans under one

---

altri simili, che sia pagato sommarliamente [*sic*], e senza fare atti precedentemente ad ogn'altro creditore anteriore, eccettochè per causa di dote."

66. Guicciardini, *Ricordi*, 101.

hundred scudi should be charged this rate. But "those who under-take large loans," by which were meant sums in excess of one hun-dred scudi, should be asked to pay 6 percent. Anyone who needed to borrow such large sums could afford, they argued, such a rate. Ten days later, the duke sent his approval: "Sta benissimo."[67] These changes, enacted with ducal consent, indicate the monte di pietà was at risk of being drained by loans: not loans to the poor given against a table knife, a cloak, a cloth hat, but by large loans authorized by the duke, who had come to see the monte almost as part of the Medici's own patrimony.

In the last years of Cosimo's reign and in the early years of Fran-cesco's, ever-growing numbers of men and women borrowed large sums authorized by the ruler from the monte di pietà. On 10 May 1576 Uberto Adimari, the camarlingo generale of the institution, be-gan a book titled "Prestati: Entrata e uscita" (Loans: Income and outgo) in which he recorded money lent and taken in on large loans, usually secured by guarantors, from that date through the end of December 1576. The loans ranged in size from twenty thousand scudi lent to Signor Oratio di Luigi Rucellai to several loans of fifty each. The borrowers included some of the most famous names in Florence (some of whom had also been borrowers in the 1560s): Ricasoli, Pitti, da Filicaia, Salviati, Gianfigliazzi, Panciatichi, Torna-quinci, Villani, Capponi, and many others. Among the members of the ruling family who repaid loans during this period were Arch-bishop Giuliano, Lorenzo di Lorenzo, Don Pietro, Cardinal Ferdi-nando (the future grand duke), Archbishop of Florence Alessandro, and Francesco di Giuliano de' Medici. The records show loan repay-ments amounting to 314,610 ducats, L. 5.11.10 from 475 different borrowers during the period. This sum came to 16,457 ducats more than the monte had lent out, so the books show the latter amount as entered into the new cash account (*conto di cassa nuovo*) as profits.[68] The tendency first established under Cosimo's reign to authorize large loans to clients thus flourished under his successor.

Cosimo's willingness to order that loans be made by the monte di pietà marked an important step in the evolving relationship between that institution and the state. The first such loans appear to have been unsecured by pawns. Unlike the dozens of loans against pawns that its three branches made every day, these large loans appear in the books of debitori e creditori or, beginning in 1576, the books of prestati; small loans against pawns were entered in the pawn books, the libri de'pegni.[69] The monte di pietà now began to be drawn into the complex world of ducal finance and into the ruler's network of patronage while continuing to offer small loans against pawns to its traditional clientele.

By the last years of Cosimo's reign, the Florentine monte di pietà had developed several banking functions, become an instrument of ducal patronage and control, and acquired reserves of capital that enabled it to offer large loans at interest. The three branches were taking in thousands of florins in interest payments on all kinds of loans; during 1569–72, for example, the monte di pietà earned over twenty-one thousand florins in interest.[70] At the same time, a final transformation took place that tied the monte definitively to ducal finance.

On several occasions in the past, depositors had used the monte di pietà as a bank in which to place money temporarily for safekeeping, later ordering payments made or giving it over as part of, say, a dowry or sales agreement. Now this precocious banking nature evolved more fully, for the duke's account was less akin to a savings than it was to a checking account. In fact, because his deposits were earning 5 percent interest, Cosimo's account most closely resembled a NOW account except that the monte, unlike a modern bank, demanded no minimum balance for an account to earn interest. The nature of the payments made against the duke's deposits makes clear

69. As noted earlier, these libri de'pegni are not extant. Throughout its first decades, the monte found it necessary to limit strictly the amount of money an individual might borrow against a pawn. The frequent reiterations that such transactions be limited to two florins suggest that this regulation was often ignored. E.g., MP 19, 4r, 12 Nov. 1506: the Eight, realizing that the capital on hand was not sufficient to provide for all the needs of the poor, "deliberaverunt quod in futuro non possit super aliquo pignore cuilibet persone mutuari ulctra florenos duos." And again, 31r, 5 July 1512: "non possit mutuari ulctra summam fl. 2 . . . pro quolibet pignore."

70. MP 4, 63–64: "li presti anno guadagnato ne'sopradetti tre anni come nel conto de'meriti a [foglio] 729: primo monte: 5,237.2.10; secondo monte: 11,575.4.1.4; terzo monte: 4,219.1.18.4: [Total]: 21,032.2.9.8."

that he was financing state activities and not merely his own household, thin though the line between the two had become. As his reign continued, he learned to exploit the monte as a source of both patronage and capital. The fullest development of the institution's fiduciary functions occurred not in the hundreds of accounts held by average depositors, but in the accounts of the duke himself.

Another example of the monte di pietà's usefulness appeared in a recommendation by the Otto di Pratica in May 1546.[71] Discussing the problem of compensating both lay and clerical owners of houses that had been ruined, the Otto wrote their provveditore Lattantio Gorini that "the opinion of the magistracy would be to deposit, at the present time, in the monte di pietà the money that has to be paid to the owners of the houses so that it might begin to accumulate interest for them at 5 percent, but that such a deposit be made in the name of the magistracy." The Otto's suggestion took account of the interest the money would earn while details of the various claims were sorted out. Equally important, it reflected civic appreciation of the monte di pietà's status as a safe place for such deposits.

Cosimo had become accustomed to keeping accounts in the monte that he could manipulate by making deposits or requesting that sums from them be paid to his creditors. He would send a letter to the institution instructing it to hand over money to his treasurer, who would use it to pay whatever expenses Cosimo had incurred. By 1570 this habit became a regular practice. Fortifications and aqueducts, whose construction and maintenance required a good deal of money in the expanded Tuscan state, received Cosimo's constant attention. Order after order reached the monte di pietà authorizing the officials to pay these expenses. In June 1570, for example, he ordered them to pay Veri de' Medici four hundred scudi taken from "the money you have on deposit for the magistracy of the consuls."[72] Part of the costs of maintaining the army were regularly paid out through Cosimo's bankers, who were in turn reimbursed by the monte di pietà, which then debited the duke's own account.[73]

71. Otto di Pratica (Principato) 102, unnumbered, 8 May 1546.
72. MP 266, Cosimo de' Medici to MP, 9 June 1570.
73. See, e.g., MP 266, Cosimo de' Medici to MP, 28 June 1570, where the monte was ordered to pay "a Luigi e Alessandro Capponi scudi 725 d'oro di cambi, o, la valuta d'essi, et a loro gli facciamo pagare per Giovanbattista d'Adda e Compagnia di Milano, per tanti che ne hanno pagati a Fabritio Ferrari nostro agente in detto luogo,

The relationship between the monte and the duke went further, for Cosimo opened a separate account for himself in which he deposited sc. 2,000 d'Italia (equal to fl. 2,142, L. 6), which in turn came from his foundry in Pisa through his agent there, Niccolò Ferrini. The entry recording this deposit bears one unique feature: the monte's officers were obliged to make whatever payments Cosimo requested, debiting the account accordingly. The duke made regular deposits such that, by September 1548, his accounts showed a balance of fl. 6,362, L. 1. During this period he ordered payments made: for example, fl. 535, L. 5 went to an "agent" of the duke; fl. 500 were paid over to his majordomo "to be paid to Giovanni Giandonati, provveditore of Arezzo, for the account for the walls of Borgo San Sepolcro."[74]

The duke used the monte di pietà to consolidate his debts. He tended to rely upon several Florentine banks, notably those of the Ricci and Salviati, to pay his creditors on receipt of an order from his treasury, and would then inform the monte di pietà to make good on his debts to his bankers. He delegated wide authority to his trusted treasurer and kinsman, Tommaso de' Medici. Writing to the monte, Cosimo commenced a set of transactions that revealed his financial acumen.

You have paid for us on the word of Messer Tommaso de' Medici, our treasurer, all the following in accordance with our orders and wishes; however, we are content that you make us debtor in these amounts in our accounts in accordance with the payments made, and we will make them good to you, that is:

25,000 scudi di moneta to Salviati at the bank in Florence on 2 July 1570
10,000 scudi di moneta to Ricci at the bank
299.6.1 scudi di moneta to Salviati at the bank

per le spese delle armature da huomini d'arme, et poneteli al conto nostro a parte delli denari rimessivi al depositario di Siena, di conto delli huomini d'arme." And again, for cavalry, 2,500 scudi on 15 July 1570.

74. MP 754, 99a–b. In the deposit entry, the bookkeepers noted that "we have to follow the will and order of the said Illustrious Lord freely." Cosimo was engaged in the construction or improvement of fortresses in Arezzo, Pisa, and Pistoia. Hale, *Florence and the Medici*, 130.

117.4.1 scudi di moneta to Ricci at the bank
4,980.2.4 scudi di moneta

TOTAL: 40,397.2.6 scudi di moneta.[75]

By late 1570 he made the process of paying his bills even more efficient. Each month an itemized payment order arrived at the monte di pietà from the palace, instructing the officials to pay whatever debts the ruler had incurred (amounts in scudi, lire, soldi, denari).[76]

650 to our majordomo for the ordinary expenses of our house
1,355.3.1.8 to our family for the payments for last September
209 for provisions
132.1 given to us in three installments
152 for alms
58.3.10 for gifts
45 for the expenses of the library of San Lorenzo
29.1.5 for the expenses of the *carrette* (small wagons)
37.-.9.4 for the work done by Monsignor Antonio Lupattini (goldsmith)
91.3.2.4 for our foundry
69.4.10 to Monsignor Giovanni the goldsmith, for work
26 to Ser Raffaello, our captain, in a loan
88.2.3 paid for several accounts and expenses

[TOTAL: 3,937.5.1]; and place this on our account, that we will make it good to you from our accounts.

Household and other expenses paid each month by the monte tended to run around four thousand scudi, as a sample for the first nine months of regular payment shows.[77]

1570   October 3,937.5.1.4
            November 3,979.2.15
            December 3,918.1.1

75. MP 266, Cosimo de' Medici to MP, July 1570.
76. MP 266, Cosimo de' Medici to MP, 2 Nov. 1570.
77. See the monthly letters from the grand duke to the MP, MP 266, Nov.–July 1570–71.

1571   January 3,900.3.6
         February 4,492.4.15.4
         March 3,980.2.11
         April 4,027.2.10.8
         May 4,014.2.3.4
         June 3,067.-.13

These payments included ordinary expenses of the ducal household and were in addition to costs of aqueducts, cavalry, infantry,
and so on, some of which Cosimo and Francesco also paid through
the monte di pietà. The monte had become a regular part of ducal
finance. Cosimo had learned how to use the liquidity of the monte di
pietà, as well as that of Florentine banks, tying it to his own interests
and streamlining state finance as a result.

Although the monte di pietà's character changed over the course
of the sixteenth century, its administration remained remarkably
static and still closely resembled the mandates of the statutes of
1496. By the late 1560s the shortcomings of the old administrative
system were evident. The personnel were overwhelmed with work;
scandal and fraud had reappeared; statute as well as ducal usurpa-
tion of power made it impossible for the eight to initiate any meaningful reform independent of the duke. Moreover, the important
business of lending to the wealthy demanded employees with responsibilities and talents for which the governing statutes had not
provided. And the growing role of the monte in state finance and
ducal patronage meant that the duke needed to keep a closer watch
over it. Intimations of change appeared in 1568 when Cosimo
granted the eight's request to raise the interest rate on large loans to
6 percent. In 1574 wholesale reform was undertaken by a special
ducal commission made up of Tommaso di Jacopo de' Medici, Alamanno di Antonio Pazzi, Giovanni di Bartolomeo Ugolini, and
Benedetto di Jacopoantonio Busini.[78] The commission pursued two
general aims: first, to regulate better all activities of the monte di
pietà, but especially its lending activities, and second, to place the
institution more firmly under ducal control.

---

78. For the following discussion of this reform, see Pampaloni, "Cenni storici,"
542–44; MP 2 Parte delli statuti, 20r–34r; and Misc. Rep., busta vii, ins. 218, "Notizie
del monte di pietà."

To accomplish the first aim the four commissioners called for more careful scrutiny of monte employees, a deep concern in the wake of the scandals and damages caused by employees in the recent past. The responsibilities of each employee were reviewed and, where necessary, reassigned and redistributed. The result was a clear division of labor, with one group of employees directing the monte's banking and large loan activities and the other overseeing its charitable services; the ledgers too began to reflect this division. Two new positions, those of *sottoprovveditore* and *camarlingo generale*, were created. The first of these offices took on the bothersome routine of day-to-day activities, allowing the provveditore to concentrate on the smooth administration of the institution as a whole. The second office replaced the old system of rotating the position of camarlingo among the three branches, entrusting it instead to a single individual who oversaw all monte finances. No doubt responding to the frustrating ease with which even lower-echelon employees had apparently defrauded the monte, the commissioners forbade the massari to leave the city without permission of the monte's officers. Transgressors were to be subject to a hefty fine equivalent to one month's salary. The old prohibition against loans secured by cloth was removed, and bookkeeping procedures were to be tightened and standardized. The grand duke himself instructed Tommaso de' Medici to order the monte not to accept jewels as collateral for loans above sc. 150, a sure sign of the ruler's close involvement and interest in these reforms even during the last months of his life. No loan was to be granted against jewels unless they were assessed at two-thirds more than the amount of the loan. The system of mallevadori—that is, of a borrower finding guarantors in lieu of a pawn for his loan— was to be carefully regulated and guidelines for accepting guarantors made stricter. New rules would govern and expedite the selling of pawns belonging to delinquent borrowers, "so that the pledges that come to the said place do not grow old, by the result of which they deteriorate" (and lose value). All these measures were aimed at the smoother running of the monte and the elimination of theft and fraud.

Still other measures tightened the bond between the ruler and the monte di pietà. First, the discretion of the employees to grant loans was strictly circumscribed, a change that merely put into writing what had been true in fact for some time. Ministers were forbidden to authorize any loan for more than one hundred florins "without the order of their Highnesses [i.e., Cosimo and Francesco] or on the authorization of our [eight] officials." The old prohibition against officials and employees holding other offices during their tenure in the monte was, with a few exceptions, lifted, thereby enabling the duke to appoint men with close connections to other Florentine institutions. Above all, the books were to be held in confidence. The ministers should "keep secret the state of the monte . . . and not hand [the books] over to anyone except to their Highnesses, nor can they show anyone the debits and credits."[79] That the monte's finances were the business of the ruler and no one else could not have been more baldly or forcefully stated.

The reforms also increased the cost of borrowing money from the monte di pietà for all but the smallest loans. First, they established a graduated scale of surcharges: for each loan up to 10 ducats, the old fee of one quattrino would remain in effect; for 10–39, it increased to five quattrini; for 40–99, to ten quattrini; for 100–299, to twenty quattrini; and 300 or over, to thirty-five quattrini.[80] Second, the interest rates, whether against pawns or secured by guarantors, were raised on loans of more than forty florins. For sums over forty but less than three hundred florins, borrowers would now pay 6 percent. Loans over three hundred would cost 7⅓ percent. The commissioners did not place a ceiling on loans. Although this last reform meant that the Medici themselves would pay higher rates on the money they borrowed, it was nonetheless a good idea. First, the money borrowed by the Medici represented less than one half of all money lent, and the more interest reaped on large loans, the more capital available for loans in the future. Second, the large number of persons seeking these large loans at 5 or 6 percent suggested that the market would bear an increase in the cost of borrowing. Third, the reforms did not increase the cost of borrowing small sums against pawns. The poor who took out these loans still paid the same rate of 5 percent and the same surcharge of one quattrino per loan, so the institution's extension of cheap credit as a form of charity continued even as its large-loan business increased dramatically.

79. MP 2, 20r.
80. MP 4, 124v, and MP 2, 14v–15v, "Ordine prescritto," 2 Nov. 1568.

Finally, the graduated scale further widened the gap between the rates paid out on deposits and the rates charged on loans, which in turn ought to mean surpluses for the monte di pietà on its banking activities. In sum, the reforms enacted in March 1574—about six weeks before Cosimo's death—codified his treatment of the monte di pietà and set it on the path of becoming an important lending institution.

7 FRAUD AND THEFT IN THE MONTE DI PIETÀ DURING THE REIGN OF COSIMO

IN 1555 COSIMO launched his forces against Siena on the pretext that the Sienese had welcomed into their territory his enemies, the French, and made the city a haven for anti-Medici exiles.[1] The subsequent conquest of Florence's longtime nemesis formed a watershed in the history of the Florentine duchy, revealing the duke's growing sense of confidence and opening new channels into which his energy and interests flowed. Cosimo understood that winning the war was one thing, but keeping control over his newly acquired territory was another altogether. Institutions like the monte di pietà would be called on to play a role in his plans to exercise authority over Siena.[2]

A prime goal among would-be absolutist rulers in Europe—among whom must be counted Cosimo de' Medici—was the rationalization of finance, particularly of the tax system which, emerging

1. In theory Cosimo's action rested on a sound legal pretext, for in March 1541 he had reached a fifteen-year agreement with the Sienese that neither city could offer safety to rebels but was instead obliged to return them to the appropriate magistracy. Otto di Pratica (Principato) 102, copy, third chapter (*capitolo*) of an agreement between Cosimo and Siena, 10 Mar. 1541 (O.S.).

2. A small but revealing example of this confidence may be seen in the ducal seals Cosimo used. Before the war his seal proclaimed his position as duke of Florence. Immediately after the fall of Siena, he commissioned a new seal which depicted him as duke of Florence and of Siena. When he became grand duke of Tuscany, he immediately adopted a seal that announced his new title. These seals are still attached to many of Cosimo's letters in the Archivio di Stato of Florence.

from its feudal or communal origins, remained disordered, lo-
calized, and inefficient.[3] In Florence the decima provided important
revenue for the dukes and had been codified early in their reign.[4]
This and other taxes flowed into the ducal coffers but did not always
prove adequate to finance the activities of the state and its ruling
house. The demands of the war and of everyday defense proved
costly, and Cosimo's armies and fortresses devoured a hefty chunk
of state revenues.[5] Payments to the duke's German Guard ate up
over sc. 425 per month. Salaries and expenses of the captain of the
Fortezza di Massa, of a captain from Arezzo and his 150 footsoldiers
in Cosimo's pay (which amounted to sc. 150 gold per month), and a
month's salary and expenses for the castellan and sixteen infantry-
men manning the fortress at Prato (sc. 48 per month) are but a fraction of the expenses that the duke's policy and lifestyle entailed.[6]

Finding the money to implement policy challenged even the most
fertile imagination. Traditional means of taxation could be shored
up and loopholes plugged, but true to Florentine tradition the duke
and his counselors began to look elsewhere for new sources of
money. What could Florentine institutions like the monte di pietà
offer? The city's history evinced a precedent for recourse by the regime to the monte di pietà's coffers in times of dire need; the duke

---

3. Diaz, *Granducato*, 4–6, 8–9, 148–62. See also Furio Diaz, "Recent Studies on
Medicean Tuscany," *Journal of Italian History* 1 (1978): 95–110. D'Addario has done
some work on the otherwise neglected issue of ducal finance under Cosimo and his
successors; see *Il problema senese nella storia italiana della prima metà del Cinquecento* (Florence, 1958). On Cosimo's political economy, see Judith Brown, "Concepts of Political
Economy: Cosimo I de' Medici in a Comparative European Context," in *Firenze e la
Toscana dei Medici nell'Europa del '500* (Florence, 1983), 1:279–92.

4. The decima, reintroduced in 1532, was levied at a rate of 10 ½ to 11 ⅔ percent
on goods and land. See Diaz, *Granducato*, 149–51. For the text of the provvisione of
14 May 1532, which reinstated this tax, see Pagnini del Ventura, *Della decima*, 1:238–
39.

5. A letter from Stefano de Rivazza, sent to Pisa to pay the expenses of Florence's
two forts there, gives some idea of the staggering expense of the ducal policy of
conquest and control. Payments to the thirty-nine officers and soldiers at the Fortezza
della Stella amounted to 1,225 ducats for a period of seven months (or 2,100 ducats
prorated for the year). Comparable outlays at the Fortezza del Falcone amounted to
over 1,136 ducats. Med. 623, ins. 3 (1558), 119, De Rivazza to Antonio de' Nobili.

6. DG, Parte antica, Recapiti di Cassa, filza 949, 1555, esp. nos. 354, 356–59.
These documents are orders from Cosimo to his treasurer-general Antonio de' Nobili
and are rich in material pertaining to ambassadorial, household, and military expenses.

surely was not ignorant of this fact. In the seventeenth century the
financial pressures of even a brief war, in which Grand Duke Ferdinando II joined a league against the pope, nearly caused the monte
di pietà and the monte comune to crash.[7]

Despite his need for cash during the war with Siena, Cosimo did
not follow the precedent of the last republic and rifle the monte di
pietà. The extant monte di pietà records not only show no unusual
activities during the 1550s, but prove that Cosimo resisted the temptation to skim money from the institution during the war. In 1667
an anonymous writer, probably one of the monte's eight officials or
the chancellor who kept its ledger (for only they and the duke were
allowed access to the "secret" books), compiled a history of the
monte and gave accurate summaries of its debits, credits and important accounts and transactions. He had before him the complete set
of ledgers, including ledgers Y for 1551–54 and Z for 1554–57.
Worthy of the compiler's attention in ledger Y were the accounts of
the Company of the Good Men of San Martino (a debit of fl. 474, L.
3.14), interest (fl. 3,952, L. 2.9.8 in the red, "there having been more
debits than credits"), and Cosimo's purchase of the Pitti palace. The
writer divided the monte's credits into those held by public or civic
institutions (*luoghi pubblici*), which together had credits of fl. 67,151,
L. 4.11.4 ("the same creditors as in the previous book X"), and those
held by private individuals (*depositi di particolari*). Book Z, according
to the writer, contained several noteworthy debtors and creditors
but, like book Y, showed no borrowing by the duke or his represen-
tatives. Public creditors held fl. 61,665, L. 2.11, nearly as much as in
the previous book, with the difference that the Misericordia had
withdrawn a deposit of over fl. 5,000. Private deposits totaled fl.
71,560, L. 5.19.6. Had the duke forced the monte to turn over some
of its funds, this writer would surely have noted such transactions.[8]

This writer's other figures, tested against those from still-extant
records, are accurate, so there is every reason to accept his credibility
for the years 1551–57 as well. Besides, Cosimo had been dead for
nearly a century when the writer compiled his report, and so he had
no reason either to fear Cosimo's ire or to sanctify his memory. The

7. Litchfield, *Emergence of a Bureaucracy*, 94, 103.
8. MP 4, 57r–59v.

writer was careful to list the accounts of the present grand duke, Cosimo II, including his debts to the monte di pietà. Thus the evidence is convincing that Cosimo did not impose forced loans on the monte di pietà to finance the war effort. Moreover, unpaid debts were always carried forward on the ledgers, and subsequent ledgers show no large debts to Cosimo accruing during the years in question.

In fact during at least part of the time in question the duke was a lender to rather than a borrower from the monte di pietà. On 19 April 1555 he ordered his treasurer-general, Antonio de' Nobili, to pay to the monte di pietà sc. 250 di moneta "for the relief of the poor," every week beginning the following day and continuing through June of that year. A receipt signed by Chiarissimo de' Medici at the monte shows that from 20 April through 28 June 1555, the monte di pietà received fl. 2,750 and entered the sums in the secret income book Z.[9] Cosimo's aid to the monte di pietà was only part of a larger plan to offer charity to the poor in time of want. From February to June 1555, Antonio de' Nobili paid nearly sc. 12,000 at Cosimo's orders to the Ufficiali della Carità "to purchase grain in order to distribute bread to the poor."[10] During the same period Cosimo continued to offer aid to a traditional Medici charity, the Company of the Good Men of San Martino.

As if conditions were not already bad enough, the disastrous flood of September 1557 caused terrible damage in the city and its contado.[11] The monte di pietà, especially its branch in Borgo Santi Apostoli only a block from the Arno, suffered the loss of or damage to many pawns, whose safety it was obliged to guarantee. Cosimo came to the rescue of some who had lost their pawns. He signed an order calling for his treasurer to pay, through Lattantio Gorini, provveditore of the Otto di Pratica, sc. 1,131 di moneta, L. 3.8 "to the monte della pietà, and to them for a number of pawns given back on

9. DG, Parte antica, Recapiti di Cassa, filza 948, no. 303, 19 Apr. 1555.

10. DG, Parte antica, Recapiti di Cassa, filza 950, no. 832, 29 Feb. 1555 (O.S.). The attached receipt confirms that the sum was actually paid. On the Company of San Martino, see DG, Parte antica, Recapiti di Cassa, filza 951, no. 717, 3 Feb. 1556 (O.S.). Also DG, Parte antica 954, no. 904, 4 Mar. 1556 (O.S.), where Antonio made a series of nine payments of fifty scudi each from 5 Mar. 1556 (O.S.) through 13 Nov. 1557 to the company.

11. On the flood, see Otto di Pratica (Principato) 198, Quattro Commessari sopra la Piena d'Arno (1557).

our orders through last September on account of the flood to a number of our court employees."[12] The monte di pietà was only one among many charities aided by the duke in the months following the flood. For instance, he paid over sc. 800 to two bakeries "for bread given to eight convents of nuns . . . for alms for the damage they suffered from the flood."[13]

Cosimo's forbearance in not approaching the monte di pietà for money at a time of need may have resulted from his appreciation of the services the institution offered the poor as well as from his astute understanding about what happens to the production of golden eggs once the goose is killed. Like any ruler at war, Cosimo displayed a voracious appetite for money. He did, however, have recourse to other resources, including one of Europe's greatest lenders, the Fugger family. In January 1557 the duke ordered his treasurer-general to "pay to the Signori Antonio Fuccheri and nephews of Augsburg residing in Venice, and for them to Messer Michele di Leonardo Mayer, their procurator, . . . three thousand scudi d'oro in oro."[14] Private lenders also accommodated the duke. He took a much larger loan of eight thousand at 12 percent from a Spaniard, Signor Luigi Martiningo, who was also on the ducal payroll, in January 1557.[15] In summer 1558, records of the ducal treasury show a series of repayments to individuals who had lent him money during the previous summer. The following list details private loans to Cosimo de' Medici during 1557–58.[16]

Creditor	Amount lent (scudi)
Sinibaldo Gaddi	1,000
Giovanni Gerini	933 ⅓
Tommaso Soderini	1,500

12. DG, Parte antica, Recapiti di Cassa, filza 954, no. 887, 1 Feb. 1557 (O.S.).

13. DG, Parte antica 954, no. 900, 28 Feb. 1557 (O.S.).

14. DG, Parte antica, Recapiti di Cassa, filza 951, no. 632, 2 Jan. 1556 (O.S.). Michele Mayer signed the receipt for the three thousand scudi, which he took in several installments in repayment of a loan.

15. DG, Parte antica 951, no. 643, 8 Jan. 1556 (O.S.). The duke continued to pay interest on the loan; see, e.g., DG, Parte antica, Recapiti di Cassa, filza 955, no. 200, 6 May 1558.

16. DG, Parte antica 955, no. 189, 28 May 1558. On this date all these creditors received half the amount due, not including interest, except for Gerini, who received sc. 460. The interest rate was not stipulated; similar loans carried 12 percent.

Creditor	Amount lent (scudi)
Agnolo Guicciardini	1,000
Giovanni and Piero Dini	1,000
Calandro Calandri	8,000
Bartolomeo Carnesecchi	700
Jacopo Capponi	600
Piero Capponi	500
Filippo Salviati	2,800
Luigi Pieri	1,400
TOTAL	19,433 ⅓

The payment order to the treasurer does not note the interest paid, but does state that payments were to be made on "capital and interest" on the amounts lent "for our service."[17]

At the same time there can be no doubt about the increasing involvement of the duke in the affairs of the monte di pietà. Nor is there any doubt that Cosimo's interest in that institution reflected his interest in all Florentine institutions, and that he embarked on a policy calculated to bring them closely under his control and to regularize their operations. His systematic approach to statecraft required the compilation of accurate statistics, and to this end he called for the census of 1551–52, the most thorough record of the population since the famous Catasto of 1427, which enumerated not only heads of households but also dependents and servants. This vigilant scrutiny was aimed at allowing the regime to keep better track of Florentines, especially when tax time rolled around.

The search for order also included imposing standards of behavior on Florentine public officials. Corruption among their ranks had been spurred by the competition for offices during the days of the commune.[18] By the early fifteenth century the ruling groups attempted to combat these evils by imposing harsh civil penalties such as fines or disqualification on those who obtained offices unfairly or who abused the powers of their magistracies. Florentines also developed the habit of entrusting sensitive posts to foreigners who, they hopefully supposed, were aloof from local partisanship. In 1429 the

17. DG, Parte antica 955, 189, 28 May 1558.
18. See Andrea Zorzi, "I fiorentini e gli uffici pubblici nel primo Quattrocento: Concorrenza, abusi, illegalità," *Quaderni storici*, n.s., 66 (1987): 725–51.

Conservatori delle Leggi came into being, charged with ensuring execution of the laws and overseeing the behavior of civic officials. Cleaning out corruption helped assure control of the city and efficient government, but conversely, or rather perversely, a ruling clique could also use false accusations of misbehavior to remove its rivals from politics.

The tradition of setting up boards of auditors (*sindaci*) stretched back at least to the late thirteenth century, when appellate judges appointed auditors to examine civic financial records.[19] From 1502, when Piero Soderini became gonfaloniere for life, through 1527, one of the Signori was probably appointed treasurer of the funds of the commune (*depositario del denaro del comune*). In 1527, sixteen *ufficiali di banco* oversaw communal payments. Since the fourteenth century, individual auditors investigated civic officers as they wound up their terms. These auditors could view the officers' records, judge disputes, and, where necessary, mete out punishments. Even the highest officers of the government were subject to this scrutiny if suspected of mishandling their offices. On rare occasions an entire Signoria was audited on the suspicion of maladministration.

Within three years of his ascent, and at a time when famine had descended on the region, Cosimo and the Magistrato Supremo turned their attention to reform and review of public officials who handled money. The duke and his advisers noted that many such officials had neglected to balance their books for years. At first the duke had ordered all such men to render an accounting to the sindaci of the monte comune, but it soon became clear that the sindaci lacked the manpower to carry out anything like a thorough audit on so large a scale. As a result the overall financial status of many magistracies remained cloudy, which in turn meant that in times of stress the public fisc could not take full advantage of any surpluses since even the officials themselves frequently could not say how much money they held. To remedy this evil, all public camarlinghi would be required to report with their balanced books to three citizens ap-

19. Pietro Rigobon, in *La contabilità di stato nella repubblica di Firenze e nel granducato di Toscana* (Grigenti, 1892), notes the city's attempts to track down fraud or incompetence in the financial dealings of officials. See esp. 56–88, 177–97. For one serious case of fraud during the ducal regime and its consequences for the state, see Carol Bresnahan Menning, "Finance and Fraud during the Reign of Cosimo I: The Case of Giuliano del Tovaglia," *Historian* 51 (1988): 1–18.

pointed as sindaci, or general auditors empowered "to review all accounts whatsoever of all ministers, officials and others whomsoever who had managed public moneys in any way whatsoever since the year 1530." The three auditors could also appoint accountants and arithmeticians to help them.[20]

A more impressive sign of the power of their office came from their license to call for examination, under penalties they themselves could set, of anyone who had had responsibility for public funds. They could even remand such persons for examination under torture. Though zeal for their office might help motivate the three sindaci, a more tangible motivation was their compensation of "two soldi for every lira that they place in the entrata," along with whatever reward the duke chose to add. The first three, Girolamo degli Albizzi, Cristofano Rinieri, and Bernardo Acciaiuoli, were confirmed by the Magistrato Supremo in May 1540. Later the same month the Magistrato declared that the sindaci held the right to proceed not only against public but also private persons. Their target was persons involved in "fraud, or who made use of their positions or of public money for themselves" or who had "lent their . . . favor" to such fraud or schemes.[21]

By the 1540s the monte di pietà was among those institutions that had begun to suffer damages from fraud, dishonesty, and incompetence. A great number of those listed as debtors at the end of each triennium were in fact employees who had, for one reason or another, cost the monte money. Several employees are among the following debtors.[22]

Name	*Amount*
Raffaello di Bartolomeo, former garzone	fl. 93, L. 632.4.7
Angiolino di Jacopo Manucci, former stimatore	fl. 31, L. 747.10
Dionigi Nasi, former massaro, 3d monte	L. 17.13

20. MS 5, 86r, 12 April 1540.
21. MS 5, 86r–v, 12 Apr. 1540; and for the confirmation, 108r, 11 May 1540; for confirmation and clarification of their powers, 110r–v, 24 May 1540.
22. See MP 744 and 746 passim. The entries under "More debtors" refer to losses from bad debts, unpaid interest, pawns sold at auction for less than the amount owed, miscellaneous damages, and so on.

Francesco di Bernardo, former camarlingo	L. 88.14.4
Niccolò di Bernardo di Ser Nigi, former camarlingo, 1st monte	L. 1,589.15
Romolo di Daniele, former stimatore	L. 15.16.8
Cosimo, former garzone	L. 12.14
More debtors and losses than creditors, 1st monte	L. 5,224.10.4
More debtors and losses than creditors, 3d monte	fl. 52, L. 2,846.18.1
Baldassare "il Bassino," former garzone	fl. 58, L. 851.13.1
Francesco di Mariotto, former stimatore	fl. 46, L. 1,128.19.8

Some of these damages were recovered from the mallevadori, or guarantors, who had agreed to be responsible for certain sums of money in the event of losses incurred during the officeholder's tenure. A credit was listed in 1533 "in compensation . . . for the account of Bassino" for fl. 58, L. 851.13.11. Another debt was partly erased by a credit entered for the damages caused by Raffaello, former garzone, in the amount of L. 630.18.4. Despite these recovered sums, the situation only worsened. Tommaso Strozzi, a former assessor at the first branch, recorded a debit of L. 22.1 in his current account, a small loss that could easily be absorbed. What must have shocked the bookkeepers was Tommaso's admission that he was short over two thousand lire "on account of several lost pawns during the time he was an assessor, as can be seen in various account books." He was also debited because of "damage to pawns that he caused" at the first branch. In total, Tommaso's actions resulted in debits to the monte of L. 2,767.–.11.[23] The institution's statutes were explicit about the duties of the stimatori, and underscored the gravity of the office by

23. MP 746, Libro di debitori e creditori, 2b, 11b. The books were quite clear that this money was in compensation for losses and damages during the tenure of these men: "Meriti per conto del Bassino. . . . Nota che e detti danari stanno per riscontro de'danni fatti el detto Bassino." And "meriti . . . per danni fatti Raffaello fu garzone. Nota ch'e sopradetti danari stanno per riscontro de'danni fatti el sopradetto Raffaello." On Tommaso Strozzi, see MP 746, 81a–b: "Tommaso Strozi fu stimatore nel primo monte dè dare addì 19 di settembre 1536 L. 22.1, di tanti restava debitore al quaderno di cassa del primo monte . . . e sono per resto d'un suo conto corrente. . . . Tommaso Strozzi . . . restava debitore al quaderno segnato C . . . e sono per più danni di pegni fecie nel monte."

requiring that each find guarantors. The stimatori were obliged to assess each pledge honestly and accurately, and were held responsible for damages resulting from their failure to do so.[24]

Losses the monte incurred due to inept or dishonest employees were so frequent and heavy that one wonders if any employee ever served his time without becoming a debtor to his employer.[25] In March 1533 the accounts of Giovanni di Niccolò Primerani, the monte's former camarlingo who had died earler that year, were found to be short by several thousand lire. The audit of his books took nearly two years.[26] The following are the debits of Giovanni Primerani:

> Giovanni di Niccolò Primerani, formerly our camarlingo, is debited on 17 March [1533, O.S.] fl. 17, L. –.6.8, himself having been made creditor for them in one of his accounts in the quaderno di cassa (cash book) Q.
>
> And on 17 March . . . for the remainder of one of his accounts, fl. 445, L. 2.12.10. Q
>
> And on 18 March . . . for so much for which he was made creditor, fl. 1,724, L. 9,028.10.7.
>
> And on that day, for so much found that he had for us from Niccolò di Ser Nigi, posted as credit (havere) in the quaderno, fl. 14.
>
> And on Dec. 10, 1535, . . . L. 3.12, to Bartolomeo Corsali for the reason stated in the book of outgo.
>
> And on Dec. 20 . . . L. 257.18.8, for one of his accounts, posted in the book of outgo.
>
> TOTAL fl. 2,200, L. 9,293.–.9
>   fl. 2,200 = L. 15,400
>
> TOTAL L. 24,693.–.9

24. The assessors "sieno tenuti alla satisfazione del danno. . . . E per ciò siano tenuti dare innanzi l'entrata loro mallevadori sufficienti di fiorini 300." MP 2, Statuti, 4r.

25. This chronic Florentine problem extended well beyond the monte di pietà. In 1567 the Pratica Segreta received a letter from Antonio de' Nobili's son begging for the duke's remission of nearly twenty-two hundred florins in debts that the late Antonio had accrued while serving the Medici. The son reminded the duke of Antonio's heavy duties, so onerous that Antonio had been obliged to hire men to help him at his own expense. Lelio Torelli passed on the word that the duke "graciously remits the entire debt that [Antonio] has with him." PS 7, Julio de' Nobili to Cosimo de' Medici, 14 Feb. 1566 (O.S.).

26. MP 746, 44a–b.

Part of this debt was reduced by applying credits to it, such as the L. 419 paid to one Domenico, garzone, and some L. 3,800 "for one of [Giovanni's] accounts in the quaderno di cassa R." But the temptation to write off the entire debit as bookkeeping sleight of hand is dispelled by a glance at the opposite page in the ledger, which shows that the monte actually collected sums from the guarantors of its late employee (and also reduced the debit by applying to it Giovanni's legitimate credits). On 20 September 1535 it took in L. 2,100 from Lorenzo Benciveni, L. 1,753 from Francesco Bonaiuto, L. 1,878.15 from Matteo Tanagli, L. 700 from Bastiano Parigialli, L. 490 from Antonio Billi and his son Francesco, and L. 235 from one Giuliano, all guarantors for Giovanni. All told, L. 12,883.4.4 in credits reduced Giovanni's debt to about half of the L. 24,693.-.9 noted above.

The monte continued to collect money to offset the losses incurred during Primerani's employment. By 1536 his debt had been reduced to fl. 1,624, L. -.2.5. Three years later he was still in debt for over fl. 1,470.[27] The next ledger showed that, by 1542, he owed over fl. 1,100. The debt continued to be slowly reduced over each three-year span, but in 1557, nearly twenty-five years after the discovery of the losses, the estate still owed the monte di pietà over fl. 600.[28]

The importance of the role played by mallevadori was especially evident in Primerani's case. The eight officials enjoyed protection from personal liability for any losses suffered by the monte di pietà during their tenure. Employees did not. The massaro, for example, was responsible for rounding up eight individuals, acceptable to the monte's eight-man governing board, who would pledge one thousand florins each on his behalf. When appointed to that position at the first branch in 1539, Bartolomeo Baroncelli met this obligation through the help of Bartolomeo di Luca Buondelmonti, Lorenzo d'Agnolo Baroncelli, Pagolo di Filippo Corsini, Pierfrancesco d'Andrea Carnesecchi, Francesco di Bartolomeo Benintendi, Francesco di Paolantonio Bandini, Mainardo di Bartolomeo Cavalcanti, and a man identified only as "Giovanni, emancipated son of Naripetti." No lengthy analysis of these surnames is needed to appreciate the lofty

---

27. MP 748, Libro di debitori e creditori, 2b, 63a.
28. MP 750, Libro di debitori e creditori, 76a, and MP 762, 6a. The latter goes into explicit detail about not only the debt but the rules for repayment. Such a debt was to be reduced by small payments every year by the heirs, until it was erased.

status of most of them. Nor should this come as any surprise, for the requirement of bond meant that only employees with influential and wealthy friends and kinsmen could serve as monte employees. Each cashier (cassiere) had to find guarantors who could pledge a total of five thousand florins; each scribe, six hundred; each assessor, from six hundred to nine hundred; even each assistant garzone needed to present acceptable mallevadori for a total of three hundred florins. In 1539, bondsmen for all monte employees at all branches guaranteed a total of fl. 129,000, evidence that the monte was serious about holding its employees, from massaro to garzone, to a high standard of integrity enforced by the mallevadori system.[29] Still the system failed to prevent losses.

Mallevadori also played a second and very different role in the monte di pietà. In May 1544 the institution began to grant large loans at 6 percent backed up by guarantors in addition to its custom of offering loans against pawns.[30] Soon petitions from subjects flooded to the duke, asking for his authorization to undertake large loans secured not, as in the past, by valuables, but by guarantors. In retrospect it is tempting to doubt the wisdom of this change. If a borrower defaulted on a loan against a pawn, the monte could auction the pawn and hope to recover its money. If a borrower with guarantors defaulted, the monte could try to collect from the guarantors, but reimbursement proved difficult and could involve costly and time-consuming lawsuits. In any case, the result was a boom in the monte's large-loan business. In 1567 the duke authorized a large loan to Montauto de' Conti di Montauto that shows both the continued reliance on guarantors for securing large loans and the duke's ability to force the monte to grant such loans at 5 rather than 6 percent: "Lend [him] the sum of 500 scudi di moneta for two years, taking from him the customary guarantors for both capital and interest at 5 percent.[31]

In January 1543 the monte's eight officials found one of their own employees, Francesco di Domenico (who was standing in for the reg-

---

29. MP 26, Deliberazioni, 120r–v.

30. Misc. Rep., busta vii, ins. 218: On 12 May 1544, "principiò il Monte a fare imprestiti anco' sopra i mallevadori con farsi pagare il frutto alla ragione di sei per-cento l'anno."

31. MP 266, Cosimo de' Medici to MP, 5 July 1567.

ular garzone at the second monte, Domenico da Cortona), guilty of fraud. This verdict stands apart from earlier renderings of accounts in the seriousness of its intent and in the atmosphere of overall reform in which it occurred. For the first time, the details of a case of intentional fraud appeared in the book of deliberations of the eight.

The eight accused Francesco of having "clandestinely and secretively" submitted the same pawn for multiple loans, of having illegally obtained cash for pawns, and of having stolen pawns from his workplace, "and thus in this way he deceived and defrauded" the monte di pietà. Under close questioning, he confessed to having spirited away pledges without having paid the cashier for them and admitted that he had done this while serving as garzone, a position that, because of its responsibilities for storing and retrieving pawns, gave him unlimited access to them. He stole a string of small pawns, such as a kerchief valued at three lire, and pawned the same black cape on at least two different occasions for fourteen lire (or two florins), the maximum that could be borrowed against a pawn at 5 percent interest.[32]

In another case the assessor Francesco di Mariotto Peccotti, who in 1534 had been discovered to have caused losses to the institution, was continually carried forward as a debtor for over one hundred florins, which amounted to "the remainder of the damages he did in the monte." His three mallevadori had been ordered to pay small amounts on an annual schedule until the entire debt was extinguished: Girolamo Boni and his son Jacopo were assessed ten florins annually, and Giovanni Amadori had to pay four florins each year "up to the sum for which they have been obligated, which was his surety for the time he served [the monte]." But this order was in vain, for the mallevadori were apparently able to evade the monte's attempts to collect the debt. The institution reaped more success in moving against Agnolo Mannucci, whose guarantors were held responsible for fl. 27, L. 5, which they made good. Though these debits were listed as damages from the time they were uncovered, it is only in the ledger of 1557–60 that the details of the repayment

---

32. MP 26, 28 Jan. 1542. "'Condemnatio Francesci Domenici gharzonnis.' . . . clandestine et occulte ut vulgo dicitur inpegnava in detto monte di piatà sua pegni [*sic*] et d'altri più volte et maxime una sua cappa nera . . . la qual medesima chappa . . . rimpegnò più et molte volte con altri pegni . . . et così faccendo in detto modo ingannava et defraudava deti monti."

plans and the names of the guarantors were spelled out.[33] By 1548 it was clear that the Florentine system of relying on mallevadori was flawed. Officials of the fisc wrote the duke that among the guarantors of "delinquents" were many who were "so poor that they don't have any way of paying a single quattrino, and this whole flaw stems from the magistrates and rectors" who failed to be careful enough in accepting persons as guarantors. This shortcoming, they continued, did "the gravest damage to the ducal camera." The remedy was to require the magistrates themselves to serve as mallevadori for mallevadori, thus avoiding "similar disorder" in the future.[34]

It was no coincidence that the monte di pietà's officials began to scrutinize the establishment's operations by the late 1550s: at precisely this time, ducal auditors and informants spread through Florence, searching for fiscal malfeasance during the recent war and moving with the vigor that came from a ducal mandate.[35] Furthermore, after the war it seemed that the poor and, consequently, the need for charity were increasing. Incidents such as the detailed investigation into the case of Francesco di Domenico, the careful ferreting out of inept or deceitful employees, and the attempts to recover damages in these cases form part of a continuing thread throughout the monte's history. But they become more meaningful when placed against the background of Cosimo's statecraft. For by the 1550s a thorough search for fraud and corruption was under way in Florence, one which affected not only the monte di pietà but the duke's most trusted advisers.

In 1556 Cosimo set up a group of four high commissioners, the Soprassindaci de'Conti della Guerra, to audit the accounts of the recent war.[36] Cosimo had probably learned the importance of such a commission from his own experiences, for he himself had been subject to regular audits during the first years of his reign. The eight ottimati who had supported his candidacy to lead Florence set up a treasury headed by an official who was appointed to a term not to exceed one year and had to look over the accounts every six months.

33. On Francesco Peccoti and Agnolo Mannucci, MP 762, 6a–b.

34. MS 1121, Suppliche, Exactori fiscali to Cosimo de' Medici, 29 July 1548; the duke responded, "Facessi."

35. MP 762, 6a–b, 258a.

36. These four were Francesco Salviati, Battista Brandini, Lorenzo della Stufa, and Niccolò Carducci.

Antonio de' Nobili too undertook with dedication the task of overseeing the examination of the finances of the duchy. "I have said," he wrote to Cosimo in the late 1550s when looking into the records of one Florentine functionary, "that I have a passion that the truth come to light for the honor of your Excellency . . . so that in the future others will learn to recognize what things must be done."[37] He kept Cosimo informed of the progress of the various investigations. After reading a report by his treasurer about the interrogation under torture at the Bargello of an official suspected of fraud, the duke noted with chilling detachment, "The important thing is to find out the truth."[38]

Cosimo expected prompt obedience and displayed impatience at delays in the audits. In May 1553, irritated that they had not yet begun to examine the books of a ducal paymaster, he chastised a team of auditors charged with the tremendous task of examining the books of virtually every public official in the duchy and headed by Giuliano del Tovaglia and Carlo Manucelli. "March and April have already passed," he wrote. "Here it is May, and you have not even begun your work. Truly we marvel at this, the more so because you have never told us a word about it."[39]

Not even Medici kin escaped the auditors' scrutiny. Giovanbattista d'Alamanno de' Medici, provveditore at Piombino, had to present his accounts and assure the auditors that the debts and credits of his predecessor in that office could be justified.[40] Even Tommaso de' Medici had to explain his expenses in entertaining the viceroy of Naples, who was Cosimo's father-in-law. Accounts of deceased officials were examined and their heirs held liable for any outstanding debts. In one case, Girolamo degli Albizzi "of blessed memory" was discovered to owe a substantial sum of money. Only part of the debt could be found: some 518 ducats were recovered from his heir Marsilio, and 200 from Luca Mini, treasurer of the bande. Thus the heirs of Girolamo were posted as debtors for the difference, which came to more than 1,348 ducats. They asked to be allowed to make

37. See Ridolfi, "Diario fiorentino di anonimo," 548–49. On Antonio de' Nobili, Med. 608, Antonio de' Nobili to Cosimo de' Medici, 836v, n.d.

38. Med. 608, minute by Cosimo de' Medici, letter of Antonio de' Nobili to Cosimo, 905r–906v.

39. Sindaci 1, no. 1, Cosimo de' Medici to the sindaci, 5 May 1553.

40. Sin. 1, to DG, 26 Nov. 1557.

good this sum in the equivalent value in arms (harquebuses, pikes, and so on), with some written off for bad debts. Most striking of all, the seven hundred–odd ducats that were recovered were paid into the duke's account in the monte di pietà.[41]

The monte di pietà began to appear regularly in the records of the sindaci as the destination for money owed the duke by his own administrators. In August 1557, for example, the auditors reported to the duke that they had uncovered a sum of money owed him and recommended that it be put into the treasury. A ducal secretary sent back a reply expressing Cosimo's wish that the money be placed instead in his account in the monte di pietà.[42] Other sums, some of them substantial, remaining in the hands of various provveditori after all expenses had been paid were ordered into the same repository. From the provveditore of the Otto di Pratica came fl. 164, L. 5.11.11. From Michele Ruberti, who was in turn paid by order of Giovanni Giandonati, provveditore of the Fortress of Arezzo, came fl. 417, L. 6.[43] Cosimo was already thinking of the monte di pietà as a treasury for ducal funds.

These cases prove that the mechanics of ducal finance were helping to construct an ever-stronger link between the duke and the monte di pietà. Why allow money owed him to lie useless in the ducal treasury when, deposited in the monte di pietà, it could accrue 5 percent interest?[44]

The monte di pietà was one of several institutions that, by the

41. Sin. 1, to DG, 26 Nov. 1557. Appointed a senator in 1532 by Clement VII, Girolamo had been one of the leading proponents of the election of Cosimo after Alessandro's assassination. He also served as *commessario* of the duke. Diaz, *Granducato*, 66, 120 n. 2; and Ricci, *Cronaca*, 296r. Sin. 1, no. 2, to Cosimo de' Medici. In examining Albizzi's accounts, the sindaci discovered some wrongdoing: one of his agents, Cosimo Casini, was thrown into the Bargello on their order, where he languished for eighteen days until his brother Girolamo petitioned the duke to release Cosimo, an old man, and to confine him in his own house under bond. Sin. 1, no. 10, 23 Sept. 1556.

42. Sin. 1, no. 2, 25 Aug. 1557.

43. Sin. 1, no. 12, Soprassindaci to Chiarissimo de' Medici, provveditore of the monte di pietà; Sin. 1, no. 12, 4 Nov. 1553, to Cosimo de' Medici; Sin. to Luca Mini, 1 Mar. 1556 (O.S.); Sin. 1, Soprassindaci to provveditore of the monte di pietà, 6 Mar. 1556 (O.S.); Sin. 1, to Marsilio degli Albizi, 6 Mar. 1556 (O.S.). These documents all contain similar language: "et gli farete mettere a entrata per il detto Camarlingo de la piatà da Sua Eccellenza Illustrissima."

44. Cosimo had, ironically, discovered a new meaning to the old idea of *lucrum cessans.*

1550s, were being made to play the role of ducal bank. Some of the duke's transactions with these institutions involved complicated transfers of funds. In one order to his treasurer-general calling for the payment of nearly sc. 175 to the Camarlingo alle Graticole del Monte, the latter was in turn "to pay fifty gold scudi to Messer Giovanfrancesco da Mantova for his upkeep and one hundred nineteen gold scudi, L. 4.17.4 to the camarlingo of the wool guild, to him so that he then pay it to the maestro and the clerics of the chorus of Santa Maria del Fiore."[45] This office too became a kind of funnel into which Cosimo ordered deposits of money to be used to pay ducal employees, who then received credits in the Graticole. In another case, the duke told Antonio de' Nobili to place over sc. 533 in the monte, at seven lire per scudo, to pay the six judges of the Ruota.[46]

The search for fraud soon uncovered a scandal in Florence. Cosimo had begun to suspect the loyalty and honesty of Giuliano del Tovaglia, who had been paymaster during the war with Siena, and before that one of Cosimo's chief auditors and provveditore of the Gabella della Carne (the office of the tax on meat). The unfortunate Giuliano was seized, tortured, and finally forced to admit that he had siphoned off thousands of ducats for himself and several fellow conspirators. More alarming was the extent of the network of fraud: he had recruited at least half a dozen men to help him. Cosimo's auditors spent months uncovering the facts and were stymied by the careful coverup that Giuliano had apparently set up. They finally reported to the duke that they suspected the validity, "with good reason," of some two thousand entries in Giuliano's books.[47] Moreover, they had to recommend to the duke a moratorium on payments by the ducal treasury, and they suggested that notice be given that no further claims stemming from war finance would be honored until they had completed their work. The duke told Antonio de' Nobili to inform "all camarlinghi of every kind that not a single denaro will be paid."[48] This single conspiracy brought about a partial halt in the financial activity of the ducal state.

45. DG, Recapiti di Cassa, filza 949, no. 381, 27 July 1555.
46. Ibid., no. 398, 27 July, 1555.
47. The details of this episode emerge from Med. 603, among other sources. See Menning, "Finance and Fraud."
48. Med. 603, Cosimo de' Medici to Antonio de' Nobili, 510r–v.

This episode helps put into context the duke's efforts to clean up corruption in the monte di pietà. Even after the triumph over Siena, Cosimo could not relax. Instead, greater watchfulness was required. No one was to be trusted blindly. Ducal control over finance must therefore be complete, and the loyalty and honesty of public officials had to be unquestionable. The latitude that public officials enjoyed in rooting out corruption could only have developed in this atmosphere and in accordance with the duke's will.

Just as Giuliano's treachery was being tracked down and auditors with sharpened pens ranged through the city, the monte di pietà uncovered a conspiracy to defraud it. In April 1558 the duke directed Ser Ieronimo de' Migliorati to write to the monte's eight officials informing them of the capture of "one Franco [Francesco di Bartolomeo da Settignano], formerly garzone at the Pazzi branch [of the monte di pietà] and presently stimatore, and of one Jacopo his son . . . and of Monna Lucrezia, Franco's wife." The duke, Migliorati stated, wanted the truth to come out. The eight were to commence interrogations of the three, who were charged with stealing from the monte di pietà, and to keep the ruler informed of the case's progress.[49] The eight began with the interrogation of Monna Lucrezia.

> Asked if she knew the reason why she had been brought in, she said no, and that she couldn't imagine why. . . . Asked if she knew Monna Caterina di Benuccio from Settignano she said yes. Asked if the said Caterina had ever brought anything from Florence to Settignano, she said no, but that Monna Caterina had accompanied her from Settignano to Florence. . . . Asked whether she [Caterina] had ever brought her [Lucrezia] pawns from Florence, . . . she said yes, . . . but that . . . there had only been a few. . . . She was warned, and told to tell things as they were . . . , that otherwise the case would proceed to torture.

Her husband, Francesco, was next. Asked why he had been brought in, he too said he did not know. His interrogators fired

---

49. The details about the following interrogations come from MP 27, Libro di partiti, 1554–59, notes of interrogations of 15 Apr., 21 Apr., 27 Apr., 5 May, 11 May 1558, 20r–v and throughout. Unfortunately, the next book in this series, MP 28, begins only in the year 1563, leaving a lacuna of three years.

questions at him, demanding to know whether he had taken the pawn of a third party without having entered it in the books. Didn't he know one Caterina from his hometown of Settignano? Hadn't she taken an assortment of pawns from Florence to Settignano? Yes, but these had all belonged to her friends, and she was doing them the favor of redeeming and retrieving the pledges while she happened to be on a trip to Florence. That was why she had brought these pawns to her own house. And all the pawns had been licitly redeemed, the original loan and interest paid. In that case, could Francesco produce receipts? He could, but they were in the monte's third branch. The officials warned him that, if he failed to be truthful, he would face torture.

The questioning of persons suspected of involvement or believed to have useful information continued. The eight had to take a hard line with one Jacopo di Domenico, who answered insolently that he did not think he had committed any wrongdoing for which he could be sent to prison. Right away they threatened him with torture. Asked if he had ever done any injury to the monte, he replied no. Did he deny having removed pawns from the monte without having paid for them? He certainly did! Did he? A witness, one of the garzoni at the branch in the Canto de' Pazzi, had seen him take a pawn away. Oh, that belonged to a friend. Did it indeed? What kind of pawn was it? Who was the friend? Jacopo didn't remember.

The assessor Francesco was questioned again. He was informed that "he had committed in the monte considerable errors and damages" and was advised "to confess everything." He persisted in his claim of innocence. His wife was questioned again, and the eight wondered whether "she had thought of other errors that she had made." She replied in the negative. A few days later the suspects were released from prison when bond was posted for them.[50] The officials took several days to investigate further before calling Francesco back for questioning. They told him they had found many receipts in his house that implicated him anew. He protested that the allegedly missing pawns were safe in the monte. The same day, Jac-

---

50. John K. Brackett, *Criminal Justice and Crime in Late Renaissance Florence, 1537–1609* (Cambridge, 1992), has shown that releasing prisoners (except those accused of political crimes) who could post bond became common during Cosimo's reign (60–61).

opo was brought in, accused of the theft of a dozen pawns, and sent to be drawn on the rope.

With this turn of events, Lucrezia confessed to having stolen eight ducats from the monte along with several items, including a little sack that she apparently hoped contained money. She brought it to a Sorella Brigida and a Signor Baldassari. The former agreed that she had received several items, including the eight ducats, from Lucrezia. Francesco remained adamant, and was subjected again to the terrible *strappado*. His hands, tied behind him, were attached to a rope which in turn was pulled, raising him up off his feet. His shoulders were probably dislocated immediately. Sometimes weights were attached to victims' feet to increase their agony as the torture was repeated. Francesco soon admitted "to having taken the pawns" and to having defrauded the monte of fl. 449. He confessed, under threat of more torment, to having stolen other pawns. Twice more threatened with the rope, he responded with the details of his thievery. He had been sure to take all the pawns early in the morning, he confided, so as to be able to operate undetected. Shown more instruments of torture, he signed his confession. He was found guilty and sentenced to be mounted on an ass and led through the city of Florence wearing a sign that said, "For having robbed the pawns." This humiliating trip would, however, be mild in comparison to the ten years forced service in the galleys to which he was condemned. His accomplice, Jacopo, was to suffer the same ride atop an ass and, in punishment for robbing the monte of forty ducats, would work the galleys for three years. All the while the hunt for corruption continued, and it was found in high places: Antonio degli Albizzi, the provveditore, admitted under threat of torture that he too had stolen pawns.

To a modern observer the brutal tactics used to extract confessions cast doubt on the suspects' guilt, and it is impossible to determine whether Francesco and Jacopo did rob the monte or whether they were merely unfortunate victims of a system that demanded scapegoats. Cosimo, however, had embarked on no wholesale purge. The search for misdeeds and fraud left room for careful consideration of individual cases, and an accusation did not always lead to conviction and punishment. In one case Alfonso della Casa, a massaro in the monte, was debited the sum of fl. 287 on account of a shortfall in the accounts of a former garzone "who did us some damages." Alfonso appealed this decision to the eight officials, who came to the conclusion that he should not be held responsible for the losses incurred by the subordinate employee, and in April 1561 they credited him with the sum of fl. 287 in order to balance his account.[51]

Nor did Cosimo exact rigorous justice from those public officials who, though their accounts came up short, had not intended to defraud. Examining one such case related to the financing of the war against Siena, Cosimo's first secretary, Lelio Torelli, distinguished between "negligence," which included errors of arithmetic and ignorance of foreign weights and measures, and "malice," which implied the intent to profit from premeditated fraud. One case concerned Matteo Castrucci, whose shortfall of nearly four hundred scudi was forgiven because he "had not erred maliciously but out of his limited intelligence and his ignorance."[52] The last resort even for those who had committed fraud with malice aforethought was to throw themselves on the mercy of the duke. An estimator at the monte di pietà, "who used to cut off the tickets from the pawns that had been pledged and then re-pawn them, and keep the money," was condemned by the Otto to the gallows and thrown into the Bargello. But in an act of princely clemency, Don Francesco de' Medici granted him his freedom.[53]

The zealous pursuit of malfeasance must be traced directly to Cosimo's personality and statecraft. He never forgot the end met by his predecessor Alessandro, and he himself had had to suppress an attempted revolt by exiles at Montemurlo.[54] Experience had conditioned the duke to expect conspiracies everywhere, and if he occasionally appears slightly paranoid, it must be remembered that paranoids may indeed have real enemies. A ducal network of spies and informers supplied him with tips, gossip, and intelligence. "Every monastery was said to contain an informer, every church, street and square," wrote John Hale in his assessment of Cosimo's vigilance. The Venetian ambassador remarked upon the duke's "retentive memory," and recorded that "if he sees a stranger he has not

---

51. MP 764, Libro di debitori e creditori, 115a.

52. Sin. 3, 1560–61, 10 Mar. 1560 (O.S.). Menning, "Finance and Fraud," cites other cases.

53. Ricci, *Cronaca*, 343v (76), 4 Feb. 1573 (O.S.).

54. For an account of this conspiracy, see D'Addario, *Formazione*, chap. 8, and Diaz, *Granducato*, chap. 1.3. One of the most detailed sources is the diary edited by Ridolfi, "Diario fiorentino di anonimo."

seen before he wants to know who he is and what he does."[55] For Cosimo, information was power. This was, after all, a prince of whom Benedetto Varchi could write, "Cosimo alone governed all, and nothing whatsoever, great or small, was done or said without his say-so."[56]

The need for careful bookkeeping was reinforced by the busy auditors whom Cosimo had ordered to review the records of Florentine institutions. The monte di pietà's bookkeepers could not be accused of taking their duties lightly; in fact, they had always tried to exercise diligence in keeping track of the institution's finances. But anyone studying the ledger for 1557–60, which coincided with the Tovaglia affair and the monte's own housecleaning, quickly discerns an intensified concern for detail and accuracy. Even accounts dating back to the first decade of the monte's history were recounted minutely, a task that must have meant long hours pouring over past ledgers, some of them forty or fifty years old. It was the bookkeepers' habit to provide several cross-references to current accounts for each entry, but the 1557–60 ledger even contains cross-references to old books in which long-standing deposits had first been entered. As an example, the monte's officials had decided in 1506 to award credit to the monastery of Santa Chiara with the understanding that the religious would use the alms to purchase grain. This gift was entered as a debit in the name of the monastery and was carried forward every year, even though the monte did not expect the nuns to repay the money. The entry for 1557 recalled the purpose of the grant, which had totaled two hundred florins, related in detail the decision reached in 1506, and included a list of grain prices and the amounts purchased.[57] Further, the list of "bad debtors" contained separate entries for each malefactor who had caused losses to the monte along with, in most cases, the nature of the loss. The case of Tommaso Strozzi was not forgotten; he was charged as a debtor for fl. 395, L. 2.-.11 "for a number of pawns that he stole." One Niccolò di Matteo, a barber, had received by error a payment of fl. 17, L.

55. Quoted in Hale, *Florence and the Medici*, 136–37.

56. Quoted in Pieraccini, *La stirpe de' Medici*, 13: "ma Cosimo solo governava il tutto, nè si diceva o faceva cosa alcuna, nè cosa grande, nè cosa piccola, alla quale egli non desse il sì o il no."

57. MP 762, 6a–b. The payments to Santa Chiara had stretched into 1508; see MP 19, 11r, 13v, and following.

1.3.8, and was duly listed as a debtor in order to balance this mistake. A former cashier, Niccolò Becchi, owed fl. 4, L. 5, "which are for four errors discovered in his entries, to the loss of Dino Compagni, massaro." Lucky Becchi! He was dead by 1557 and no longer had to be troubled about this debt; the problem was now his heirs'. The duke's accounts required special care: the bookkeepers discovered an error to Cosimo's disadvantage, and so, to rectify it, they solemnly credited the duke with one denaro.[58]

The atmosphere of caution and watchfulness did not dissipate in the 1560s as the monte di pietà continued to seek out and punish those who had caused it damage. The arrest and interrogation in 1569 of one Giulio, a wool washer, echoed that of the conspirators of 1558–59. Asked if he knew why he had been incarcerated, he replied, "I don't know unless you tell me." He soon discovered that flippancy was a mistaken tactic. Under pressure of constant questioning and threats, he confessed that "in the past days he went to the lenders [the monte di pietà] and saw that someone was pawning a cape. . . . He later returned to the [monte] saying that the said pawn was his, and thus they had the receipt rewritten." He tried to recruit an accomplice, but the first man he approached refused. A Jew, here no doubt placed in the traditional role of the enemy of the monte, agreed to enter the scheme. For all his efforts Giulio turned out to be a mediocre criminal: he profited by a mere fourteen lire. Further wrongdoing he denied. Just to be sure, the interrogators ordered him pulled on the rope twice, but he never admitted any more misdeeds. The fourteen lire had cost him a great deal of suffering.[59]

In 1569 a list of the debtors of the monte included a number of employees who had caused it losses. Nicolaio di Girolamo Cioni, former massaro at the third branch, still owed just under fl. 1,000, a sum for which his guarantors were responsible. His successor Alfonso della Casa did not seem to be an improvement on him, for his debt to the monte stood at over fl. 640 "for the account of the administration of his office." Giovanbattista Primerani's old debt "for the remainder of losses caused" came to just over fl. 624. Giovanni da Villole, former garzone, was a debtor for over fl. 400 for the

58. On Becchi, MP 762, 7a–b. For the credit of one denaro, MP 762, 257a–b.
59. MP 28, Libro di partiti, interrogation of Giulio Purgatore, 15 Jan. 1568 (O.S.).

same reason. Francesco di Bartolomeo, one of Giovanni's colleagues, owed nearly fl. 450, which he admitted having obtained illegally while working for the monte. Other miscellaneous bad debts cost the monte over fl. 836.[60] Other employees owed smaller amounts.

Although Cosimo and his successors attacked the problems of fraud and incompetence, they never succeeded in eliminating them. In 1606, for example, the monte di pietà's provveditore, Simone Franceschi, had apparently grown too old and ill to carry out his duties. His replacement, Carlo Catastini, turned out to be inept and "unsuited to the office." Catastini instead received an appointment in the ducal household (*maestro della casa del palazzo*) and was replaced before he could do much damage to the monte di pietà.[61] High office in the monte required financial and organizational abilities, and a man might be placed there only to be removed should his talents prove insufficient for the task.

There is only one explanation for the continued pursuit of fraud: Cosimo viewed the monte di pietà as an arm of ducal finance, and robbing the monte had become the moral equivalent of robbing the ducal treasury. The eight officials would never have pursued so aggressively those whom they suspected of stealing from the monte on their own initiative. After all, prior to Cosimo's reign, employees had been reprimanded, debited, even dismissed for damages they had caused, but there are no lurid tales of merciless interrogations and torture by the strappado. As Cosimo's stake in the monte di pietà grew, his interest in keeping the institution honest grew accordingly.

60. MP 768, Libro di debitori e creditori, 554a.
61. Ricci, *Cronaca* 60r, 540, 30 Oct. 1606. Ricci says delicately that Catastini was transferred from the monte di pietà, "not being suited to such an office."

8 FROM FLORENCE TO SIENA AND BEYOND: THE MEDICI AND THE MONTE DI PIETÀ

COSIMO'S EXPLOITATION of the Florentine monte di pietà formed an effective part of his larger policy of control. More effective still was his application of the lessons he had learned governing Florence to the administration of the duchy, especially the newly conquered city of Siena. While in the treaty of 1555 Cosimo had agreed to concede to Siena some of its traditional autonomy, he had every intention of placing the city under his own jurisdiction. Two sets of laws, the first dating from 1561 and the second from ten years later, helped accomplish this goal.[1]

Turning his attention to the Sienese monte di pietà in June 1568, the duke wrote to his treasurer there, Niccolò Panciatichi, "Advise us whether in that city of Siena there is a monte di pietà that might lend money to the poor against pawns as is done here and, if there is, give us information on the mode of functioning and the governance of such a pious place. . . . And moreover, there being a monte di pietà, we will wish to know what possessions [*mobili*] it has and how much it lends."[2]

Such a lending institution had been established in Siena in 1472, several decades before Florence's monte di pietà was founded. *Monte*

---

1. Elena Fasano Guarini, "The Grand Duchy of Tuscany at the Death of Cosimo I: A Historical Map," *Journal of Italian History* 2 (1979): 529.

2. Med. 232, Registro terzo di lettere di Sua Eccellentia Illustrissima, 5v, Cosimo de' Medici to Niccolò Panciatichi, 6 or 1 June (one of the two numbers has been written over the other) 1568.

in Siena had long meant any form of collected funds for trade or mutual assistance. By the late fourteenth century, the city had created a Monte dei Paschi (or Pascoli), originally designed to administer pasture lands in the Maremma district; the communally owned domain around Siena itself was administered by the Dogana dei Paschi. Siena received revenue from rents on these lands for sheep grazing. The union of the Monte del Sale (salt tax ministry), Monte del Biado (grain tax ministry), and Dogana dei Paschi by the end of the century resulted in the "monte comune, sale, e paschi."[3] The predecessors of Siena's monte di pietà, then, were secular and civic rather than religious and charitable.

The Sienese monte di pietà began with capital of thirty-two thousand florins and offered loans of up to eight florins at the cost of 7½ percent per annum, 50 percent higher than the normal Florentine rate of 5 percent. Later known as the monte dei paschi (the name under which, as a bank, it still exists today), the Sienese establishment broke from the stereotypical Italian monte di pietà in two ways. First, unlike most others including the Florentine one, the Sienese monte di pietà's creation did not coincide with legislation mandating the expulsion of the Jews, and Jewish moneylenders continued to carry on a lively business.[4] Second, the Franciscans, avid promoters of monti di pietà, played but a small role in founding the institution in Siena, although several brothers, including Bernardino of Siena, preached in its behalf.

Only five years after the Sienese monte di pietà's beginning, the city fathers found it necessary to make a compact with several Jewish moneylenders, a sure sign that the monte was failing to meet the needs of the city's poor. The plague in 1478 and the continued attacks of the Dominicans hurt it. Its directors displayed supposedly typical Renaissance values when, in 1481, despite its fiscal woes, they appropriated money from its slim resources to commission a fresco for its premises, a decision perhaps admirable from the point of view of aesthetics but not from the point of view of fiscal priorities. By 1483 it had a large number of debtors but no means for calling in their debts. Attempts to lower its interest rate to 5 percent and to infuse it with additional capital fell short. An audit of its records in

---

3. *Il monte dei Paschi di Siena* (Siena, 1955), 19–21.

4. N. Piccolomini, ed., *Il monte dei paschi di Siena e le aziende in esso riunite* (Siena, 1891), 1:171; Cassandro, *Gli ebrei*, 72–74; and *Monte dei paschi di Siena*, 24–25.

1501 reported that it had become "greatly cut off from its capital, and for this reason it was unable anymore to succor the poor citizens."[5] The institution was certainly in existence in the early 1550s, for in 1554 its records note the election of its officers and arrangements to sell off pawns.[6]

Cosimo surely knew that the Sienese monte di pietà had in fact ceased to operate. When the Medici conqueror made his first visit to Siena in October 1559, the citizens, suffering from the effects of the recent war, begged him to see to the reestablishment of their defunct charitable institution.[7] Cosimo's source in Siena confirmed that the Sienese monte no longer functioned; replying to one of his agents, the duke wrote that he had "learned from your letter that in that city of Siena there is no monte di pietà," and then expressed his desire "to create one." This unambiguous language suggested that, even if the monte had never been officially legislated out of existence, it was so moribund that Cosimo's informants could detect no flicker of life. The duke asked them for more information "so that we can take up with you such ways and means as seem to us convenient" for the monte's revival. He ordered his agent, Ser Federigo de' Conti di Montauto, to inform the balìa of Siena that he had "resolved to create in that city a monte di pietà that will lend money against pawns for the populace, to avoid the poor's having to be consumed by the inordinate usury of the Jews who are lending today, and for the convenience of the citizens as well, who can be supported in times of need."[8]

Aware of the misery that had followed the war, Cosimo was genuinely concerned with the well-being of his new subjects. In a letter illustrative of both his love for minutiae and his attention to charity, he wrote to his treasurer in Siena, "We understand that at the baths of San Filippo [in Siena] it is customary that everyone who bathes pay two soldi every day. . . . And because poor persons come there

5. Piccolomini, ed., *Monte dei paschi di Siena*, supp., 3; see also Cassandro, *Gli ebrei*, for the persistence of Jewish moneylending in Siena despite the presence of the monte di pietà (72–74).

6. Melis, "Motivi di storia bancaria," 61–63. Melis disproves the long-held thesis that the institution died in 1511 but cannot show much vigor in its operations for the entire first half of the century.

7. Piccolomini, ed., *Monte dei paschi di Siena*, 2:9–10.

8. Med. 232, two letters, Cosimo de' Medici to Federigo de' Conti da Montauto, 10 June 1568.

who sometimes have no means of paying, we commission you to give orders that from now on all those who are truly poor will not be made to pay anything."[9] Far be it from Cosimo to deprive the poor of their baths!

But Cosimo was a crafty statesman, and his motives ran deeper than the waters of the baths of San Filippo. At the same time that he asked for information about Siena's monte di pietà, he sought information of another sort, and these two different requests hint that establishing a monte in Siena was part of a larger strategy. He sent his men in Siena a list of young Sienese noblemen, asking for "true information on the quality, life and habits" of each. Answers were to be gathered in the utmost secrecy. Several months later Cosimo drew up a company of men-at-arms chosen from this list, having appointed each man on the basis of the information his agents in Siena had supplied. Several years later he would include some of Siena's aristocracy in his elite new order, the Knights of Santo Stefano, with himself as the company's head. He followed the same procedures in other cities, including Arezzo.[10] It is no coincidence that, while he was decrying the usury of the Jews and asserting his determination to help the poor, he was preparing to create an armed band of vassals handpicked from Siena's elite.

Cosimo's defeat of Siena did not cause universal rejoicing among the powerful rulers of Europe, particularly the emperor Charles V and the king of France, Henry II. When the Sienese revolted against the Spanish in July 1552, they placed themselves under the protection of the French crown. Cosimo, eager to stir up trouble, within weeks signed a pact of nonaggression with the French while quietly agreeing with Charles to move against Siena, having been promised compensation should he win. Victory, however, "will be a hard nut to crack," Cosimo acknowledged. He cracked that nut only to find himself confronted with Philip II, the new king of Spain, who had no intention of allowing so juicy a prize as Siena to fall to the Florentine duke. In the end Cosimo outmaneuvered Philip and received Siena from him in fief. But he had to be on the lookout for signs of danger from both France and Spain, a fact that made his securing Siena all the more vital.[11]

---

9. Med. 232, 28r, 14 Oct. 1568.

10. Med. 232, 18r–v, Cosimo de' Medici to the captain of justice in Siena, 11 Aug. 1568; and 35r, 6 Dec. 1568.

11. For the preceding discussion, see Giorgio Spini, "The Medici Principality and

The monte di pietà could be useful in this plan, for his experience with the Florentine establishment had convinced him that it was more than just a charitable pawnshop. He sent his agents an exhaustive set of instructions for setting up the new Sienese monte. Above all, the Florentine monte di pietà was to serve as a model. The duke himself would appoint the two most important officers, the camarlingo and the massaro, yet another sign that he meant to watch closely over the daughter institution. The board of directors and less important employees would be chosen by the local balìa. The duke ordered certain civic groups and charities, including the Quattro Conservatori dello Stato, the Spedale (hospital) della Scala, the Opera del Duomo and the Mercanzia, to help provide capital for the enterprise by depositing funds in the new monte at 5 percent interest. By the end of three years, Cosimo believed, these measures would set the institution on a solid footing, all books would be balanced, all creditors repaid. In effect the duke had imposed forced loans on these Sienese institutions, no doubt a more popular approach than imposing them on individuals. He hoped, nonetheless, that private persons "gratis and for the love of God" would lend money to Siena's revived monte. In return for this favor, the monte would pay such persons 5 percent interest after three years, its financial condition permitting. Thus the Sienese monte's reliance on the Florentine model was almost complete.[12]

Cosimo continued to follow the progress of the Sienese monte di pietà as it began to collect its capital. Hearing that it needing more funding, he ordered the Spedale della Scala to lend it two thousand ducats for several months. He appointed Egidio di Bartolomeo de' Veccha massaro and debated whom to name as camarlingo, before nominating Aldiere della Casa. When the revived Sienese monte di pietà opened its doors to serve the poor on 1 August 1569, Cosimo wrote to his agents there expressing his pleasure and his hope that the inhabitants would find the monte useful and convenient.[13]

---

the Organization of the States of Europe in the Sixteenth Century," *Journal of Italian History* 2 (1979): 420–47; the quotation about the difficulty of victory comes from p. 428.

12. Med. 232, 28v, 14 Oct. 1567.

13. From Med. 232: on Cosimo's concern, see his letter to Federigo da Montauto, 49r, 3 Mar. 1569, and to the depositario of Siena, 57r, 20 Apr. 1569; on the spedale, to that institution's overseers, 66r–v, 23 May 1569. On Veccha and Aldiere della Casa,

The duke's interest in the Sienese monte di pietà did not end with its opening, however. Report after report reached him from Siena. He followed the monte's progress and noted that the Sienese had begun to place deposits in the institution. He granted his appointee as camarlingo the second post of cassiere for his own treasurer in Siena, with Cosimo informing the treasurer that "we wish this office to depend on us." This dependency resulted not only from Cosimo's prerogative to appoint whomever he wished, but also from his promise to pay 140 ducats of the total salary of 300 himself. He personally urged Aldiere to see that all employees presented the proper guarantors against fraud or loss: once again, his experience in Florence molded his attitude toward Siena.[14]

Cosimo's desire to control the monte di pietà of Siena had precedents elsewhere in Tuscany. His powerful Pratica Secreta heard a petition in 1550 from Pisans asking that their charitable pawnshop be allowed to lend money at 7 percent. The petitioners pointed out that in many areas both merchants and pious houses lent "not only at 7 percent, but at ten and 12 percent."[15] Cosimo's own ambassador to Pope Julius III had heard the pontiff say that he tolerated this rate of interest, the Pisans told the duke, because only in this way could the even higher interest rates of the Jews be avoided.

Writing to the duke about this petition and on behalf of the Pratica Segreta, Jacopo Polverini agreed that "removing the Jew from Pisa is a holy enterprise, and it would be better to remove him from the entire dominion, because . . . allowing the Jews to stay can only lead to evil effects." Nonetheless, Polverini felt, 7 percent was simply too high an interest rate. "Usury," he wrote, "[is] prohibited by divine law, and neither popes nor princes can permit it, nor should they tolerate it." The duke read these remarks with interest, concurred that the Pisans ought to use other methods to supply their monte di pietà with capital, and refused their request.[16] In the case of Pescia too, Cosimo's son Francesco reviewed with the Pratica Segreta the proposed statutes for a new monte di pietà, setting the

---

see one letter to Federigo and one to Aldiere, 83v–84r, 16 July 1569. On the reopening of the institution, see Cosimo to the depositario of Siena, 86v, 7 Aug. 1569.

14. Med. 232, 102r, 15 Dec. 1569, and 28v, 14 Oct. 1568.
15. PS 1, no. 115, 4 Sept. 1550.
16. Ibid.

interest rate for loans at 5 percent, "considering that Florence, Arezzo, Volterra and the greater part of the other monti of the states of Your Highness lend at five percent."[17]

Officials of monti di pietà throughout Tuscany asked ducal advisers to aid them in reforming their institutions. Franco di Quinti, for example, wrote the Otto di Pratica for help in correcting "the disorder" of the charitable pawnshop in Montevarchi.[18] In Arezzo, reform of the monte di pietà was but a part of overall civic reform. Four citizens, together with Brancazio Rucellai, the Florentine captain of the city, reviewed and reformed the monte by order of the duke's Pratica Segreta in 1562. "It would be good," the Pratica noted, "to balance the accounts of the monte [di pietà] and to review completely the state it is in," and it recommended that the Aretine city council select two auditors for this task. The Pratica oversaw the fine-tuning of the institution's bylaws, with a special eye to ensuring their conformity with Florentine law.[19] In 1570 after a thorough review, members of the Pratica reconfirmed the statutes of the Pisan monte di pietà despite the fact that its rate on loans had risen to 7½ percent, a rate that, when proposed for the new monte at Pescia, they had called usury. The Pratica wanted only one change. Located in a university town, the Pisan monte had apparently become a virtual secondhand book store as students flocked to it to pawn their books. The Pratica did not think it "reasonable that one can lend against books since scholars can make use of other possessions of theirs, and he who pawns books has little desire for study, and that is a damnable and dishonorable thing."[20] In 1571 the Florentine captain in Prato forwarded to the Pratica Segreta a review of the statutes of the Pratese monte di pietà. The Pratica decided to limit the amount lent to a total of eight thousand scudi at 5 percent, but permitted the institution to request an increase if the needs of the poor demanded it.[21]

This emerging strategy of control over provincial monti paralleled what may be seen in Florence. Cosimo, who had called for the Si-

17. PS 8, no. 69, 24 Nov. 1570.
18. Otto di Pratica (Principato), Lettere 100, 3 April 1559.
19. PS 6, no. 68, 558r. On Sept. 12, 1562, Lelio Torelli noted approvingly, "Tutto sta bene." See further tinkering with the monte's operations in PS 8, no. 4, Mario Tolosani to Francesco de' Medici, 15 Aug. 1567.
20. PS 8, no. 68, 29 Nov. 1570. Lelio Torelli noted, "Sta bene tutto."
21. PS 9, no. 12, 28 June 1571.

enese monte di pietà's establishment, had ordered its statutes "to conform to those of the monte di pietà of Florence," designated the sources of a good portion of its "monte," or start-up capital, appointed its most important officers, and paid part of their salaries. As Cosimo himself put it to Federigo, "We have drawn up the instructions as to how to undertake and govern this monte [in Siena]," and he allowed himself to pronounce it "a praiseworthy work."[22] By authorizing it to pay the same 5 percent interest on deposits that had allowed its Florentine mother institution to attract thousands of depositors, he both offered his Sienese subjects the same investment opportunity as their counterparts in Florence and insured the Sienese monte a steady influx of deposits. Finally, Cosimo established an institution that not only pleased God by addressing the needs of the poor, but also—once it had accrued sufficient capital—might serve as an instrument of ducal finance and control, just as the Florentine monte did. Cosimo's treatment of Tuscan monti di pietà shows that the consolidation of his territorial state meant control and consolidation of originally distinct institutions.[23]

Cosimo soon took his control over the Sienese monte one step further. He informed Federigo that "the profits made in the recent Abbondanza be deposited in the Sienese monte di pietà."[24] The monte in Siena now mirrored yet another feature of the Florentine one: it would serve as a repository for some of the profits of other civic institutions. Indeed, the money Cosimo provided to pay for his newly created corps of men-at-arms in Siena was to be placed in the Sienese monte di pietà for safekeeping, a sign that he expected it to serve as a sort of financial clearinghouse just as the Florentine monte did. The sum involved was substantial: forty-eight hundred ducats had been needed to purchase arms and horses for the men. The duke also urged his treasurer to make sure that the monte turned away no depositor. In answer to a question from Federigo, Cosimo wrote, "It appears to us that the monte della pietà cannot and should not refuse to accept in deposit the entry of the four thousand scudi

---

22. Med. 232, 28v, 14 Oct. 1568.

23. This point has been suggested by Fasano Guarini in both *Lo stato mediceo* and "Grand Duchy" (521), where she speaks of the need to see states as "territorial complexes. We need to reconstruct their overall organizational structures . . . [and to analyze] the process of assimilation and the network of links that arose . . . among social and political entities that were originally quite distinct."

24. Med. 232, 28r, 14 Oct. 1568.

that you say the heirs of Messer Salvitio Mandoli want to deposit there," for otherwise the money would simply go elsewhere.[25] About the same time in 1570, the administrators of Prato's various pious establishments had to place their surpluses in their city's monte di pietà, an order that surely bears Cosimo and Francesco's stamp.[26]

In 1570 the Florentine ruler made a decision whose long-term impact on the Sienese monte di pietà he could not have discerned. Henceforth it could make large loans to cattle breeders in the Maremma,[27] thus including the institution in Cosimo's vision of the Tuscan political economy and, consciously or not, reaching back to the connections between the original Sienese monte and the Maremma. So involved did the Sienese monte di pietà become in agribusiness loans that in the seventeenth century a second monte had to be created to insure that the needs of the monte's traditional clientele—the poor—could be met. In 1623 the grand duke created a Monte non Vacabile de'Paschi (that is, a monte with perpetual capital that paid interest on nonredeemable shares) of two hundred thousand scudi. Every year it was to receive an additional ten thousand scudi in revenues from the Maremma pastures. Sienese could purchase, for one hundred scudi each, a share yielding 5 percent. With this development the Sienese monte was permitted to invest its capital, a vital step on the road to its eventual destination as a full-fledged bank. By the nineteenth century its business was multifold, but still reflected the action of Cosimo three hundred years earlier. It served as a pawnshop, an agricredit institution, and a reinvestment company interested in mortgages. It plowed half its profits back into business but remained true to its charitable mission by giving the rest to charity and public works.[28]

The year 1570 also brought a decisive order that demonstrated the maturity of Medici thinking about Siena's new monte di pietà. Cosimo and Francesco informed Federigo that they had written to the officers of the Sienese pious institution that any net profits be transferred to an account at 5 percent in its name in the Florentine monte di pietà. Cosimo saw no sense in "their holding onto [the

25. Med. 236, 36r, 17 Oct. 1570. More deposits came from other sources.
26. A.G.B., "Monte della pietà," 104.
27. *Monte dei paschi di Siena*, 30–31.
28. Ibid., 60–63.

money] without [receiving] interest."²⁹ The benefits of this policy were threefold: the Sienese foundation would profit by earning interest on its excess capital; the Florentine foundation would add to its own liquidity by holding these funds; and those whose interests were well served by healthy monti di pietà in Florence and Siena would benefit.

Into this last category fell, above all, Duke Cosimo de' Medici. It was he and his successors, in fact, who most benefited from well-endowed monti in their state. In 1570, shortly after the Sienese establishment began operation, Cosimo and his son and heir Francesco began to pay their regular household expenses through accounts in the Florentine monte di pietà. Infusions of capital from other monti like the one in Siena were carefully earmarked for specific purposes by the duke. For example, in 1571 he wrote to an aide that he had decided to purchase a large amount of grain in Grossetto, for which he needed twelve thousand ducats. The source of this cash? Redemptions and profits from the Sienese monte di pietà.³⁰

The establishment of the Sienese monte di pietà demonstrates vividly the Medici duke's ingenuity in extracting every possible advantage from Tuscan institutions and in propagating those institutions that he found especially useful. The revival of Siena's monte di pietà occurred at a time when the ruler of Florence was consolidating his control over a city captured only a decade earlier. It also came at a time when the Medici were bringing the Florentine monte di pietà into the network of their patronage and vigorously exploiting its usefulness as an instrument of ducal finance. Cosimo's treatment of the Sienese monte di pietà also shows that he saw Tuscany as an economic entity whose institutions could be supportive not only of each other, but of his own interests and of the Tuscan economy and population.

The last years of Cosimo's reign, in fact the years during which he gradually withdrew from active statecraft in favor of his heir, also marked the years when Medici use of the Florentine monte di pietà expanded. To what degree the impetus behind this expansion bore Francesco's stamp cannot be known, but much of the correspon-

29. Med. 236, 59r, 9 Jan. 1571 Note that, although by this time Cosimo had formally abdicated in favor of Francesco, much documentation still proceeded through him.

30. Med. 236, 107v, 1 May 1571.

dence from the chancery to the monte di pietà still carried the ducal seal (updated to a grand-ducal seal in 1569) and Cosimo's own signature, never a model of legibility but even more idiosyncratic as the years took their toll on his health.

Medici involvement in the monte di pietà historically had taken several forms. In the institution's early years, they could place money freely in the monte di pietà and, through such a charitable act, hope to win God's grace. The sole example of such an act took place on 29 July 1496, when Monna Lisabetta, widow of Braccio di Conte di Nicola di Messer Veri de' Medici freely deposited fl. 881, L. 1.13 for a term of ten months.[31] After Lisabetta withdrew her deposit in 1498, not a single Medici ever offered a voluntary loan to the monte. The general lack of interest displayed by the family in making deposits gratis in the monte di pietà reflected the attitude of the Florentine patriciate as a whole.

Later the Medici could make money by placing interest-earning deposits in the monte. Like other shrewd patricians, the Medici sometimes found the monte a safe repository for restricted money like dowry payments, albeit often on a short-term basis. Lorenzo d'Attilio de' Medici made the first private deposit at interest held by a Medici. In March 1544 Lorenzo invested L. 2,800 at 5 percent interest to be repaid upon his demand. He made more deposits, which along with interest brought his total to L. 4,700.10.[32] Lorenzo closed out his account over the next three years, but he opened a new one for a purpose that was carefully noted in the ledger. In March 1546 he stood as creditor for fl. 200 at 5 percent placed in the monte by his nephew Attilio di Veri de' Medici. Should he for some reason never make use of this sum, Lorenzo declared that "it be paid to Clemenza, his daughter, when she marries or becomes a nun." In case of Clemenza's death prior to such an event, "it must be paid to Monna Beatrice, his wife, as part of the restitution of her dowry."[33]

As duke, Cosimo de' Medici confronted unique problems of personal and state finance, and his fiscal responsibilities required tremendous liquidity and quick access to his own money as well as to

---

31. MP 721, 3a–b.

32. MP 752, 125a. Lorenzo was named a senator in the Forty-Eight for Santa Croce, along with Jacopo di Lazzero de' Medici in March 1556. Ricci, *Cronaca*, 297v, 8.

33. MP 754, 166b, 98a–b.

loans. The monte di pietà served as a convenient clearinghouse for his expenses. Above all he found highly attractive the monte's accrual of large amounts of cash by the late 1540s and learned to authorize loans from these reserves to himself and his friends. Finally, the Medici strengthened their hold over the monte di pietà by controlling the organs that exercised jurisdiction over it and by placing friends and kinsmen on its board of eight directors and in its important paid positions.

Medici accounts in the monte di pietà were significant both for the sums involved and for the impact the ruling family's use of the monte had upon state finance. The monte's ledgers from 1548 on reveal growing Medici interest in the charitable pawnshop (see Appendix A, Table 13, Overview of Medici Accounts). This growing interest stemmed from a sudden burst of enthusiasm among Tuscans for investment in the monte: in 1542 only 77 creditors were listed; three years later there were 133, and the increase continued over the next years as well, with 387 creditors listed in 1563. From five in November 1548 and seven in 1557, Medici accounts rose to ten in 1560; there were still ten in 1563. A more revealing trend is the changing nature of those accounts. In 1548, two Medici were debtors; in 1557, there were three. By 1560 there were four Medici accounts showing a debit, two of which belonged to Cosimo. Three years later, there were six, the two new ones charged to Attilio de' Medici, but the amounts of money in the other accounts had risen steadily. A dawning realization of the potential of the monte as a source of loans lay behind the Medici's growing participation in it.

Very shortly after Lorenzo d'Attilio's deposit in the monte, his better-known kinsman Duke Cosimo made his first deposit. This entry illuminated a tentative connection between the monte di pietà and ducal finance. First, Cosimo himself was credited with this initial deposit of fl. 2,142, L. 6 (changed from sc. 2,000 d'Italia), even though the money came not from his personal wealth but from the foundry at Pisa and had been handed over to the monte's provveditore, Chiarissimo de' Medici, by Cosimo's agent Niccolò Ferrini. Second, the stipulation that the monte was to abide by the duke's will in paying out money from this account illustrated the potentially vital role played by the provveditore and showed why it was crucial for that post to be held by a trusted individual. More deposits augmented the original sum, continuing the precedent of depositing surpluses from other "public" sources in the monte: two deposits, for example, of fl. 750 each were received from Bastiano d'Altopascio, the procaccio of Pisa.[34]

If the late 1540s saw Cosimo establish a current account, the same period also saw him discover the monte as a source of credit. In late December 1547, "on the word of his Excellency," the monte paid fl. 7,500 (calculated from sc. 7,000 d'Italia) to Girolamo Miglioretti, an official of the wardrobe, through Messer Pierfrancesco Ricci, Cosimo's majordomo. The entry did not reveal the use to which Miglioretti was to put this large sum. Regardless of its purpose, the loan was charged to Cosimo himself, who promised "to make good the interest at the rate of 5 percent, as is paid on the deposits we hold." Interest for 10⅗ months came to fl. 331, L. 1.15 when the ledger was balanced in November 1548, and Cosimo, not having paid this sum, was posted forward as a debtor for fl. 7,831, L. 1.15.[35]

This loan was the first of many that Cosimo took from the monte di pietà. It was not limited to a specific term, and although the duke promised to pay interest of 5 percent, he was not obliged to do so within any given period of time. In the case of this loan, Cosimo paid no interest at all during the remaining eleven months of the triennium. The most powerful man in Tuscany had thus received this large loan at the same rate paid by those who took small loans against pawns.

Cosimo's accounts continued to be active over the years. The value of his current account, fl. 1,790, L. 5 in the black as of November 1548, rose and fell as he added or withdrew money. Over the next three years he deposited nearly fl. 6,000 all told, but after making several withdrawals (including sc. 1,000 d'Italia or fl. 1,071, L. 3 for his majordomo Ricci) he found himself with a credit of fl. 4,885, L. 1.2.4 in November 1551. His debit, listed as a separate account, increased to just over fl. 9,000, not because of further loans but because of the accrual of over fl. 1,174 in unpaid interest.[36] Furthermore, in late 1551 he owed the monte di pietà an additional fl. 68, L. 1.7.4, the result of having overdrawn a deposit created from taxes

34. MP 754, 99b.
35. MP 754, 130a–b.
36. MP 756, 54a–b, 66a–b.

collected in his domain. The total amount moved into and out of his accounts from 1548 came to more than fl. 33,000.[37]

Because the ledgers covering most of the 1550s are missing, it is unclear just how it occurred to Cosimo to use the monte di pietà to help finance the purchase of the Pitti palace, which the numerous Pitti heirs had determined to divide, along with its gardens, among themselves.[38] In November 1557 the monte's bookkeeper noted that Cosimo, basically by overdrawing a monte di pietà deposit, had been "consigned to us as debtor [by] our predecessors" for fl. 5,775, L. 6.4.10, "for a separate account of money made good for his Excellency to the Pitti for the account of the purchase of the palazzo, on which his Excellency, as long as he does not have [it] paid to us, must make good the interest at a rate of 7 percent as is paid to the said Pitti." Interest paid to the Pitti in late February 1560 came to fl. 311, L. –.15.2, bringing Cosimo's indebtedness to fl. 6,087, but on the same day he had his treasurer, Antonio de' Nobili, pay fl. 130 into his account, "which money he paid us so that it be given to Andrea di Luca Pitti for the remainder of his portion . . . and in diminution of the debt [posted] opposite." Cosimo was, therefore, "consigned as debtor to the new officials" in November 1560, for fl. 5,957.[39]

The role of the duke's treasurer, Antonio de' Nobili, in providing for the deposit of fl. 130 exemplified the ingenuity of Cosimo's manipulation of the monte. Antonio now held his own current account in the monte (usually running a deficit) from which he paid certain expenses as the duke directed. Among the payments Antonio made from this account was one of fl. 130 "paid to Andrea di Luca Pitti . . . for the remainder of [his] portion of the palace."[40] In effect Cosimo had through his treasurer transferred credit from one account to another, a means of financial manipulation that began to appear often in his and in Antonio's monte accounts. When he had Antonio pay out the fl. 130 to Andrea Pitti, the credit was not only transferred to and then subsequently debited from Cosimo's own account, but had to be transferred to Antonio's account from an-

37. MP 756, 54a–b, 66a–b, 225a–b, 244a–b. See, e.g., the last two references for a large number of transactions totaling over fl. 22,565 and fl. 11,148 each.

38. MS 4, 1 Apr. 1538, Divisio domus seu palatij de Pittis, 56v.

39. MP 762, 67a–b, 258a–b. The interest rate of 7 percent was apparently the result of the deal struck by Cosimo with the Pitti.

40. MP 762, 145a.

other source in order to place enough money in that account to cover the transaction. In fact, a credit for fl. 130, "for so much of which he was a creditor in the cash book B of the second monte," was posted to Antonio's account, credited "in two entries, to pay to Andrea Pitti." Thus the payment of the fl. 130 in interest due Andrea Pitti involved a set of transfers among several accounts. Then Antonio had his own account debited for this sum, transferring it to the duke's account for the Pitti palace, from which the monte di pietà, at the ruler's order, paid it to the Pitti and debited Cosimo's account accordingly. The language in the ledger shows that many of these transactions involved an exchange made on paper rather than in coins. The idiom used is usually *fare* or *farne buoni* (to make good an amount owed), and it implies a fiduciary transfer rather than payment in currency.[41] A further detail reveals the advantage of this kind of manipulation: the process actually happened in the reverse order, with Cosimo paying fl. 130 to Andrea Pitti and debiting his own account on 29 February 1560, and Antonio de' Nobili "receiving" this sum only a month later.[42] Cosimo enjoyed the most useful advantage of credit: the float between his agreement to pay a debt and the actual transfer of cash or credit out of his own accounts.

The techniques that the duke used—maintaining a current account (*conto currente*), transferring credits among accounts and to his own creditors as payment, enjoying an overdraft—had been in existence for at least two centuries in Italy. Private banks in Venice and their clients had, by the early fourteenth century if not before, discovered and accepted the utility of bank money, that is, a deposit placed in a bank and transferable to other accounts or even other banks. The Venetian state sometimes accepted or made payments through such transfers, which were usually made orally in the Veneto, though not in Tuscany, where they were written out. Some Venetian banks permitted good customers to overdraw their accounts. Andrea Barbarigo, for instance, overdrew his account periodically for sums as high as eight hundred ducats and for several months at a time. In Florence in the fifteenth century, wealthy men sometimes paid workers not in cash but in what amounted to a check drawn on a local bank. The workers could then cash the written draft at the

---

41. Edler, *Glossary*, 116–17. For the latter, the monte di pietà's ledgers use the term *recò*.

42. MP 762, 145a–b, 67a–b.

bank on which it had been drawn. In some cases an employer set up a current account in a bank through which he then paid expenses by issuing payment orders.[43] Cosimo's use of his current account in the monte di pietà was, therefore, not an innovation in itself. What was new was his regular use of these mechanisms exercised through an institution never intended as an arm of ducal finance.

It is not necessary to follow each such transaction to appreciate the growing sophistication of Cosimo's financial strategies. He made almost innumerable payments of interest to the Pitti heirs, each time taking advantage of short-term overdrafts in the ways exemplified by the payment of fl. 130 to Andrea Pitti. In November 1560 the debt on the palace stood at fl. 5,957. Three years later it had decreased somewhat, totaling fl. 5,645, L. 6.4.10. Finally, in October 1568 Cosimo paid off the debt, closing out this account.[44] This payment did not signal the end of Cosimo's large debits in the monte di pietà, for by this time he had begun to borrow much larger sums.

The usefulness of an account held by the trusted treasurer-general, Antonio de' Nobili, had already emerged in the financing of the Pitti palace. The early 1560s brought about experiments to extend the utility of such an account. It appeared in the monte's records for the first time on 27 February 1558 as a debit in Antonio's name.[45]

> Antonio de' Nobili, treasurer-general of his Excellency . . . is debited through February 27 [1558 N.S.] . . . fl. 1,131, L. 3.18, . . . to give them to Lattantio Gorini, *pagatore* of the Salviati [Company] of the court of his Excellency, to reimburse us for many pawns returned to the employees on account of the flood, as his Excellency has ordered said Lattantio.

This first debit was followed by others of fl. 1,400 "to Pietro della Pegna, a Spaniard"; fl. 14,000 "given in credit to Messer Francesco Grifoni, by order of his Excellency"; fl. 1,500 "to Messer Battista

---

43. On Venice, see Reinhold C. Mueller, "The Role of Bank Money in Venice, 1300–1500," *Studi veneziani*, n.s., 3 (1979): 47–96. On Florence, Goldthwaite, *Building of Renaissance Florence*, 305–6.

44. MP 768, 11a–b.

45. For the following discussion of Antonio de' Nobili's account, see MP 762, 145a–b.

Concini, secretary of his Excellency"; fl. 130 for Andrea di Luca Pitti; and fl. 363, L. 2.6.8 to Antonio Gorini.

Although a total of fl. 18,524, L. 6.4.8 was transacted in debits alone over this period through Antonio's account, a series of deposits kept the account in the black most of the time. Income came in the form of fl. 14,000 "made good by Reverend Messer Francesco Grifoni, monsignore of Altopascio"; fl. 4,013, L. 3.18 "for so much for which his Excellency is made debtor in his current account by an order of the said Antonio, given to Antonio degli Albizzi, our provveditore"; fl. 130 from Antonio's account in the cash book B of the second monte; and fl. 363, L. 2.6.8 from the duke. Thus with total credits of fl. 18,524, L. 6.4.8, Antonio's account balanced.

In early 1559 Cosimo enjoyed credits in the monte di pietà of fl. 5,075, L. −.7.11.[46] Over the next three months seven deposits raised this sum to fl. 7,593, L. 4.16.4. The income came from the consolidation of several diverse accounts as well as from money collected by the auditors for the accounts of the war with Siena, grain (*ritratti di grani*), and oxen (*ritratti de'buoi*). For the most part this income went into—and quickly out of—the account to finance Cosimo's activities, including the purchase of the Pitti palace and other property.

Sums transferred from ledger to ledger and from account to account; payments and deposits authorized by the duke or by his treasurer; over eighteen thousand florins moved in each side of the account—there can be no doubt that the years after the war against Siena had raised the level of fiscal sophistication of the duke, certainly where the monte di pietà was concerned.

In 1566 Cosimo was listed as a substantial debtor of the monte in several separate accounts. His debit in the purchase of the palace amounted to fl. 5,645, L. 6.4.10 in November 1566. His current account ran a deficit of about fl. 9,356, L. 4.2. Another account showed that Cosimo had borrowed from the monte di pietà fl. 6,000 "to be repaid at our [the monte's] pleasure along with interest of 5 percent." In addition, Don Francesco de' Medici had borrowed fl. 2,000, for which amount he was carried forward as debtor in November 1566. Finally, the duke's treasurer-general, Antonio de' No-

46. MP 762, 215a–b.

bili, owed fl. 1,687, L. 6. for various expenses and loans associated with state finance.[47]

Cosimo's current account in the monte served some of the functions of a modern checking account on which he could run as large a deficit as he liked. Yet evidence shows that he was reluctant to abuse this privilege. His debt to the monte, standing at some fl. 9,356 in 1566, was sizable, but although the account was extraordinarily active over the next three years, and his debit grew, Cosimo made good on his obligation by ordering a deposit in April 1568 of fl. 15,568, reducing his debt to L. −.5.1. Most of this debt had accrued in his current accounts through the interest he owed on certain loans, especially on loans the monte had granted his family and friends on his own orders. A loan of fl. 1,200 to the sons of Carlo Anzoni, for example, accrued interest of fl. 262, L. 3.10 for which Cosimo had agreed to be responsible.

Cosimo's record of paying his debts testifies to his sense of fiscal responsibility: he was willing to float a debt, but he proved again and again his intention to make good on his financial obligations. The duke's sense of responsibility did not, however, prevent him from occasionally ignoring his obligation to pay interest on time on sums he had borrowed. For example, a debit of fl. 6,000 in 1566 rose to over fl. 7,000 by 1569 because Cosimo paid no interest during the three years. A second loan of fl. 3,000 along with interest accrued over several months raised the total Francesco owed to fl. 5,037, L. 3.10. If Francesco followed his father's example in ignoring the due dates of interest payments, he also ultimately followed his example of fiscal responsibility, for the prince paid off his debt in November 1568.[48]

On 12 December 1567 the duke deposited fl. 53,571, L. 3 "from Messer Tommaso de' Medici his treasurer" in the monte.[49] This deposit, the largest ever belonging to an individual up to this time, seems at first glance to contradict the rule that Florentine patricians

47. On the Pitti palace, MP 768, 1b, 11a–b: "sono per quella resta a pagare della conpera del . . . Palazzo." On the current account, MP 768, 1b, 21a–b. On the six thousand and two thousand in loans, MP 768, 2b. On Antonio de Nobili's accounts, MP 768, 11a–b.

48. MP 768, 244a–b.

49. MP 768, 333a–b. This sum represents the translation into florins of fifty thousand scudi d'Italia at the prevailing rate of L. 7.10 per scudo; each florin was worth seven lire.

did not deposit large sums in the monte. Upon closer scrutiny, the rule holds true after all. The debit page opposite lists the huge sum of fl. 60,591, L. −.15, "for so much which His Most Illustrious Excellency has been made debtor in quaderno E where he was a debtor for sc. 50,000 d'Italia, made good to the Salviati [Company]." Cosimo had taken the fifty thousand scudi as a loan prior to his deposit of the equivalent in florins in the monte. That debit, therefore, represented outgo in the form of a loan already noted in the book E and now posted to the duke's account. Interest brought the debt to fl. 60,667, L. 3.4, but even as the debt accrued interest, the deposit did likewise, earning fl. 2,581, L. 2.4 through 29 November 1568. At that time the total credit of fl. 56,152, L. 5.4 was applied to the duke's debit, leaving fl. 4,513, L. 5.1, for which the duke was posted forward as debtor to the monte di pietà when the ledger was balanced at the end of the triennium in December 1569.[50] It is an interesting commentary on the amount of capital the monte had accrued during his reign that Cosimo could casually take a loan of sc. 50,000 with no damage to the institution, whereas forty years earlier the last republic had taken a third of this sum and nearly bankrupted it.

In July 1568 a debit of fl. 6,055, L. 1.3.8 stood in Cosimo's name in a different account, paid by the monte di pietà "for his Most Illustrious Excellency to the Salviati [Company]." Through 30 December of that year, Cosimo's debt reached fl. 34,670, L. 1.3.8. Some of this money went to several persons, including a German jeweler who had sold seven emeralds to the duke. The fl. 1,071, L. 3 that the jeweler received was paid for the monte di pietà by the Salviati bank, which was then credited by the institution when it debited Cosimo's account for that sum.[51] The largest part of this figure, fl. 21,000, went to Tommaso de' Medici in his capacity as treasurer.

What was Tommaso de' Medici doing with all this money? Other monte di pietà accounts, which may at first appear to be simple deposits, reveal the purposes of some of the transactions undertaken for the duke by the treasurer. The duke had a number of creditors of all types who often were satisfied through these monte payments. For example,

50. MP 768, 333a–b, 565a–b.
51. MP 768, 489a–b.

> Simone di Domenico di Bartolomeo Manzini, stationer, is cred-
> ited on 28 May 1568 six hundred florins, for him from the
> most Illustrious and Excellent Lord Duke . . . from Messer
> Tommaso de' Medici, his treasurer, for the price of a mill and
> two millstones and their appurtenances, situated in the diocese
> of Fiesole . . . , which is to be reinvested in property in the city
> or contado of Florence.[52]

Simone's account earned over forty-seven florins in interest, most of
which he withdrew in adherence to a typical pattern. Restrictions on
the disposition of deposits in the monte di pietà whose origins were
in land sales were common. Many such transactions involved land
acquired from dowries or inheritances and were subject to any restrictions contained in the dotal contracts or wills. In Simone's case,
no mention of a dowry can be found, but that absence does not
mean the land had not been part of a dowry. In any event, the entry
stated clearly the conditions on his deposit, forbidding him to remove the capital—the interest was freely available to him—except
for investment in land. The duke's strategy in financing property
acquisitions, first seen in the case of the Pitti palace, was continued
in this and in other similar transactions through the monte di pietà.

Much of the money Tommaso de' Medici paid out on ducal orders
went to creditors of this nature. Five brothers from the Cantucci
family, who sold several farms to the duke, received fl. 3,800. In the
same way, Cosimo paid fl. 680 "for goods purchased" from Andrea
di Simone Piero del Garbo, who was free to do as he pleased with
the money.[53] There can thus be no doubt that some of the money
Cosimo enjoyed in loans from the monte di pietà went to pay his
private debts rather than those incurred in his capacity as head of
state.

Opposite these large debits were, as usual, credits applied to this
account. Cosimo had had over fl. 9,000 posted to this account from
an earlier balance. Two more deposits brought the credit side of his
account, in December 1568, to fl. 11,214, L. 3.9.4. Posted against his
debits, this sum left Cosimo fl. 23,455, L. 4.14.4 in the red, for which
amount he was posted forward as debtor in November 1569.[54]

52. MP 768, 380a–b.
53. MP 768, 354a–b, 387a–b.
54. MP 768, 489a–b.

Finally, Cosimo held a separate account, placed in the monte, "to hold in deposit, with the interest of 5 percent." After just under a year, the deposit of fl. 3,000 had earned interest of fl. 147, which Cosimo left untouched. He was posted forward as creditor for fl. 3,147 when the books were balanced.[55]

In sum, Cosimo enjoyed over fl. 123,500 in loans and "overdrafts" from the monte di pietà from November 1566 through that same month of 1569. During this period he made deposits of over fl. 91,700. All told his own transactions in the monte came to more than fl. 215,000, not including the tens of thousands of florins the institution lent out to his friends and relatives on his command. There can be no question that the monte di pietà had, by the end of Cosimo's career, been made an important part of the machinery of both ducal and private Medicean finance.

It is worth noting the growing participation in the monte by the duke's children, for it shows how the idea of the monte's utility was ingrained in Cosimo's progeny and successors. On 24 November 1569,

> the most Illustrious Lord Don Pedro [Pietro] de' Medici, son of
> . . . Duke Cosimo, is credited . . . fl. 5,642, L. 6, for him from
> Raffaello and Battista Spinoli, and for them from the Ricci
> [Company] . . . , which they paid by order of . . . the duke,
> and they, for the most Illustrious Signor Don Gratia of Toledo,
> to make good the dowry of the most Illustrious Lady Dionora
> of Toledo, his daughter, and wife of the said Don Pedro,
> which we have to hold in deposit while giving 5 percent inter-
> est, and the said money may not be removed, either the capital
> or the interest, except by order of the most Illustrious and Ex-
> cellent Lord Duke.[56]

A second deposit brought the capital to fl. 11,000, and in a few days it earned interest so that Don Pedro was posted forward as creditor for fl. 11,046 in late November 1569.

Pietro and Francesco were not the only children of the ruling house to have recourse to the monte for relief of debts. Isabella di Cosimo de' Medici received fl. 12,000 by order of her father early in

---

55. MP 768, 411a–b.
56. MP 768, 527a–b.

1568, "paid . . . to several of her creditors by her order . . . [and] to return to us within the next three years [at the rate of] one thousand florins every three months . . . and moreover, she has had consigned to us several jewels as security for the said sum." In 1569 she took a further fl. 2,000 in loans, but also paid her first three installments of fl. 1,000 each on time. With interest she still owed fl. 11,449 in November 1569.[57] Isabella's loan from the monte was yet another example of creative Medici manipulation of the resources of an institution they had come to value.

57. MP 768, 464a–b.

9 CONCLUSIONS

THE MONTE DI PIETÀ in Florence began to offer charity in the form of low-cost loans to the poor in 1496. There was nothing special about the Florentine institution at its inception to set it apart from other Italian monti di pietà. In fact, its late founding marked the Florentines as a bit backward when it came to innovation in helping the needy, since monti di pietà had been in existence for more than thirty years. Its early development, though important to our understanding of Florentine society and politics in the early sixteenth century, was unremarkable in the context of the history of Italian monti di pietà. Its financial difficulties at the outset mirrored those of similar institutions; the Florentine monte profited little from the experiences of others. In fact the Sienese example, wherein the charitable foundation was ruined by incompetence, dishonesty, and lack of support, seemed to have had little impact in Florence, where the monte slowly accrued capital but also began to suffer losses from inept employees and fraud. Monti in other areas of Italy, such as the Veneto, also began to offer interest on deposits. Even the use made of the monte di pietà as a source of loans by the more powerful classes was familiar in other cities—for example, in Milan.

The Florentine monte's uniqueness lies elsewhere. It had, from its inception, subtle and tenuous connections to the state, beginning with the communal statutes that gave it life, continuing with the republic's backing of its directors and the judicial orders to place certain fines and other funds in its coffers, and culminating, during the republic, with the seizure of thousands of florins of its resources in 1529. This connection shaped its destiny. Inherent in the monte's creation was the idea of its dependence on, and possible contributions to, the Florentine state. Once it had amassed a huge reserve of capital after the 1530s, the monte's potential usefulness to the dukes grew accordingly.

The ledgers show that Florence's elite did not rush to make unconditional deposits in the monte di pietà at 5 percent interest, although the few patricians who did so held a disproportionately large percentage of the monte's credits. Toward the end of Cosimo's reign the patriciate did place many conditional deposits in the monte di pietà for stated reasons, often for dowries. In these cases, depositing money in the monte was one tactic in a greater financial scheme. A very few, above all the duke himself, who needed access to cash for many frequent transactions, maintained accounts holding as much as several thousand florins. Establishment, however, of this type of account was motivated by convenience and security rather than by the attraction of a return of 5 percent. For the elite the monte di pietà was an excellent source of loans. Where else could Florentines find capital, available at 5 percent, later at 6 percent (still a bargain)? By appealing to the duke for authorization of large loans, those who had the sovereign's ear could take advantage of the resources of an institution originally designed to offer loans at low cost to the poor.

That, in the minds of those able to ask favors of the duke, the monte was good for loans but not for investing (except for conditional deposits) is evident merely from the paucity of free deposits from the elite and the crowds of elite borrowers. This conclusion was also spelled out clearly in three requests to the duke or his son late in 1568. In the first, Andrea Avignonesi from Montepulciano, "most faithful servant of your most Illustrious Excellency," found himself in dire need. He had just married off a daughter and a niece, and was beset by other family burdens. Lacking money to make good on his dotal and other obligations, he hit upon the idea of coming to Florence "to seek out money at interest." After two weeks of futility, he took recourse "to the kindness of Your Excellency, begging him that in his goodness . . . he deign to accommodate [Andrea] with five hundred or six hundred scudi from the monte di pietà for one year, or two, with his giving qualified security, and paying the usual interest." Andrea underscored the importance of this loan by adding that familiar paternal lament: he still had "three other girls to marry off."[1] The duke consented. This petition proves that large monte di pietà loans were available to, and understood to be available by, even some provincials like Andrea from Montepulciano. He knew that the only source of a loan the size of the one he was contemplating was the capital city, and he spent, he claimed, two weeks seeking a lender. No doubt he was discouraged by prevailing interest rates on the open market or, even if determined to undertake such a costly loan, was denied credit. The monte di pietà, with its controlled low rates, was the answer.

Even more explicit was a petition on behalf of Portia, widow of Messer Andrea di Fernando de Angulo. She had two thousand scudi invested in the monte di pietà,

> where with such a low return [*ove con si basso emolumento*] she cannot sustain herself and her many children, and having made arrangements in Bologna to put [the money] in a secure place at a reasonable profit, and, however, it being necessary to take it out of the said monte and bring it to Bologna, for all this she has given this information to His Most Serene Highness, to beg him that it may please him to commission or order the camarlingo or the provveditore of the said monte di pietà that they pay her the said dowry.[2]

Portia's forthright description of the monte's return on her deposit makes clear a motive that must have lurked behind many such petitions to the ruler. For persons trying to survive on interest earnings, 5 percent was an inadequate return on an investment.

The third petition came on behalf of Monna Ginevra de' Carnesecchi, widow of Giuliano di Piero di Messer Luca Pitti, who enjoyed sole usufruct of certain of her husband's assets, including his share of profits from the sale of the Pitti palace. By contract, the proceeds had been deposited in the monte di pietà, and the heirs were free to use the interest as they wished. But Ginevra complained that the principal could only be withdrawn if it was to be invested in another piece of property. "Otherwise," she shrewdly noted, "there would be no more interest, except that which the monte di pietà

1. MP 266, Petition for Andrea Avignonesi to Cosimo de' Medici, 20 Dec. 1568.
2. MP 266, Petition for La Portia to Cosimo and Francesco de' Medici, 20 Feb. 1570.

pays at five percent." Her petition asked the duke to permit her to withdraw her inheritance from the monte di pietà in order to reinvest it, because she knew that this rate was not a particularly good one. The duke consented, as long as she offered security.[3] Monna Ginevra made explicit the fact that the monte was a secure investment, but not an especially lucrative one. These qualities made it desirable only for investments where security was the paramount consideration.

Historians who purport to see the structures of modern banking in the monte di pietà are only partly correct. By the early fourteenth century, banks offered three kinds of accounts to their clients: savings accounts, time deposits, and bank deposits (the latter a form of fiduciary money transferable to one's creditors).[4] Florence's monte di pietà, by the 1540s, offered all three of these as well. Hundreds, even thousands, of Tuscans maintained small deposits, tantamount to small savings accounts, that earned 5 percent interest. The duke himself kept a large account that he learned to manipulate, ultimately ordering virtually all household expenses and salaries to be paid through it, while the principal earned interest. He also was a debtor of the monte di pietà in separate accounts. The duke used his current accounts to transfer credits to his own creditors or from account to account. Some Florentines with substantial deposits in the institution, mostly widows or minors, must have lived to a large degree off the interest their money earned; their monte credits represented a kind of primitive trust fund, administered, in the case of minors, by the Office of the Pupilli, whose treasurer was, from the late 1490s, a monte di pietà employee. The monte di pietà of Rome made another contribution to modern finance: in 1788 it issued a note for 130 scudi that is apparently the first paper money printed in Italy.[5]

As a charitable institution the monte succeeded despite the heavy demands made upon it after the 1540s by large-scale borrowers. Its determination to live up to the requirement that it divest itself of all profits once its debts and salaries had been paid was short-lived and

3. MP 266, Petition for Ginevra de' Carnesecchi to Cosimo de' Medici, n.d., but from late 1568 or early 1569.
4. See Mueller, "Role of Bank Money," 47.
5. Parsons, "Economic Significance," 9. Parsons's article includes a facsimile of this note.

did not survive into Cosimo's reign. For the first three decades of its existence, it shopped about for worthy recipients of charity and settled credits upon poor undowered girls, a needy convent, another local monte di pietà, and, finally, the Company of the Good Men of San Martino. Because of the troubles of the last republic, the monte had to stop this practice as its own resources dwindled. In the ducal era it occasionally granted small credits to local charitable institutions. But the custom of handing over all surpluses to the poor whose interest payments on loans had created them had fallen into disuse by the time the dukes entered the scene.

The main culprit in this development was not Medici tyranny but the last republic, whose demand for money in 1530 came close to dealing a death blow to the monte di pietà. It was ironic that the Medici, who had a history of opposition to monti di pietà, turned the monte's fortunes around by allowing it to pay 5 percent interest on deposits. There is no evidence for supposing that Alessandro intended the monte to acquire a mass of surplus capital that he and his successors would thereafter exploit; this was no elite conspiracy. The documents are quite clear that the purpose of temporarily raising the interest rates on loans and allowing the monte to pay interest on deposits was to permit the foundation to recover from the "disorder" into which it had stumbled, and that the duke was concerned with the pitiful lot of Florence's poor. Moreover, the impact of this change was not immediate, and its revolutionary nature, though perhaps hinted at as early as the 1540s, emerged convincingly only in the 1550s and thereafter when hordes of Florentines came to the monte to make deposits. The accrual of large reserves of liquid assets, then, was an unexpected consequence of the reforms of 1534–35 and not the result of the "structures" of the monte di pietà. It took the acumen of Cosimo I to perceive the uses to which such capital might be applied.

Intended or not, the changes resulting from alterations in the monte's bylaws favored the development of large-scale lending by making available the capital for inexpensive secured loans. The monte succeeded in building up capital only after receiving permission to pay 5 percent interest on deposits. It offered a safe, conservative investment for depositors who were unable or unwilling to place their money in more lucrative ventures, or who sought to diversify their investments by putting some money into the reliable monte di pietà, some into riskier schemes. These deposits, plus the profits made through the monte's charitable lending, created the basis for its big-time loans to the Medici and their clients. Of all the monte's activities, these loans had the broadest impact on ducal finance and on the character of the monte itself.

The mere availability of capital for lending through the monte di pietà constituted a necessary but not a sufficient cause for the development of that activity. It was, in fact, not the structures of the institution—designed, after all, as a charitable pawnshop—but the continuing efforts of the Medici to establish an absolute state in early modern Tuscany that provided the real impetus for its involvement in its most important banking activity, the granting of large loans at the duke's order. The tremendous demands of ducal finance in the enlarged Medicean state, coupled with the remarkable consolidation of that state by the single-minded Cosimo I, resulted in an exhaustive, purposeful search for sources of money, a search that formed part of the greater plan to rationalize state finance. For the ordinary subject, the limit on loans against pawns from the monte di pietà remained two florins. But for those who, invoking ties of friendship, kinship, loyal service, or political interests, could persuade the duke to authorize a loan, the monte handed over thousands of ducats at an unprofitable rate for the institution. Only in a state ruled by a prince who saw himself as above the law could the monte di pietà turn into a major lending institution for the patriciate and an arm of ducal finance, all the while carrying on its original mission of offering cheap loans to the poor against pawns.

Recent and ongoing scholarship on Cosimo's duchy has argued that Cosimo developed a political economy, that is, he understood the economy could, to some degree, be controlled by the state in order to enrich both people and sovereign.[6] By centralizing control of the guilds in the Pratica Segreta and Magistrato Supremo, Cosimo removed the guilds' historic autonomy and demonstrated his understanding that the economy operated under a system of laws.

Cosimo was also, despite his momentous victory over Siena, an indifferent soldier. Son of one of the few bona fide military heroes Florence ever produced, he reverted to the focus of his clan: mercantile and financial interests. His use of the monte di pietà illustrates both his developing sense of political economy—the monte di

6. For this argument, see Brown, "Concepts of Political Economy."

pietà was not the hub of this wheel, of course, only one spoke—and his realization, according to Spini, that "to dominate a city of capitalists he must himself become the greatest Florentine capitalist."[7] Perhaps manager rather than capitalist better describes Cosimo's role, but either way the point is clear.

One of the most important themes concerning the development of the Florentine monte di pietà was its relationship to the various Florentine states from the Savonarolan republic to the Medicean grand duchy. Several years before Cosimo received the title of grand duke of Tuscany in 1569, he had begun to lose his fierce energy for governing and formally abdicated in favor of Don Francesco while still keeping his hand in government. But he had succeeded in creating the basis for a bureaucratized, well-organized state to which he had closely tied various institutions of city and district alike, including those that predated his rule, and particularly Tuscan monti di pietà.[8] By the late 1560s the monte had become so much an organ not only of patronage but of state finance that it behaved like a ducal bank, even to the point of handling the monthly payroll and debiting the duke's accounts accordingly. As a source of loans to foreign potentates whom the ruler wished to cultivate, the institution bankrolled an important part of Tuscan foreign policy.

The Florentine state in its several forms kept close control over the monte, exercising important powers beyond the latitude that the statutes permitted the eight officials. The eight themselves were elected, at first by the Great Council and later by other organs; as soon as Alessandro took over the city, he usurped the right to control the choice of the monte's eight officers. The tightened hold Cosimo placed over the choice of the eight and of important monte employees comprised a part of his overall pattern of control.

The tightest bonds between monte and state were fashioned by Cosimo as the institution became important for its liquidity. The duke placed the full force of the new regulatory boards, like the

7. Spini, "Medici Principality," 425 for the quotation, and 425–27 for this discussion.

8. Fasano Guarini, in "Grand Duchy," 528–29, emphasizes the rational consolidation of Cosimo's territorial state, though she also notes the limits of that consolidation. Still, "the structures [of the grand duchy] certainly reflect the impact of Cosimo I's personal actions." She concludes that her map of Tuscany in 1574 "represents not the beginnings but the most mature stage in the process by which the strong territorial state of Tuscany was formed."

Soprassindaci, behind an investigation of it and other Florentine institutions. Throughout its history the monte had suffered losses from bad debts, inept employees, and fraud, so it quickly became caught up in the hunt for corruption that began after the end of the war with Siena. It was in Cosimo's interest to eliminate graft in an institution that helped underwrite ducal finance.

Of course no one had foreseen this development, and it was by no means an inevitable result of the monte's relationship to the state. In an era where the distinction between public and private wavered and blurred, the monte had become firmly entrenched as an adjunct to the ducal treasury. All that remained for the Medici was the single-minded refinement of this truth. One sign of their diligence in assuring that the monte di pietà would continue to serve the duke's needs was the completion, just before his death, of reform of its administrative structures, streamlined to accommodate the big-loan business.

The scope of this book does not include an examination of the Florentine monte di pietà after the time of Cosimo I. It is nevertheless worth noting that the monte, so changed by Cosimo's rule, did not fade away as did his own interest in governing. The Florentine monte di pietà outlived not only Cosimo but also his line.

The period from the mid-sixteenth through the seventeenth centuries, while no longer viewed as a period of economic disaster in Italy, was nonetheless characterized by decline.[9] Florence did not escape this decline, which stood in contrast to the resurgence of political energy that Cosimo's reign had brought. Many Florentine aristocrats, truly worthy of that name by the late sixteenth century, withdrew from commerce and industry in favor of investments in land and turned their talents toward winning posts in the ducal

---

9. See the debate on the economic trends of the sixteenth century in Carlo Cipolla, "The So-Called 'Price Revolution': Reflections on the Italian Situation," and the reply by Alexandre Chabert, in "More about the Sixteenth-Century Price Revolution," in Peter Burke, ed., *Economy and Society in Early Modern Europe: Essays from "Annales"* (New York, 1972). Cipolla discounts the notion that a vicious spiral of inflation, spurred by New World bullion, characterized this period. Instead, price fluctuations compared favorably to those of Rostow's "century of 'monetary stability,'" the nineteenth. Chabert, while conceding that "revolution" is too dramatic a term, nonetheless disputes Cipolla's findings. It is wise to place this debate against the background of Braudel's "upper limit," that line "between possibility and impossibility . . . established for every period." See *Capitalism and Material Life*, esp. preface, ix–x.

household or the bureaucracy. Inflation in the cost of various important commodities, ranging from grain to dowries, contributed to the decline. Taxes, especially indirect taxes and those levied on the contado, grew more onerous by the late sixteenth century.[10]

Nothing reversed this decline in the seventeenth century. Rather the general "pauperization of European society" continued, a phenomenon exacerbated in Italian cities by crises in trade and manufacturing.[11] In Florence, for example, the number of wool workshops declined from eighty-four to forty-six by the early seventeenth century. The result was the impoverishment of the most marginal classes. In 1621 two lists, drawn up at ducal command, illustrated the problems of the poor. Of 244 cases, most were men, a sure sign of the difficulty of finding employment. Growing fears of vagabonds and of the restlessness they brought led to their classification as criminals.

So serious were these problems that new institutions were set up to cope with them. The Opera dei Poveri Mendicanti, created in 1621–22 to end vagabondage, merely fell back on the old medieval notion that some persons were forced to beg, while others did so out of laziness. The mendicant poor were to be offered the choice of hard work, internment in the Opera, or expulsion from the territory. But the directors of the Opera quickly saw that the sheer numbers of the poor were far larger than they had imagined. The elegance and richesse of courtly society contrasted ever more starkly with the growing misery of the poor. The grand duke and his friends continued to divert money from the monte di pietà for their own political, social, and economic needs just at the time when that institution's liquidity might have been put to use to help the very group for which it had been created—the poor.

Cosimo's heir Francesco lacked not only what Hale calls his predecessor's "coolly architectonic approach to government" but also his

10. See Litchfield, *Emergence of a Bureaucracy*, chaps. 1–3. By the mid-sixteenth century the size of the ducal retinue reached about 280. D'Addario ("Burocrazia") adds that all ducal employees numbered no more than one thousand; their salaries and expenses cost the duke about sc. 55,500 annually: 27,000 for salaries of officials *di dentro*, 25,000 to the *giusdicenti* of the *dominio*, and 3,200 for the *giudici della Ruota* (372–73).

11. Ludovico Branca, "Pauperismo, assistenza, e controllo sociale a Firenze (1621–1632): Materiali e ricerche," *ASI* 141 (1983), 421; for the following discussion, see esp. 421–34.

political energy, drive, and creativity.[12] Fortunately for the dynasty, the structures built by Cosimo held firm and survived Francesco's mediocrity until the succession of Ferdinando in 1587 restored some vigor to the governance of Tuscany. The establishment of a sound bureaucracy insured continued attention by a prototype civil service whose members carried on regardless of who ruled. The efficiency of this bureaucracy is evident in the pattern of careful reform that altered the monte di pietà again in 1583. The monte had acquired a momentum of its own, and occasional tinkering with its statutes merely fine-tuned its operation. By 1589 the grand duke ordered the monte di pietà of Prato to deposit its excess capital in Florence's monte. Earlier Cosimo had obliged the Sienese monte to do the same thing, but Prato's case was different in one important point: its deposits in Florence would earn no interest.[13]

The tendency of the grand dukes to view the monte di pietà as a source of liquid capital continued into the seventeenth century and was especially notable under Cosimo II. This continuity was prompted by the fiscal woes that threatened the realm: by the time the Medici line died out, the funded public debt stood at about sc. 14 million[14]

A different motive prompted the revisions of 1616, reforms that must be placed against the backdrop of post-Reformation Europe. It is tempting to equate the Church's loss of political power north of the Alps with a loss of spiritual and political power in Italy as well, but such an assumption does not hold. Though Cosimo strove mightily to free himself from papal domination, he succeeded only after a bitter struggle. A hostile pope was a serious enemy, and Cosimo worked hard to place his own relatives in important church positions, to court those prelates who were friendly to him or at least lukewarm to Rome, and to cement such alliances through patronage. As a Catholic prince at a time of religious ferment and war, he also exercised some leverage with the popes.[15]

12. Hale, *Florence and the Medici*, 147.
13. A.G.B., "Monte di pietà," 104.
14. See Litchfield, *Emergence of a Bureaucracy*, chaps. 1 and 6. Luigi Dal Pane, *La finanza toscana dagli inizi del secolo XVIII alla caduta del granducato* (Milan, 1965), 38 and 19, refers to the "chronic ill of public finance" and notes that interest payments on the debt ate up income from the gabelles on salt, iron, and flour, and from the decima.
15. Cosimo was kept abreast of the events of the Reformation by many sources, including Florentine diplomats. The letters from his ambassador in Brussels during

It is likewise simple to overlook the Church's ongoing concern with issues easily dismissed as "medieval," like usury. Although the Church remained steadfast in its condemnation of this evil throughout the early modern age, the issue lay relatively quiet during the sixteenth century, overshadowed by that astonishing set of events, the Protestant and the Catholic reformations. The institution that emerged from the Council of Trent was invigorated by the resounding confirmation of Church doctrine, and it set off on a path of reconquest and conservative entrenchment as the best means to win back lost souls and to hold firmly those who might waver. The spiritual battle for the souls of European Christians reincarnated old issues and invested them with new importance. One of these issues, and one that closely affected the monte di pietà, was the question of usury.

Within two months of the monte reforms of 1574 an archepiscopal synod in Florence issued a denunciation of all usury, including the interest charged by the monte di pietà on loans and paid out by it on deposits. That the monte often realized a profit beyond what it required for its own expenses cannot be doubted. An ecclesiastical condemnation of such profit making threatened the interests of the new grand duke, Francesco; reacting with alarmed vigor, he requested an end to the condemnation. The pope complied, but the resurrection of this issue sounded, as Pampaloni suggested, a "peal of alarm."[16] The monte depended on the public's confidence: the evaporation of this trust would strike at the institution's very existence. The only way to nurture public faith in the monte as a bank was to ensure that no papal prohibitions, indeed no doubts or questions whatsoever, would raise the specter of usury.

The early years of the seventeenth century saw the opening of a new chapter in the canonical debate over the monte's lending activities. The canon lawyer Girolamo Confetti stated that conscientious consideration disapproved of the monte's practices, which Confetti called, in the most unflattering terms, "haggling" (*negoziazione*). The grand duke replied by creating a commission, drawn up, according

---

the 1550s-70s are full of news (and rumors) about Protestant and Catholic affairs. Giovan Battista Guicciardini, *Lettere di Giovan Battista Guicciardini a Cosimo e Francesco de' Medici scritte dal Belgio dal 1559 al 1577* (Brussels, 1949).

16. Pampaloni, "Cenni storici," 545.

to one reminiscence, "in order to quiet consciences," to determine ways to evade such condemnation.[17] Of the monte's activities the most difficult to defend canonically was no longer its collection of interest on loans but its payment of interest to depositors. The depositors themselves, and not the monte or its borrowers, ran the risk of usury by accepting earnings on money that they invested voluntarily.[18] The commission, demonstrating the unique creativity that Italian entrepreneurs had typically shown when trying to get around canonical restrictions on business practices, decided to establish a monte non vacabile. Instead of depositing money, persons wishing to open interest-earning accounts had to purchase *luoghi di monte*—shares, essentially—at one hundred scudi each. Each share returned 5 percent interest. Because one had to purchase the luoghi, each such transaction took the form of a sale, the undertaking of which entitled the purchaser to make a profit licitly. In 1609 Ferdinando approved this method of keeping the canonists happy. The archbishop of Florence concurred that this plan avoided the taint of usury, and the Senate of Forty-Eight approved it in April 1616. Printed shares, with an engraving of Jesus displaying his wounds in each of the upper corners and the Medici coat of arms in the middle, quickly began to circulate.[19]

17. Acquisti e Doni 281, 2. Sitting on the commission of Teologi, Canonisti, Dottori e Gentiluomini were "il Padre fra Francesco Pitti Aretino dell'Osservanza, Confessore di S.A.; il padre Leonardo Coquét Francese Agostiniano, confessore di Madamma Serenissima; il padre Fra Vincenzio Civitella, Dominicano Lettore dello Studio di Pisa; Messer Girolamo Confetti, canonista; Messer Geri Spini, e Messer Niccolò dell' Antella, utriusque Juris Doctores; Messer Giulio de' Nobili e Messer Luigi Gaddi, Intelligenti e pratichi degl'ordini, costumi, e usanze della Città di Firenze." They were convened "per quietare le coscienze."

18. Monti in the Veneto engaged in similar attempts to make canonically licit the payment of interest on deposits. On one hand, because depositors did not incur any risk in placing money in the monte, and because they might redeem it at their pleasure, they could be committing usury by accepting interest. By the same token it was honorable and Christian to "lend" money to the monte; such a good deed deserved some kind of reward beyond a spiritual one, because such persons could have invested their funds in a more lucrative venture. The compromise reached stated that only money depositors had intended to invest in business or other active ventures could licitly earn a modest return. Obviously such a determination was impossible to make. See Pullan, *Rich and Poor*, chap. 5.

19. An extant certificate for two shares issued on 15 Sept. 1625 to Pompeo di Fabio Sperandi is held by the Rare Book Room at the Hatcher Graduate Library, University of Michigan, Ann Arbor. Sperandi paid "one hundred scudi for each share at seven lire per scudo" and was guaranteed 5 percent in interest per annum, payable every six months.

The effect of this change upon the monte was, however, not salutary in the long run. Florentines questioned whether the shares were
adequately secured, no doubt having in mind the disappointing histories of other Florentine monti. The new plans also complicated the
process of withdrawing deposits, an effect that did nothing to shore
up public confidence in the institution. New deposits continued to
increase, but at a slower pace after 1616. By 1620 the provveditore
reported total credits in excess of 3 million ducats. The institution
still attracted deposits, including one from the duke of Bavaria
amounting to some 15,000 scudi, and another from Eleonora Galigai
of France for 200,000 scudi.[20] The monte continued to pay interest
promptly. The grand duke kept to the practice of authorizing loans
to those whom he wished to patronize, and extended substantial
loans to foreigners, a practice Cosimo had followed only in a limited
way. Unfortunately for the monte, one of the heftiest loans—a total
of some 300,000 ducats—went in 1583 to the Spanish crown, whose
pattern of fiscal irresponsibility in the late sixteenth century is too
well known to describe at length here. At the rate of $7\frac{1}{3}$ percent, the
monte was due interest of nearly 22,000 ducats the first year alone.
Needless to say, the Spaniards defaulted and the monte never recovered all its principal, let alone any interest.

The Spanish default presaged unsettled times for the monte di
pietà of Florence, and by the mid-seventeenth century it was in serious trouble. The major cause of its difficulties seems to have been
its adverse cash flow, with huge reserves flooding out to large borrowers. As a result the monte was left with insufficient liquidity to
pay interest promptly to its shareholders. Finally the exigencies of
the Thirty Years War drove the grand dukes to raid the coffers of
the monte di pietà, just as their republican forebears had done a
century earlier during the siege of Florence. The result was the
same: the monte almost crashed.[21] Interest rates on deposits were
reduced to an unattractive $1\frac{1}{2}$ percent, and shares dropped to 75
percent of their face value. These drastic measures allowed the
monte to survive, but did nothing to attract investments in it. Money
taken in fell far short of expenses. The monte had begun to absorb

20. For the figures of 1620, Miscellanea Medicea 472, ins. 19, cited by Pampaloni,
"Cenni storici," 548, n. 79. Pampaloni suggests, however, that this figure is too high
by one-third, because it omitted certain debits. On the foreign deposits, Miscellanea
Medicea 460, ins. 8, cited ibid., 549, nn. 83 and 84.
21. Litchfield, *Emergence of a Bureaucracy*, chap. 6.

the major portion of state revenues, an irony in view of its role during Cosimo's reign when it contributed to state finance. Taking on more and more the role of a funded public debt, the monte di pietà and the public debt were finally united officially under the Habsburgs. At the same time, Grand Duke Leopold ordered the monte to return to its initial function of offering loans to the poor against small pawns. In 1781 a new ministry was created to supervise the monte in its functions as a benevolent establishment. But in the following year the monte di pietà per se ceased to exist and was replaced by the Azienda dei Presti ed Arruoti. Soon thereafter, the monte's credits and property were consigned to the Bigallo for the use and relief of poor girls there.[22] The new Azienda dei Presti was restructured from the ruins of the old monte di pietà, but freed from its predecessor's debts, it could start anew with the granting of small loans to the poor.

The Napoleonic age temporarily brought Tuscany under French domination. The monte's successor institution survived and was still functioning at the time of the Lorrensian restoration.[23] The stress and dislocation of the Napoleonic Wars, however, had upset the Azienda's finances. Despite several attempts to reform it, the Azienda teetered on the brink of bankruptcy; it had, in the minds of most Tuscans, outlived its usefulness. With the unification of Italy and a new emphasis on national rather than regional institutions, the Azienda lost its unique position in Florence, and with it, its identity as an institution.[24]

The rapid decline and the drawn-out expiration of the monte di pietà of Florence take on a logical cast when placed against the background of European history from the sixteenth to the nineteenth century. The years under Cosimo had been the monte's golden years: it attracted thousands of depositors, offered loans at interest to rich and poor alike, enjoyed remarkable liquidity, and, because it served him in so many important ways, received careful attention from one of Italy's most talented rulers. Machiavelli noted the difficulties of state building, especially for a prince who had conquered a

---

22. See Pampaloni, "Cenni storici," 554–57.
23. Ibid., 560.
24. Article 97 of the Acts of the Congress of Vienna of 1815 deals with the debts and property of the surviving monte of Milan, by then known as the Mont-Napoléon. I am grateful to Ralph R. Menning of Heidelberg College for this reference.

formerly free land. The demands of statecraft tested Cosimo's *virtù*. He had to adapt institutions to his own needs and did so successfully. His successors became entangled in a different trap altogether, tending to fall victim to the complacency against which Machiavelli tried to warn princes who inherited a well-functioning state. With the possible exception of Ferdinando, none had Cosimo I's taste or talent for statesmanship. Further, the Medici as dukes faced a problem common among European royalty: whom can a grand duke and his children marry? By Cosimo's own time, the Medici signaled their equality with the ruling houses of Europe by marrying into them. One has only to consider the bloated and repulsive Gian Gastone, the last Medici grand duke, never opening letters for fear of having to answer them, seldom leaving the sanctuary of his bed until his death in 1737, to see that complacency and inbreeding had ruined the Medici and their state with them.[25] They failed to continue the vigilant watch over all institutions that Cosimo had kept so well. Perhaps we should not wonder at the eventual downfall of both Cosimo's dynasty and the institutions, like the monte di pietà, upon which his state depended, but we should instead respect the tremendous momentum he imparted to them, and their remarkable longevity in the face of decades of neglect and ineptitude in government.

25. See Harold Acton, *The Last Medici* (London, 1980; orig. pub. London, 1932), 203–53.

APPENDIX A.
TABLES

Table 1.
Monte di pietà directors, 1530–1575

1530–33[a]	Zanobi di Leonardo Bartolini	Lorenzo di Filippo Strozzi
	Luigi di Gianfrancesco Pazzi	Tanai di Piero de' Nerli
		Vittorio d'Antonio Landi
	Luigi Soderini	Filippo d'Antonio Baroncini
	Larione Martelli	
1530–33[b]	Bartolomeo Valori	Averardo d'Alamanno Salviati
	Filippo d'Alessandro Machiavelli	Filippo di Filippo Strozzi
	Bernardo di Carlo Gondi	Giuliano di Franco del Zecheria
	Giovanfrancesco d'Antonio de' Nobili	Luigi di Francesco Pieri
1533–36	Agostino di Francesco Dini	Matteo di Lorenzo Strozzi
	Niccolò di Bartolomeo del Croscia	Giovanni di Filippo dell'Antella
	Niccolò di Battista Dini	Francesco d'Antonio Nori
	Jacopo di Ms. Bongianni Gianfigliazzi	Filippo di Benedetto Nerli
1536–39	Uliveri di Simone Guadagni	Lapo di Bartolomeo del Tovaglia

Table 1.—*continued*

1536–39	Giuliano di Piero Capponi
	Raffaello di Francesco de'
	  Medici
	Luigi di Piero Guicciardini
		Alessandro di Leonardo
		  del Caccia
		Averardo di Alamanno
		  Salviati
		Francesco di Niccolò Valori[c]
		Federigo di Roberto de'
		  Ricci[d]

1539–42	Roberto di Donato
	  Acciaiuoli
	Jacopo di Ms. Bongianni
	  Gianfigliazzi
	Francesco di Bartolomeo
	  Buonagratia
	Giovanfrancesco d'Antonio
	  de' Nobili
		Cristoforo di Bernardo
		  Rinieri
		Francesco di Girolamo
		  Rucellai
		Gherardo di Bartolomeo
		  Bartolini
		Giovanni di Niccolo Giraldi

1542–45	Migliotto di Bardo de'
	  Bardi
	Raffaello di Luca
	  Torrigiani
	Ottaviano di Lorenzo de'
	  Medici
	Alessandro di Niccolò
	  Antinori
		Girolamo di Giovanni
		  Morelli
		Federigo di Roberto de'
		  Ricci
		Lorenzo di Matteo Strozzi
		Piero di Niccolò Chezioni

1545–48	Filippo d'Alessandro
	  Machiavelli
	Agostino di Francesco Dini
	Andreuolo di Niccolò Zati
	Prinzivale di Ms. Luigi
	  della Stufa
		Francesco di Pierantonio
		  Bandini
		Girolamo di Piero
		  Guicciardini
		Bartolomeo di Zanobi
		  Carnesecchi
		Pierantonio di
		  Giovanfrancesco de'
		  Nobili

1548–51	Taddeo di Francesco di
	  Ser Guiducci
	Bernardo d'Andrea
	  Carnesecchi
	Girolamo di Francesco da
	  Sommaia
		Bindo d'Antonio Altoviti
		Jacopo di Uliveri Guadagni
		Lorenzo di Mo. Giovanni
		  Pasquali
		Sinibaldo di Taddeo Gaddi

Table 1.—*continued*

1548–51	Bongianni di Gherardo Gianfigliazzi	
1551–54	Ms. Agnolo di Ms. Antonio Niccolini	Ippolito di Giovanni Buondelmonti[c]
	Giovanni d'Antonio Gerini	Girolamo di Luca degli Albizzi
	Bastiano di Zanobi da Montauto[c]	Francesco di Ms. Luigi della Stufa
	Agostino di Piero del Nero	Bartolomeo di Zanobi Carnesecchi
	Federigo di Roberto de' Ricci[d]	Luigi di Giuliano Capponi[d]
1554–57	Lorenzo di Mariotto Gondi	Giovanni Zanchini
	Giovanni Battista di Tommaso Ginori	Ridolfo di Roberto Serristori
	Piero d'Alamanno Salviati	Simone di Jacopo Corsi
	Giovanni d'Agostino Dini	Marcello di Giovanni Acciaiuoli
1557–60	Tommaso Cavalcanti	Pierfrancesco di Salvi Becherini
	Averardo Serristori	Tommaso di Ms. Giovanvitale Soderini
	Francesco di Bartolomeo Zati	Niccolò di Matteo Berardi
	Lione di Filippo de' Nerli	Filippo d'Averardo Salviati
1560–63	Andrea di Tommaso Alamanni	Giovanni di Bartolomeo Ugolini
	Bongianni di Jacopo Gianfigliazzi	Piero di Gino Capponi
	Pierfilippo di Francesco Pandolfini	Brancatio di Ms. Niccolò Rucellai
	Lorenzo di Piero Ridolfi	Luca di Raffaello Torrigiani
1563–66	Simone di Jacopo Corsi	Marabotto d'Antonio Rustichi
	Jacopo di Uliveri Guadagni	Piero di Ms. Matteo Niccolini
	Agnolo di Niccolò Biffoli	Lodovico di Giovanni Ridolfi
	Agostino di Piero del Nero	Alessandro di Giuliano Capponi

Table 1.—*continued*

1566–69	Carlo di Roberto Acciaiuoli	Lorenzo del Vigna
	Camillo di Matteo Strozzi	Jacopo di Lorenzo Giacomini
	Agnolo di Girolamo Guicciardini	Piero d'Agostino Dini
	Giovanbattista di Tommaso Cavalcanti	Francesco d'Alessandro Rinuccini
1569–72	Bartolomeo di Bernardo Gondi	Alamanno di Tommaso da Filicaia
	Alamanno d'Antonio de' Pazzi	Giovanni di Giuliano de' Ricci
	Benvenuto di Lorenzo Machiavelli	Bartolomeo di Larione Martelli
	Cristofano di Giovanni Spini	Filippo di Guasparre da Ricasoli
1572–75	[*illeg.*] to di Francesco di Diaceto	Chiarissimo di Bernardo de' Medici
	Daniello di Giovanni degli Alberti	Benedetto di Jacopo Busini
	Niccolò di Giovanni Manelli	Giovanni di Jacopo Morelli
	Antonio di Donato Malegonelle	Napoleone di Girolamo Cambi

[a]Served during the last republic.   [b]Appointed by Clement VII.
[c]Deceased in office.   [d]Appointed to replace deceased.

Table 2.
Families with more than one appointment
to monte di pietà board, 1530–1575

Surname	Dates appointed
Acciaiuoli	1539, 1554, 1566
Capponi	1536, 1551, 1560, 1563
Carnesecchi	1545, 1548, 1551
Cavalcanti	1557, 1566
Corsi	1554, 1563
Dini	1533, 1545, 1554, 1566
Gianfigliazzi	1533, 1539, 1548, 1560
Gondi	1530, 1554, 1569
Guadagni	1536, 1548, 1563
Guicciardini	1536, 1545, 1566
Machiavelli	1530, 1545, 1569
Medici	1536, 1542, 1572
Morelli	1542, 1572
Nerli	1533, 1557
del Nero	1551, 1563
Niccolini	1551, 1563
Nobili	1530, 1539, 1545
Ricci	1536, 1542, 1551, 1569
Ridolfi	1560, 1563
Rucellai	1539, 1560
Salviati	1530, 1536, 1554, 1557
Serristori	1554, 1557
Strozzi	1530, 1533, 1542, 1566
della Stufa	1545, 1551
Torrigiani	1542, 1560
Valori	1530, 1536
Zati	1545, 1557

Table 3.
Families with one appointment to
monte di pietà board, 1530–1575

Surname	Date	Surname	Date
Alamanni	1560	Ginori	1554
Alberti	1572	Giraldi	1539
Albizzi	1551	di Ser Guiducci	1548
Altoviti	1548	Malegonelle	1572
dell'Antella	1533	Manelli	1572
Antinori	1542	Martelli	1569
Bandini	1545	da Montauto	1551
Bardi	1542	Nori	1533
Bartolini	1539	Pandolfini	1560
Becherini	1557	Pasquali	1548
Berardi	1557	Pazzi	1569
Biffoli	1563	Pieri	1530
Buonagratia	1539	Ricasoli	1569
Buondelmonti	1551	Rinieri	1539
Busini	1572	Rinuccini	1566
della Caccia	1536	Rustichi	1563
Cambi	1572	Soderini	1557
Chezioni	1542	da Sommaia	1548
del Croscia	1533	Spini	1569
di Diaceto	1572	del Tovaglia	1536
da Filicaia	1569	Ugolini	1560
Gaddi	1548	del Vigna	1566
Gerini	1551	Zanchini	1554
Giacomini	1566	del Zecheria	1530

Table 4.
The first eighteen depositors with
interest-bearing accounts, 1539–1542

Name	Principal	Interest earned
Pietropagolo di Mariotto, blacksmith	L. 402.10	L. 78.2 (withdrawn)
Monna Fiametta	1,427.4	132.4
Two women	324.7	36.7
Caterina Dannovoli	490	55.9.4 (withdrawn)
Giovannni Soldi	0	75.15.4[a]
Maria e Francesca	151	11
Capitani del Bigallo	386.10	36.10
Fra Giovanbattista di Jacopo	232.3.4	22.3.4
Maria di Bartolomeo Manzuoli	1,823.3	80.3
Jacopo di Dominico Castellini	467.10	17.10
Alessandro Masini	79	4
Caterina di Giovanni Falconi	63	3
Lisabetta di Jacopo Rapacci	748.5	37.8
Gostanza di Francesco, cloth merchant	1,099.10	8.10
Lucrezia del Fabrino	196	49.10
Pippa di Giovanni da Muzzi	357	12.2.6
Monna Caterina di Lattanzio	352.18.4	2.18.4
Monna Lena da Cepperello	0	176.6.4 (withdrawn[b])
TOTAL	L. 8,600.1.8	838.19.4

Source: MP 750, 77b, 73a.
Notes: Amounts are in lire, soldi, denari; unless otherwise noted, these amounts were on the books as of 17 Nov. 1542.
[a]The deposit and interest were withdrawn prior to 17 Nov. 1542.
[b]The original deposit of fl. 200 (L. 1,400) was withdrawn prior to 17 Nov. 1542; the interest was given as a credit to Giannozzo di Dominico Stradi, who withdrew it for unstated purpose.

Table 5.
Accounts of heirs, 17 November 1563

Heirs of	Accrued interest	Total value of account
Benedetto Arrigucci	21, L. —	156, L. 5.18
Antonio Alamanni	7, L. —	52, L. 4
Domenico di Parente	1, L. 2.16	11, L. 1.16
Giovanni Latrona	2, L. 2.7	17, L. 4.10
Lorenzo di Niccolò della Rena	87, L. 5.5	666, L. 1.10
Jacopo di Francesco Nucci	12, L. 2	102, L. 1.10
Buonaccorso Pitti	a	1,086, L. 3.7.6
Giuliano Pitti	a	375, L. —
Giuliano Celli	15, L. 3.17.4	162, L. 4.4
Monna Francesca	3, L. —	22, L. 6.5
Capitano Bartolomeo Greco	11, L. 3.10	78, L. 3.10
Guasparre di Giovanni	16, L. 2.6	121, L. 2.16
Filippo Altoni	134, L. 2	936, L. 2
Giuliano di Piero	19, L. 4–.14	97, L. 1.10
Averone	104, L. —	306, L. –.8.6
Tommaso Carducci	75, L. 4.13	675, L. 4.13
Alessandro Camerotti	140, L. 4	1, L. 104.6
Girolamo Squilli	1, L. 4.13	31, L. –.3
Piero Mariscotti	13, L. —	122, L. 2
Gostino Capitani	19, L. 1.16	105, L. 6
Michele Pulinari	—, L. 6.10.6	7, L. 4.8
Daniele di Carlo Strozzi	123, L. 2.14.6	859, L. 1.3
Ser Niccolò di Bernaba	6, L. 1.8	46, L. 6
Girolamo Villani	10, L. 6.14	101, L. 2.14.4
Francesco d'Andrea	38, L. 3	(withdrawn)
Bartolomeo di Jacopo Corriere	23, L. 4.3	167, L. 1.15.10
Piero Baldegli	184, L. 6.2.8	1,490, L. –.8
Giovanbattista Filiarchi	29, L. 5.13.4	287, L. 5
Giovanbattista Pitti	a	1,101, L. 5.13.11
Francesco Vernacci	7, L. —	87, L. —
Domenico Dardano	9, L. 6	159, L. 6
Benedetto di Giovanbattista	3, L. 1.10	53, L. 1.10
Giovanni di Domenico	2, L. 4	42, L. 4
Messer Bartolomeo di Prinzivalle Cambi	3, L. 3.10	7, L. 3.10

Table 5.—*continued*

Heirs of	Accrued interest	Total value of account
Michele di Battista	1, L. 2.10	21, L. 2.10
Piero di Giovanni Bruzzi	19, L. —	419, L. —
Monte di Bilicozzo Gatti	—, L. 4.15	20, L. 4.15
Messer Pierfrancesco Cecchi	27, L. —	1, L. 577
Francesco di Mariotto	3, L. 1	101, L. 4
Michele di Francesco	11, L. 5.13.4	295, L. 5.13.4
Giovanni di Francesco	94, L. —	438, L. 6.10
Don Basilio Lapi	2, L. –.1	126, L. 4.9
Vincenzio Galli	1, L. —	131, L. —
Ser Lorenzo Ricchi	—, L. 3	104, L. 3
Baccio di Simone	[b]	13, L. 6.10.4
Filippo di Francesco	[b]	90, L. —
Filippo di Manete	[b]	133, L. —
Monna Lessandra di Simone	[b]	150, L. —
Piero di Girolamo	70, L. —	785, L. 5.6.8
Piero di Michele	[b]	168, L. —
Jacopo	[a]	320, L. —
TOTAL 51 ACCOUNTS		fl. 13,981, L. 1.17.11

Source: MP 764.

Note: Amounts are in florins, lire, soldi, denari.

[a]The Pitti accounts represented the sums left to these heirs from the proceeds of the sale of the family's palace; no interest was entered in the books for them. The account of Jacopo, which accrued from the sale of a house, also yielded no interest according to the books.

[b]These accounts were interest-earning accounts, but were opened too late to have accrued calculable interest.

Table 6.
Sample of creditors, 1566–1569

Creditor and type of deposit	Account
Monna Sandra di Domenico Scarpellino, free deposit at 5%	fl. 20, L. 3 fl. 1, L. 3.10 (int.) −fl. 21, L. 6.10 0
Monna Ginevra, widow of Lorenzo di Dino, carpenter, free deposit at 5%	fl. 16, L. 2.5 fl. 1, L. 4.4 (int.) −fl. 17, L. 6.9 0
Hospital de'Pellegrini de'Preti on Via San Gallo, conditional deposit at 5%, from the duke for houses purchased from it; principal to be reinvested only in real estate	fl. 405 fl. 270 fl. 80, L. 1 (int.) −fl. 170 −fl. 270 −fl. 315, L. 1 0
Giovanni di Matteo Gamberelli, conditional deposit at 5%, to be paid to his daughters upon their marriages or entry into a convent	fl. 39 L. 3.10 (int.) −fl. 39, L. 3.10 0
Monna Domenica di Domenico da Rostolena di Mugello, free deposit at 5%	fl. 18, L. 2.10 fl. 2, L. 5.10 (int.) fl. 21, L. 1
Monna Maria di Domenico Pedoni, conditional deposit at 5%, to be paid equally among Lena di Pasquino Pedoni, Maria di Lorenzo Pedoni, and Francesca di Lorenzo Dorelli when they marry	fl. 30, L. 4.5 fl. 4, L. 3.10 (int.) fl. 35, L. −.15
Margherita di Lorenzo da San Piero a Sieve, conditional deposit at 5%, to be paid by Fra Marcantonio Aiardo, prior of Santa Maria Maggiore, in accordance with Piero Lasessesi of Verona, executor of the will of Messer Matteo Monna of Verona, to be paid when Margherita marries	fl. 10, L. 1.10 fl. 1, L. 3.10 (int.) fl. 11, L. 5

Table 6.—*continued*

Creditor and type of deposit	Account
Sabatino di Simone Gancalardi of Barberino di Mugello, conditional deposit at 5%, deposited for him by his mother and controlled by her	fl. 25, L. 3.10 fl. 3, L. 1.10 (int.) −fl. 28, L. 5 o
Monna Caterina di Simone Barbassi di Gattaia, free deposit at 5%	fl. 14, L. 4 fl. 14, L. 2 fl. 3, L. 1. (int.) fl. 32
Heirs of Domenico Mainardi of S. Gimignano, conditional deposit at 5%, placed by order of Office of Pupilli	fl. 128 fl. 19, L. 1.10 (int.) fl. 147, L. 1.10
Morgante, dwarf of his Excellency, conditional deposit at 5%, placed by order of Pupilli	fl. 102 fl. 15 (int.) fl. 117
Antonio di Girolamo di San Benedetto di Romagna, free deposit at 5%	fl. 11, L. 1.5 fl. 11, L. 4.10 fl. 1, L. 5.5 (int.) −fl. 1, L. 4.11 fl. 22, L. 6.19
Alessandro di Dino Canacci, conditional deposit at 5%, capital to be reinvested only in real estate	fl. 160 fl. 7, L. 4.13 (int.) −fl. 167, L. 4.13 o
Monna Ginevra di Battista di Zanobi, master weaver, free deposit at 5%	fl. 154, L. 3.10 fl. 50 fl. 50 fl. 25, L. 3.10 (int.) −fl. 127, L. 1.10 fl. 152, L. 5.10
Noferi de' Rossi from Pistoia, and Monna Ortensia his wife, deposit at 5%, to be reinvested only in real estate (withdrawn, with sc. 450 posted against failure to reinvest it within one year)	fl. 482, L. 1 fl. 54, L. 1.8 (int.) −fl. 536, L. 2.8 o
Monna Maria de' Corsi, wife of Alamanno Martelli, free deposit at 5%	fl. 203, L. 2.6 fl. 30 (int.) −fl. 20 fl. 213, L. 2.6

Table 6.—*continued*

Creditor and type of deposit	Account
Monna Lena di Lazzero Frasconi da Rimaggio, free deposit at 5%	fl. 25
	fl. 3, L. 1.10 (int.)
	fl. 28, L. 1.10
Maestro Giovanbattista Arrighi, friar at Santo Spirito, free deposit at 5%	fl. 50
	fl. 5, L. 2.16 (int.)
	−fl. 55, L. 2.16
	0
Monna Diamante di Domenico, carpenter, free deposit at 5%	fl. 21.
	fl. 2, L. 5 (int.)
	−fl. 2, L. 3.10
	fl. 21, L. 1.10
Betta di Damiano del Riva, conditional deposit at 5%, placed by the Otto di Guardia e Balìa for her dowry	fl. 50
	fl. 3, L. 6.10 (int.)
	−fl. 53, L. 6.10
	0
Maddalena and Gostanza di Battista di Domenico, conditional deposit at 5%, placed for them as part of their inheritance and to be removed only to pay for their dowries	fl. 50
	fl. 3 (int.)
	−fl. 53
	0
Lorenzo di Bastiano del Soldato, miller, free deposit at 5%	fl. 100
	fl. 1 (int.)
	−fl. 101
	0
Marco di Matteo Palmieri, free deposit at 5%	fl. 120
	fl. 50
	fl. 4 (int.)
	−fl. 174
	0
Niccolò di Giovanni Boni, conditional deposit at 5%, capital to be reinvested only in real estate, from the duke for the purchase of a house	fl. 200
	fl. 25 (int.)
	−fl. 15, L. 2.6.8
	fl. 209, L. 4.13.4
Tommaso di Benozzo, cloth weaver, free deposit at 5%, placed in the monte as his inheritance	fl. 500
	fl. 400
	fl. 107, L. 3.10 (int.)
	−fl. 490
	fl. 517, L. 3.10

Table 6.—*continued*

Creditor and type of deposit	Account
Maddalena, daughter of Messer Tommaso de' Medici, conditional deposit at 5%, placed in the monte by Tommaso, to be paid with interest only for her dowry, or to be paid in part to her convent if she becomes a nun, and the rest to be paid to Tommaso or, in the event of his prior demise, to his sister (withdrawn at Tommaso's order for other investments at 7% in Maddalena's name)	fl. 321, L. 3 fl. 29, L. 2.10 (int.) − fl. 169, L. 4.18 − fl. 181, L. −.12 — 0
Vincenzio di Filippo da San Miniato, free deposit at 5%	fl. 240 fl. 10, L. 6 (int.) − fl. 250, L. 6 — 0
Giovanni di Mendoza, soldier, free deposit at 5%	fl. 48 fl. 9, L. 1 (int.) fl. 4, L. 1.10 − fl. 61, L. 2.10 — 0
Francesco di Domenico Anichini, merchant, conditional deposit at 5%, from his wife's dowry, capital to be reinvested only in real estate in the duchy	fl. 450 fl. 56, L. 1.15 (int.) − fl. 52, L. 3.10 — fl. 453, L. 5.5
Ser Domenico di Gianmaria Buonaccorsi da Fucecchio, free deposit at 5%	fl. 100 fl. 3, L. 5.5 (int.) − fl. 103, L. 5.5 — 0
Maria, Ginevra, Cassandra, and Caterina, daughters of Agnolo Biliotti, conditional deposit at 5%, opened by their mother, to be removed only for their dowries or to pay to their convent if they become nuns, to be divided equally	fl. 400 fl. 38, L. 2 (int.) — fl. 438, L. 2
Monna Ippolita d' Alessandro Rinuccini,	fl. 600

Table 6.—*continued*

Creditor and type of deposit	Account
wife of Bernardo Machiavelli, free deposit at 5%, to be withdrawn at her pleasure without the intervention of judges or magistrates (her husband affirmed that this was her money, to be disposed of freely by her, and to go to her sons upon her death)	fl. 53, L. 5.5 (int.) −fl. 45 fl. 608, L. 5.5
Monastery and nuns of Santa Monaca, conditional deposit at 5%, given by Monna Lucretia di Bartolomeo Panciatichi, to be used for the walls of the monastery	fl. 62 fl. 5, L. 4.10 (int.) fl. 67, L. 4.10
Church, formerly the Badia, of San Bartolomeo a Cappiano di Fucecchio, bishopric of Lucca, conditional deposit at 5%, deposited by Monsignor Lorenzo Pagni, to be reinvested only in real estate (the money was withdrawn, however, when the contract of liberation was revoked, "apostolic consent not having arrived")	fl. 210 fl. 3 (int.) −fl. 3 −fl. 210 0
Giovanni di Biagio di Frosino, cloth weaver, free deposit at 5%	fl. 107, L. 3 fl. 4 (int.) −fl. 8 fl. 103, L. 3
Heirs of Capt. Francesco d'Agnolo Deviarelli of Arezzo, from Messer Agnolo Biffoli, treasurer of his Excellency, and for him from the Ricci [Company] as their inheritance (due the deceased for services rendered)	fl. 200 fl. 18, L. 3.10 (int.) −fl. 10 fl. 208, L. 3.10
Bartolomeo di Pierfrancesco Fiorentino, free deposit at 5%	fl. 80 fl. 7, L. 2.6 (int.) fl. 87, L. 2.6
Monna Francesca di Lazzero, cloth weaver, free deposit at 5%	fl. 33, L. 2.6.8 fl. 3 (int.) fl. 36, L. 2.6.8

Table 6.—*continued*

Creditor and type of deposit	Account
Domenico d'Antonio di Raffaello, shoemaker at Settignano, from Jacopo and Bartolomeo Cignoni, conditional deposit at 5%, to be reinvested only in real estate	fl. 70 fl. 2, L. 6.5 (int.) − fl. 72, L. 6.5 0
Pietro d'Alessandro da San Casciano, free deposit at 5%	fl. 35 fl. 2 (int.) − fl. 37 0
Monna Margherita d'Andrea di Frosino da Torsoli, free deposit at 5%	fl. 48, L. 3 fl. 4, L. 3 (int.) − fl. 4, L. 6.10 fl. 47, L. 6.10
Monna Cammilla di Matteo Biliotti, wife of Piero Scarlatti, conditional deposit at 5%, to be reinvested only in real estate (she withdrew the money to invest in monte shares at 4% but which she was able to purchase at a discounted price)	fl. 270 fl. 30 (int.) fl. 10, L. 6. (int.) − fl. 207, L. 3.10 fl. 103, L. 2.10
Monna Marietta, widow of Antonio Ruchetti, goldsmith, conditional deposit at 5%, Marietta to have free usufruct of interest with capital to be withdrawn only to pay the dowries of the two daughters of her nephew	fl. 80 fl. 7, L. 2.6 (int.) − fl. 4, L. 3.10 fl. 82, L. 5.16
Monna Marietta di Santi Petrucci, widow of Piero, a merchant, free deposit at 5%	fl. 50 fl. 1, L. 1.10 (int.) − fl. 51, L. 1.10 0
Andrea di Simone Piero del Garbo, conditional deposit at 5%, from Tommaso de' Medici for his Excellency, for the price of goods purchased by him, to be reinvested only in real estate in the city or contado of Florence	fl. 680 fl. 62, L. 2.6 (int.) − fl. 50 fl. 692, L. 2.6

Source: Samples taken from MP 768, 212a–216b, 284a–289b, 349b–354b.

Table 7.
Number of pawns pledged by branch,
December 1545–November 1548

Month	First branch	Second branch	Third branch	Total pawns
Dec. 1545	1,824	2,414	a	4,238
Jan. 1546	2,134	2,152	a	4,286
Feb.	1,611	2,055	1,146	4,812
Mar.	1,466	2,202	1,536	5,204
Apr.	763	1,766	2,184	4,713
May	1,109	2,196	2,528	5,833
Jun.	446	1,619	2,188	4,253
Jul.	1,129	1,495	2,203	4,827
Aug.	1,500	1,033	2,090	4,623
Sep.	1,399	656	2,129	4,184
Oct.	1,770	664	2,307	4,741
Nov.	1,536	357	2,002	3,895
Dec.	1,301	1,347	1,182	3,830
Jan. 1547	1,216	2,081	786	4,083
Feb.	1,012	1,705	307	3,024
Mar.	1,132	1,862	173	3,167
Apr.	1,300	1,872	675	3,847
May	1,222	1,956	665	3,843
Jun.	1,261	1,714	658	3,633
Jul.	747	1,633	1,754	4,134
Aug.	643	1,382	1,737	3,762
Sep.	862	1,597	1,741	4,200
Oct.	528	1,886	2,125	4,539
Nov.	819	1,923	1,290	4,032
Dec.	2,490	1,061	934	4,485
Jan. 1548	1,876	1,332	2,384	5,592
Feb.	1,542	1,164	2,042	4,748
Mar.	1,655	797	2,223	4,675
Apr.	1,984	369	2,654	5,007
May	2,090	954	2,369	5,413
Jun.	1,843	2,914	896	5,653

Table 7.—*continued*

Month	First branch	Second branch	Third branch	Total pawns
Jul.	1,677	2,474	707	4,858
Aug.	1,759	2,286	603	4,648
Sep.	1,759	2,562	572	4,893
Oct.	1,936	2,849	686	5,471
Nov.	2,066	2,785	588	5,439
TOTAL	51,407	61,114	50,064	162,585

ªNo figures provided.

Table 8.
Number of pawns redeemed by branch,
December 1545–November 1548

Month	First branch	Second branch	Third branch	Total pawns
Dec. 1545	1,206	1,402	a	2,608
Jan. 1546	996	1,192	a	2,188
Feb.	1,590	1,149	a	2,739
Mar.	1,999	1,594	962	4,555
Apr.	1,920	2,042	1,561	5,523
May	1,931	1,747	1,458	5,136
Jun.	1,068	1,761	1,503	4,332
Jul.	1,024	2,335	1,558	4,917
Aug.	882	2,064	1,517	4,463
Sep.	1,007	1,495	1,699	4,201
Oct.	1,372	1,719	2,062	5,153
Nov.	1,625	1,045	1,689	4,359
Dec.	1,211	1,037	1,759	4,007
Jan. 1547	1,113	971	1,798	3,882
Feb.	889	982	858	2,729
Mar.	1,241	2,525	877	4,643
Apr.	1,567	1,695	1,469	4,731
May	1,473	1,616	1,446	4,535
Jun.	1,465	1,453	1,238	4,156
Jul.	1,449	1,440	1,663	4,552
Aug.	1,240	1,747	1,122	4,109
Sep.	1,462	1,437	1,209	4,108
Oct.	1,129	1,853	1,457	4,439
Nov.	567	1,423	934	2,924
Dec.	1,375	2,128	975	4,478
Jan. 1548	883	2,274	1,214	4,371
Feb.	777	1,791	1,213	3,781
Mar.	1,408	1,609	1,845	4,862
Apr.	1,026	798	1,526	3,350
May	2,593	1,067	1,948	5,608
Jun.	1,428	1,050	2,155	4,633

Table 8.—*continued*

Month	First branch	Second branch	Third branch	Total pawns
Jul.	1,120	1,050	1,650	3,820
Aug.	1,157	1,166	137	2,460
Sep.	1,329	1,546	1,288	4,163
Oct.	1,707	851	1,118	3,676
Nov.	1,340	1,419	[a]	2,759
TOTAL	47,569	54,473	44,908	146,950

[a]No figures provided.

Table 9.
Debts charged to each massaro, 1499–1563
This table shows the amount lent out on pawns, less amount received in redemptions and interest.

Year	First branch	Second branch	Third branch
1499	fl. 6,379, L. 15,838.1 (Lorenzo Guidotti)	—	—
1503	fl. 9,472, L. 35,776.7 (Giovanni Scolari)	fl. 6,538, L. 48,267.3 (Giovanfrancesco Lapaccini)	—
1506	fl. 6,951, L. 33,898.10 (Giovanni Scolari)	fl. 7,246, L. 59,261.11 (Domenico Lapaccini)	fl. 6,893, L. 35,485.12 (Dionigi Nasi)
1509	fl. 5,849, L. 42,231.5 (Giovanni Scolari)	fl. 6,421, L. 52,192.18 (Domenico Lapaccini)	fl. 5,711, L. 48,456.14 (Dionigi Nasi)
1512	fl. 7,042, L. 46,461.15 (Giovanni Scolari)	fl. 8,137, L. 52,462.12 (Domenico Lapaccini)	fl. 6,675, L. 63,812.7 (Dionigi Nasi)
1515	fl. 4,011, L. 55,864.9 (Giovanni Scolari)	fl. 6,169, L. 63,425.1 (Domenico Lapaccini)	fl. 3,502, L. 80,011.12 (Dionigi Nasi)
1518	fl. 2,829, L. 55,563.14 (Giovanni Scolari)	fl. 4,369, L. 74,990.6 (Domenico Lapaccini)	fl. 2,091, L. 80,515.12 (Dionigi Nasi)
1521	fl. 4,602, L. 59,300.7 (Giovanni Scolari)	fl. 5,548, L. 62,457.18 (Alessandro Rinuccini)	fl. 3,773, L. 76,012.11 (Giovanni Neri)
1524	fl. 1,830, L. 63,674.9 (Giovanni Scolari)	fl. 3,176, L. 70,463.14 (Alessandro Rinuccini)	fl. 1,494, L. 78,624.1 (Dionigi Nasi)
1527	fl. 897, L. 105,086 (Giovanni Scolari)	fl. 1,240, L. 99,267.18 (Alessandro Rinuccini)	fl. 928, L. 114,332.17 (Neri Compagni)
1530	fl. 356, L. 75,272.9 (Giovanni Scolari)	fl. 425, L. 74,511.6 (Alessandro Rinuccini)	fl. 220, L. 94,308.4 (Neri Compagni)
1533	fl. 35, L. 67,910.4 (Girolamo Coni)	fl. 37, L. 67,248.12 (Francesco Rinuccini)	fl. 4, L. 72,165.1 (Dino Compagni)
1536	fl. 6, L. 70,480 (Girolamo Coni)	fl. 16, L. 84,199 (Francesco Rinuccini)	fl. 9, L. 90,955.0.6 (Dino Compagni)
1539	fl. — L. 76,333.5 (Bartolomeo Baroncelli)	fl. 16, L. 109,995.5 (Francesco Rinuccini)	fl. 4, L. 99,186.5 (Dino Compagni)
1542	fl. — L. 77,464.14 (Bartolomeo Baroncelli)	fl. 16, L. 119,210.11 (Francesco Rinuccini)	fl. 4, L. 107,476.12 (Dino Compagni)
1545	fl. — L. 130,097.7 (Bartolomeo Baroncelli)	fl. — L. 154,415.15 (Francesco Rinuccini)	fl. — L. 141,312.14 (Dino Compagni)
1548	fl. 25,682, L. 4.10 (Bartolomeo Baroncelli)	fl. 25,020, L. 4.18 (Francesco Rinuccini)	fl. 23,163, L. –.19 (Nicolaio Cioni)
1551	fl. 25,486, L. 3.4 (Antonio Miniati)	fl. 34,148, L. 1.16 (Francesco Rinuccini)	fl. 40,389, L. 5.2 (Nicolaio Cioni)
1554	n.a.	n.a.	n.a.

Table 9.—*continued*

Year	First branch	Second branch	Third branch
557	fl. 22,447, L. − 4.3 (Antonio Miniati)	fl. 31,236, L. 5.2.8 (Francesco Rinuccini)	fl. 28,459, L. 1.9.8 (Alfonso della Casa)
560	fl. 20,571, L. 2.10 (Antonio Miniati)	fl. 26,278, L. 6.18 (Francesco da Filicaia)	fl. 22,714, L. 2.18 (Baldo Taddei) fl. 7,375, L. 2.6.8 (N. Coni, old massaro)
563	fl. 29,080, L. 6.10 (Vincenzio Rucellai)	fl. 21,194, L. 5.8 (Francesco da Filicaia)	fl. 30,263, L. 5.7.8 (Baldo Taddei)

Table 10.
Number of pawns pledged by branch, 1567–1569

Month	First branch	Second branch	Third branch	Total pawns
Jan. 1567	1,795	2,228	a	4,023
Feb.	1,406	1,777	a	3,183
Mar.	920	1,689	916	3,525
Apr.	756	2,227	2,323	5,306
May	624	1,884	2,160	4,668
June	1,113	1,833	1,904	4,850
July	801	1,792	1,952	4,545
Aug.	385	1,594	1,583	3,562
Sep.	203	1,627	1,744	3,574
Oct.	199	1,963	2,041	4,203
Nov.	103	1,626	1,804	3,533
Dec.	96	1,523	1,645	3,264
Jan. 1568	1,564	492	1,842	3,898
Feb.	1,540	412	1,428	3,380
Mar.	1,650	454	1,798	3,902
Apr.	2,060	690	1,832	4,582
May	2,258	789	2,031	5,078
June	2,246	470	2,014	4,730
July	2,342	490	2,236	5,068
Aug.	2,394	368	2,003	4,765
Sep.	2,233	250	1,905	4,388
Oct.	2,926	297	2,274	5,497
Nov.	2,625	125	2,160	4,910
Dec.	2,344	254	1,906	4,504
Jan. 1569	2,469	279	2,128	4,876
Feb.	1,950	1,857	419	4,226
Mar.	2,150	2,144	483	4,777
Apr.	2,207	2,451	806	5,464
May	2,458	2,488	878	5,824
June	2,775	2,910	644	6,329
July	2,649	2,749	388	5,786
Aug.	2,721	2,930	342	5,993
Sep.	2,784	2,917	237	5,938
Oct.	3,500	3,417	286	7,203
Nov.	2,865	2,821	203	5,889
Dec.	2,637	2,590	429	5,656
Total pawns pledged	65,748	56,407	48,744	170,899

Table 10.—*continued*

Month	First branch	Second branch	Third branch	Total pawns
Total outgo (loans on pawns plus salaries & expenses)	L. 107,854.4.3	L. 166,586.5.10	L. 95,707.4.8	
Adjustments	—	+ 2,793.3.3[b]	+ 3,206.–.14.8[b]	
TOTAL	L. 107,854.4.3	L. 169,581.6.8	L. 98,913.5.2.8	

[a]No figures provided in the ledgers.

[b]The bookkeepers at the second and third branches added this sum to balance their ledgers, these branches having had more income than outgo.

Table 11.
Number of pawns redeemed by branch, 1567–1569

Month	First branch	Second branch	Third branch	Total pawns
Jan. 1567	1,600	1,287	318	3,205
Feb.	1,720	1,605[a]	404	3,729
Mar.	2,409	2,268	510	5,187
Apr.	2,605	2,018	800	5,423
May	2,168	1,555	923	4,646
June	2,466	1,931	1,119	5,516
July	1,782	1,718	1,079	4,579
Aug.	1,140	1,584	1,167	3,891
Sep.	709	1,813	1,258	3,780
Oct.	695	2,137	1,788	4,620
Nov.	106	1,625	1,357	3,088
Dec.	612	1,847	1,540	3,999
Jan. 1568	580	1,992	1,120	3,692
Feb.	702	1,763	1,327	3,792
Mar.	720	2,028	1,381	4,129
Apr.	1,211	1,995	1,859	5,065
May	1,096	1,958	1,566	4,620
June	1,284	1,400	1,616	4,300
July	1,220	1,132	1,543	3,895
Aug.	1,146	673	1,322	3,141
Sep.	1,490	925	1,529	3,944
Oct.	1,790	[b]	1,831	3,621
Nov.	1,490	132	1,146	2,768
Dec.	1,546	669[c]	1,680	3,895
Jan. 1569	1,516	340	1,240	3,096
Feb.	1,376	365	1,460	3,201
Mar.	1,782	792	1,718	4,292
Apr.	2,037	1,020	1,997	5,054
May	2,081	1,100	1,973	5,154
June	1,796	1,320	1,683	4,799
July	1,691	2,510	1,062	5,263
Aug.	1,700	[b]	810	2,510
Sep.	1,880	1,513	622	4,015
Oct.	2,337	2,101	575	5,013
Nov.	2,289	1,837	252	4,378
Dec.	2,342	1,827	442	4,611
		+3,20?[d]		3,20?
Total pawns redeemed	55,114	53,98?	44,017	153,11?

Table 11.—*continued*

Month	First branch	Second branch	Third branch	Total pawns
Total income from re-demptions, sales, & sundry items)	L. 96,045.—.3	L. 169,581.6.8	L. 98,913.5.2.8	
Adjustments	+ 11,809.4ᶜ	—	—	
TOTAL	L. 107,854.4.3	L. 169,581.6.8	L. 98,913.5.2.8	

ᵃIncludes 620 redeemed "in January and February."
ᵇNo figures provided in the ledgers.
ᶜIncludes 367 redeemed in "November and December."
ᵈListed as "from Sept. through June"; the last digit is illegible.
ᵉThe bookkeeper added this amount to balance the ledger, the first branch having had more outgo than income.

Table 12.
Documented large loans, 1564–1574

Borrower	Amount (sc.)	Rate	Term
Ciro Alidosio	3,000	5%	4 yrs.
Alamanno di Bernardo de' Medici	300	5%	
Antonio di Bernardo Albizzi	1,200	5%	3 yrs.
Ms. Lionardo de' Nobili	400	5%	
Don Francesco de' Medici	10,000	5%	a
Ciro Alidosio	2,000	5%	1 yr.
Don Francesco de' Medici	15,000	5%	a
Cosimo de' Medici	6,000	5%	a
Cosimo de' Medici	3,000	5%	a
Sr. Montauto de' Conti di Montauto	500	5%	2 yrs.
Bartolomeo Amannati	450	5%	
Traiano Bobba, ducal cameriere	200	5%	
Andrea Avignonesi of Montepulciano	500	5%	2 yrs.
Bartholome Romero	15	5%	
Cristoforo Mandruzo, cardinal of Trent	10,000	5%	1 ½ yrs.
Felice d'Arcangelo Gattai, ducal barber	240	5%	
Carlo di Roberto Acciaiuoli	1,400	6%	2 yrs.
Sr. Mario Sforza	3,000	6%	1 yr.
Antonio di Bartolomeo Lanfredini	1,500	6%	5 yrs.
Monna Lucrezia de' Pucci	450	6%	2 yrs.
Community and men of Pietro Santo	300	6%	
Bartolomeo Volterra Greco	600	6%	
Ms. Giuseppe Bono Siciliano	500	6%	1 yr.
Marchese Carlo Trolio and Cammillo Malespini	300	6%	3 yrs.
Antonio Angeli, bishop-elect of Massa	800	6%	4 yrs.
Don Francesco de' Medici	40,000	5%	

Table 12.—*continued*

Borrower	Amount (sc.)	Rate	Term
Filippo d'Antonio Giannetti	700	5%	
Isabella de' Medici	4,000	5%	
Francesco Buti, cashier at the *scrittoio*	500	5%	
Raffaello de' Medici	1,000	6%	2 yrs.
Ser Jacopo Offredo	600	6%	3 yrs
Alessandro Milanese	200	6%	1 yr.
Ms. Raffaello de' Medici	400	5%	2 yrs.
Filippo Spina	2,000	5%	
Ms. Bartolomeo Concini, ducal secretary	1,500	5%	
Cornelio Merman', jeweler	1,500	5%	
Nuns of Foligno	150	5%	
Several brothers, to monachate their sister	500	5%	
Nuns of the Poverine (prioress: Zanobia de' Gherardi)	300	5%	
Barbara Geralda	100	5%	
Isabella de' Medici	12,000	5%	4 yrs.
Ms. Lorenzo Ridolfi	4,000	6%	2 yrs.
Hospital of San Paolo	2,000	5%	
Amerigo di Cammillo Antinori	300	6%	3 yrs.
Opera and operai of Santa Maria Novella	100	5%	
Giovanni di Bernardo Capponi	1,500	6%	2 yrs.
Cammillo di Gerardo de' Pazzi	400	6%	2 yrs.
Capt. Giovanni Fierenberger, German Guard	1,000	6%	5 yrs.
Ma. Lisabetta Altoviti, widow of a de' Nerli	500	6%	1 yr.
Francesco di Niccolò Baldovinetti	250	6%	1 yr.
Monna Maria, widow of Niccodemo Salviati	150	5%	2 yrs.
Giovan di Cristophya	1,000	6%	3 yrs.
Ms. Piero Ardinghelli, knight	2,000	6%	1 yr.

Table 12.—*continued*

Borrower	Amount (sc.)	Rate	Term
Francesco di Lorenzo of Santa Croce	400	6%	
Domenica di Donato Bonsi	30	5%	
Ser Agnolo Familla, ducal chancellor	100	5%	1 yr.
Michele di Giache Spagnuolo, artilleryman	120	5%	
Andrea Tartaglia da Palaia	200	6%	2 yrs.
Ms. Chiarissimo de' Medici	700	6%	3 yrs.
Colonel Luigi Dovara	2,000	6%	1 yr.
Simone di Dinozzo Lippi	200	6%	1 yr.
Nuns of Santa Ursula	200	6%	1 yr.
Ms. Andrea Minerbetti, knight	736	6%	1 yr.
Isabella de' Medici	2,000	6%	
Ms. Giulio del Caccia	1,000		
Antonio Francesco di Raffaello di Gratia, sottoprovveditore of monte di pietà	36		1 yr.
Lionardo Busini	200		2 yrs.
Mondragone	3,500		5 yrs.
Bongianni Gianfigliazzi	1,000		2 yrs.
Raffaello de' Medici, *balio* of Florence	400		2 yrs.
Capt. Francesco Bruni da Volterra	300		1 yr.
Sr. Sinolfo Otterio	700		1 yr.
Antonella degli Alessandri	250		3 yrs.
Luigi di Jacopo Gianfigliazzi	500		1 ½ yrs.
Cosimo Bonsi, podestà of Castiglione Fiorentino	200		½ yr.
Sr. Piero de' Marchesi del Monte, Castellano of Fortezza di Pisa	500		1 yr.
Giovanbattista Bicicai da Galatea	500		2 yrs.
Filippo d'Antonio Giannetti del Mucione	700		3 yrs.

Table 12.—*continued*

Borrower	Amount (sc.)	Rate	Term
Ricciuolo Scudiere	400		4 yrs.
Monna Alessandra de' Ricasoli	500		
Vescovo del Borgo	1,000		3 yrs.
Brothers of San Francesco d'Ogni Santi	500		2 yrs.
Polidoro Castelli	500		5 yrs.
Magistrato de' Consolati	500		
Lisabetta Malespina, widow of chancellor Carlo Mariscotto	600		3 yrs.
Ms. Andriano Tassoni	500		4 yrs.
Illma. Dona Violante, wife of Domenico di Jacopo Offredi, daughter of Domenico Sforza	600		3 yrs.
Agnolo, Pietropagolo and Giovanni, sons of Pagolo di Agnolo Serristori	200		1 yr.
Monna Cassandra, former wetnurse	300		3 yrs.
Giovanni di Piero Ulivieri	650		5 yrs.
Piero Caramanti, physician	200		1 yr.
Belicozzo Gondi	350		
Giulio de' Baroni de' Ricasoli	500		1 yr.
Messer Bernardo Miniati	200		2 yrs.
Francesco d'Alessandro del Caccia	2,100		2 yrs.
Francesco di Raffaello	70		2 yrs.
Candido Vagnucci da Cortona	400		2 yrs.
Bartolomeo di Francesco Caprini, armorer	60		2 yrs.
Francesco di Carlo Bati	150		
Monks of Cestello	1,000		
Fra Carlo Venatio	500		50 mos.
Colonel Aloysius	2,000		1 yr.
Abbess and nuns of Spirito Santo	200		1 yr.
Piero Rabini	60		2 yrs.

Table 12.—*continued*

Borrower	Amount (sc.)	Rate	Term
Cammile Federico Genezzo	100		3 yrs.
Donato Tornabuoni	1,500		3 yrs.
Guglielmo Giramonti	700		
Lionardo Socrano	100		1 yr.
Francesco de' Medici of Athens	100		
Ms. Giuliano Brunozi of Pistoia	500		3 yrs.
Lattantio Dovitii da Bibbiena	600		1 yr.
Bernardino di Giovanni Naldini	500		1 yr.
Matteo di Benedetto Palmerini	150		2 yrs.
Cardinal [Ferdinando] de' Medici	6,000		3 yrs.
Carlo di Bartolomeo Panciatichi, ducal cameriere	1,000		3 yrs.
Monna Maria, daughter of Ubertino Strozzi and wife of Piero Gianfigliazzi	500		5 yrs.
Traiano Bobba, ducal cameriere	3,500		3 yrs.
Guido Mannelli	1,000		
Vincentio Chieli d'Anghiara	733		6 mos.
Simone e Lionardo di Salvestro del Sale	800		1 yr.
Aldello and Postumio Placidi	800		[a]
Ms. Giovanni Gori, of the ducal wardrobe	100		1 yr.
Sr. Pierfrancesco de' Conti di Montedogli	300		2 yrs.
Ms. Francesco Strozza	200		1 yr.
Sons of Sr. Gualterotto de' Bardi	2,000		2 yrs.
Ms. Alessandro and Aldo Buonlemapo (?)	(illegible)		7 mos.
Galeotto di Piero de' Pazzi	400		1 yr.
Piero Buoninsegni	600		1 yr.

Table 12.—*continued*

Borrower	Amount (sc.)	Rate	Term
Ms. Aurelio Manni, ducal *fiscale*	800		2 yrs.
Pagolo, called Papone	50		1 yr.
Ms. Francesco de' Medici of Athens	100		1 yr.
Filippo di Filippo della Luna	200		
Pierfilippo di Vincentio Gianfigliazzi	150		2 yrs.
Capt. Martino Martini	300		2 mos.
Sra. Donna Isabella de' Medici Orsini	10,000		
Giuseppe Bono	400		1 yr.
Cosimo de' Medici	50,000		
Matteo Castrucci	300		2 yrs.
Bartolo di Luigi Vetraro, veneziano	400		
Margherita, widow of Francesco di Santa Croce	200		1 yr.
Fabio Segni	150		2 yrs.
Luigi Somentio	500		
Matteo di Jacopo	200		2 yrs.
Carlo Pitti	5,000	6 ⅓%	2 yrs.
Raffaello Niccolini	1,500		1 yr.
Cosimo, Hypolito, and Camillo Lioni	1,800		1 yr.
Federigo di Monsignor Domenico Toscanelli	525		1 yr.
Enea Vaino	500		2 yrs.
Vincentio d'Andrea Alamanni	3,500		1 yr.
Tommaso di Roberto Bonsi	2,000		1 yr.
Giovanbattista di Lucantonio degli Albizzi	1,000		1 yr.
Alessandro di Francesco Alessandri	500		1 yr.
Francesco Baldovinetti	1,200		1 yr.
Bartolomeo d'Antonio del Vigna	1,000		

Table 12.—*continued*

Borrower	Amount (sc.)	Rate	Term
Ridolfo di Gabriello de' Rossi	200		1 yr.
Lorenzo di Lorenzo Carnesecchi	200		1 yr.
Girolamo Mannelli	130		2 yrs.
Monna Fiammetta di Lionetto Tornabuoni	400		
Benedetto di Jacopantonio Busini	800		1 yr.
Bartolomeo di Giovanni Arrighi	500		3 yrs.
Taddeo Taddei	300		3 yrs.
Giovanni di Simone Peruzzi	250		
Giovanbattista and Antonio Mogliani	170		
Filippo di Filippo della Luna	300		3 yrs.
Benedetto Tornaquinci	400		1 yr.
Tommaso Baldracani, knight of Santo Stefano	500		1 yr.
Agnolo Agolanti	300		2 yrs.
Vincentio Ambrogi of Spain	20,276, 10s. 8d.		
Don Pietro de' Medici	6,000		6 mos.
Filippo d'Antonio Neroni	150		
Ridolfo, Jacopo, and Pierantonio di Pierantonio Guasconi	350		
Piero di Tommaso Salvetti	500		2 yrs.
Giovanni di Lorenzo Ridolfi	800		2 yrs.
Bernardo Manetti	400		2 yrs.
Giovanni d'Andrea Dazi	300		
Lorenzo d'Alessandro Arrighi	100		18 mos.
The Bishop of Arezzo	500		18 mos.
Bernardo del Riccio	200		1 yr.
Alessandro di Giovanni Federighi	1,500		1 yr.
Capt. Corbize Corbizi	100		1 yr.
Giuseppe di Lorenzo, ducal barber	1,550		1 yr.

Table 12.—*continued*

Borrower	Amount (sc.)	Rate	Term
Lionardo di Bernardo Brabatti	400		3 yrs.
Piero Lotti	1,000		1 yr.
Carlo Campagni	300		1 yr.
Francesco Buontalenti, knight of Santo Stefano	300		1 yr.
Ms. Piero di Ms. Luigi Ridolfi, knight of Santo Stefano	200		
Ceser de Giovanni Guazzonn	100		1 yr.
Gherardo Frescobaldi	1,000		1 yr.
Andrea da Veragano	150		3 yrs.
Giovanbattista di Mariotto Bertini	500		2 yrs.
Giorgio di Niccolò Benlighieri	100		3 yrs.
Luigi Capponi Stufa	700		1 yr.
Luigi Guazani	80		
Don Pietro de' Medici	3,000		
Michelangelo Orlandi, knight of Santo Stefano	200		4 yrs.
Francesco Grazini	100		1 yr.
Rev. Monsignor Fra Michele Bonelli, cardinal	10,000		4 yrs.
Filippo di Giovanni Rucellai	1,000		1 yr.
Signor Giovanni Vitelli	2,000		1 yr.
Heirs of Ms. Francesco Vinta	200		2 yrs.
Capt. Piero Fatii	200		4 yrs.
Berto Berti da Pescia	300		1 yr.
Heirs of Lorenzo Strozzi	10,000		no limit
Conte Antonio Avogadro	350		1 yr.
Giovanfrancesco di Piero Avanzati	120		8 mos.
Zanobi di Jacopo di Ser Guglielmi	300		2 yrs.
Guglielmo di Jacopo Corsini	200		
Bartolomeo di Giovanni Arrighi	400		5 yrs.
Lorenzo Giovanni	400		
Alvaro Mendez, Portuguese, knight of San Jacopo	30,000		6 mos.

Table 12.—*continued*

Borrower	Amount (sc.)	Rate	Term
Domenico di Giovanni Altoviti	180		
Torello di Giovanbattista de' Nobili	150		2 yrs.
Bartolomeo degli Alessandri	1,100		
Giannozzo di Gherardo da Cepperello	400		18 mos.
Jacopo di Pagolo Mormorai	2,000		2 yrs.
Giovanni di Raffaello Mazzinghi	500		
Aurelio Fregoso	2,000		50 mos.
Ser Jacopo Offredi, knight of Santo Stefano	200		2 yrs.
Signor Aniballe Dovara	100		
Girolamo Mannelli, knight of Santo Stefano	200		2 yrs.
Altobranco di Lorenzo Buondelmonti	400		2 yrs.
Cornelio di Francesco Altoviti	3,000		1 yr.
Pagolo di Raffaello Benciveni	150		3 yrs.
Livio da Cossa	100		1 yr.
Lorenzo Sanpietro a Panzano	300		3 yrs.
Calvano di Giovanni Oradini	400		3 yrs.
Niccolò da Ferrara	200		3 yrs.
Cosimo di Luigi Pitti	110		2 yrs.
Girolamo Ugurgier of Siena	400		4 yrs.
Piero di Giovanbattista of Panzano	250		3 yrs.
Alessandro d'Andrea Tartaglia	150		3 yrs.
Cardinal de' Medici	6,000		6 mos.
Dianora Filipetri Fortunati	500		
Bernabò Malespina	200		
Guid'Ascanio Borboni de' Marchesi del Monte Santa Maria	800		2 yrs.
Pierantonio Anselmi	300		1 yr.
Domenico Simoni	300		6 yrs.
Cardinal Simoncelli	5,000		

Table 12.—*continued*

Borrower	Amount (sc.)	Rate	Term
Don Pietro la Rocca	1,000		1 yr.
Andrea di Manfredi Macinghi	400		3 yrs.
Bastiano Confetto	150		1 yr.
The Bishop of Borgo	500		3 yrs.
Jacopo di Lorenzo Mannucci	500		1 yr.
Guido d'Alessandro Guidi	700		
Clemente Cotti, captain of the Bande	400		5 yrs.
Vincentio di Rinieri Ser Nigi	400		2 yrs.
Giovanfranco Corsini	300		
Simoniello de Monte	1,500		4 yrs.
Cardinal de' Medici	20,000	5%	40 mos.
TOTAL LOANS ISSUED	249		
TOTAL VALUE	427,291, 10s.8d.		

Sources: MP 266, Filza di Atti di Cancelleria, Suppliche et Mandati, compiled by Francesco di Guglielmo Ciacchi, provveditore of the monte; MP 768; and Monte di Pietà del Bigallo 1, Filza Prima di Prestati e di Suppliche dal 1572 al 1575. The loans contained in this file are only those actually approved.

Notes: The interest rate and term are given only if stated explicitly. As of 1568, borrowers receiving over 100 sc. were supposed to pay 6 percent.

ªRepayable to the monte upon its demand.

Table 13.
An overview of Medici accounts in
the monte di pietà, 1548–1563

Accounts	Amount
Medici accounts on the books as of November 1548 (in florins)	
Cosimo de' Medici	1,790, L. 5
Cosimo de' Medici	−7,831, L. 1.15
Lorenzo d'Attilio de' Medici	462, L. 2
Giuliano di Giovani de' Medici	−1,200, —
Attilio de' Medici	77, L. −.19.11[a]
Medici accounts as of November 1557	
Cosimo de' Medici	981, L. 4.13.7
Cosimo de' Medici	−5,775, L. 6.4.10
Jacopo di Lazzero de' Medici	405, L. 3.19.8
Attilio di Veri de' Medici	321, L. 1.2
Tommaso di Jacopo de' Medici	1,600, —
Nannino di Giovanni de' Medici	−110, —
Alessandro di Jacopo de' Medici	−252, L. 4.5
Medici accounts as of November 1560	
Cosimo de' Medici	−5,957, —
Cosimo de' Medici	−6,333, L. 6.12.2
Jacopo di Lazzero de' Medici	400, —
Tommaso di Jacopo de' Medici	1,605, L. 2
Nannina di Giovanni de' Medici	−76, L. 2
Alessandro di Jacopo de' Medici	−78, L. 4.5
Chiarissimo di Bernardo de' Medici	111, L. −.8
Nicola di Tanai de' Medici	363, L. 5.5
Attilio di Veri de' Medici	326, L. 6
Attilio di Veri de' Medici	840, L. 2.17
Medici accounts as of November 1563	
Cosimo de' Medici	−5,645, L. 6.4.10
Cosimo de' Medici	−9,356, L. 1.14.2
Chiarissimo di Bernardo de' Medici	113, L. −.8
Ms. Tommaso di Jacopo de Medici	1,610, L. —
Attilio di Veri de' Medici	−102, L. 3.2.8
Nannina di Giovanni de' Medici	−36, —
Alessandro di Jacopo de' Medici	−123, L. 4.12
Cosimo de' Medici	256, —
Attilio di Veri de' Medici	50, —
Attilio di Veri de' Medici	−6, L. 6.10.5

[a]Attilio de' Medici was cassiere of the monte; only his personal accounts in the institution are listed here.

APPENDIX B.
A NOTE ON
FLORENTINE MONEY

ONE DIFFICULTY in unraveling the finances of Florentine institutions is the confusing proliferation of several different kinds of money, some actual coins and some moneys of account. The actual coins of the Florentines included the famous gold florin as well as silver and copper coins.[1]

Like other Florentine institutions the monte di pietà dealt with moneys of account and real coins, among which was the occasional counterfeit or foreign coin. The bylaws of 1496 required that certain currencies be used for various transactions and record keeping, though references to these currencies were sometimes vague. When making a loan on a pawn, for instance, the massaro had to make up a receipt, "saying in the said receipt what money [the camarlingo] pays, that is, florins larghi in oro, lire, soldi and denari."[2] Even this can be misleading, since at first glance it seems to suggest that the camarlingo actually paid out lire, soldi and denari, an impossibility since lire/soldi/denari referred to a money of account, although the denaro by itself was a real *biglione* coin (billon, or base silver; see

---

1. Much of the following discussion comes from Carlo Cipolla, *Money in Sixteenth Century Florence* (Berkeley, Calif., 1989; orig. pub. as *La moneta a Firenze nel Cinquecento* [Bologna, 1987]); Edler, *Glossary*; and Goldthwaite, *Building of Renaissance Florence*, esp. 301–5 and the appendix, as well as from the information contained in the monte di pietà's ledgers. I am grateful to Richard Goldthwaite for his generous help with this section.

2. This and the following references to the monte di pietà's statutes come from MP 1, Statuti, chaps. 8, 15–16.

below). Lire, which did not exist as real coins, were subdivided into soldi (20 per lira) and denari (12 per soldo, or 240 per lira). The monte's camarlingo had to keep his books of income and outgo in "fiorini larghi in oro, lire, soldi, e denari di moneta vecchia." Moreover, the borrowers who redeemed their pawns had to repay their loans in "those same moneys [i.e., the same kind of coins] in which their loans were made."

Around the time of the monte di pietà's creation, Florence's coinage had evolved but little from its medieval origins. The Florentines used a 24-karat gold florin, or *fiorino*, containing about 3.5 grams of gold and hardly changed since its appearance in 1252. Their best silver coin was the groat, or *grosso*, whose weight was reduced over time but whose fineness remained stable at 958.333/1000. References to grossi are to real coins. Also in circulation were base silver coins, the *quattrino* and *denaro* (four denari to one quattrino), referred to as *picciolo*, whose fineness and weight declined over time. Quattrini with a higher content of silver were called "white money" (*moneta bianca*), while those with a higher content of copper were called "black money" (*moneta nera*). Naturally, the relative value of silver and gold coins fluctuated in response to a number of factors, including the weight and fineness of each. Different silver coins would also change in value relative to each other for the same reasons, as would different gold coins.

As for the florin, its dominance in Europe had spanned the period from 1252 until the 1340s, when the collapse of several big Florentine banks and the Black Death caused economic crisis and a loss of confidence. Thereafter the Venetian *ducato*, or gold ducat, gained preeminence. As a result of the automatic association in people's minds of the Venetian ducat and good money, Florentines often referred to their own florin as a ducat, a habit that explains the interchangeable use in the sixteenth century of these two terms in the books of the monte di pietà and other institutions.

The early sixteenth century saw the emergence of the gold *scudo* in Florence. In an application of what would later be called Gresham's law, the scudo issued by Alessandro, of inferior fineness to the old ducat or florin, drove out the older money (bad money drives out good). Alessandro also set the gold scudo equal to L. 7, with the ducat or florin equal to L. 7.5. The problem was that these two gold coins were too close in value, and thus it was difficult to keep them both in circulation.

In 1537 the new ruler Cosimo I ordered the minting of a gold scudo. Carlo Cipolla notes that this coin became "the prevalent gold piece in the Florentine state. The old fiorino, for all practical purposes, gradually disappeared from the scene."[3] However, it did not disappear from people's minds or from the ledgers of many Florentine institutions, including the monte di pietà, which still referred frequently to ducats, florins, and scudi through the lifetime of Cosimo I.

At the beginning of the monte di pietà's ledger for 1496–99, the bookkeeper listed the alms collected from several sources as

(1) fl. 512 *larghi d'oro in oro* and
(2) L. 791.16.8 *piccioli in grossi* and
(3) L. 1,884.18.7 *piccioli di moneta nera in quattrini.*

The *fiorino largo d'oro in oro*, also known as the *fiorino largo d'oro*, or *fiorino d'oro in oro*, or *fiorino di oro*, was an actual gold coin minted from 1422 until 1530 but in circulation for a good number of years thereafter.[4] "Largo" refers to the coin's larger diameter—an attempt to persuade people of its competitiveness with the Venetian ducat—but it was not otherwise a "larger" florin in the sense of containing more gold.

The second currency listed above, L. 791 *piccioli in grossi*, is more complicated. The word *in* signals that the following currency, grossi, refers to a real coin. The figure of 791.16.8 is the expression in lire, soldi, denari (a money of account) of a sum of actual coins, namely, grossi. The third currency, lire *piccioli di moneta nera in quattrini*, can be understood in a similar way. The quattrini were real coins, and here they are expressed in lire, soldi and denari, the money of account.

The monte di pietà's record keepers had to convert the values of different coins into one money of account so as to be able to add and subtract them. For the conversion of the second currency above, the L. 791.16.8 piccioli in grossi, the process was twofold. First, this sum was converted into fiorini larghi di grossi, that is, the actual coins,

---

3. Cipolla, *Money*, 18.
4. Yet another florin, the *fiorino di suggello*, appears on rare occasions in the monte di pietà's accounts. Before the mid-fifteenth century it had been a sealed and weighed coin, but after that time it became a money of account for silver.

the grossi, were expressed in florins of account larghi at a rate of L. 5.11 per florin. Thus the first step:

L. 791.16.8 piccioli in grossi
@ L. 5.11 per florin

= fl. 142.11.7 larghi di grossi.

The second computation converts these 142 florins into the equivalent in fiorini larghi d'oro in oro, which, by the monte's reckoning, were worth 10¾ percent more.

fl. 142.11.7 larghi di grossi
= fl. 128 d'oro in oro
+ a remainder of L. 4.19 di moneta nera.

This step completes the conversion to fiorini larghi d'oro in oro from lire piccioli in grossi. Lines one and two, now expressed in the same currency, total fl. 640 d'oro in oro plus L. 4.19 di moneta nera.

The monte di pietà's bookkeeper did not explain the method by which he converted the sum in the third line, L. 1,884.18.7 piccioli di moneta nera, but gave the equivalent as L. 1,389.17.7 di moneta nera vecchia. The latter is thus worth about 35.6 percent more than the former. In any case, the sum of all three figures, originally in different coins, has now been calculated to equal fl. 640 d'oro in oro plus L. 1,389.17.7 di moneta nera vecchia.

After 1530, the monte di pietà's ledgers refer to four different moneys. First and second, the ledgers still used the florin, probably out of habit, interchangeably with the ducat. Third, lire still appeared in the ledgers, reaching seven to the florin/ducat by midcentury. From 1521 through 1545 the ledgers were balanced in lire. Finally, the *scudo d'oro* appeared, usually called the *scudo d'Italia* in the monte's books, probably to distinguish it from the French scudo, the *écu*. This coin was valued just over 7 percent higher than the florin. For example, a loan granted by the monte di pietà to the bishop of Arezzo came to one thousand scudi d'Italia, which the ledgers changed to 1,071 florins and 3 lire.

BIBLIOGRAPHY

Published Primary Sources

Adriani, Giovanni Battista. *Scritti varii editi ed inediti di G. B. Adriani e di Marcello suo figliuolo.* Ed. Adolfo Bartoli. Bologna: Gaetano Romagnoli, 1871.

Alighieri, Dante. *La divina commedia: Inferno.* Ed. Natalino Sapegno. Florence: La Nuova Italia, 1955.

——. *Inferno.* Trans. John Ciardi. New York: Mentor, 1982. Orig. pub. New York, 1954.

Aquinas, Thomas. *Summa Theologica.* 60 vols. London: Blackfriars, 1975.

Azzi, Giustiano degli. "Un frammento inedito della Cronaca di Benedetto Dei." *Archivio storico italiano* 110 (1952): 99–111.

Bellinazzi, Anna, and Claudio Lamioni, eds. *Carteggio universale di Cosimo I de' Medici. Archivio di Stato di Firenze: Inventario.* Vol. 1. Florence: Giunta Regionale Toscana: Nuova Italia, 1982.

Bernardino of Siena. *Le prediche volgari.* 5 vols. Ed. Ciro Cannorozzi. Florence: Libreria Editrice Fiorentina, 1934; repr. Florence, 1957.

Bonfantini, Mario, ed. *Le sacre rappresentazioni italiane: Raccolta di testi dal secolo XIII al secolo XVI.* Milan: Bompiani, 1942.

Borghini, Vincenzo. *Discorsi di Monsignore don Vincenzo Borghini.* 2 vols. Florence: Filippo e Jacopo Giunti e Fratelli, 1584.

Brucker, Gene, ed. *Two Memoirs of Renaissance Florence: The Diaries of Buonaccorso Pitti and Gregorio Dati.* New York: Harper Torchbooks, 1967.

Busini, Giovambattista. *Lettere di Giovambattista Busini a Benedetto Varchi sopra l'assedio di Firenze.* Ed. G. Milanesi. Florence: Le Monnier, 1860.

Compostella, Piero, ed. *Il monte di pietà di Milano: Libro giornale (1506–1535) e ordinazioni capitolari (1497–1580).* Milan: Banca del Monte di Milano, 1973.

Dei, Benedetto. *La cronica dall'anno 1400 all'anno 1500*. Ed. Roberto Barducci. Istituto per la Storia degli Antichi Stati Italiani, Fonti e studi, 1. Monte Oriolo, Italy: Francesco Papafava, 1984.

Fachard, Denis, ed. *Consulte e pratiche, 1505–1512*. Université de Lausanne, Publications de la Faculté des Lettres, 29. Geneva: Librairie Droz, 1988.

Ficino, Marsilio. *The Letters of Marsilio Ficino*. 2 vols. Trans. Language Department of the School of Economic Science, University of London. London: Shepheard-Walwyn, 1975.

Guibert of Nogent. *Self and Society in Medieval France: The Memoirs of Abbot Guibert of Nogent*. Ed. John Benton. New York: Harper Torchbooks, 1970.

Guicciardini, Francesco. *History of Italy*. Ed. and trans. Sidney Alexander. New York: Collier, 1969.

——. *Ricordi*. Ed. Raffaele Spongano. Florence: G. C. Sansoni, 1951.

——. *Storia d'Italia*. Ed. Costantino Panigada. 5 vols. Bari: Giuseppe Laterza e Figli, 1929.

Guicciardini, Giovan Battista. *Lettere di Giovan Battista Guicciardini a Cosimo e Francesco de' Medici scritte dal Belgio dal 1559 al 1577*. Ed. Mario Battistini. Bibliothèque de l'Institut historique belge de Rome, 2. Brussels: 27 Montagne de la Cour, 1949; Rome: Academia Belgica, 1949.

Landucci, Luca. *Diario fiorentino dal 1450 al 1516, continuato da un anonimo fino al 1542*. Florence: G. C. Sansoni, 1883. Repr. 1985.

Lapini, Agostino. *Diario fiorentino di Agostino Lapini dal 252 al 1596*. Ed. Giuseppe Odoardo Corazzini. Florence: G. C. Sansoni, 1900.

Machiavelli, Niccolò. *History of Florence and the Affairs of Italy*. Ed. Felix Gilbert. New York: Harper Torchbooks, 1960.

——. *Lettere*. Ed. Franco Gaeta. Milan: Giangiacomo Feltrinelli, 1961.

——. *Opere complete*. Palermo: Fratelli Pedoni Lauriel, 1868.

——. *The Prince and the Discourses*. Ed. Max Lerner. Trans. Luigi Ricci, rev. E. R. P. Vincent. New York: Modern Library, 1950.

——. *Il principe*. Ed. Sergio Bertelli. Milan: Giangiacomo Feltrinelli, 1969.

Masi, Bartolomeo. *Ricordanze di Bartolomeo Masi calderaio fiorentino dal 1478 al 1526*. Ed. Giuseppe Odoardo Corazzini. Florence: G. C. Sansoni, 1906.

Medici, Cosimo I de'. *Lettere*. Ed. Giorgio Spini. Florence: Vallecchi, 1940.

Medici, Giovanni de' [Leo X]. "Tre documenti: Instructione al Magnifico Lorenzo." Ed. Tommaso Gar. *Archivo storico italiano* (Appendix 1) 1 (1842–44): 293–306.

Meneghin, Vittorino, ed. *Documenti vari intorno al Beato Bernardino Tomitano da Feltre*. Studi e testi francescani, 35. Rome: Edizioni Francescane, 1966.

Migliore, Ferdinando Leopoldo del. *Firenze, città nobilissima illustrata*. Florence: Stamperia della Stella, 1684.

Morandini, Francesca, ed. "Statuti e ordinamenti dell'Ufficio dei Pupilli e

Adulti nel periodo della Repubblica Fiorentina (1388–1534)." *Archivio storico italiano* 114 (1956): 92–117.

Morini, Ugo, ed. *Documenti inediti o poco noti per la storia della Misericordia di Firenze*. Florence: A cura della Venerabile Arciconfraternita, 1940.

Nerli, Filippo de'. *Commentarj de'fatti civili occorsi dentro la città di Firenze dall'anno MCCXV al MDXXXVII*. Augusta [Florence]: D. R. Mertz e G. J. Majer, 1728.

Pampaloni, Guido. "I ricordi segreti del mediceo Francesco di Agostino Cegia (1495–1497)." *Archivio storico italiano* 115 (1957): 188–234.

Pius II [Enea Silvio Piccolomini]. *Memoirs of a Renaissance Pope: The Commentaries of Pius II*. Ed. Leona C. Gabel. New York: G. P. Putnam's Sons, 1959.

Rabelais, François. *Oeuvres complètes*. Ed. Guy Demerson. Paris: Editions du Seuil, 1973.

Ricci, Giuliano de'. *Cronaca (1532–1606)*. Ed. Giuliana Sapori. Documenti di Filologia, 17. Milan: Riccardo Ricciardi, 1971.

Ridolfi, Roberto, ed. "Diario fiorentino di anonimo delle cose occorse l'anno 1537." *Archivio storico italiano* 116 (1958): 544–60.

Rucellai, Giovanni. *Giovanni Rucellai ed il suo Zibaldone*. Vol. 1, *Il Zibaldone quaresimale*. Ed. Alessandro Perosa. Studies of the Warburg Institute, 24. London: Warburg Institute, 1960.

Savonarola, Girolamo. *Prediche e scritti*. Ed. Mario Ferrara. Milan: Ulrich Hoepli, 1930.

Segni, Bernardo. *Storie fiorentine di Messer Bernardo Segni, gentiluomo fiorentino, dall'anno MDXXVII al MDLV colla vita di Niccolò Capponi*. 3 vols. Milan: Società Tipografica de'Classici Italiani, 1118: 1805.

Strozzi, Alessandra. *Lettere di una gentildonna del secolo XV ai figliuoli esuli*. Ed. C. Guasti. Florence: G. C. Sansoni, 1877.

Vespasiano da Bisticci. *Le vite*. 2 vols. Ed. Aulo Greco. Florence: Istituto Nazionale di Studi sul Rinascimento, 1970–76.

Vettori, Francesco. *Scritti storici e politici*. Ed. Enrico Niccolini. Scrittori d'Italia, 252. Bari: Giuseppe Laterza e Figli, 1972.

Secondary Sources

Acton, Harold. *The Last Medici*. Rev. ed. London: Thames and Hudson, 1980. Orig. pub. London, 1932.

Ady, Cecilia. *Lorenzo dei Medici and Renaissance Italy*. New York: Collier, 1962. Orig. pub. New York, 1955.

A.G.B. "Il monte di pietà." In *Pel calendario pratese del 1848: Memorie e studi di cose patrie*, 98–114. Prato: Guasti, 1847.

Albertini, Rudolf von. *Firenze dalla repubblica al principato: Storia e coscienza politica*. Trans. C. Cristofolini. Biblioteca di cultura storica, 109. 2d ed.

Turin: Giulio Einaudi, 1970. Orig. pub. as *Das florentinische Staatsbe-wusstsein im Übergang von der Republik zum Prinzipat.* Bern, 1955.

Annibaldi, G. "I banchi degli ebrei ed il Monte di Pietà di Gesi." *Picenum seraphicum* 9 (1972): 89–129.

Ariès, Philippe. "Richesse et pauvreté devant la mort." In Michel Mollat, ed., *Etudes sur l'histoire de la pauvreté.* 2 vols. Publications de la Sorbonne. "Etudes" Series, 8. Paris: Sorbonne, 1974.

Balestracci, Duccio. "I libri impegnati al monte di pietà senese: Una fonte indiretta per la storia dell'alfabetismo nel xv secolo." *Alfabetismo e cultura scritta. Seminario permanente. Notizie*, Nov. 1982: 14–16.

Becker, Marvin. "Aspects of Lay Piety in Early Renaissance Florence." In Charles Trinkaus and Heiko Obermann, eds., *The Pursuit of Holiness in Late Medieval and Renaissance Religion.* Studies in Medieval and Reformation Thought, 10. London: E. J. Brill, 1974.

——. "The Republican City State in Florence: An Inquiry into Its Origins and Survival (1280–1434)." *Speculum* 35 (1960): 39–50.

Bertelli, Sergio. "La crisi del 1501: Firenze e Cesare Borgia." In S. Bertelli and G. Ramakus, eds., *Essays Presented to Myron P. Gilmore.* 2 vols. Villa i Tatti, 2. Florence: Nuova Italia, 1978.

Bonfil, Robert. "The Devil and the Jews in the Christian Consciousness of the Middle Ages." In Shmuel Almog, ed., *Antisemitism through the Ages.* Oxford: Pergamon Press, 1988.

Booth, Cecily. *Cosimo I, Duke of Florence.* Cambridge: Cambridge University Press, 1921.

Borsook, Eve. "Art and Politics at the Medici Court, 1: The Funeral of Cosimo I de' Medici." *Mitteilungen des Kunsthistorischen Institutes in Florenz* 12 (1965): 31–54.

Brackett, John K. *Criminal Justice and Crime in Late Renaissance Florence, 1537–1609.* Cambridge: Cambridge University Press, 1992.

Branca, Lodovico. "Pauperismo, assistenza, e controllo sociale a Firenze (1621–1632): Materiali e ricerche." *Archivio storico italiano* 141 (1983): 421–62

Braudel, Fernand. *Capitalism and Material Life, 1400–1800.* Trans. Miriam Kochan. New York: Harper Colophon, 1973. Orig. pub. as *Civilisation matérielle et capitalisme.* Paris, 1967.

——. *The Mediterranean and the Mediterranean World in the Age of Philip II.* Trans. Sian Reynolds. New York: Harper and Row, 1972–73. Orig. pub. as *La Méditerranée et le monde méditerranéen à l'époque de Philippe II.* 2d rev. ed., Paris, 1966.

Brown, Judith. "Concepts of Political Economy: Cosimo I de' Medici in a Comparative European Context." In *Firenze e la Toscana dei Medici nell'Europa del '500.* Vol. 1. Florence: Leo S. Olschki, 1983.

Brucker, Gene. *The Civic World of Early Renaissance Florence.* Princeton, N.J.: Princeton University Press, 1977.

——. *Renaissance Florence*. New York: Wiley, 1969. Reprint with supplements, Berkeley, 1983.

——. "Tales of Two Cities: Florence and Venice in the Renaissance." *American Historical Review* 88 (1983): 599–616.

Bullard, Melissa. *Filippo Strozzi and the Medici*. Cambridge: Cambridge University Press, 1980.

——. "Marriage, Politics and the Family in Florence: The Strozzi-Medici Alliance of 1508." *American Historical Review* 84 (1979): 668–87.

Burckhardt, Jacob. *The Civilization of the Renaissance in Italy*. 2 vols. Trans. S. G. C. Middlemore. New York: Harper and Row, 1958. Orig. pub. Bern, 1860.

Butters, Humfrey. *Governors and Government in Early Sixteenth-Century Florence, 1502–1519*. Oxford: Clarendon Press, 1985.

Cantagalli, Roberto. *Cosimo I de' Medici, granduca di Toscana*. Milan: U. Mursia, 1985.

Capecchi, Ilvo, and Lucia Gai. *Il monte della pietà a Pistoia e le sue origini*. Florence: Leo S. Olschki, 1976.

Cassandro, M. *Gli ebrei e il prestito ebraico a Siena nel Cinquecento*. Quaderni di "Studi senesi," 42. Milan: Giuffré, 1979.

Cassirer, Ernst, "Giovanni Pico della Mirandola." In Paul Oskar Kristeller and Philip P. Wiener, eds. *Renaissance Essays from the "Journal of the History of Ideas."* New York: Harper and Row, 1968. Orig. pub. in vol. 2 (1942) of that journal.

Cassuto, Umberto. *Gli ebrei in Firenze nell'età del Rinascimento*. R. Instituto di Studi Superiori Pratici di Perfezionamento di Firenze. Sezione di Filosofia e Filologia, 40. Florence: Leo S. Olschki, 1965.

——. *La famille des Médicis et les juifs*. Paris: Durlacher, 1923.

Chabert, A. R. E. "More about the Sixteenth-Century Price Revolution." In Peter Burke, ed., *Economy and Society in Early Modern Europe: Essays from "Annales."* Trans Keith Folca. New York: Harper and Row, 1972.

Chabod, Federico. "Was There a Renaissance State?" In Heinz Lubasz, ed., *The Development of the Modern State*. Main Themes in European History, ed. Bruce Mazlish. New York: Macmillan, 1964. Orig. pub. as "Y a-t-il un état de la Renaissance?" In *Acts du colloque sur la Renaissance*, 57–74. Paris, 1958.

Chiaudano, Mario. "Un contributo alla storia dei monti di pietà e della banca in Italia: L'istituto S. Paolo di Torino." *Archivo storico italiano* 124 (1966): 250–56.

Chittolini, Giorgio. *La formazione dello stato regionale e le istituzioni del contado: secoli xiv e xv*. Turin: Giulio Einaudi, 1979.

Ciardini, M. *I banchieri ebrei in Firenze nel secolo XV e il monte di pietà*. Florence: Gozzini, 1975.

Cipolla, Carlo. "The Economic Decline of Italy." In Brian Pullan, ed., *Crisis and Change in the Venetian Economy in the Sixteenth and Seventeenth Centu-*

ries. London: Methuen, 1968. Orig. pub. as "Il declino economico dell'Italia." In *Storia dell'economia italiana*. Turin, 1959.

——. *Money in Sixteenth-Century Florence*. Berkeley: University of California Press, 1989. Orig. pub. as *La moneta a Firenze nel Cinquecento*. Bologna: Il Mulino, 1987.

——. "The So-Called 'Price Revolution': Reflections on 'the Italian Situation.'" In Peter Burke, ed., *Economy and Society in Early Modern Europe: Essays from "Annales."* New York: Harper and Row, 1972.

Clarke, Paula C. *The Soderini and the Medici: Power and Patronage in Fifteenth-Century Florence*. Oxford: Clarendon Press, 1991.

Cochrane, Eric. *Florence in the Forgotten Centuries, 1527–1800: A History of Florence and the Florentines in the Age of the Grand Dukes*. Chicago: University of Chicago Press, 1973.

Cohn, Samuel K., Jr. *Death and Property in Siena, 1205–1800: Strategies for the Afterlife*. Baltimore: Johns Hopkins University Press, 1988.

——. *The Laboring Classes in Renaissance Florence*. New York: Academic Press, 1980.

Compostella, Piero. *Il monte di pietà di Milano: Le origini (1486–1518)*. Milan: Banca del Monte di Milano, 1966.

——. *Il monte di pietà di Milano: L'istituto nella storia milanese attraverso i secoli xv e xvi*. Milan: Banca del Monte di Milano, 1973.

Connell, William J. "Il 'libro di possessioni, fitti, socciti et amezi' di Messer Iacopo Melocchi." *LDF: Bolletino della ricerca sui libri di famiglia in Italia* 1 (June–Sept. 1988): 20–22.

Cooper, Roslyn Pesman. "The Florentine Ruling Group under the 'Governo Popolare,' 1494–1512." *Studies in Medieval and Renaissance History* 7 (o.s. 17): 71–181.

Corsi, Domenico. "Il secondo monte di pietà di Lucca (1493–1502)." *Archivio storico italiano* 126 (1968): 389–408.

Couturier, Edith. "The Philanthropic Activities of Pedro Romero de Terreros: First Count of Rigla (1753–1781)." *Americas* 32 (1975): 13–30.

D'Addario, Arnaldo. "Burocrazia, economia, e finanze dello stato fiorentino alla metà del Cinquecento." *Archivio storico italiano* 121 (1963): 362–456.

——. *La formazione dello stato moderno in Toscana da Cosimo il Vecchio a Cosimo I de' Medici*. Lecce: Adriatica ed. Salentina, 1976.

——. "Note di storia della religiosità e della carità dei Fiorentini nel secolo XVI." *Archivio storico italiano* 126 (1968): 61–147.

——. *Il problema di Siena nella storia italiana della prima metà del Cinquecento (La Guerra di Siena)*. Florence: Le Monnier, 1958.

Dal Pane, Luigi. *La finanza toscana dagli inizi del secolo XVIII alla caduta del granducato*. Studi e ricerchi di storia economica italiana nell'età del Risorgimento. Milan: Banca commerciale italiana, 1965.

de Roover, Florence Edler. "Restitution in Renaissance Florence." In *Studi in onore di Armando Sapori*. 2 vols. Milan: Istituto Editoriale Cisalpino, 1957.

de Roover, Raymond. "'Cambium ad Venetias': A Contribution to the History of Foreign Exchange." In *Studi in onore di Armando Sapori*. Milan: Istituto Editoriale Cisalpino, 1957.

———. "Labour Conditions in Florence around 1400: Theory, Policy and Reality." In Nicolai Rubinstein, ed., *Florentine Studies: Politics and Society in Renaissance Florence*. Evanston, Ill.: Northwestern University Press, 1965.

———. *Money, Banking and Credit in Medieval Bruges*. Cambridge, Mass.: Medieval Academy of America, 1948.

———. *The Rise and Decline of the Medici Bank, 1397–1494*. New York: W. W. Norton, 1966.

Diaz, Furio. *Il granducato di Toscana: I Medici*. In *Storia d'Italia*, ed. Giuseppe Galasso, vol. 13.1. Turin: UTET, 1976; repr. 1982.

———. "Recent Studies on Medicean Tuscany." *Journal of Italian History* 1 (1978): 95–110.

Dickens, A. G. *Reformation and Society in Sixteenth-Century Europe*. New York: Harcourt, Brace and World, 1966.

Dillen, Johannes G. van, ed. *History of the Principal Public Banks*. Contributions to the History of Banking, 1. The Hague: Martinus Nijhoff, 1934.

Doria, Giorgio. "Conoscenza del mercato e sistema informativo: Il know-how dei mercanti genovesi nei secoli xvi e xvii." In Aldo De Maddalena and Hermann Kellenbenz, eds., *La repubblica internazionale del denaro tra XV e XVII secolo*. Annali dell'Istituto Storico Italo-Germanico, 20. Bologna: Il Mulino, 1986.

Duby, Georges. *The Early Growth of the European Economy: Warriors and Peasants from the Seventh to the Twelfth Century*. Trans. Howard B. Clarke. Ithaca, N.Y.: Cornell University Press, 1974.

Dupré Theseider, Eugenio. "I papi medicei e la loro politica domestica." In *Studi fiorentini* 7. Libera Cattedra di Storia della Civiltà Fiorentina. Unione Fiorentina. Florence: G. C. Sansoni, 1963.

Edler, Florence. *Glossary of Medieval Terms of Business: Italian Series, 1200–1600*. Cambridge, Mass.: Medieval Academy of America, 1934.

Elliott, J. H. *Imperial Spain, 1469–1716*. New York: St. Martin's Press, 1963.

Fasano Guarini, Elena. "The Grand Duchy of Tuscany at the Death of Cosimo I: A Historical Map." *Journal of Italian History* 2 (1979): 520–36.

———. *Lo stato mediceo di Cosimo I*. Florence: G. C. Sansoni, 1973.

———, ed. *Prato: Storia di una città*. Vol. 2, *Un microcosmo in movimento (dal 1494 al 1815)*. Prato and Florence: Le Monnier, 1986.

Fioravanti, Gianfranco. "Polemiche antigiudaiche nell'Italia del Quattrocento: Un tentativo di interpretazione globale." *Quaderni storici*, n.s., 64 (1987): 19–37.

Galluzzi, R. *Istoria del granducato di Toscana sotto il governo di casa Medici.* 7 vols. Capolago: Elvetica, 1841–42.

Garrani, Giuseppe. *Il carattere bancario e l'evoluzione strutturale dei primogenii monti di pietà: Riflessi della tecnica bancaria antica su quella moderna.* Istituto di Economia Aziendale dell'Università Commerciale L. Bocconi, ser. 1, no. 13. Milan: Giuffré, 1957.

Ghinato, Alberto. "I monti di pietà, istituzione francescana." *Picenum seraphicum* 2 (1982): 7–62.

Gilbert, Felix. "Bernardo Rucellai and the Orti Oricellari." *Journal of the Warburg and Courtauld Institutes* 12 (1949): 101–31.

——. *Machiavelli and Guicciardini: Politics and History in Sixteenth Century Florence.* Princeton, N.J.: Princeton University Press, 1965.

——. "The Venetian Constitution in Florentine Political Thought." In Nicolai Rubinstein, ed., *Florentine Studies: Politics and Society in Renaissance Florence.* Evanston, Ill.: Northwestern University Press, 1968.

Gilmore, Myron P. *The World of Humanism, 1453–1517.* New York: Harper and Row, 1952.

Goldthwaite, Richard. *The Building of Renaissance Florence: An Economic and Social History.* Baltimore: Johns Hopkins University Press, 1980.

——. "Local Banking in Renaissance Florence." *Journal of European Economic History* 14 (1985): 5–55.

——. "The Medici Bank and the World of Florentine Capitalism." *Past and Present* 114 (1987): 3–31.

——. *Private Wealth in Renaissance Florence: A Study of Four Families.* Princeton, N.J.: Princeton University Press, 1968.

Hale, John R. "The End of Florentine Liberty: The Fortezza da Basso." In Nicolai Rubinstein, ed., *Florentine Studies: Politics and Society in Renaissance Florence*: 501–32. Evanston, Ill.: Northwestern University Press, 1968.

——. *Florence and the Medici: The Pattern of Control.* London: Thames and Hudson, 1977.

Herlihy, David, and Christiane Klapisch-Zuber. *Tuscans and Their Families.* New Haven: Yale University Press, 1985. Orig. pub. as *Les toscans et leurs familles*, Paris, 1978.

Holmes, George. *Florence, Rome, and the Origins of the Renaissance.* Oxford: Clarendon Press, 1986.

Holzapfel, P. Heribert. "Le origini dei monti di pietà." *La Verna* 1 (1905): 407–12, 603–11, 667–73; 2 (1906): 86–95, 164–68, 343–52, 470–76, 547–52; 3 (1907): 25–33, 293–97, 681–92, 743–56. Orig. pub. as *Die Anfänge der Montes Pietatis*, Munich, 1903.

Jones, Rosemary Devonshire. *Francesco Vettori, Florentine Citizen and Medici Servant.* London: Athlone Press of the University of London, 1972.

Kent, Dale. *The Rise of the Medici: Faction in Florence, 1426–1434.* Oxford: Oxford University Press, 1978.

Kent, Francis William. *Household and Lineage in Renaissance Florence: The Family Life of the Capponi, Ginori, and Rucellai.* Princeton, N.J.: Princeton University Press, 1977.

Kirshner, Julius. "From Usury to Public Finance: The Ecclesiastical Controversy over the Public Debts of Florence, Genoa, and Venice (1300–1500)." Ph.D. diss., Columbia University, 1970.

Klapisch-Zuber, Christiane. "The Griselda Complex: Dowry and Marriage Gifts in the Quattrocento." Trans. Lydia Cochrane. In Christiane Klapisch-Zuber, ed., *Women, Family and Ritual in Renaissance Italy,* 213–46. Chicago: University of Chicago Press, 1985. Orig. pub. as "Le complexe de Griselda," in *Mélanges de l'Ecole Française de Rome* 94 (1982): 7–43.

Lane, Frederic C. "Venetian Bankers, 1496–1533: A Study in the Early Stages of Deposit Banking." *Journal of Political Economy* 45 (1937): 187–206.

Larner, John. "Europe of the Courts." *Journal of Modern History* 55 (1983): 669–81.

Litchfield, R. Burr. *Emergence of a Bureaucracy: The Florentine Patricians, 1530–1790.* Princeton, N.J.: Princeton University Press, 1986.

——. "Officeholding in Florence after the Republic." In Anthony Molho and John A. Tedeschi, eds., *Renaissance: Studies in Honor of Hans Baron.* DeKalb, Ill.: Northern Illinois University Press, 1971.

Little, Lester K. *Religious Poverty and the Profit Economy in Medieval Europe.* Ithaca, N.Y.: Cornell University Press, 1978.

——. "L'utilité sociale de la pauvreté volontaire." In Michel Mollat, ed., *Etudes sur l'histoire de la pauvreté.* 2 vols. Paris: Sorbonne, 1974.

Lopez Yepes, José. *Historia de los montes de piedad en España.* 2 vols. Madrid: Confederacion Española de Cajas de Ahorros, 1971.

McLaughlin, Terence P. "The Teaching of the Canonists on Usury." *Mediaeval Studies* 1 (1939): 81–147, and 2 (1940): 1–22.

Malowist, Marian. "Capitalismo commerciale e agricoltura." In *Storia d'Italia: Annali.* Vol. 1. Turin: Giulio Einaudi, 1978.

Mandich, Giulio. "Il fiorino di conto a Firenze nel 1382–1464." *Archivio storico italiano* 14 (1988): 155–81.

Maragi, M. "Cenni sulla natura e sullo svolgimento storico dei monti di pietà." *Archivi storici delle aziende di credito* 1 (1956): 291–314.

Marks, L. F. "La crisi finanziaria a Firenze dal 1494 al 1502." *Archivio storico italiano* 112 (1954): 40–72.

——. "The Financial Oligarchy under Lorenzo." In E. F. Jacob, ed., *Italian Renaissance Studies: A Tribute to the Late Cecilia M. Ady.* London: Faber and Faber, 1960.

Martines, Lauro. *Lawyers and Statecraft in Renaissance Florence.* Princeton, N.J.: Princeton University Press, 1968.

———. *Power and Imagination: City States in Renaissance Italy.* New York: Alfred A. Knopf, 1979.

Mazzone, Umberto. *"El buon governo": Un progetto di riforma generale nella Firenze savonaroliana.* Florence: Leo S. Olschki, 1978.

Melis, Federico. "Motivi di storia bancaria senese: Dai banchieri privati alla banca pubblica." *Monte dei Paschi di Siena, Note economiche* 5 (1972): 47–65.

Meneghin, Vittorino. *Bernardino da Feltre e i monti di pietà.* Vicenza: L.I.E.F. Edizioni, 1974.

———. *I monti di pietà in Italia dal 1462 al 1562.* Vicenza: L.I.E.F. Edizioni, 1986.

Menning, Carol Bresnahan. "Finance and Fraud during the Reign of Cosimo I: The Case of Giuliano del Tovaglia." *Historian* 51 (1988): 1–18.

———. "Loans and Favors, Kin and Clients: Cosimo I de' Medici and the Monte di Pietà." *Journal of Modern History* 61 (1989): 487–511.

———. "The Monte's 'monte': The Early Supporters of Florence's Monte di Pietà. *Sixteenth Century Journal* 23 (1992): 303–18.

———. "'Una tal laudabile opera': The Monte di Pietà in Late Renaissance Florence." Ph.D. diss., Brown University, 1986.

Milano, Attilio. *Storia degli ebrei in Italia.* Turin: Giulio Einaudi, 1963.

Molho, Anthony. "Cosimo de' Medici: *Pater Patriae* or *Padrino?*" *Stanford Italian Review* 1 (1979): 5–33.

———. *Florentine Public Finances in the Early Renaissance, 1400–1433.* Cambridge, Mass.: Harvard University Press, 1971.

———. "Investimenti nel monte delle doti di Firenze: Un'analisi sociale e geografica." *Quaderni storici* 21 (1986): 147–70.

———. "A Note on Jewish Moneylenders in the Late Trecento and Early Quattrocento." In Anthony Molho and John Tedeschi, eds., *Renaissance: Studies in Honor of Hans Baron.* DeKalb, Ill.: Northern Illinois University Press, 1971.

Molho, Anthony, and Julius Kirshner. "The Dowry Fund and the Marriage Market in Early Quattrocento Florence." *Journal of Modern History* 50 (1978): 403–38.

Monaco, Michele. "La questione dei monti di pietà al Quinto Concilio lateranense." *Rivista di studi salernitani* 4 (1971): 86–136.

Il monte dei paschi di Siena: Historical Notes. Siena: Monte dei Paschi di Siena, 1955.

Monti, Gennaro Maria. *Le confraternite medievali dell'alta e media Italia.* 2 vols. Venice: Nuova Italia, 1927.

Mueller, Reinhold C. "The Role of Bank Money in Venice, 1300–1500." *Studi veneziani,* n.s., 3 (1979): 47–96.

Muzzarelli, Maria Giuseppina. "Un bilancio storiografico sui monti di pietà: 1956–1976." *Rivista di storia della Chiesa in Italia* 33 (1979): 165–183.

———. "Luoghi e tendenze dell'attuale storiografica italiana sulla presenza ebraica fra XIV e XVI secolo." *Società e storia* 24 (1984): 369–94.

Najemy, John M. *Corporatism and Consensus in Florentine Electoral Politics, 1280–1400.* Chapel Hill: University of North Carolina Press, 1982.

———. "Guild Republicanism in Trecento Florence: The Successes and Ultimate Failures of Corporate Politics." *American Historical Review* 84 (1979): 53–71.

Nardi, Jacopo. *Istorie della città di Firenze.* 2 vols. Florence: Le Monnier, 1858.

Nelson, Benjamin N. *The Idea of Usury: From Tribal Brotherhood to Universal Otherhood.* 2d ed. Chicago: University of Chicago Press, 1969. Orig. pub. Princeton, N.J., 1949.

———. "The Usurer and the Merchant Prince: Italian Businessmen and the Ecclesiastical Law of Restitution, 1100–1500." *Journal of Economic History* 7, Supp. 7 (1947): 104–22.

Noonan, John T. *The Scholastic Analysis of Usury.* Cambridge: Cambridge University Press, 1957.

Obermann, Heiko. "Discovery of Hebrew and Discrimination against the Jews: The *Veritas Hebraica* as Double-Edged Sword in Renaissance and Reformation." In Andrew C. Fix and Susan C. Karant-Nunn, eds., *Germania Illustrata: Essays on Early Modern Germany Presented to Gerald Strauss.* Sixteenth Century Essays and Studies, 18. Kirksville, Mo.: Sixteenth Century Journal, 1992.

Origo, Iris. *The Merchant of Prato: Francesco di Marco Datini, 1335–1410.* New York: Alfred A. Knopf, 1957.

Pagnini del Ventura, Giovanni Francesco. *Della decima e di varie altre gravezze imposte dal comune di Firenze.* 2 vols. Bologna: Forni, 1967; orig. pub. Lucca, 1765.

Pampaloni, Guido. "Cenni storici sul monte di pietà di Firenze." *Archivi storici delle aziende di credito* 1 (1956): 525–60.

Papi, Massimo D. "Studi e problemi sull'antigiudaismo medievale." *Archivio storico italiano* 135 (1977): 141–63.

Parsons, Anscar. "Bernardine of Feltre and the *Montes Pietatis.*" *Franciscan Studies* 22, n.s. 1 (Mar. 1941): 11–32.

———. "The Economic Significance of *Montes Pietatis.*" *Franciscan Studies* 22, n.s. 1 (Sept. 1941): 3–28.

Passerini, Luigi. *Storia degli stabilmenti di beneficenza e d'istruzione elementare gratuita della città di Firenze.* Florence: Le Monnier, 1853.

Pastor, Ludwig. *History of the Popes.* 40 vols. Trans. R. Kerr. London: Kegan Paul, 1908.

Perrens, François T. *Histoire de Florence.* Paris: Maison Quantin, 1889.

Piccolomini, N., ed. *Il monte dei paschi di Siena e le aziende in esso riunite.* 4 vols. Siena: L. Lazzeri, 1891.

Pieraccini, Gaetano. *La stirpe de' Medici di Cafaggiolo.* 2 vols. Florence: Vallecchi, 1924.

Potter, G. R., and Denis Hay, *The Renaissance*. Vol. 1 of *New Cambridge Modern History*. Cambridge: Cambridge University Press, 1957.

Pullan, Brian. *Rich and Poor in Renaissance Venice: The Social Institutions of a Catholic State*. Oxford: Basil Blackwell, 1971.

Quaglioni, Diego. "I giuristi medioevali e gli ebrei: Due 'consultationes' di G. F. Pavini (1478)." *Quaderni storici*, n.s., 64 (1987): 1–18.

Queller, Donald. "The Civic Irresponsibility of the Venetian Nobility." In Robert Lopez, Vsevolod Slessarev, and David Herlihy, eds., *Economy, Society, and Government in Medieval Italy: Essays in Memory of Robert L. Reynolds*. Kent, Ohio: Kent State University Press, 1969.

Raby, R. Cornelius. *The Regulation of Pawnbroking*. New York: Russell Sage Foundation, 1924.

Ranke, Leopold von. *History of the Popes: Their Church and State*. Trans. E. Fowler. 3 vols. Rev. ed. New York: P. F. Collier, 1901.

Ricci, Giovanni. "Povertà, vergogna, e 'povertà vergognosa.'" *Società e storia* 5 (1979): 305–37.

Richelson, Paul W. *Studies in the Personal Imagery of Cosimo I de' Medici, Duke of Florence*. Garland Series of Outstanding Dissertations in the Fine Arts. New York: Garland Press, 1978.

Rigobon, Pietro. *La contabilità di stato nella repubblica di Firenze e nel granducato di Toscana*. Grigenti: Salvatore Montes, 1892.

Rinieri de' Rocchi, A. "Compagnia dei disciplinati." In L. Lazzeri, ed., *Siena e il suo territorio*. Siena: R. Istituto dei Sordo-Muti, 1862, repr. Siena: Arnaldo Forni, 1989.

Rocke, Michael J. "Il controllo dell'omosessualità a Firenze nel XV secolo: Gli 'Ufficiali di notte.'" *Quaderni storici*, n.s., 66 (1987): 701–23.

Roth, Cecil. *The Last Florentine Republic*. London: Methuen, 1925.

Rubinstein, Nicolai. "Firenze e il problema della politica imperiale in Italia al tempo di Massimiliano I." *Archivio storico italiano* 116 (1958): 5–35, 147–77.

———. *The Government of Florence under the Medici, 1434–94*. Oxford: Clarendon Press, 1966.

———. "Politics and Constitution in Florence at the End of the Fifteenth Century." In E. F. Jacob, ed., *Italian Renaissance Studies: A Tribute to the Late Cecilia M. Ady*, London: Faber and Faber, 1960.

———. "I primi anni del Consiglio Maggiore di Firenze (1494–99)." *Archivio storico italiano* 112 (1954): 151–94.

Saalman, Howard. *The Bigallo: The Oratory and Residence of the Compagnia del Bigallo e della Misericordia in Florence*. New York: New York University Press, 1969.

Salter, F. R. "The Jews in Fifteenth Century Florence and Savonarola's Establishment of a *Mons Pietatis*." *Cambridge Historical Journal* 5 (1935–37): 193–211.

Sandri, Leopoldo. "Saggio bibliografico di scritti sull'attività bancaria nei secoli xvi e xvii." *Archivi storici delle aziende di credito* 1 (1956): 405–18.

Spicciani, Amleto "The 'Poveri Vergognosi' in Fifteenth-Century Florence." In Thomas Riis, ed., *Poverty in Early Modern Europe*. Alphen aan den Rijn: Sijthoff, 1981.

Spini, Giorgio. *Cosimo I de' Medici e l'indipendenza del principato mediceo*. Collana storica a cura di E. Codignola, 52. Florence: Vallecchi, 1945.

———. "The Medici Principality and the Organization of the States of Europe in the Sixteenth Century." *Journal of Italian History* 2 (1979): 420–47.

———. "Questioni e problemi di metodo per la storia del principato mediceo e degli stati toscani del Cinquecento." *Rivista storica italiana* 58 (1941): 76–93.

Staley, Edgcumbe. *The Guilds of Florence*. Chicago: A. G. McClurg, 1906.

Steegman, Mary G. *Bianca Cappello*. London: Constable, 1913.

Stephens, John N. *The Fall of the Florentine Republic, 1512–1530*. Oxford: Clarendon Press, 1983.

Stumpa, Enrico. "Le istituzioni e la società." In Elena Fasano Guarini, ed., *Prato: Storia di una città*. Vol. 2: *Un microcosmo in movimento (dal 1494 al 1815)*. Prato: Le Monnier, 1986.

Toaff, Ariel. *The Jews in Medieval Assisi, 1305–1487: A Social and Economic History of a Small Jewish Community in Italy*. Biblioteca dell'*Archivum Romanicum*, ser. 1, vol. 148. Florence: Leo S. Olschki, 1979.

Todeschini, Giacomo. *La ricchezza degli ebrei: Merci e denaro nella riflessione ebraica e nella definizione christiana dell'usura alla fine del Medioevo*. Biblioteca degli "Studi Medievali," 15. Spoleto: Centro Italiano di Studi sull'Alto Medioevo, 1989.

Touring Club Italiano. *Firenze e dintorni*. 6th ed. Guida d'Italia del T.C.I., vol. 12. Milan: Touring Club Italiano, 1974.

Trexler, Richard C. "Adolescence and Salvation in the Renaissance." In Charles Trinkhaus and Heiko Obermann, eds., *The Pursuit of Holiness in Late Medieval and Renaissance Religion*. Leiden: E. J. Brill, 1974.

———. "The Bishop's Portion: Generic Pious Legacies in the Late Middle Ages in Italy." *Traditio* 28 (1972): 397–450.

———. "Charity and the Defense of Urban Elites in the Italian Communes." In Frederic Cople Jaher, ed., *The Rich, the Wellborn, and the Powerful: Elites and Upper Classes in History*. Urbana: University of Illinois Press, 1973.

———. "The Foundlings of Florence, 1395–1455." *History of Childhood Quarterly* 1 (1973): 259–84.

———. *Public Life in Renaissance Florence*. New York: Academic Press, 1980.

Ugolini, Piero. "Il podere nell'economia rurale italiana." In *Storia d'Italia: Annali*. Turin: Giulio Einaudi, 1978.

Usher, Abbott Payson. *The Early History of Deposit Banking in Mediterranean*

Europe. New York: Russell and Russell, 1967; orig. pub. Cambridge, Mass., 1943.

Villari, Pasquale. *The Life and Times of Niccolò Machiavelli*. Trans. Linda Villari. 2 vols. New ed. New York: Greenwood Press, 1968; orig. pub. 1892.

Vitale, Vito. *Breviario della storia di Genova*. 2 vols. Genoa: Società Ligure di Storia Patria, 1955.

Weinstein, Donald. "Critical Issues in Civic Religion." In Charles Trinkhaus and Heiko Obermann, eds., *The Pursuit of Holiness in Late Medieval and Renaissance Religion*. Leiden: E. J. Brill, 1974.

——. "Hagiography, Demonology, Biography: Savonarola Studies Today." *Journal of Modern History* 63 (1991): 483–503.

——. *Savonarola and Florence: Prophecy and Patriotism in the Renaissance*. Princeton, N.J.: Princeton University Press, 1970.

Winspeare, F. *Isabella Orsini e la corte medicea del suo tempo*. Biblioteca dell'*Archivio storico italiano*, 12. Florence: Leo S. Olschki, 1961.

Zanetti, Paolo. "Intervento politico, riorganizzazione istituzionale, pratica amministrativa del principato medìceo nell'area pisana (1532–1574)." *Archivio storico italiano* 146 (1988): 183–215.

Zorzi, Andrea. "I fiorentini e gli uffici pubblici nel primo Quattrocento: Concorrenza, abusi, illegalità." *Quaderni storici*, n.s., 66 (1987): 725–51.

INDEX

Library of Congress Cataloging-in-Publication Data

Menning, Carol Bresnahan.
  Charity and State in late Renaissance Italy : the Monte di pietà
of Florence / Carol Bresnahan Menning.
      p.   cm.
  Includes bibliographical references and index.
  ISBN 0-8014-2773-8
    1. Monte di pietà (Florence, Italy)—History.   2. Pawnbroking—
Italy—Florence—History.   3. Charities—Italy—Florence—History.
4. Finance—Italy—Florence—History.   5. Medici, House of.
I. Title.
HG2093.I6M46   1993
361.7'632'094551—dc20   92-56788